The Prado Guide

Edition
Museo Nacional del Prado

Coordination
Área de Edición del Museo
Nacional del Prado

Editor
María Dolores Jiménez-Blanco

Production
Museo Nacional del Prado Difusión

Translation
Philip Sutton
Laura Suffield
Jenny Dodman

Copy Editor
Diana Davies

Design
Mikel Garay

Layout
gráfica futura

Prepress
Lucam

Printer
Brizzolis, arte en gráficas

First edition, March 2009
Second edition revised, May 2009
Third edition revised, January 2011
Fourth edition revised, 2012

Authors
Brief History of the Museo del Prado
and Spanish Painting: Alberto Pancorbo.
Italian Painting: María Dolores Jiménez-
Blanco, pp. 220-243; José María Riello,
p. 219 and pp. 244-295; Diego Blanca,
pp. 295-305. Flemish Painting: Diego
Blanca, pp. 307-343; José Juan Pérez
Preciado, pp. 344-371. Dutch Painting:
Ángel Aterido. French Painting: Ángel
Aterido, pp. 381-391; Diego Blanca,
pp. 392-401. German Painting: Ángel
Aterido. British Painting: Diego Blanca.
Drawing, Sculpture and Decorative Arts:
Raquel González Escribano

Photographers
José Baztán and Álvaro Otero and
Photographic Archive of the Museo
Nacional del Prado. Philip Sayer
pp. 8-9 and 16

Cover image
Diego Velázquez, *Las Meninas*
or *The Family of Philip IV* (detail), 1656.
Madrid, Museo Nacional del Prado

Image details
Index: Francisco de Goya, *Half-
submerged Dog*, 1819-23. Spanish
Painting: Francisco de Goya, *St Isidore's
Meadow*, c. 1788. Italian Painting: Fra
Angelico, *The Annunciation*, c. 1425-28.
Flemish Painting: Joachim Patinir,
Charon crossing the River Styx, c. 1520-24.
Dutch Painting: Pieter Claesz, *Still Life*,
1637. French Painting: Nicolas Poussin,
Parnassus, c. 1631-33. German Painting:
Albrecht Dürer, *Adam*, 1507. British
Painting: Lawrence Alma Tadema,
Pompeian Scene (The Siesta), 1868.
Drawings: José de Ribera, *St Cecilia*,
c. 1645-50. Sculpture and Decorative
Arts: Giambologna, *Allegory of Francesco
I de' Medici*, 1560-61.

GOBIERNO
DE ESPAÑA

MINISTERIO
DE EDUCACIÓN, CULTURA
Y DEPORTE

BENEFACTOR DEL PROGRAMA
DE ATENCIÓN AL VISITANTE

The Prado Guide

MUSEO NACIONAL DEL PRADO

Introduction

The Museo del Prado is considered by many to be the greatest public collection of paintings in the world. From the time of its foundation in 1819 the Museum attracted to Madrid the most refined and sensitive art lovers of the 19th century. In the Prado's tranquil galleries they discovered Velázquez and Goya and through them the entire Spanish School, which from that point onwards enjoyed a new esteem among critics and art historians worldwide. In addition to the key works by those painters, to whose list of names we should add El Greco, the Museum also houses extremely important holdings of the work of other European artists as a result of the collecting interests of the Spanish monarchy. It is consequently impossible to gain a profound knowledge of the work of Titian, Rubens or Bosch without visiting this venerable institution.

During the course of its existence and over the almost two hundred years that have passed since 1819, the Museo del Prado has been able to reinforce its collections to a significant degree, becoming one of the most established and highly appreciated institutions of its kind in Europe. For this reason, and bearing in mind the importance of its historical roots in the formation of its collections, the Museum is fully aware that its story is an ongoing one, with a marked emphasis on the future to come. This was demonstrated in 2007 with the inauguration of a new, modern building that has given the Prado the installations and services required by major museums in the 21st century. It is also demonstrated through the publication presented here.

Over the course of its history the Prado has produced many notable publications. Despite this, it has lacked an official guide to its collections of the type published by many of the principal museums in Europe and America over the past few decades with the aim of summarising the most important works in their collections in a single volume. Like those guides, the present volume aims to be of use to the non-specialist visitor and to bring the Museum closer to an ever broader public and one increasingly interested in obtaining clear, precise information on the works in the Prado's collections.

Given the range and quality of the collections housed by the Prado, the selection of works in this guide can only represent a summary from which some important paintings have inevitably had to be excluded. Nonetheless, we are confident that the final result offers an exact portrait of a Museum whose founding aim was not to present an indiscriminate gathering of works from different periods and cultures but one that owes its excellence and renown to the unique nature of its collections, determined as they were by the personal tastes of the Spanish monarchs and the historical circumstances through which modern Spain evolved. The present guide thus achieves its intention of being representative not by giving equal weight to the different chapters of which it is made up but rather by reflecting the pronounced differences that exist between the artists and schools represented in the Prado. It is thus not surprising that Velázquez occupies a key position in terms of both quantity and quality, or that due to his special historical connection with the Museum's identity he is the only artist to be devoted a specific chapter on his relationship with the Museo del Prado. In this regard, Velázquez is followed by Goya, El Greco, Titian, Bosch and Rubens, who, as I noted above, should be considered the foundation stones of the collection.

With the aim of creating a formal structure in which to appreciate the large number of works – around four hundred – included in this guide, we have followed the now standard model used in other guides to international museums referred to above. The works are thus grouped into chapters devoted to the most important national schools: Spanish, Italian, Flemish, Dutch, French, German and British. In addition, there are two further chapters, on works on paper, and on sculpture and the decorative arts. Finally, and with the aim of facilitating an understanding of the historical context of the individual works within the overall panorama of art history, the guide includes introductory texts that focus on developments within each school and which refer to periods or artistic movements as well as to artists who made particularly important contributions to the evolution of the art of their day, or who occupy a pre-eminent position within the Prado's holdings.

Finally, it should be noted that all the works included are carefully illustrated and most have brief accompanying texts that aim to inform the reader on the story narrated in the painting, the artistic personality of its creator, its importance within the collection as a whole, or other issues considered interesting in each case. The inevitable restrictions of space in a guidebook of this type have not prevented its authors from recounting the mythological or biblical sources of some works, or from including references to many of the leading figures of the early modern age. Such references are essential given that the history of the Prado is inseparable from the history of European culture, and to lose oneself in its rooms or in the pages of this guide enables the visitor or reader to learn more about some of the most important and stirring as well as the most subtle and delightful episodes in that history.

Visitors to the Museum, whether members of the general public or experts, continue to grow in number, as does the interest in the works that it houses. The intention of this guide is to accompany and enlighten all those who have the pleasure of personally visiting the galleries of the Prado as well as those who wish to learn more about its collections from further away, in the hope that they will be encouraged to visit us at a future date.

Miguel Zugaza Miranda
Director, Museo Nacional del Prado

Brief History
of the Museo del Prado

Detail of the Eastern side of the Museo del Prado building

The institution we now know as the Museo del Prado was first opened to the public on 19 November 1819 under the name of the Museo Real de Pinturas (Royal Museum of Paintings), having been created at the behest and under the patronage of King Ferdinand VII (reigned 1808–1833). The Musée du Louvre, the first public museum and the model for all those created afterwards, had been inaugurated in 1793. Although it was a royal museum, the Prado shared the Louvre's objective of exhibiting the art treasures which had until then been known and enjoyed only by a very small group of members of the royalty, the aristocracy and the church. The notion of making art public had its roots in the Enlightenment and its development in the Revolution, and like many other ideas, it was spread through the whole of Europe by the Napoleonic invasions. As early as the turn of the nineteenth century, a need had already been perceived for a museum in the Spanish Court which would bring together the major art works kept in poor condition elsewhere in the country, but the first truly concerted attempt to create a museum of paintings came after the Napoleonic invasion. It was Joseph Bonaparte who issued a decree in 1809 whereby a museum of painting, the Museo Josefino, was to be set up in Madrid. The first site considered for the future museum was Buenavista Palace, near today's Plaza de Cibeles, but the difficulties involved in adapting this building led in 1811 to a new proposal. This was to use a building on the Prado de San Jerónimo which had been designed by Juan de Villanueva. Begun in 1785 under the auspices of the Count of Floridablanca, an enlightened politician who was first secretary of state to Charles III, it was originally intended to be a Cabinet of Natural History and an Academy of Sciences, but was never actually used for that purpose. Instead, it was to become the home of the Museo Real de

Pinturas, the predecessor of today's Museo del Prado, which took its name from the meadow (*prado*) where the building stood.

With the end of the Spanish War of Independence, the withdrawal of the French, and Ferdinand VII's arrival in Madrid as king in 1814, the conditions for creating an art museum were highly favourable. In the months immediately following his arrival, the king made all the necessary arrangements for the museum, and thus the Prado was established under King Ferdinand VII's patronage and paid for out of his own pocket. In this, the Museo del Prado was clearly distinguished from the Louvre: the Louvre was established at the height of revolutionary fervour with art works that were nationalised crown property or had been confiscated from the church and the nobility; the contents of the Museo del Prado, by contrast, came from the works in the Royal Collection. This was to define its peculiar character and the special quality of its contents. The Museo del Prado is not an encyclopaedic museum that preserves and exhibits representative examples of every period, place, school and tendency in world art. It also differs from the Louvre in that it did not grow up under the shadow of the Napoleonic empire, which brought art from Italy, Greece, Egypt and Mesopotamia to France. The Museo del Prado was born of the love of art, the collector's enthusiasm and the personal tastes of the monarchs who reigned in Spain from the fifteenth century onwards. The Prado, one of the world's most important art galleries, is neither the most grandiose nor the most complete of the great museums, but it is perhaps the most eloquent, and its collections are possibly those with the greatest substance and coherence, not because they are exhaustive but because of the enthusiasm and fervour of those who brought it into being.

Although the museum dates from the early years of the nineteenth century, the history of its collections, which are its true essence, begins four centuries earlier. It is the history of royal collecting since the fifteenth century, when Ferdinand and Isabella, with their preference for Flemish painters, laid down some of the precepts that would be followed by future royal collectors. Their grandson, Emperor Charles V, continued to collect works by the principal Flemish artists, such as Van der Weyden, Van Eyck and Anthonis Mor, but his attention was also drawn to Italian artists like Titian, who became the portraitist of both the emperor and his son, Philip II, under whom the royal painting collection received its first great impetus in the sixteenth century. Thanks to these two monarchs and to Mary of Hungary (1505–1558), the sister of Charles V and governor of the Netherlands, the Prado possesses an exceptional collection of works by Titian, an artist who subsequently had an enormous influence on the path taken by the Royal Collection and on the development of Spanish painting as a whole. Philip II also inherited his predecessors' taste for Flemish art, purchasing works by Van der Weyden, Bouts, Patinir, Campin, Gossaert, David, and above all Bosch, of whose work the Prado has the finest collection in the world. To these we must add the works of his court portraitists, Anthonis Mor and Sánchez Coello, who created a characteristic type of official portrait whose influence lasted until the eighteenth century, and the works of the many artists, mainly Italians, working on the most important artistic project of the age, the decoration of the monastery of El Escorial.

The Museo del Prado in 1857, photography by Charles Clifford

The other great milestone in the history of the Royal Collection came with Philip IV, whose reign, from 1621 to 1665, coincided with one of the climactic moments in Spanish painting. Not only was Philip IV the patron of Velázquez, but he was also an indefatigable collector who commissioned numerous works expressly for the decoration of his royal palaces. Large decorative cycles were created for the Torre de la Parada, with major contributions from Rubens and Velázquez, and for the new Buen Retiro Palace. Philip IV's passion for collecting is clear from the works he acquired at the sale of the estate of King Charles I of England, another of history's great collectors, whose collection was auctioned off in London after his execution in 1649. Among the significant works purchased by Philip IV at the auction were Mantegna's *Death of the Virgin*, Tintoretto's *The Washing of the Feet*, Dürer's *Self-Portrait*, Raphael's *Holy Family, called 'The Pearl'*, and Veronese's *Moses Saved from the Waters*.

After the death of Charles II, the last of the Spanish Habsburgs, the arrival of a new dynasty led also to a change in artistic taste. The Bourbons, who reigned in Spain from 1700 onwards, brought French artists and a greater interest in the more classicist Italian art. Philip V purchased the important collection of the painter Carlo Maratta, with works by the Carracci, Sacchi and Poussin. His second wife, Isabella Farnese, was in her turn responsible for enlarging the Spanish Royal Collections with works by eighteenth-century Flemish and Dutch painters, and by classicising Italian artists who had not hitherto been represented, such as Domenichino, Guercino, Guido Reni and Crespi. Perhaps her most important contribution, however, was her purchase of a large number of works by Murillo while the court was resident in Seville

View of the main gallery around 1897, photography by J. Laurent y Cia

between 1729 and 1733. There had been hardly any paintings by Murillo in the Royal Collection until that point, but he was to be well represented from then on thanks to these acquisitions and others made later by Charles IV. In 1742, Philip V and his wife also bought the set of sculptures which had been assembled in Rome in the second half of the seventeenth century by Queen Christina of Sweden. Together with the works acquired in Rome by Velázquez under commission from Philip IV, these were to form the basis of the Museo del Prado's collection of classical sculpture. With the Bourbons, the last two great masters of the late Baroque in Europe, Corrado Giaquinto and Giovanni Battista Tiepolo, also came to Spain to work on the decoration of the royal palaces. Tiepolo's time in Spain coincided with that of another of the great artistic figures of the day, Anton Raffael Mengs, who introduced classicist academicism into the country. The reign of Charles IV was another great period for the painting collection. Besides having Goya and Paret under his patronage, he enriched the Royal Collections with works by Barocci, Andrea del Sarto and Raphael, also adding pieces by Spanish artists like Ribera, Ribalta and Juan de Juanes. Charles IV was succeeded by his son, Ferdinand VII, who, as we have seen, was the founder of the Museo del Prado.

When the museum first opened, it had 311 works on display, all by Spanish artists. This number quickly increased with the arrival of paintings from the royal palaces, which were requested for the museum with the king's support. The monarch furthermore covered the institution's expenses, since it was still a royal possession, although it was open to the public. By the time of the inventory of 1827, the museum already had more than 4,000 pictures.

Main gallery of the Museo del Prado in 2008

In accordance with its royal status, the first directors of the museum were members of the higher nobility with connections in the royal palace. The first to be appointed, for instance, was the Marquess of Santa Cruz, steward to the royal household and councillor of the Royal Academy of Fine Arts; he was assisted by an artistic adviser and a *conserje mayor* (senior caretaker). Both these posts were filled by court painters.

The death of Ferdinand VII on 29 September 1833 led to the first great crisis for the institution, since the king's will allowed for all his personal property to be freely disposable. This meant that the works in the museum ran the risk of being divided up among his heirs. The problem remained unresolved until 1843, when Isabella II was declared upon her thirteenth birthday to have come of age. The queen set up a committee to assess her father's will which advised her to avoid breaking up the artistic patrimony by buying the objects intended for the service and adornment of the royal palaces that had fallen to her sister, Infanta María Luisa Fernanda, in their father's inheritance. These included the art works in the museum. The committee also proposed that the Museo del Prado should be incorporated into the Crown, thereby ceasing to be the personal property of the monarch, and so preventing a repetition of the inheritance problem. However, this was not actually done until 1865.

Four years after the death of Ferdinand VII, with his will still unresolved, an event took place which was to be of enormous importance for the future of the Museo del Prado. On 31 December 1837, the Museo Nacional de Pintura y Escultura (National Museum of Painting and Sculpture) was created, clearly differentiated from the royal museum by name and, above all, in being the property of the State. Commonly known as the Museo de la Trinidad, since it was housed in the Convent

The Museum during the Spanish civil war in October 1936. Photography by Hauser & Menet

of the Trinity on Madrid's Calle de Atocha, the new museum was created for the purpose of the conservation and exhibition of art works from the monasteries which had been suppressed in the provinces of Madrid, Toledo, Avila and Segovia as a result of the disentailment of ecclesiastical property. It was also intended to house the contemporary art works acquired by the State, most of which had won awards at the National Exhibitions of Fine Arts, first held in 1856. Unlike the royal museum, the Museo de la Trinidad was directed not by an aristocrat but by a committee of professors. This new approach was to spread to the Museo Real in 1838, when José de Madrazo, a painter rather than a nobleman, was appointed director, introducing a long phase of artist directors which lasted right up to 1960.

The last third of the nineteenth century brought vast changes. As we have seen, the Prado became the property of the Crown in 1865. It thus ceased to be the property of the monarch, which effectively prevented its contents from being divided up through inheritance. In 1872, the revolution which deposed Isabella II and sent her into exile led to the end of the Crown's patrimony and its appropriation by the State, which meant that the Prado now became national property. From that moment on, there was little sense in having two national museums of painting and sculpture in a country that could barely afford one. The Museo de la Trinidad was therefore wound up that same year, and its collections joined those of the Museo del Prado, intensifying the problem of insufficient space which had dogged the institution since its very earliest days. The solution was sought in new plans to enlarge the museum building and in a policy of depositing the works in a number of different places, which led to a series of

Installation of the *Guernica*, by Pablo Picasso, in the Casón del Buen Retiro, 1981

cataloguing and conservation problems that were not to be fully resolved until the last quarter of the twentieth century. Two other important changes took place in the late nineteenth century. One was the approval of a new ruling for the museum in 1876, in which it was stipulated that the director of the Museo del Prado had to be a painter, a member of the San Fernando Academy of Fine Arts, and the winner of a medal at a National Exhibition of Fine Arts. The other took place in 1894, when the Museo de Arte Contemporáneo (Museum of Contemporary Art) was created. Most of the nineteenth-century works kept at the Museo del Prado were moved there.

The early decades of the twentieth century brought the Prado's first temporary exhibition, which was held in 1902 and featured works by El Greco. They also brought the creation of the Real Patronato (Royal Board of Trustees) in 1912, with the purpose of improving the museum's management, making it more scientific in character and bringing it into closer contact with society. One of the trustees' first initiatives was to set up a committee with the mission of carrying out an exhaustive inventory of the museum's possessions, ascertaining the exact whereabouts of each one. Another was to supervise the first extension to the Villanueva building, which was built between 1914 and 1923.

In 1936, the Civil War brought the worst crisis yet faced by the Museo del Prado, which was forced to close on 30 August of that year. Shortly before, the government had formed a special board to protect the Prado's art works, and work had started on safeguarding the building against possible damage. On 20 September 1936, in a gesture laden with symbolism, the Republican government appointed Pablo Picasso as director of the Prado. Not long afterwards, it

Extension building of the Museo del Prado, designed by architect Rafael Moneo and opened in 2007

was decided to move the most important works from the Museo del Prado to Valencia, and later, as the war progressed, to Catalonia. The International Committee for the Salvation of Spanish Art Treasures, which was made up of experts from various countries, was created in 1939. Its aim was to evacuate the works to Geneva under the protection of the League of Nations, an operation which took place in February that year. The works from the Prado were exhibited in Geneva, and the new government negotiated their return to Spain once the war was over. The first pieces arrived in Madrid in May 1939. The Prado reopened on 7 July, and the last of the works were returned in September.

Now that the war was over and the collection was back in Madrid, the main problem facing the museum, apart from the evident economic penury of the nation as a whole, was the recurrent one of the lack of adequate space to conserve and exhibit its collections. To alleviate the problem, two further extensions were added to the Villanueva building, the first between 1954 and 1956, and the second between 1964 and 1968. As the century wore on, however, it became increasingly apparent that the Prado needed not only to enlarge its exhibition space but also to adjust to the new demands being made on museums, including those deriving from an increased number of visitors in the wake of the tourism boom and the growing interest in art. It was thus recognised that the changes needed were not merely of a material nature, such as improved climate controls and additional spaces in which to offer necessary new visitor services. What was also required was a completely new approach to the museum. A technical committee was therefore formed in 1971 with the task of producing a full report on the modernisation of the Prado, establishing new criteria for the arrangement of the facilities, the refurbishment

The *Nineteenth Century* in the new exhibition rooms of the new building, 2007-08

of the buildings and the conservation of the collections. From then on, the Prado was abreast with the times. The number of temporary exhibitions increased, improvements were made in the conservation and restoration of the works, and the museum developed its facility as a research centre, as well as gradually improving its visitor services. To bring all this about, extra space still had to be found. Further extensions to the Villanueva building were no longer a satisfactory solution, so it was proposed instead that new buildings should be added to the museum. The scheme crystallised when the Casón del Buen Retiro, the former ballroom of the Buen Retiro Palace, was allocated to the Museo del Prado. Once refurbished, it was used to house the museum's nineteenth-century collection, opening to the public in 1981. That same year, it also became the home of *Guernica*, Picasso's emblematic painting, after its arrival in Spain from the Museum of Modern Art in New York. This work, together with the rest of the Picasso legacy, was transferred eleven years later to the Museo Nacional Centro de Arte Reina Sofía, a contemporary art museum whose creation necessitated a redistribution of the State art collections. Under an agreement reached in 1995, the nineteenth- and twentieth-century works were therefore reassigned between the Museo Nacional del Prado and the Museo Nacional Centro de Arte Reina Sofía. It was in the 1990s that the modernisation of the Prado started to be pursued most strongly, following the example of other great museums like the Louvre. The process culminated in 2007, requiring a new administrative status which would give the Prado greater autonomy and enable it to increase its staff, renovate the Casón del Buen Retiro, and carry out an ambitious project to enlarge the museum by incorporating the former cloisters of the monastery of Los Jerónimos.

Contents

THE SPANISH PAINTING COLLECTION

24 Romanesque Painting
28 Gothic Painting
32 Hispano-Flemish Painting
36 Bartolomé Bermejo
38 The Dawn of Renaissance Painting:
   Pedro Berruguete and Juan de Flandes
42 Renaissance and Mannerism
48 Luis de Morales
50 The Spanish Painters of Philip II
54 El Greco
60 El Greco. High Altar of the College
   of Doña María de Aragón
64 Juan Bautista Maíno
66 Sánchez Cotán and the Birth of the Still Life
   in Spain
70 The Still Life of the Golden Age
74 Ribalta and Painting in Seventeenth-century Valencia
76 Ribera
84 Andalusian Painting in the Seventeenth Century
86 Zurbarán
90 Alonso Cano
94 Velázquez and the Museo del Prado
96 Velázquez. Seville and the Early Years at Court
100 Velázquez. The First Journey to Italy
104 Velázquez. Years of Maturity
110 Velázquez. Philosophers and the 'People of Pleasure'
114 Velázquez. The Last Years
122 The Salón de Reinos
128 Painters in Seventeenth-century Madrid
132 The High Baroque Painters
140 Murillo
148 Eighteenth-century Spanish Painters
154 Meléndez and the Spanish Still Life Tradition
   in the Eighteenth Century
158 Paret and Cabinet Painting

162 Goya

166 Goya. Tapestry Cartoons

170 Goya. Religious Painting

172 Goya. Royalty, Nobility, the Enlightened and the People
of Madrid

186 Goya. The Black Paintings and Goya's Last Works

194 Nineteenth-century Painting. Neoclassicism

196 Romanticism

202 History Painting

210 Realism and its Evolution towards the Fin-de-siècle

THE ITALIAN PAINTING COLLECTION

220 Renaissance

226 Raphael

232 The Sixteenth Century in Florence and Rome

244 Venice

248 Titian

254 Titian and the Habsburgs

264 Tintoretto

270 Veronese

274 The Bassano

276 Italian Painters at the Spanish Court

278 The Bolognese Painters

282 Caravaggio and Naturalism

286 Other Artistic Centres: Florence, Genoa and Ferrara

290 Luca Giordano and Neapolitan Painters

296 Eighteenth-century Italian Painting

302 The Tiepolo

THE EARLY NETHERLANDISH
AND FLEMISH PAINTING COLLECTION

308 Southern Netherlandish Painting of the Fifteenth
and Sixteenth Centuries

312 Van der Weyden and his Circle

320 Bosch

326 Patinir and Sixteenth-century Netherlandish Painting

338 Pieter Bruegel the Elder

340 Anthonis Mor

344 Jan 'Velvet' Brueghel and Flemish Cabinet Painting
350 The Series of the Five Senses
354 Rubens
364 Van Dyck
370 Jordaens

THE DUTCH PAINTING COLLECTION

374 Seventeenth-century Painting in Holland

THE FRENCH PAINTING COLLECTION

382 La Tour and the Beginning of the Baroque in France
386 Poussin
390 Claude Lorraine
392 French Painters at the Spanish Bourbon Court
396 The Rococo
400 Nineteenth-century French Painting

THE GERMAN PAINTING COLLECTION

404 Dürer and the German Renaissance
414 Anton Raffael Mengs

THE BRITISH PAINTING COLLECTION

420 The Apogee of British Painting

THE DRAWING COLLECTION

432 Drawings and Prints by Goya

THE SCULPTURE
AND DECORATIVE ARTS COLLECTION

440 Ancient Sculpture
450 Modern Sculpture
454 Nineteenth-century Sculpture
458 The Dauphin's Treasure
460 The *Pietre Dure* Collection
462 The Medal and Miniature Collection

The Spanish Painting Collection

Of all the collections in the Museo del Prado, that of Spanish painting is the largest and most complete, and constitutes the nucleus of the museum's holdings. Its importance lies not only in that it offers a survey of painting in Spain over a period of eight centuries, from the Romanesque murals of the twelfth century to the first decade of the twentieth, but also in that it preserves numerous masterpieces by Spanish artists regarded as painters of universal genius, such as El Greco, Ribera, Murillo, Zurbarán, and above all Velázquez and Goya. The Prado possesses the world's finest collections of these last two painters. It is not by chance that the Prado's inauguration coincided with the international discovery of the 'Spanish School' in general, and of the most emblematic of its painters, Velázquez, in particular. Indeed, the characteristics regarded as typical of the 'Spanish School' can largely be said to be those associated with the most outstanding paintings by these artists at the Prado.

The Spanish paintings at the Museo del Prado came principally from the Royal Collections, and were later augmented by the collections of the Museo Nacional de Pintura y Escultura, otherwise known as the Museo de la Trinidad, which was closed down in 1872. These art works came mainly in their turn from the religious institutions and monasteries which had been disentailed in the first decades of the nineteenth century. This enabled the Prado to round off its collection with a series of great religious works, including such artistic landmarks as Pedro Berruguete's cycle of paintings, originally at Santo Tomás in Ávila, and a magnificent group of works by El Greco. A large number of nineteenth-century pieces also arrived from the Museo de la Trinidad. These were the prizewinners at the National Exhibitions of Fine Arts, which had been purchased and deposited at the museum by the State. Ever since its creation in 1819, moreover, the Museo del Prado had devoted considerable effort to enriching its collection of Spanish painting, reinforcing its strong points and filling in its lacunae. The reason for these gaps lay in the preference of some of the Spanish monarchs for foreign artists, especially Flemish and Italian ones, though it was precisely these royal preferences which gave the Museo del Prado one of the world's finest collections of early western painting. The very first work acquired for the Prado was a Spanish one. José de Ribera's *The Trinity* [57] was bought by King Ferdinand VII himself in 1820, only a few months after the museum's inauguration. Spanish too was the first work given to the museum by a private donor, Velázquez's *Christ on the Cross* [75], which entered the Prado in 1829 after the king had received it as a gift from one of the heirs of the Countess of Chinchón. Efforts to improve the collection of Spanish painting have been constant, and they continue today with a large number of important works by Spanish artists still entering the museum in the twenty-first century.

Romanesque Painting

The earliest Spanish paintings at the Museo del Prado were not acquired until well into the twentieth century, when international historiography began to develop an interest in and appreciation of the painting of the Middle Ages. The Spanish monarchs, who built up over the centuries what would later be the core of the Prado's collection, showed no interest in the medieval art of the Iberian Peninsula, and it was not until the creation of a royal board of trustees for the museum in 1912, and at the express insistence of its members, that discussions started to be held on the need to enrich the collections with examples of the Spanish painting of the twelfth, thirteenth and fourteenth centuries. It was not until 1920 that a group of important medieval paintings were eventually transferred to the Prado from the Museo Arqueológico Nacional, and only in 1948 was the public first shown an example of Spanish Romanesque painting, the murals from the chapel of Santa Cruz de Maderuelo (Segovia) [2], bequeathed to the museum two years earlier. This caused consternation both among those who believed that the addition of the work would detract from the collection and destroy its coherence, and among those who found the paintings too close to modern art. Among the latter was the director of the Prado himself, the painter Fernando Alvarez de Sotomayor, who thought that exhibiting the paintings was tantamount to a justification for hanging Picasso in the Prado. In 1957, the trustees brokered an agreement between the Spanish Ministry of National Education and the Metropolitan Museum of Art in New York whereby six of the frescoes from the chapel of San Baudelio in Casillas de Berlanga (Soria) [1], which had been removed and taken to the United States in 1926, were ceded by the American museum to the Prado for an indefinite period. In return, the Metropolitan received the custody of the apse of the church of San Martín in Fuentidueña, near Segovia. Although few in number, these pieces are of exceptional importance, since the works at the Prado are the two finest examples of murals in Castilian Romanesque painting, together with those of San Isidoro in León. Their quality is comparable with the best work in Catalonia, the primary focal point of European Romanesque painting.

1

Mural painting from
San Baudelio in Casillas
de Berlanga (Soria)
Hare Chase

First third of the 12th century.
Fresco and tempera transferred
to canvas. 185 x 360 cm
P7265

The fragment formed part of
the lower tier of decoration
of the Mozarabic chapel of San
Baudelio, which also included
other scenes preserved at the
Prado, such as the *Stag Hunt,* a
Soldier or *Hunter*, and an *Elephant*,
together with an image identified
as a curtain. The group's great
singularity within European
painting is that it represents
hunting scenes in a sacred space.
Some specialists have explained
this oddity by attributing a
profane character to it, seeking
parallels both in the Muslim
miniature and in the mosaics

of antiquity, which abound on
the Castilian tableland. Others,
on the other hand, adduce solely
Christian precedents and see
the paintings as imbued with
religious symbolism. They
claim that these hunting scenes
and representations of animals,
with their monumentality and an
eye for nature that is exceptional
for the period, are intimately
related to the scenes from the
life of Christ shown in the upper
part of the chapel, so creating
an iconographic discourse which
ascends from the earthly to
the divine.

2

Mural paintings from the chapel of Santa Cruz de Maderuelo (Segovia)

c. 1125. Fresco and tempera transferred to canvas, 498 x 450 cm (group)
P7269-P7287

The group from Santa Cruz de Maderuelo is a magnificent example of Romanesque religious painting, with close technical and iconographic links with the church of Santa María in Taüll (Lérida) and the paintings in the upper part of the chapel of San Baudelio in Berlanga. This suggests that itinerant artists might have brought the influence of Lombard painting to Castile after passing it through the filter of Catalan Romanesque. The

way these paintings are arranged in the museum reconstructs the space of the original chapel, with its rectangular plan, barrel vault and flat end wall. Scenes from the Old and New Testament are arranged in a complex but strongly unified iconographic programme executed in a linear style with exquisite draughtsmanship. The illustration shows one of the lunettes of the chapel with *The Creation of Adam* (P7825) and *The Fall of Adam and Eve* (P7428).

Gothic Painting

The transition from Romanesque to Gothic in Spanish painting was a gradual one. What characterises Gothic painting in Spain is the evolution of the earlier Romanesque forms in combination with French and Italian influences, and the peculiarity of its use of Mudejar decorative elements. Despite the persistence of archaic features, the conceptual nature of Romanesque art was attenuated because of a heightened awareness of the real world, which gave rise to closer observation of nature, a growing interest in the expression of sentiment, and a more humanised mode of representation.

Initially, two interpretations of Gothic reached Spain. One originated in France and was based on the tradition of western painting, while the second, of Italian origin, was related to Byzantine models. The French influence was the first to become widespread, giving rise to the so-called Franco-Gothic style, represented by the *St Christopher Altarpiece* [4] in the Museo del Prado. The Italian influence made its appearance in the late fourteenth century and grew over the next two hundred years, eventually replacing Franco-Gothic completely. It showed a greater concern with the representation of space and more detailed anatomical study, while at the same time according more importance to light in relation to both volume and colour. Although there are various tendencies within this overall style, the best represented at the Prado is the Florentine, which is characterised by the plasticity of its compositions, its interest in emphasising the details of the human body, and the monumentality and solemnity of its figures. Jaime Serra's panels of *St Mary Magdalene and St John the Baptist* [3] belong to this Italianate style and illustrate its development in Catalonia, while the *Altarpiece of Archbishop Sancho de Rojas* [5] by Juan Rodríguez de Toledo is an example of its influence in Castile.

Finally, the *Altarpiece of the Life of the Virgin and of St Francis* [6] by Nicolás Francés belongs to the International Gothic style, which fuses French and Sienese characteristics. Whilst incorporating the idealising tendency of the Italian masters, the style also displays a narrative sense and a taste for anecdote and secondary subjects which point to the influence of the French miniature.

3 →
JAIME SERRA
Barcelona, documented
between 1358 and 1390

Histories of St Mary Magdalene and St John the Baptist
1356–59. Tempera on panel,
280 x 92 cm (each panel)
P3106-3107

These panels come from the shrine of Nuestra Señora de Tobed, in the province of Saragossa. They are the side panels of an altarpiece whose central panel showed the Virgin and Child together with the donor, Henry of Trastámara, the king of Castile since 1366, who had taken refuge in Aragon. He commissioned the work from the Catalan painter Jaime Serra, a representative of the Italo-Gothic tendency. These panels, with their triangular canopies, are made up of several scenes running from top to bottom, with a predella below. On the left, the panel of the Magdalene shows *The Supper in the House of Simon* in the upper tier, *The Marys at the Sepulchre* and *Noli Me Tangere* in the middle, and *The Death of the Magdalene* below, with St Peter, St Dominic and a bishop saint in the predella. On the right, the panel of St John the Baptist represents *The Dance of Salome* above, *The Beheading of the Baptist* in two episodes in the centre, and a posthumous miracle beneath, with a female saint, St Lawrence and St Paul in the predella.

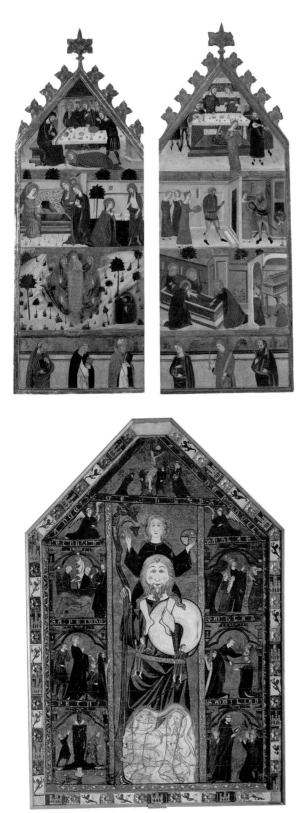

4 ←
St Christopher Altarpiece
14th century. Tempera on panel,
266 x 184 cm
P3150

A fine example of Castilian
Franco-Gothic painting,
this work presents the linear
refinement characteristic
of the style, which is closely
related to the miniature.
The taste for monumentality
is evident in the large figure of
the saint, who is crossing a river
full of fish with the Christ Child
on his shoulders. Culminating
in a representation of Calvary,
the panel also shows scenes
from the lives of St Peter,
St Blaise and St Millán. The cult
of the latter, a saint from La
Rioja, is not widespread outside
the region, which indicates
that the work might come
from a church or monastery in
that area. The border of castles
and lions raises the possibility
of a royal donation.

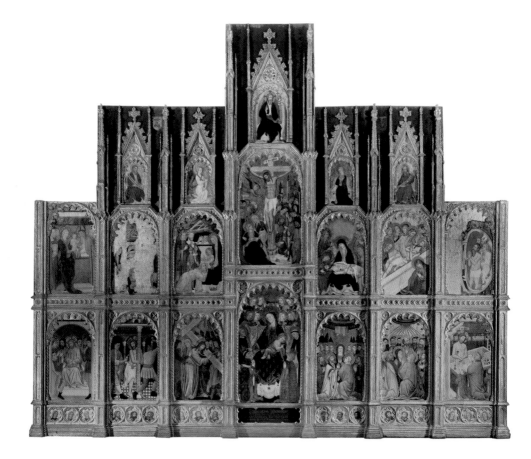

5
JUAN RODRÍGUEZ
DE TOLEDO
Toledo, active between 1395
and 1420

*Altarpiece of Archbishop
Sancho de Rojas*

1412–15. Tempera on panel,
532 x 618 cm
P1321

This altarpiece was painted for the convent of San Benito el Real in Valladolid, but it has been moved and dismantled so often that it is impossible to determine the original structure of the group. The central panel shows the Virgin and Child with St Benedict and St Bernard, as befits a Benedictine monastery, along with portraits of the archbishop of Toledo, Don Sancho de Rojas (c. 1381–1422), the patron of the altarpiece, and Prince Fernando de Antequera (1380–1416), the future Ferdinand I of Aragon, who is being crowned by the Christ Child. Don Sancho and Don Fernando fought together against the Muslims during the conquest of Antequera in 1410. The work is a fine example of the diffusion in Castile of the Tuscan models introduced to Toledo by Gerardo Starnina and Niccolò di Antonio. The influence here comes not from Sienese painting, as is the case in Catalonia, but from Florentine models, with a somewhat Giottesque feeling for form and volume, and a preference for serenity and monumentality over movement.

6

NICOLÁS FRANCÉS
Documented in León before
1434–1468

*Altarpiece of the Life of
the Virgin and of St Francis*

c. 1445–60. Tempera
on panel, 557 x 558 cm

P2545

This altarpiece from La Bañeza
(León) has been preserved
virtually intact. Its delicate
refinement and its numerous
scenes of extraordinary
iconographic value make it
one of the masterpieces of
International Gothic in Castile.
The side panels show scenes
from the lives of the Virgin
and St Francis, while figures
of apostles and prophets appear
in the predella. The enthroned
Virgin who presides over the
central panel is surrounded
by angels, while the Child
in her lap plays with a bird tied

to a piece of string. Above her
is the scene of the *Assumption*,
and the altarpiece culminates,
as is customary, with a *Calvary*.
With great narrative skill,
the painter brings considerable
liveliness to the scenes through
the use of anecdotal details,
which compensate for the
stylised expression of some
figures.

Hispano-Flemish Painting

The Museo del Prado has a very rich collection of Hispano-Flemish painting, a tendency which led to a radical renewal of Spanish painting from the mid-fifteenth century onwards. Because of the close political and economic ties between Flanders and the Crown of Castile, the techniques, forms and models of Flemish art were able to penetrate Spain through imported art or foreign artists working in the Iberian Peninsula. The principal technical novelty of this school was the use of oil paint, since mixing oil with the pigments allowed for richer colouring, finer chromatic nuances and a broader tonal range.

The Spanish sensibility was highly receptive to these Flemish models, which came to be profoundly identified with Hispanic devotional tastes. Their heightened drama tinged with melancholy was very well received in the Iberian Peninsula, and so too were their spatial coherence, their taste for the concrete, their pleasure in folds of rich fabric, and their minute reproduction of detail, all of which became characteristic features of Hispanic art. In addition, the Flemish influence was introduced on certain occasions by German artists, which led to painting of greater expressiveness and pathos and with more angular folds in the cloth, very different from the flowing curves of the drapery of the International Style. The Museo del Prado has some magnificent examples of this in the works of Fernando Gallego.

7
FERNANDO GALLEGO
Salamanca, documented
between 1468 and 1507

Pietà, or the Fifth Sorrow
c. 1470. Oil and tempera
on panel, 117.8 x 111 cm
P2998

In the works of Fernando Gallego, one of the main representatives of the Hispano-Flemish style in Castile, the expressiveness of the Flemish models is accentuated. He exaggerates the characters' severe expressions and the angular folds of the draperies, as clearly seen in the garments and cloak of the Virgin in this panel. Some features of his work also look back to International Gothic and the work of the German engravers. In this *Pietà*, one of his early pieces, the grim faces of Christ and the Virgin are represented with great harshness and profound pathos, heightened by such details as Christ's half-closed eyes. Clearly visible here is the hard and expressive draughtsmanship of this painter, whose mastery is considerable notwithstanding his violent contrasts. Alongside the central figures, but on a smaller scale, the donors contemplate the scene in an attitude of prayer against a stylised landscape background typical of International Gothic. Unusually for the period, the painter's signature appears beneath the figures of Christ and the Virgin.

8

ANONYMOUS HISPANO-
FLEMISH ARTIST

St Michael the Archangel

c. 1495. Oil and tempera
on panel, 242 x 153 cm
P1326

Executed by an unknown
Hispano-Flemish painter,
this picture shows the fall of the
rebel angels as the subject had
taken form in northern Europe
around the year 1400. The
theme of the struggle between
good and evil may owe something to the original function
of the picture, which once hung
in the hospital of San Miguel in
Zafra (Badajoz). St Michael, the
leader of the celestial forces, raises his sword to smite the dragon.
The angelic choirs are deployed
along the top while the struggle
between the good angels and
the rebels is seen on the sides.
Below, the latter have been
turned into monstrous demons.
Reflected on the shield is a figure who has been interpreted as
either the kneeling donor or the
artist himself. On either side, a
demon and the figure's guardian
angel prepare to do battle.

9

MASTER OF SOPETRÁN
Active c. 1470

The First Marquess of Santillana or his Son, the First Duke of El Infantado

c. 1470. Oil and tempera
on panel, 103 x 60 cm
P2576

10

MASTER OF THE VIRGIN OF THE CATHOLIC MONARCHS

The Virgin of the Catholic Monarchs

c. 1491–93. Tempera
on panel, 123 x 122 cm
P1260

Because it originally came
from the royal chamber at the
monastery of Santo Tomás in
Avila, this panel was traditionally
attributed to Pedro Berruguete,
who painted other works for
the same monastery. However,
and despite the presence
of certain features which relate
it to Fernando Gallego, there
is no documentary evidence
to permit the identification
of the artist who, like Gallego
and Berruguete, was faithful
to the Hispano-Flemish style.
In this painting, ceremonial
in character, the Virgin Mary is
enthroned with the Child in her
arms as she receives the homage
of Ferdinand and Isabella and
their two children. The Catholic
monarchs are shown lower down
but on the same scale as the
Virgin, and do not look towards
her. As was customary, Ferdinand
the Catholic appears in the most
important position, to the right
of the Virgin and Child. Next
to him is Prince Juan protected
by St Thomas. Queen Isabella
of Castile, who financed the
monastery, is given slightly
more space than the king, and is
placed closer to the Virgin. She
is protected by St Dominic.
Next to her is a princess, almost
certainly her eldest child, Isabella.
The picture is completed by
two other Dominicans kneeling
behind the monarchs and their
children, probably St Peter
the Martyr and the inquisitor
of Aragon, Pedro de Arbués.

Bartolomé Bermejo

Owing to the relations existing between Italy and the Crown of Aragon, the Flemish influence in Aragon, and above all in Catalonia and Valencia, was combined with that of the Italian Quattrocento. This added complexity to the pictorial panorama of Spain while also paving the way for the later arrival of Renaissance painting. Despite the primacy of colour and a closer study of light, the use of gilding to enhance the colour against a gleaming background was often retained, constituting a highly characteristic feature of Spanish art at that moment. It was especially common in Aragon, perhaps as a result of Moorish influence, and is illustrated by the Prado's *St Dominic of Silos enthroned as Bishop* by Bartolomé Bermejo [11], the principal representative of the Hispano-Flemish style in the lands of the Crown of Aragon. This work, the central panel of the altarpiece of Santo Domingo de Silos in Daroca (Saragossa), is one of the masterpieces of fifteenth-century Spanish painting. Although it is only one fragment of the whole altarpiece, it produces a rare impression of completeness, and is outstanding for its technical perfection, its precise study of material qualities and its meticulous treatment of detail. Bermejo's arrival in Daroca from Valencia in about 1474 has been credited with introducing and spreading the technique of oil painting and the Flemish style to Aragonese Gothic painting. Bermejo achieves extraordinary effects of transparency and glazing in the drapery and the throne, and he treats the saint's facial features with minute attention to detail. St Dominic, who founded the monastery of Silos (Burgos) in the eleventh century and was its first abbot, is here represented as a bishop with all the attributes. He is seated on a Gothic throne, a symbol of power, on which the seven virtues are arranged in the form of polychrome sculptures. The cope is embroidered with the images of seven saints. Surrounded by this brilliant and highly decorative robe, the bishop, hieratic, majestically frontal and almost sculptural in his severity, directs his impassive gaze at the viewer.

11
BARTOLOMÉ BERMEJO
Cordova, c. 1440–Barcelona, 1500

St Dominic of Silos enthroned as Bishop
1474–77. Oil and tempera on panel, 242 x 130 cm
P1323

The Dawn of Renaissance Painting: Pedro Berruguete and Juan de Flandes

In 1472, the Italian artist Paolo de San Leocadio arrived in Valencia under the protection of Cardinal Rodrigo de Borja, later Pope Alexander VI (from 1492 to 1503). This painter is credited with the introduction to Spain of the mature forms of the Quattrocento, which greatly influenced the painters of the Valencian region, subsequently the focal point of the Spanish Renaissance. A modified version of the same forms was brought to Castile a decade later by Pedro Berruguete [13], an artist born in Palencia and trained in Italy, where he became familiar with classical models and worked for Federico da Montefeltro, duke of Urbino. He returned to Spain at the start of 1480, bringing with him a classicist decorative repertoire, a severe sense of form and great mastery in the representation of the human figure. Unlike San Leocadio [12], however, Berruguete's personal taste, allied with the demands of those who commissioned work from him, led him to combine the features of the Italian Renaissance with those of earlier Castilian painting, itself based on Hispano-Flemish, Gothic and Mudejar styles. From all this, there emerged a personal style mid-way between that of Flanders and Italy.

Another of the main figures responsible for introducing the Renaissance to Castile, though this time in its northern variant, was Juan de Flandes (John of Flanders), a painter who arrived in the region in 1496 to work for Isabella the Catholic (reigned 1474–1504). His style bore a close relationship to that of the Bruges School and the painting of Hans Memling [266], Gérard David [276, 277], and Jan van Eyck [258], but it also reflected something of the Italian Renaissance in its taste for idealised beauty, its delicate use of light and the inclusion of Italian decorative and architectural elements. When Isabella died in 1504, Juan de Flandes chose to remain in Castile, adapting his style to the requirements of his new commissions. He moved in 1505 to Salamanca, where he painted the altarpiece of the university chapel of El Estudio, and he then left in 1509 for Palencia, where he was engaged on the paintings for the high altar of the cathedral. This group, unfinished at his death, included the *Crucifixion* [15], which was situated in the centre of the predella. It was also while in Palencia that he executed the high altar for the church of San Lázaro in Palencia, which contained the *Resurrection of Lazarus,* also in the Prado [14].

12
PAOLO DE SAN LEOCADIO
Reggio Emilia, 1447–Valencia, 1519

The Virgin of the Knight of Montesa
c. 1475. Oil and tempera on panel, 102 x 96 cm
P1335

13
PEDRO BERRUGUETE
Paredes de Nava, Palencia,
c. 1445/1450–Madrid (?), 1503

St Dominic Guzmán
presiding over an Auto-da-fé
c. 1493–98/99. Oil on panel,
154 x 92 cm
P618

This work comes from the
sacristy of the convent of Santo
Tomás in Avila, and not, as
formerly believed, from the
same convent's *St Dominic*
Altarpiece, the origin of three
other panels in the Prado with
scenes of the saint's life. St
Dominic Guzmán (1170–1221),
the founder of the Dominican
order, was entrusted by
Innocent III with the task
of eradicating the Albigensian
heresy. He here presides
over the auto-da-fé in which
Raimundo de Corsi is abjuring
heretical beliefs. Corsi appears
at the foot of the steps in a
yellow sanbenito bearing the
words 'condemned heretic'.
In a single scene, Berruguete
shows the whole process of
trial, sentence and execution
as though it were taking place
in the period when the picture
was painted. The setting,
the costumes and the actions
of the figures all point to the
artist's desire to make his
work a faithful reflection of
life in the times of Ferdinand
and Isabella. The formal
Italian influence evident in the
coherence of the perspective
contrasts with this content.

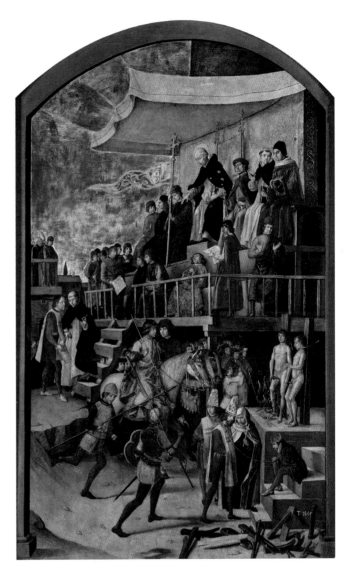

14
JUAN DE FLANDES
Southern Netherlands,
c. 1465–Palencia, 1519

The Resurrection of Lazarus
c. 1510–18. Oil on panel,
110 x 84 cm
P2935

Like *The Agony in the Garden*,
The Ascension and *The Descent
of the Holy Ghost*, all in the
Prado, and four other panels
at the National Gallery of Art
in Washington, this painting
formed part of the retable
of the high altar of the church
of San Lázaro in Palencia.
It shows Lazarus rising from
his tomb at Christ's bidding
with two black pearls for
eyes, his arm resting on
the edge of the sepulchre.
Although the gospel says
that it was his sister Martha
who was present at this event
(*John*, 2: 38-44), the figure
shown here is remarkably
similar to the Magdalene in
the same artist's *Crucifixion*,
also in the Prado [15]. Her face
and that of Christ are tender
and melancholy in contrast
with those of the spectators,
who witness the miracle from
beneath a round arch in a
ruined wall.

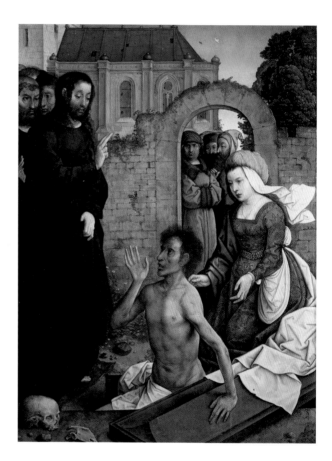

15
JUAN DE FLANDES
Southern Netherlands,
c. 1465–Palencia, 1519

The Crucifixion
1509–18. Oil on panel,
123 x 169 cm
P7878

The low viewpoint and the extensive landscape in the background are reminiscent of Mantegna's *Crucifixion*, but Juan de Flandes reduces the number of characters and creates a composition of great solemnity and balance in which vertical lines predominate. Christ has already died and darkness is covering the sun. Arranged in a semicircle around him are St John, the Virgin, the two Marys and the Magdalene, with the mounted centurion and another horseman behind them. Completing the semicircle in the right foreground is a a lancer, darkly outlined against the landscape, his back to the viewer. On the ground is the skull of Adam, traditionally said to have been buried on Golgotha, and here symbolising the redemption of all human sinners. The precious stones evoke Paradise, and the piece of coral symbolises the blood of Christ. Very common in Juan de Flandes's work, these features show a debt to Jan van Eyck.

Renaissance and Mannerism

It is difficult to apply the categories of Italian art to the eccentric art of Spain, and particularly so in the case of the Renaissance. Despite its enormous influence, this style was very short-lived in its canonical form, even in Italy, and in fact constituted only a brief moment in the career of a handful of artists.

What reached the Iberian Peninsula of the Italian Renaissance was often assimilated only superficially. It appeared in works arbitrarily, and was mixed in with Nordic influences and the Hispanic substratum. Various regional schools briefly flourished, their styles varying in accordance with the force or clarity with which the Italian innovations were grasped, and depending on whether they were kept pure or combined to a greater or lesser degree with earlier forms of painting.

The purest focal point was Valencia, because of the persistence there of a Quattrocento tradition which provided a seedbed for the Leonardesque influences brought in by Fernando Llanos and Fernando Yáñez de la Almedina [16], Spanish artists who worked in Italy. Moreover, close contacts with Italy favoured the circulation of prints after compositions by Raphael, and also explain the presence in Valencia of four paintings by Sebastiano del Piombo [199, 200], which were sent over by Jerónimo Vich y Valterra (1459–1535). Two other focal points, less forceful but also important, were Toledo and Seville, both closely linked to their respective cathedrals in a clearly medieval arrangement.

The taste for foreign artists of the early Spanish Habsburgs prevented a local centre of Renaissance art from forming around the court. This also explains why Spanish Renaissance painting is very unevenly represented at the Prado, whose basic nucleus consists of the Royal Collections. The works from the Toledo school joined the Prado with the collections of the Museo de la Trinidad, a museum which housed the art works confiscated from the church in the disentailments of the nineteenth century. The works from the Valencian school did, on the other hand, belong to the Royal Collection, but were bought much later under the Bourbons.

As for Mannerism, it could be said that all Spanish Renaissance art has something of a Mannerist nature owing to the lateness of its development. This time lapse, indeed, meant that the influences reaching Spain were no longer properly Renaissance but Mannerist.

16
FERNANDO YÁÑEZ
DE LA ALMEDINA
Almedina, Ciudad Real,
c. 1475–1540

St Catherine
1505–10. Oil on panel,
212 x 112 cm
P2902

The painter here departs from the descriptive tradition of the Middle Ages to create a symbolic representation of great force and beauty. The episodes in the life of the young woman from Alexandria who stood up to the Emperor Maxentius in the third century are here replaced by the elegant figure of the saint with all her attributes. The crown alludes to her noble origin, the spiked wheel is the instrument of her torture, the palm is that of martyrdom, and the book symbolises her wisdom, with which she converted some of the emperor's philosophers to Christianity. Against a background of severe Renaissance architecture, the saint presents a monumental and almost sculptural figure whose face, with its delicate smile and mysterious and melancholic remoteness, reveals a clear Leonardesque influence. Richly attired, she displays a mixture of Italianate features, such as the pearl necklace, and Hispanic ones, like the tunic decorated with Cufic letters in the Mudejar tradition.

17 ↓
ALEJO FERNÁNDEZ
Germany (?), Documented
between 1496 and 1545/46

The Flagellation
c. 1508. Oil on panel,
49 x 35.4 cm
P1925

Though of German origin, this artist took the surname of his father-in-law, Pedro Fernández, a painter from Cordova. His work is a good example of the joint use of elements from Flemish art and the Italian Renaissance. The complex classical portico is based on a design by the architect Donato Bramante. Partly in ruins, it provides a setting for action involving characters from a very different tradition, that of the expressive world of Quentin Massys and other Flemish artists. This is clearly seen in Christ's executioners, who are anatomically correct but whose faces and expressions are caricaturesque.

18 →
JUAN VICENTE MASIP
Valencia, c. 1475–1550

The Visitation
c. 1540. Oil on panel, 60 cm
in diameter
P851

This small tondo and its companion piece, *The Martyrdom of St Agnes*, also at the Prado, formed part of an altarpiece in the chapel of Santo Tomás de Villanueva at San Julián, a convent of Augustinian nuns in Valencia. The composition is inspired by paintings by Raphael, which Masip knew from the prints then circulating in Valencia, mostly the work of Marcantonio Raimondi. The main scene of the Visitation is accompanied in the background landscape by the Baptism of Christ, thereby linking the two main events in Christ's relationship with the Baptist. The work illustrates the mature style of this painter of monumental figures, in particular his firm and elegant draughtsmanship, warm colours, and use of chiaroscuro that denotes the influence of Sebastiano del Piombo [199, 200].

19
PEDRO MACHUCA
Toledo, c. 1490–Granada, 1550

The Descent from the Cross
c.1520. Oil on panel,
141 x 128 cm
P3017

This Spanish painter and architect trained in Italy, possibly under Michelangelo himself. Upon his return to Spain in 1520, he introduced the Mannerist style both to painting and, as master of works of Charles V's palace in Granada, to architecture. The Mannerist character of this work can be seen in the nervous attitudes and forced postures of the figures, the coolness of the nocturnal light with its notes of intense colour, and the contrasting chiaroscuro that gives the scene a sense of mystery. The light is focused on the Michelangelesque body of Christ and on the figure of the Magdalene. Unusual details like the child with a gumboil and the strange character in short breeches, both on the right of the picture, are also typical of Mannerism.

20
JUAN CORREA DE VIVAR
Mascaraque, Toledo,
c. 1510–Toledo, 1566

The Annunciation
1559. Oil on panel, 225 x 146 cm
P2828

This late work no longer displays the serenity and expressive restraint which characterise the early paintings of this artist under the influence of his master, Juan de Borgoña. On the contrary, a noticeable mark has been left here by Mannerism, which Correa discovered thanks to the presence in Toledo of Alonso Berruguete, Diego de Siloé and Pedro Machuca [19]. However, Raphael is still an influence, especially in the figure of God the Father, who is similar to the one who appears to Noah in the Stanza d'Eliodoro in the Vatican. Mannerist tendencies are apparent in the dynamic composition, the slender figures and their artful movements, and above all in the serpentining sophistication of the archangel Gabriel, who recalls a Mercury by Parmigianino. Mannerist too are the spatial distortions and iridescent colours, which contrast with the serene faces of the Virgin and Gabriel.

21
JUAN DE JUANES
Valencia (?), c. 1510–Bocairente,
Valencia, 1579

The Last Supper
c. 1562. Oil on panel,
116 x 191 cm
P846

The Last Supper was the
central panel of the predella
from the high altar of San
Esteban in Valencia. It is the
most significant, and most
monumental, work executed by
Juan Vicente Masip's son, Juan
de Juanes, an artist who was long
regarded as the most important
Spanish Renaissance painter. He
was also one of the few who won
recognition outside Spain, thanks
to his similarities to Raphael.
The composition of this panel
is inspired by Leonardo's *Last
Supper*, but Juanes represents

Christ raising the Host at the
moment of its consecration,
a scene which is very common
in the Spanish iconographic
tradition. The influence of
Raphael [189] can be clearly
seen in the expressiveness of
the apostles, and is also evident
in the exquisite draughtsmanship
and the rich and brilliant
colouring. On the table, the
painter shows the chalice
preserved in Valencia Cathedral,
said by legend to be the Holy
Grail, the vessel used by Christ
at the Last Supper.

Luis de Morales

22
LUIS DE MORALES
Badajoz, c. 1510–1586

The Birth of the Virgin
c. 1560–70. Oil on panel,
69·2 x 93·2 cm
P7859

The Bible makes no mention of the birth of the Virgin, and the subject of this panel is based on the apocryphal proto-gospel of St James. It is an exceptional work within Morales's production, since it is the only one known on this theme, and the number of figures is unusual for him. The centre of the composition is occupied by St Anne who, exhausted after giving birth, is helped by a young woman to sit up and drink the broth she is offered. Further to the left, the wet nurse suckles the newly born Virgin. At the right of the picture, an elegant and mysterious figure, oblivious to the scene, holds a basket of fruit and looks directly at the viewer.

The distinctive character of the paintings of Luis de Morales, known from an early date as 'the Divine' because of the religious intensity of his works, was the result of a union of Nordic and Italian features. His predominantly religious subjects came from the late medieval tradition, and he painted them with a Flemish eye for minute detail combined with Italian-style colouring and a masterly use of Leonardesque *sfumato*, which he learned from the Renaissance-style art he saw in Valencia. His work appealed to the intellectual spirituality of clergymen like Fray Luis de Granada (1504–1588), and St John de Ribera (1532–1611), bishop of Badajoz, who was one of Morales's principal clients. Morales's portrait of him is preserved at the Museo del Prado. However, Morales also connected with the profound popular devotion of sixteenth-century Spanish society. His delicate images were much sought after and he received numerous commissions, obliging him to run a large and active workshop, but despite his many clients and his empathy with the spirituality of his time, Morales, like El Greco, never managed to secure royal patronage. Most of the works by him at the Prado are modern acquisitions or bequests; those which come from the Royal Collections were purchased under the Bourbons.

23
LUIS DE MORALES
Badajoz, c. 1510–1586

The Virgin and Child
1568. Oil on panel, 84 x 64 cm
P2656

Morales specialised in religious images of great intimacy, especially paintings of Christ's Passion and, as here, of the Virgin and Child. This work is the most beautiful of the many versions of the subject painted by Morales or his workshop, and is considered the prototype for all the others. Morales reduces the elements of the composition to a minimum, creating a devotional icon intended to evoke tenderness and compassion. The Virgin is framed by a black background from which only the stone bench on which she sits emerges. Perhaps foreseeing the sufferings of the Passion, she turns a melancholy gaze on her Son. The Child returns her gaze, searching with one hand for his mother's breast while clutching her veil with the other. The transparency of the veil is rendered with great subtlety.

The Spanish Painters of Philip II

Like his predecessors, Philip II (reigned 1556–1598) had a preference for Flemish and Italian painting, especially Venetian. He acquired very few works by Spaniards, and the number of Spanish artists who worked for him was small, for the honour was achieved only by those whose versatility allowed them to adapt to his demands. One who did was Juan Fernández de Navarrete, nicknamed '*El Mudo*' ('the Dumb') because he had never learned to speak after going deaf at the age of three. This was the painter chosen by Philip II for the decorative programme at the monastery of El Escorial. The programme was intended to reflect the ideas of the Counter-Reformation, although the work was largely finished by Italian artists owing to Navarrete's early death. Most of Navarrete's work, all of it religious, is preserved at the monastery itself, but the Museo del Prado holds a small panel which served to demonstrate his skills to the monarch [26].

Alonso Sánchez Coello also managed to adapt to requirements at court and to the taste of Philip II, who followed his father, Emperor Charles V (reigned 1519–1556), in commissioning portraits from Titian [213-215] and Anthonis Mor [287]. Coello, a pupil of the latter, was the artist who (*continues on page 52*)

24
ALONSO SÁNCHEZ COELLO
Benifairó de les Valls, Valencia, 1531/32–Madrid, 1588

The Infantas Isabella Clara Eugenia and Catherine Micaela
c. 1575. Oil on canvas, 135 x 149 cm
P1138

25
Prince Carlos
c. 1558. Oil on canvas, 109 x 95 cm
P1136

192.
137

Coello painted Philip II's children on numerous occasions, and this is the latest of the three surviving portraits of this pair of princesses, the king's daughters by his third wife, Isabel of Valois. Isabella Clara Eugenia (1566–1633) and Catherine Micaela (1567–1597) are stiffly dressed in the adult fashion of the time. The purpose of this type of portrait was to reflect the healthy growth of the royal offspring, so demonstrating that the succession was secure, and also to arrange dynastic marriages, which made them into official portraits as severe and distant as those of the monarchs themselves. The portrait of Carlos, on the other hand, is one of the first executed by Coello at the Spanish court after his return from Flanders. It shows Prince Carlos (1545–1568), the eldest child of Philip II and his first wife, his cousin Maria Manuela of Portugal (1526–1545). It is the most serene and elegant of all the portraits painted of this prince, who was sick and weakly from birth probably because of the consanguinity of his parents. He is shown here as the heir to the Crown. In the landscape seen through the window, which was uncovered during a restoration carried out in 1990, Jupiter watches an eagle carrying one of the Pillars of Hercules, a symbol of the Spanish monarchy.

(*continues from page 50*) defined the Spanish court portrait, adopting the formulae devised by the Habsburg court while assimilating elements from both Titian and the Florentine portraitists. The iconographic models he created, which persisted until well into the seventeenth century, were solemn and imposing official images whose aim was to dignify the sitter. Distanced by their pomp and majesty, their cold elegance and their lack of vitality, the sitters are presented as institutions rather than people, which perfectly suited the character and style of Philip II's government. Coello painted a large number of portraits, as well as numerous replicas and copies of works by other portraitists, which were destined for the many royal residences and for other European courts linked to the Habsburg crown [24]. Upon Coello's death in 1588, Juan Pantoja de la Cruz, who had trained in his workshop, became the leading portraitist of the end of Philip II's reign and the early years of Philip III (reigned 1598–1621), perpetuating the iconographic formulae established for royal portraiture [27].

26
JUAN FERNÁNDEZ DE
NAVARRETE, 'EL MUDO'
Logroño, c. 1538–Toledo, 1579

The Baptism of Christ
c. 1567. Oil on panel,
48.5 x 37 cm
P1012

This work, the earliest of all those known to be by the hand of Navarrete, was executed shortly after his return from Italy. Its purpose was to demonstrate the painter's skill to Philip II. The influence of Michelangelo and the Roman Mannerists is evident in the cold and jarring colours and in the robust anatomies of Christ and St John the Baptist. Also detectable are traces of Flemish influence, especially in the landscape. As Navarrete's work evolved, he looked more towards the Venetian painters of the sixteenth century, and above all Titian [208 ff.], whose works at El Escorial he restored, though he was also influenced by the Bassano family [230] and Sebastiano del Piombo [199, 200]. His colouring became more sensual, his manner more pictorial and his lighting more audacious, but he never lost his narrative clarity, a certain grandiose severity, and the decorum which Philip II demanded for the religious images at El Escorial.

27
JUAN PANTOJA DE LA CRUZ
Valladolid, c. 1553–Madrid,
1608

Queen Margaret of Austria
c. 1606. Oil on canvas,
207 x 122 cm
P2563

This work forms a pair with
a portrait of Philip III by
the same artist, also preserved
at the Prado. Pantoja de la
Cruz faithfully follows the
practice of his master Coello,
intensifying the remoteness
and sophistication of the
model characteristic of the
Habsburg dynasty. He takes
advantage of the fashion
of his time, richer and more
luminous than that of Philip
II's reign, to dwell on the
sumptuousness of fabrics,
which he renders in great
detail, and on the richness of
jewels. It is perhaps because
of this that his female
portraits, and particularly this
one of Queen Margaret, are
among his best, successfully
transmitting the concept
of majesty through a figure of
great solemnity with features
bordering on the abstract. Her
triangular silhouette reflects
the fashion for geometry,
and on her breast she wears
one of the most important
of the dynastic jewels, the
so-called *Joyel Rico*, made up
of a large steel blue diamond
with the '*Peregrina*' pearl for
a pendant. Margaret of Austria
married Philip III in 1599
and bore eight children, one
of whom was the future King
Philip IV.

El Greco

Regarded as a singular artist even in his own time, Domenicos Theotocopoulos, called El Greco, was admired by some and vilified by others for the formal extravagance of his work and his peculiar way of depicting religious subjects. His art was dismissed outright during the eighteenth century and part of the nineteenth, and although he is earlier than either Velázquez or Goya, with whom he forms the trio of the Spanish School's great masters, he was the last to be rediscovered. Trained in the Byzantine icon painting tradition, El Greco travelled first to Venice and then throughout Italy in order to assimilate the western style of painting. He succeeded to perfection, but when he failed to achieve the recognition in Rome that he thought he deserved, he travelled to Spain in search of a court that would make him its principal artist. In this too he failed, since Philip II (reigned 1556–1598) judged neither his *Martyrdom of St Maurice* nor his *Allegory of the Holy League* to be suitable for El Escorial. He then settled in Toledo, where he created an oeuvre with a distinct character of its own.

El Greco has been described in many ways – as a Greek disciple of Titian's, for instance, or as the painter whose work best reflected the religious spirit and Hispanic values of society under Philip II, but also as a philosopher, as an intellectual and as a sensitive and idiosyncratic artist who painted with great freedom, creating an extremely personal style whose peculiarity has more to do with Mannerist formalism than with Spanish art. So singular is this style, with its expressionism and subjectivism, that avant-garde pictorial movements of the twentieth century were keen to claim it as a precedent.

Two magnificent examples of the few surviving works painted by El Greco before he arrived in Spain are in the Museo del Prado, together with examples from every stage of his career in Spain. There are pictures belonging to the altarpieces he painted for churches and monasteries, portraits of the intellectual and political personalities of Toledo, and versions of small or medium-sized devotional works whose iconography he repeated time and again for private clients, and which helped him to maintain his workshop. The portraits belonged to the Royal Collections, the religious works come mainly from the Museo de la Trinidad, and a third group, which includes *The Adoration of the Shepherds* from Santo Domingo el Antiguo [37], are modern acquisitions.

28
EL GRECO
Candia, Crete, 1541–Toledo, 1614

The Trinity
1577–79. Oil on canvas, 300 x 179 cm
P824

This work formed part of the main altarpiece of the convent of Santo Domingo el Antiguo in Toledo, established by Doña María de Silva. Doña María was a Portuguese noblewoman who came to Spain in the service of Empress Isabella of Portugal, the wife of Charles V. The first works commissioned from El Greco in Toledo were three altarpieces for this convent, together with *El Expolio* (*The Disrobing of Christ*) for the cathedral. These commissions owed much to Don Diego de Castilla, dean of the cathedral and executor of María de Silva's will. El Greco had befriended his son, Luis de Castilla, at the court of Alessandro Farnese in Rome. El Greco here bases his composition on a print by Dürer, but eliminates nearly every reference to the Passion, reducing the importance of Christ's wounds and imbuing the relationship between father and son with as much tenderness and emotion as a *Pietà*. The colours are Venetian, but the influence of Michelangelo is evident in the monumental forms of Christ's body, while the beauty of the figures and their gentle expressions give the work a grave serenity.

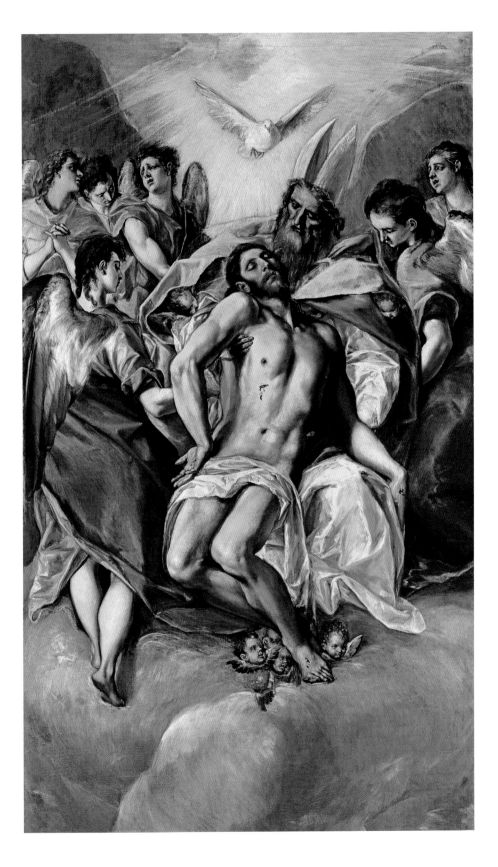

29
EL GRECO
Candia, Crete, 1541–Toledo,
1614

The Annunciation
1570–72. Oil on panel,
26.7 x 20 cm
P827

Because of its small size, this
panel might be a preparatory
study or a workshop model.
Like *The Flight into Egypt*, it
belongs to El Greco's final
period in Venice. It shows
his assimilation of Venetian
models; its composition and
colouring have been related
to Titian's *Annunciation* in
Treviso Cathedral, while the
impeccable creation of space
by means of the paving and the
perspective of the street visible
in the background are strongly
reminiscent of Tintoretto.
The Virgin kneels on a dais at
a prie-dieu with accentuated
curves, and is surprised in her
reading by the presence of the
angel, who appears to her on a
cloud. The Byzantine tradition
persists in the matched colours
and the golden tones of the
angel's tunic, as well as in
the beam of light traversing the
clouds upon which the dove of
the Holy Spirit descends.

30
EL GRECO
Candia, Crete, 1541–Toledo, 1614

The Flight into Egypt
c. 1570. Oil on panel,
15.9 x 21.6 cm
P7772

This small panel is a departure
from El Greco's usual style.
Because of its debts to Venetian
painting, it was once attributed
to Tintoretto and also to Jacopo
Bassano. Executed towards
the end of his stay in Venice, it
shows that the artist had already
left behind the Byzantine
pictorial tradition and was
concerned with constructing
lifelike spaces. His sources
were other artists' engravings,
from which he created an

original composition with an
unusual diagonal movement
from the right, where the
Virgin and Child can be seen
on a donkey, to the left, where
St Joseph pulls on the animal's
reins, encouraging it to cross
the bridge. In this way, the
sacred scene acquires a narrative
and anecdotal character.
In 1904, the Basque painter
Darío de Regoyos saw shades
in this picture of 'the most
impressionist modern painting'.

31
EL GRECO
Candia, Crete, 1541–Toledo, 1614

Fable

c. 1580. Oil on canvas,
50.5 x 63.6 cm
P7657

A singular work on account of its enigmatic nature, this was probably the first version of the subject painted by El Greco, and the most luminous and colourful of them all. In the centre of the composition is a figure whose face is strongly illuminated by the ember which she is blowing into flame to light a taper. The picture could be a recreation of a work by the Greek painter Antiphilus, who was praised by Pliny the Elder in his *Natural History* for his success at capturing the luminosity of a live ember.

However, it could also be an allegory in which the monkey, which gazes with intelligence as it mimics the gesture of the central figure, would symbolise painting as an imitation of the real, or it might contain a moral allusion to fire as sexual desire, which can be fanned into flame by the merest breath. It is quite possibly a little of everything – an allegory, a caricature, a genre scene, a moral lesson, and also a reflection on painting that demonstrates the artist's virtuosity with colour and light.

32
EL GRECO
Candia, Crete, 1541–Toledo, 1614

Aged Gentleman
c. 1587–1600. Oil on canvas, 46 x 43 cm
P806

33
EL GRECO
Candia, Crete, 1541–Toledo, 1614

Jerónimo de Cevallos
1613. Oil on canvas, 64 x 54 cm
P812

34
EL GRECO
Candia, Crete, 1541–Toledo, 1614

The Nobleman with his Hand on his Chest

c. 1580. Oil on canvas,
81·8 x 65·8 cm
P809

El Greco's ability to assimilate the tradition of the Spanish portrait, with its combination of sobriety, aloofness and attention to detail, within a Venetian pictorial technique brought him a recognition in the field of portraiture that he failed to achieve with the rest of his oeuvre. Even his detractors conceded he had produced some fine works in this genre. The portrait seen here, one of his earliest studies of a Spanish gentleman, establishes a prototype of a bust outlined against a neutral ground, with dark clothes to emphasise the sitter's wealth, while the light concentrates on the face and hands, which are framed by the ruff and by the cuffs, and on certain details of discreet ornamentation, such as the handle of the sword or the half-concealed chain. Owing to its personification of the values of the Spanish Christian knight and of Spanish painting itself, the work has generated a great deal of literature. The elegant hand with outstretched fingers has been variously interpreted as a sign of repentance or of self-assertion, a vow (this possibility is reinforced by the unsheathed sword), a mark of distinction, a rhetorical gesture or an effective pictorial strategy. Though traditionally taken to be an unknown sitter, the nobleman has been tentatively identified as Juan de Silva, notary major of Toledo.

El Greco

High Altar of the College of Doña María de Aragón

This altarpiece is one of the largest commissions ever received by El Greco, and he was paid more money for it than for any other work. It was commissioned from him in 1596 by the College of La Encarnación in Madrid, an Augustinian seminary founded in 1590. The college was better known by the name of its founder, Doña María de Córdoba y Aragón, lady-in-waiting to Queen Anna of Austria and daughter of Don Alvaro de Córdoba, master of the king's horse under Philip II. El Greco designed the shape of the altarpiece and was responsible for its architectural structure as well as its paintings and sculptures. However, we do not know exactly which paintings it comprised, and the sculptures and framing structure of the altarpiece have been lost. Even so, it is important when looking at one of El Greco's paintings for an altarpiece to bear in mind that it was painted as part of a group whose full meaning was revealed only when the altarpiece was viewed as a whole. In this case, the vicissitudes of the convent, which was secularised, disentailed and converted into a debating chamber for the Cadiz Parliament of 1814, led to the dismantling of the altarpiece and the dispersal of its pieces. *The Adoration of the Shepherds* at the Museum of Art in Bucharest is agreed by virtually all authorities to have belonged to it, as do *The Annunciation* and *The Baptism of Christ* at the Prado [35, 36]. Three other works in the Prado, *The Crucifixion*, *The Resurrection* and *Pentecost*, may also have formed part of it.

El Greco fully develops his most characteristic style in this altarpiece which he produced in the final phase of his artistic career. It was then that he distanced himself completely from the triumphant naturalism of the painting of his time, and in so doing aroused the wonder of both his contemporaries and succeeding generations for his extraordinary freedom of conception and execution. El Greco never abandoned his excellent grasp of anatomy and extraordinary skill at expressing movement within the markedly vertical format of these pictures, but he nevertheless elongated the figures and made bold attempts at foreshortening. The paintings clearly depict an ascent from the earthly to the celestial in which the artist breaks away from the traditional representation of perspective by making space airily immaterial. Together with the intensity of the colour contrasts, the powerful but eerie light and the vibrancy of the brushwork, this contributes to the creation of images of great spiritual and expressive force.

Proposed reconstruction of the altarpiece by J.M. Pita Andrade and M. Almagro Gorbea, 2001.

35
EL GRECO
Candia, Crete, 1541–Toledo, 1614

The Annunciation (High Altar of the College of Doña María de Aragón)
1597–1600. Oil on canvas, 315 x 174 cm
P3888

36
EL GRECO
Candia, Crete, 1541–Toledo,
1614

*The Baptism of Christ
(High Altar of the College
of Doña María de Aragón)*
1597–1600. Oil on canvas,
350 x 144 cm
P821

This painting shares
the chromatic audacity of the
Annunciation from the same
altarpiece [35], as well as the
spatial abstraction and elongated
figures typical of late works by
El Greco. Here, however, the
verticality of the composition is
accentuated both by the format
of the canvas and by the verticals
formed by the figures in the
foreground. The gospel passage
of the Baptism is represented on
an earthly plane and on a celestial
one, united by the Holy Spirit.
On the earthly plane, Christ,
is framed by a cloak of red, the
liturgical colour of sacrifice
and martyrdom. On the right is
St John the Baptist clothed in a
camel skin, and near him is an
axe on a treetrunk, a commonly
used iconographical symbol that
alludes to one of the Baptist's
sermons: 'And now also the
axe is laid unto the root of the
trees: therefore every tree which
bringeth not forth good fruit
is hewn down, and cast into
the fire' (*Matthew*, 3:10). On
the celestial plane, the Father,
represented as the Pantocrator,
together with all the angelic
hierarchy, solemnises the
occasion with his right hand
raised in blessing, whilst in the
other is a transparent sphere
that represents the world.
In evocation of the Trinity,
the gleaming light is centred
on the white garments of God
the Father, the dove of the Holy
Spirit and the figure of Christ.

37
EL GRECO
Candia, Crete, 1541–Toledo, 1614

The Adoration of the Shepherds
1612–14. Oil on canvas,
319 x 180 cm
P2988

One of the most important
works in El Greco's late
production, this painting formed
part of the altarpiece for the
artist's family burial chapel at
the church of Santo Domingo el
Antiguo in Toledo. The subject,
a symbol of resurrection and
eternity, had been represented
by the painter before. As the
Virgin reveals Jesus to the
shepherds, she gazes at her son
with infinite tenderness, while
St Joseph looks on with an
expression of amazement and
the shepherds are overcome with
emotion. This time, however,
the choice of theme was of
special significance because
the painting was to accompany
the remains of the artist, who
probably portrayed himself in
the shepherd in the foreground.
With a less busy composition
than the paintings for the Doña
María de Aragón altarpiece
[35, 36], El Greco here uses a
wide range of pictorial resources.
Space returns, and there is even
an architectural reference in
the vaulted passageway above
the Virgin, whose delicate face
contrasts with the recoiling
head and imprecise contours
of the nearest shepherd. The
characters are arranged around
the Child, the true focus, whose
light dramatically illuminates
the whole scene, including the
celestial plane, and so creates
an atmosphere of unreality.

Juan Bautista Maíno

A Spanish artist with a Milanese father, Maíno's production was small because he largely neglected painting after he entered the Augustinian order in 1613. The Museo del Prado holds all of his most outstanding works: the ten paintings which formed part of the *Altarpiece of the Four Holy Feasts*, painted for the Dominican convent of San Pedro Mártir in Toledo; the only known portrait by his hand [38]; *The Recapture of Bahia in Brazil* [95], painted for the Salón de Reinos (Hall of Realms); and *St Dominic in Soriano*, an iconography of his own creation which enjoyed great success. Although virtually nothing is known of his initial apprenticeship, he may have trained in Madrid before going to Italy, where he encountered the naturalism of Caravaggio and his followers and the Roman-Bolognese classicism of the Carracci and Guido Reni. Upon his return to Spain, he introduced a new style which gave primacy to direct observation of reality. He thus broke away from the intellectual elaboration of Mannerism, and also from the art of El Greco. Maíno's naturalism is tempered by the decorum demanded of paintings in Spain, which allowed no daring realism like that of Caravaggio's late work. Instead he followed the Caraveggesque tendency in its brighter and more colourful form, as developed by painters like Orazio Gentileschi [239] and Carlo Saraceni. Around 1620, he was appointed as drawing master to the future Philip IV (reigned 1621–1665), and he established himself at court, where he wielded an enormous influence over Spanish painting. Proof of this is the fact that when a public competition was convened in 1626 for a painting of the *Expulsion of the Moriscos*, he was one of those who awarded the commission to Velázquez (the painting is now lost). Above all, Maíno helped to introduce the naturalist style to Spain, a pictorial tendency that would predominate for much of the seventeenth century.

39
JUAN BAUTISTA MAÍNO
DE CASTRO
Pastrana, Guadalajara,
1581–Madrid, 1649

The Adoration of the Kings
1612–14. Oil on canvas,
315 x 174 cm
P886

This work belongs to the *Altarpiece of the Four Holy Feasts*, where it was arranged on the first tier alongside an *Adoration of the Shepherds*. The second tier contained *The Resurrection* and *Pentecost*, also in a markedly vertical format; completing the altarpiece were four works in a horizontal format showing saints in broad landscapes. It is a good example of Maíno's technique, characterised by close and concise brushwork and a strong descriptive vocabulary resulting in a masterly rendering of materials and superb still-life details, such as the receptacles in which the kings have brought their gifts. The whole scene is lit with a bright intense light that rounds out the volumes and strongly delineates the shadows, though without creating the enveloping darkness from which figures emerge in the purest Caravaggism. The intensification of Maíno's brilliant colouring in this work is reflected in the costumes, such as Balthasar's multicoloured shawl and Melchior's damask cloak.

38
JUAN BAUTISTA MAÍNO
DE CASTRO
Pastrana, Guadalajara,
1581–Madrid, 1649

Portrait of a Gentleman
1613–18. Oil on canvas,
96 x 73 cm
P2595

Sánchez Cotán and the Birth of the Still Life in Spain

The still life was born as an independent genre almost simultaneously in Northern Italy, the Netherlands and Spain at the end of the sixteenth century. This development is certainly related to the growing Baroque taste for the faithful representation of nature, but it is also related to the revival of ancient erudition and rhetoric, since it is an attempt to emulate and surpass Zeuxis, the famous Greek painter of antiquity who painted grapes of such realism that the birds tried to peck at them. The first still lifes recorded in Spain were painted by Blas de Prado, but none of his work has come down to us. The painter of the earliest still lifes to have survived, Juan Sánchez Cotán, seems to have undergone his training with this artist in Toledo. In the early years of the seventeenth century, Sánchez Cotán defined the Spanish still-life genre, giving it a character of its own which persisted throughout nearly the whole of the historical development of the so-called Spanish School. In his still lifes humble objects are monumentalised and given a dignity and profundity of their own, their volumes accentuated by dramatic lighting. These features distinguished it not only from the more vibrant and theatrical Italian model, but also from the cold precision of the French and the exuberance of the Flemish. Because Sánchez Cotán was a Carthusian monk, some commentators have seen a transcendent and almost religious value in these works, but this may not have been intentional on the part of the painter, and his contemporaries would almost certainly have failed to detect it. What they admired about him was his virtuosity and precision in representing reality, but while he enjoyed some success among a certain cultured circle, the still life continued to be regarded as a minor genre. The Museo del Prado preserves one of the few extant pieces by Sánchez Cotán, possibly the earliest Spanish still life to have survived [40]. The museum also holds examples of still lifes by Juan van der Hamen [42, 43]. Taking Sánchez Cotán's austere still lifes as a model, Van der Hamen created subtle and elaborate spatial compositions, introducing elements of refinement that encapsulated life at court. The *Still Life with Cardoon, Francolin, Grapes and Lilies* by Felipe Ramírez [41], of whose life nothing is known, shows the effect and the persistence of Sánchez Cotán's model. The Prado's works by these two artists are modern acquisitions, since the Spanish kings preferred still lifes from the Netherlands, the only exception being those by Van der Hamen.

40
JUAN SÁNCHEZ COTÁN
Orgaz, Toledo, 1560–Granada,
1627

*Still Life with Game,
Vegetables and Fruit*

1602. Oil on canvas, 68 x 89 cm
P7612

Sánchez Cotán's still lifes are characterised by a rigorously geometrical composition, here determined by the sober architecture of what appears to be a larder. Simple food – fruit, vegetables and small game – is picked out by an intense light from the side, which rescues it from the deep and magnetic darkness of the back of the cupboard, creating strong shadows whose tenebrism is contemporaneous with Caravaggio's. The painter combines his astonishing ability to capture reality, manifest in every detail of the objects, with a careful abstract composition in which nothing is left to chance. The dominant element is the cardoon, a characteristic feature of all his works, whose curves are counterposed by the rigid right angles of the cupboard. This early composition with its range of items is one of the painter's most complex as there are progressively fewer objects in his later works.

41 ←
FELIPE RAMÍREZ
Toledo, documented between
1628 and 1632

*Still Life with Cardoon,
Francolin, Grapes and Lilies*
1628. Oil on canvas, 71 x 92 cm
P2802

This painting by Ramírez
is an example of the enormous
influence exerted on Spanish
painting by the still lifes
of Sánchez Cotán [40].
Executed a quarter of a
century after Sánchez Cotán's
earliest works, it faithfully
reproduces all the features of
his still lifes and may be a copy
of a lost original. However,
Ramírez uses a different
brushwork consisting of
short parallel strokes, and he
includes two elements which
are absent from any extant
work by Sánchez Cotán. These
are the lilies and the golden
cup, a sharp contrast with the
humble objects of the earlier
artist's compositions.

42 ↑
JUAN VAN DER HAMEN
Madrid, 1596–1631

*Still Life with Sweets
and Glass Vessels*
1622. Oil on canvas, 52 x 88 cm
P1164

In this early work, the influence
of the still lifes of Sánchez
Cotán can be clearly seen in the
tenebrist intensity of the light
and in the importance assumed
by the black background from
which the objects emerge. It
is also apparent in the carefully
devised composition, which
becomes more complex in Van
der Hamen's later work. What
differentiates him from Sánchez
Cotán, however, is the type of
object depicted. No longer are
they simple foodstuffs but rich

delicacies typical of a feast at
court, presented in fine vessels
in a variety of materials and
forms. This allows the artist to
display his mastery at rendering
textures, as can be seen not only
in the gleams and transparencies
of the glass and porcelain,
but also in the stickiness of
the crystallised fruit and the
brittleness of the wafers. Two
flies buzz around the flask, which
is full of *aloja*, a sweet drink of
Moorish origin made from water,
honey and aromatic spices.

43
JUAN VAN DER HAMEN
Madrid, 1596–1631

Still Life with Artichokes,
Flowers and Glass Vessels
1627. Oil on canvas, 81 x 110 cm
P7907

From 1626 onwards, Van der Hamen produced more complex compositions with a larger number of objects, which are often – as in this case – stepped by height and depth, an arrangement with precedents in Roman antiquity. The background is now less dark and the flowers make the composition less severe, distancing it from Sánchez Cotán's model [40]. Retained, on the other hand, are the taste for detail, the virtuosity in the rendering of textures, and the individualised treatment of each of the objects. Within the artist's career, it signifies a point of perfect equilibrium between the compositional sobriety of his first still lifes and the more complex arrangements of his later work. It can be classed among the very finest of the known pieces by this artist's hand, and one of his most satisfactory compositions.

The Still Life of the Golden Age

In the seventeenth century, the genre of the still life, practically non-existent until then, began to acquire great importance all over Europe. Its development was related to the Baroque taste for the accidental and the desire of artists to show their skill at illusionism, but also to the emergence of a bourgeois urban clientele who demanded new subjects and motifs. In general, the Spanish still life of the Golden Age followed the model established by Juan Sánchez Cotán [40], maintaining its characteristics of austerity and restraint, together with the dignifying of objects and the accentuation of volume by dramatic lighting. This formula was subjected to highly personal treatment by Zurbarán (see the chapter on the painter's work in this guide) [64], but otherwise remained constant for much of the century. The Spanish still life was thus clearly differentiated from its exuberant Flemish counterpart, pulsating with colour and highly influenced by the painting of Rubens, which was favoured by the Spanish kings and chosen by them for the decoration of their palaces. Hardly any Spanish still lifes therefore entered the Royal Collections. If we add the fact that there were even fewer still lifes in the Museo de la Trinidad, which had mainly religious works, it explains why there was such a small number in the Prado before the mid-twentieth century. It was then that the originality and quality of the Spanish still life began to be valued, and the Prado strove hard to fill this gap in its collection. One of the most important results of their efforts was the acquisition in 2006 of forty works from Rosendo Naseiro's collection of Spanish still lifes, resulting in a formidable collection. It includes works from the first half of the seventeenth century by artists such as Juan Fernández (El Labrador) [45], Juan de Espinosa [44] and Tomás Hiepes [46, 47], who confirm the distinctive features of the Spanish still life and its debt to naturalism. But there are also other works, like the flower pieces of Juan de Arellano [48], which show how outside influences were assimilated in Spain after the mid-seventeenth century, above all from the Flemish flower pieces and garlands of Daniel Seghers and the paintings of the Italian artist Mario Nuzzi, resulting in a move towards a more exuberant Baroque.

44
JUAN DE ESPINOSA
Documented between 1628 and 1659

Still Life with Apples, Plums, Grapes and Pears
c. 1630. Oil on canvas, 76 x 59 cm
P702

Juan de Espinosa – who is not to be confused with Juan Bautista de Espinosa, a painter known to be responsible for a very fine still life executed in 1624 – excelled at the depiction of fruit. His still lifes, however, are less austere than El Labrador's, and rely far less on chiaroscuro. This picture combines plums and apples with different types of grape, which have the gleam and transparency of precious stones. He thus creates an interplay of textures and colours, heightened by the juxtaposition of the deep red of the earthenware jar and the shine of the metal dish, in which one can see the reflection of the apples.

45
JUAN FERNÁNDEZ, 'EL
LABRADOR'
Documented between 1630
and 1636

*Two Hanging Bunches
of Grapes*
Oil on canvas, 29 x 38 cm
P7905

El Labrador specialised in paintings of fruit, and his most characteristic ones depict grapes. The Prado holds several examples in which the artist uses tight brushwork and contrasted light to create a powerful effect of illusion. The two bunches here hang from two cords, as in the still lifes of Sánchez Cotán [40], rather than from the vine, as in other works by the artist. On one of the bunches, he has painted a fly to emphasise the ripeness of the grapes, a detail which an informed viewer of the period would have interpreted as a reference to the brevity of life, and also as a quotation from the classical painter Zeuxis, said to have painted grapes so real that the birds flew down to peck at them.

46
TOMÁS HIEPES
Valencia, c. 1610–1674

*Delft Fruit Bowl
and Two Vases of Flowers*
1642. Oil on canvas, 67 x 96 cm
P7909

47
TOMÁS HIEPES
Valencia, c. 1610–1674

Two Fruit Bowls on a Table
1642. Oil on canvas, 67 x 96 cm
P7910

Hiepes is the main
representative of Baroque
still-life painting in Valencia,
although his compositions
have a somewhat archaic
quality when compared with
the work produced at that
time in Madrid. Within
the still-life painting of
his period, this artist has
a personality of his own,
manifest in the rigorously
symmetrical composition
of these two pieces, a format
he rarely altered throughout
his production, and in the
neutral background against
which the ceramic vessels,
fruits and flowers stand out.
The high viewpoint and
the closeness of the objects
to the viewer give them
a monumental character,
and the artist renders them
minutely, individualising
each fruit, leaf and flower.
The same attention to
minute detail is evident in
the meticulous reproduction
of the pattern on the ceramics,
and in the virtuosity of the
rendering of the folds in
the delicate lace tablecloths.

48
JUAN DE ARELLANO
Santorcaz, Madrid,
1614–Madrid, 1676

Flowers in a Crystal Vase
1668. Oil on canvas, 83 x 62 cm
P7921

This picture is a mature work of Arellano, the greatest Spanish flower painter of the seventeenth century. This sub-genre within the still life attained considerable importance in Flanders, and it spread from there to the rest of Europe, most notably to the court of Spain. Arellano, whose work draws inspiration from the finest of the Flemish flower painters, has devised here a composition which shows his inventiveness. Behind the apparently disorganised arrangement of the flowers, which fill practically the whole picture, is a closely studied and very subtle symmetry. The large variety of species shown in this work are all perfectly differentiated and identifiable, and their freshness makes them look newly cut, contributing both colour and verisimilitude to the painting.

Ribalta and Painting
in Seventeenth-century Valencia

In the sixteenth century, Valencia was the foremost centre of Renaissance painting in Spain, and it maintained its status in the seventeenth century as one of the focal points of artistic creation on the Iberian Peninsula, together with Seville and Madrid. The economic importance of this region attracted a large number of artists, who executed mainly religious works. During the first half of the seventeenth century, Valencia was imbued with the Counter-Reformation spirit of St John de Ribera (1532–1611), who was one of the principal clients of Luis de Morales [22, 23]. After arriving from Badajoz in 1569, St John de Ribera served as archbishop of Valencia until his death, and the art produced in the city under his influence bore the stamp of his severe dogmatism. Despite pressures to maintain the familiar conventions, the profoundly religious art of Valencia nonetheless evolved from pious Romanism in the tradition of Juan de Juanes [21] towards naturalism, which became the dominant trend in the city. The main figure at that time was Francisco Ribalta [50], a painter from Catalonia who trained at El Escorial and was heavily influenced in his work by the artists employed there, such as Pellegrino Tibaldi, Romulo Cincinato, Vicente Carducho, and above all Navarrete, 'El Mudo' [26]. Ribalta settled in Valencia in 1599, almost certainly at the behest of Archbishop Ribera. There he produced work of an increasingly personal nature which combined his training in El Escorial with the influences of Caravaggio and of Sebastiano del Piombo [199, 200], some of whose paintings could be seen in the city. Pedro Orrente, on the other hand, spent only a few years in Valencia, but left a profound mark on subsequent local painting.

49
PEDRO ORRENTE
Murcia, 1580–Valencia, 1645

The Crucifixion
Oil on canvas, 153 x 128 cm
P1016

Orrente was a hugely successful artist in his day. By 1600 he was settled in Toledo, where he was praised by El Greco and copied by Sánchez Cotán. Called 'the Spanish Bassano', he was greatly admired for his adherence to the formulas established by the celebrated family of Venetian artists [230], whom he met during a stay in Venice between 1602 and 1605. In this *Crucifixion*, which came to the Prado from the Buen Retiro Palace, Christ has already expired and the sky has been symbolically shrouded in darkness. The scene thus becomes a nocturne in which the tenebrist light, which creates a dramatic chiaroscuro, is centred on the bodies of Jesus and the good thief turning towards him, and on the face of the Virgin. By contrast, the bad thief, who averts his face so as not to look at Christ, is left in shadow. The pathetic gestures of the Virgin, the Magdalene and St John make this a highly theatrical image.

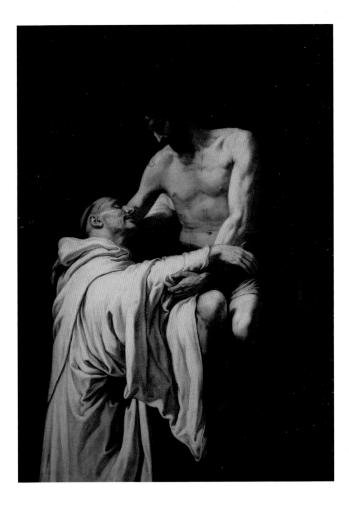

50
FRANCISCO RIBALTA
Solsona, Lérida, 1565–Valencia,
1628

Christ embracing St Bernard
c. 1626. Oil on canvas,
158 x 113 cm
P2804

This major work, painted for the charterhouse of Portacoeli, near Valencia, shows the devotional intensity of which the artist was capable. The painting narrates the mystic vision of St Bernard, the founder of the Cistercian order, as described in one of the most popular devotional works of the Baroque, the *Flos sanctorum* or *Libro de la vida de los santos* (Book of the Lives of the Saints) by Pedro de Ribadeneyra. In the vision, Christ frees his arms from the cross to embrace the saint as a sign of his love for him. Ribalta creates a scene full of tenderness and joy, expressed in Christ's loving gaze and the happiness of the saint. The idealised herculean beauty of Christ, transmitted via Sebastiano del Piombo from Michelangelesque models, is paired with the naturalism of the saint. The tenebrist lighting emphasises the volumes of the main figures and the expressive folds of the saint's habit. Recent cleaning has revealed the presence of two additional figures, possibly angels.

Ribera

José de Ribera is one of the great masters of Spanish Golden Age painting. He is also the artist who exerted the greatest influence in his own time, both through his pictures and through his facility as a draughtsman [366] and printmaker, which allowed his compositions to circulate throughout Europe. He travelled to Italy in the first decade of the seventeenth century and was in Rome in 1612, where he painted in the Caravaggesque manner. Four years later he had settled in Naples, which was then under Spanish rule. His entire pictorial career unfolded there, and his work left a profound mark on the painting of southern Italy. He received commissions not only from Neapolitan ecclesiastical institutions but also from Spanish notables residing in the city, especially the viceroys of Naples and their court. Although he spent most of his life in Italy, he always considered himself Spanish – he was known as '*lo Spagnoletto*' – and was greatly admired in Spain, where his influence on contemporary artists extended to Velázquez, Zurbarán and Murillo. This explains why the Museo del Prado holds a large number of his canvases, among them several masterpieces, most of them originating in the Royal Collections. There have been occasional attempts to classify Ribera as the chief exponent of tenebrist naturalism and of the harsh religiosity of the Counter-Reformation, which exalts martyrdom and suffering, as well as of the supposed starkness of the Spanish, but such a classification ignores the many other resources of an artist who after the 1630s was to achieve a highly personal synthesis of naturalism and classicism.

51
JOSÉ DE RIBERA
Játiva, Valencia, 1591–Naples, 1652

The Resurrection of Lazarus
c. 1613–16. Oil on canvas,
171 x 289 cm
P7768

Acquired by the Museo del Prado in 2001, this work has been dated to the artist's Roman period, which would make it not only the earliest painting by Ribera in the Prado, but the only one executed prior to his Neapolitan period. Like many artists who had moved to Rome, most of them from France or the Netherlands, Ribera in his early phase is faithful to the tenets of Caravaggio. The miracle of the resurrection of Lazarus is told in a harshly naturalist manner and the figures are modelled on ordinary people. An intense and dramatic light contributes to the narrative by emphasising the hand of Christ pointing towards Lazarus and the vigorous gesture of Lazarus as he returns to life.

52
JOSÉ DE RIBERA
Játiva, Valencia, 1591–Naples, 1652

Democritus (?)

1630. Oil on canvas, 125 x 81 cm
P1121

This figure has always been assumed to represent one of the philosophers of antiquity. Some have identified him with Archimedes, the Sicilian mathematician, because of the compasses he holds in his right hand and the geometrical diagrams on the paper in his left. Others have inclined towards Democritus, who was generally shown laughing. Like Caravaggio, who used ordinary people to represent the saints, Ribera modelled his philosopher from the life.

This is probably the earliest of Ribera's 'ragged philosophers', a genre he largely invented and which became very popular in seventeenth-century Italy. Standing out from the predominantly brown tones of the picture are the whites of the edge of the shirt and the papers forming part of the still life in the lower left corner. His skill in depicting naturalist detail can also be observed in his rendering of the philosopher's old and wrinkled flesh and ragged clothes.

53
JOSÉ DE RIBERA
Játiva, Valencia, 1591–Naples,
1652

St James the Elder
1631. Oil on canvas, 202 x 146 cm
P1083

This figure, who has been
identified as St James the
Apostle on the basis of his
pilgrim's staff, may have
formed a pair with a painting
of St Roch of a similar
size and composition, also
preserved at the Museo del
Prado. Although portrayed
in simple clothes, which are
depicted with minute realism,
St James has a dignified
and almost heroic air, thanks
in part to his posture and to
the sobriety of the flight of
stone steps.

54
JOSÉ DE RIBERA
Játiva, Valencia, 1591–Naples, 1652

Isaac and Jacob
1637. Oil on canvas, 110 x 291 cm
P1118

The picture shows the moment when Jacob, his arm covered with a sheep's skin in imitation of the hairiness of his brother Esau, deceives his blind father Isaac in order to obtain his blessing, and so assure himself of the birthright he had bought from his brother for a plate of lentils. Ribera emphasises and individualises the gestures and expressions of each character. The mother encourages Jacob to go ahead with the deception while looking at the viewer and pointing to the action, a very Baroque motif. Jacob holds out his arm to his father, who feels it with both hands, a look of concentration on his face, while on the left Esau, oblivious to what is going on, returns from hunting. The work still displays features proper to the naturalism of the early years of the century, such as the contrasted passages of light and dark. However, there are already clear signs of Ribera's evolution towards a painting with its roots in Venetian colour, which he here combines with his profound love for palpable reality. This is appreciable in the qualities of the fabrics, the lamb's skin and the flesh tones, and it reaches full expression in the still life to the right of the composition.

55
JOSÉ DE RIBERA
Játiva, Valencia, 1591–Naples,
1652

The Martyrdom of St Philip
1639. Oil on canvas,
234 x 234 cm
P1101

Until the second half of the
twentieth century, this was
believed to be a depiction of
the martyrdom of the apostle
St Bartholomew, who was flayed
alive, and the painting was thus
held up as a clear example of the
cruelty inherent in Ribera's work.
In fact, the figure represents
St Philip, who died tied to a cross,
and the scene contains no blood
or explicit violence. Rather than
the more dramatic moment of the
martyrdom itself, the artist chooses
to show the preparations for it,
which allow him to demonstrate
his compositional mastery in
a complex setting marked by

foreshortenings and typically
Baroque diagonals. The main
diagonal is formed by the boldly
modelled body of the saint, who
resigns himself to his suffering.
A counterpoint is provided by the
strain of the executioners' efforts
to raise him. The scene is shown
with a low viewpoint that lends
monumentality to the figures
and reveals a large area of brilliant
blue sky, illuminated by a warm
and radiant sunlight. The painting
demonstrates the artist's variety
of pictorial resources both in its
sumptuous colours and in the light
and vibrant brushwork, a novelty
for Ribera.

56
JOSÉ DE RIBERA
Játiva, Valencia, 1591–Naples,
1652

Jacob's Dream
1639. Oil on canvas,
179 x 233 cm
P1117

Forming a pair with *St Peter freed by an Angel*, also at the Museo del Prado, this work was once attributed to Murillo on chromatic grounds, and also because its serene representation of this biblical scene jarred with the commonly held idea of Ribera's painting. Jacob, tired by his journey, sleeps by the wayside in Haran and dreams of a ladder to Heaven on which rows of angels are climbing up and down.

In most Baroque interpretations of this scene, the artist focuses on the extraordinary vision by placing the emphasis on the angels. By contrast, Ribera focuses on the vigorous figure of the patriarch. Like any weary traveller, Jacob lies propped against a stone with his blanket over him. The ladder of angels practically dissolves in the halo of diffuse light above his head, rising into a blue sky that occupies over half the picture.

57
JOSÉ DE RIBERA
Játiva, Valencia, 1591–
Naples, 1652

The Trinity
c. 1635. Oil on canvas,
226 x 118 cm
P1069

Acquired by King Ferdinand
VII in 1820, one year after the
museum's inauguration, this
work is inspired by the same
Dürer print which provided
the basis for El Greco's
Trinity, also in the Prado
[28]. Unlike El Greco, Ribera
here shows an imperturbable
Father presenting us with the
sacrifice of his Son. The work
is divided into two parts that
are given very different pictorial
treatments. In the upper part,
God the Father, impassive

and timeless, is surrounded by
warm and sumptuous colour. In
the lower part, the inert body
of the dead Christ is treated
with dramatic tenebrism.
The Father's rosy-hued face
contrasts with the paleness of
Christ's, which is nearly ashen.
A few thin trickles of blood
run down from his wounds,
leaving a slight stain on the
loincloth and shroud. This
subtle dramatic effect would
have been greatly to Counter-
Reformation taste.

58
JOSÉ DE RIBERA
Játiva, Valencia, 1591–Naples,
1652

The Magdalene

1641. Oil on canvas, 182 x 149 cm
P1103

The Museo del Prado has a
series of four pictures by Ribera
showing penitent saints in
landscape settings. They reveal the
fascination felt by the Catholic

societies of the seventeenth
century for the lives of these saints,
whose representation combines
prayer, penitence, solitude and
life amidst nature. They show a
child, St John the Baptist (P1108);
an old man, St Bartholomew
(P1100); an old woman, St Mary
of Egypt (P1106); and the girl in
this work, who has been identified
as the Magdalene, a woman of
extraordinary beauty who retired
from the world to do penance after
a life of sin. The four paintings
have a diagonal composition

emphasised by a tree trunk,
and the monumental figures stand
out against a dark background
contrasting with the sky which
opens out in one corner of the
composition. The contrast is
especially great in this painting,
the most luminous of the four. The
chromatic richness of the fabrics,
and especially the sumptuous red
of the saint's voluminous cloak,
enhance her devout expression and
delicate features, which are in stark
contrast to her coarse penitent's
undergarment.

Andalusian Painting in the Seventeenth Century

During the sixteenth century, Seville became Europe's leading port and the main economic, social and cultural centre of Spain. This made it a magnet for all the artists who planned to travel to the New World or earn commissions from the city's numerous convents and religious foundations. Most of these artists were of Flemish origin and thus the painting of Seville, and by extension of Andalusia, became characterised by rigorous draughtsmanship, a taste for detail, and smooth, enamelled brushwork. Furthermore, it was of an intensely devotional nature, in which great pains were taken to maintain decorum in the depiction of religious events. It was therefore tightly controlled both formally and iconographically by the ecclesiastical authorities, who could allow no deviations from dogma in a city that was the gateway to the Indies.

The main figure in Seville in the first part of the seventeenth century was the painter and theorist Francisco Pacheco (1564–1644). A practitioner of realist detail in the Flemish tradition, Pacheco was the master of Velázquez [68 ff.] and Alonso Cano [65-67], as well as father-in-law to the former. Juan de Roelas (c. 1560–1624), the other leading artist of the time, was trained in Venice, and became a pioneering figure in the art world of Seville. His reformed Mannerism introduced Venetian sensuality, a certain chiaroscuro, and a greater sensitivity to the real, paving the way for naturalism. Some of the features of his style, such as the Venetian brushwork and the greater interest in reality and everyday detail, were passed on to Francisco Herrera the Elder [59]. Unlike his predecessors, however, Herrera clearly reflected his assimilation of Caravaggio's naturalism, which gradually imposed itself on the earlier Flemish late Mannerism until it became the dominant style in Seville. It was in this naturalist tradition that Zurbarán [60-64], Alonso Cano and Velázquez learned their trade.

At that time, the Spanish court showed little interest in the painting produced in Seville, and the Prado therefore has no works by this school from the Royal Collections. Those to be seen in the museum are either recent acquisitions or belong to periods spent outside Seville by its principal artists.

59
FRANCISCO DE HERRERA
THE ELDER
Seville, c. 1590–Madrid, c. 1654

*St Bonaventure receives
the Habit from St Francis*
1628. Oil on canvas, 46 x 84 cm
P7134

This work belongs to the decorative cycle of the church of the Franciscan College of San Buenaventura in Seville, a commission Herrera shared with the young Zurbarán. It shows the saint being received into the order in the presence of St Francis himself. Evident here is the harsh and expressive naturalism of this artist, who combines a certain tenebrism with an energetic, loose and vibrant brushwork of Venetian origin. Venetian too is the use of tonal harmonies, which here take the form of a limited range of chestnuts and golds against which only the splash of red on the back of St Francis's chair stands out. The marked horizontality of the composition, which retains a touch of the late Mannerism predominating in Seville in the early years of the century, is further articulated by the line of monks receding into the background.

Zurbarán

Of all the great Golden Age masters, Francisco de Zurbarán was perhaps the painter who evolved least. Throughout his career, he maintained the profound Caravaggesque influence predominant in the Seville of his apprenticeship, which he experienced at the same time as Velázquez and Alonso Cano. His technique, the candour of his scenes and his skill at representing religious feeling made him the perfect interpreter of the devout Seville of the Counter-Reformation. This allowed him to secure commissions from nearly all the orders present in Andalusia and Extremadura, and made him the painter *par excellence* of saints and the monastic life. In 1634 he was invited to court, probably at Velázquez's suggestion, to take part in the decoration of the Buen Retiro Palace, for which he painted two battle scenes [94] (one of which has disappeared) and ten pictures of the Labours of Hercules. All were destined for the Salón de Reinos (Hall of Realms), and entered the Museo del Prado from the Royal Collections. The Spanish kings did not hold his work in great esteem, preferring a more Baroque and theatrical style of painting. The rest of the works by Zurbarán at the Prado, with the exception of *St Elizabeth of Hungary*, are therefore modern acquisitions or donations.

As a result of his contact with the works in the Royal Collections, the painting Zurbarán brought back to Seville upon his return from Madrid was rather more luminous and colourful, and was somewhat influenced by Bolognese classicism, though far less than Ribera or Velázquez. However, he never abandoned either chiaroscuro or the static monumentality of his figures, and his limitations are apparent when it comes to complex compositions and the treatment of linear perspective. His best works are therefore those with simple compositions, especially his figures of saints or monks, either alone or in pairs. Zurbarán also had a special gift for endowing his faces with a spiritual quality and for giving his inanimate objects a mysterious corporeity. These features, together with his ability to render tactile qualities and the subtle richness of his colouring, make him a magnificent painter of still lifes [64]. He was overshadowed in the Seville of the 1650s by the growing success of Murillo's gentler and more Baroque work. He therefore decided to move back to Madrid, where he died in 1664.

60

FRANCISCO DE ZURBARÁN
Fuente de Cantos, Badajoz, 1598–Madrid, 1664

St Peter the Apostle appearing to St Peter Nolasco
1629. Oil on canvas, 179 x 223 cm
P1237

The Museo del Prado holds two of the pictures from the cycle painted by Zurbarán and his workshop for the convent of the Mercedarians in Seville. The cycle narrates the life of St Peter Nolasco, the founder of the order, who was canonised the year this work was painted. The paintings in the Prado depict the saint's two visions, one of the Celestial Jerusalem (*The Vision of St Peter Nolasco*) and this one of St Peter on the cross. The saint is surprised in his austere cell by the apparition of his patron, the apostle St Peter, who presents himself upside down, the manner in which he was crucified, to console him for not being able to visit his tomb in Rome, and to encourage him to continue his apostolic mission in Spain. Painted during the first phase in Zurbarán's career, two basic characteristics of the artist's mature work are already discernible. One is the representation of the supernatural with the forms of the natural, and the other is his sensitive handling of textures, especially of white habits such as the one the saint is wearing here.

61
FRANCISCO DE ZURBARÁN
Fuente de Cantos, Badajoz,
1598–Madrid, 1664

*A Painter before Christ
on the Cross*
c. 1630–35. Oil on canvas,
105 x 84 cm
P2594

As is the case with many of
Zurbarán's compositions, this
picture is based on prints or
images by other artists. Here,
however, the artist has replaced
the figure of the donor, which
would normally appear by
the cross, with another that
may well be a self-portrait,
and was traditionally identified
as St Luke the Evangelist,
the patron saint of painters.

63 →
FRANCISCO DE ZURBARÁN
Fuente de Cantos, Badajoz,
1598–Madrid, 1664

Agnus Dei
c. 1635–40. Oil on canvas,
36 x 62 cm
P7293

In several paintings, Zurbarán represented the lamb as a sacrificial victim and therefore as a symbol for Christ, whose death would redeem mankind from sin. Of all those paintings, this is the one of greatest refinement. A young ram is shown with its legs bound, a sign of its helplessness, and an expression of meekness. The painter reduces the elements to the essentials and his range of colour to a luminous patch on an indeterminate grey surface, which stands out against the darkness of the background. However, the work also exemplifies Zurbarán's technical skill at rendering details and textures, such as the lamb's moist muzzle, the eyes with their delicate lashes, the roughness of the horns, and the springy texture of the wool, made slightly dirty in order to emphasise the realism still further.

62 ↑
FRANCISCO DE ZURBARÁN
Fuente de Cantos, Badajoz,
1598–Madrid, 1664

St Elizabeth of Portugal
1640. Oil on canvas,
184 x 98 cm
P1239

St Elizabeth of Portugal, the daughter of Peter III of Aragon and wife of King Denis of Portugal, here personifies the 'miracle of the roses', a miracle also associated with St Elizabeth of Hungary and St Casilda, who were likewise painted by Zurbarán. The queen used to carry money in her clothing to give to the poor. Her husband had forbidden her to give alms, and when she chanced to encounter him, the contents of her lap were miraculously transformed into roses. The saint's individualised face is close to portraiture, and Zurbarán renders her rich apparel and jewels with his habitual precision, creating a virtuoso range of textures, the colours of which stand out against a dark background.

64
FRANCISCO DE ZURBARÁN
Fuente de Cantos, Badajoz,
1598–Madrid, 1664

Still Life
c. 1635–40. Oil on canvas,
46 x 84 cm
P2803

The few still lifes painted by Zurbarán are among the most popular in all of Spanish painting. This one is exceptional in that it does not show fruit, flowers or any perishable element that would mark the passage of time. Nor does it appear to have any recognisable symbolic significance, although the ceramics may be a reference to St Justa and St Rufina, the patron saints of Seville, who were the daughters of a potter. It is more likely, however, that the artist chose the vessels for their narrative neutrality, and because of the opportunity it gave him to transform ordinary motifs into something extraordinary. The protagonist might be said to be the light, which makes the vessels surge up from the dark background, modelling them with Zurbarán's characteristic attention to sculptural volume, and further increasing the work's ability to mystify and fascinate the viewer.

Alonso Cano

Less famous than his contemporaries Zurbarán and Velázquez, this versatile artist was equally renowned in his own time as a sculptor, a maker of altarpieces, and an architect. The works by him in the Museo del Prado are less numerous than those by other masters of his generation, and belong to his periods in Madrid, when he devoted himself mainly to painting. Cano received his initial training from his father, an altarpiece maker, before entering the workshop of Francisco Pacheco (1564–1644) alongside the slightly older Velázquez. Few paintings remain from that first phase in Seville, and none is in the Museo del Prado. In 1638, when he had already won a reputation as an artist in Seville, he was summoned to court by Olivares to serve as a court painter and royal adjutant. As in Zurbarán's case, the invitation probably owed something to the intervention of Velázquez. His contact with Velázquez in Madrid and his proximity to the Royal Collections as their restorer, particularly after the fire at the Buen Retiro Palace in 1640, gave him an intimate knowledge of Venetian painting. He then distanced himself from naturalism, and his work fell mainly under the influence of the sixteenth-century Venetian painters and Van Dyck [313, 314]. There thus emerges a personal style that differs surprisingly from those of his contemporaries. What sets him apart is his exquisite and balanced sensitivity, his taste for serene beauty and his conscious search for perfection, for he was the most idealistic of the Spanish Baroque masters and, together with Velázquez, the most classical. Noteworthy too is his taste for drawing and for the nude, as shown by a drawing at the Prado, one of the few female nudes of the Spanish Baroque painting [367]. The paintings by Alonso Cano preserved at the Prado reveal a delicacy that is exceptional for the Spain of his period. These works did not enter the Royal Collections until the time of the Bourbons, even though Cano had been employed at court. Others were acquired by the museum still later.

65
ALONSO CANO
Granada, 1601–1667

The Virgin and Child
c. 1646. Oil on canvas,
162 x 107 cm
P627

This fine example of Alonso Cano's numerous paintings on Marian subjects represents a type of religious image that makes the divine familiar by bringing it closer to the worshipper. This type of image was much appreciated in Spain, as the later success of Murillo shows [110 ff.]. In this case, the viewer witnesses the shared intimacy of the Virgin and Child through the look they exchange. The classical composition derives from a well-known engraving by Dürer which Cano interprets with exquisite delicacy, endowing the faces with a serenity and sweetness that relate them to Raphael's Madonnas [187, 188]. The technique exhibits great similarities with that of Cano's own *Miracle of the Well* [66], and the influence of Titian is to be seen in the colouring. The figures are set in a nocturnal landscape of blue tones, against which the gentle pinks of the Virgin's flesh and tunic stand out.

66
ALONSO CANO
Granada, 1601–1667

The Miracle of the Well
1638–40. Oil on canvas,
216 x 149 cm
P2806

Shortly after arriving in Madrid, Elizabeth of Bourbon, the wife of Philip IV, commissioned this picture from Alonso Cano for the high altar of the church of Nuestra Señora de la Almudena. It soon became one of the most highly praised works in Madrid, partly because of its subject matter. It tells the story of the miracle of the son of St Isidore, Madrid's patron saint, and of his wife St Mary de la Cabeza, who was restored to life by the Virgin of La Almudena after drowning in a well. Cano demonstrates his skill as a narrator in his precise description of the action and his inclusion of a variety of human types and attitudes. Although he had only fairly recently arrived in Madrid, he had already abandoned the draughtsmanlike style he cultivated in Seville, and had assimilated Venetian models. In his free and loose technique, it may be possible to discern the influence of Velázquez, the only painter with whom Cano can be compared.

67
ALONSO CANO
Granada, 1601–1667

The Dead Christ supported by an Angel

c. 1646. Oil on canvas,
180 x 120 cm
P629

The Museo del Prado holds two versions of this subject by Alonso Cano. In this one, the very beautiful body of Christ, reminiscent of Michelangelo, is gently supported by an angel who looks sorrowfully at the viewer as though confronting us with the tragedy of the scene. On the right of the picture is a landscape with a city, and on the left are the symbols of the Passion – the nails, the crown of thorns and, standing out against the dark background, the golden gleam of the basin in which the sponge rests. The artist presents the drama with restraint and balance, avoiding pathos. This allows him to linger on the nude, one of his favourite themes. Christ's body, on which scarcely any trace of blood remains, is perfectly proportioned in accordance with the classical ideal. The painter uses all the expressive possibilities of light, contrasting the inert whiteness of Christ's body, only slightly less white than the shroud, with the pink flesh of the angel and the darkness of the background. The scene is thus suffused with an atmosphere of stillness and mystery.

Velázquez and the Museo del Prado

The Prado contains many great works by such masters as Bosch, Titian, Rubens and Goya, but if the museum were to be identified with a single artist, it would surely be Diego Velázquez. Exhibited at the Prado are some fifty of the approximately one hundred and twenty paintings known to be by the artist, including his most outstanding and ambitious works. Velázquez even occupies the centre of the Prado in a physical sense, since the most pre-eminent place in the museum, the great basilica-style hall on the main floor, has been dedicated to him since 1899, and it is around *Las Meninas*, his supreme masterpiece, that the rest of the collection is organised, rather as though Velázquez's work were both its summation and its culmination. Velázquez studied the Royal Collections, and in them he assimilated the 'Spanish taste' created by the Habsburg monarchs. Thanks to the very works by Mor, El Greco, Titian, Tintoretto, Ribera and Rubens which now hang alongside his own at the Museo del Prado, he was able to enrich his painting to a prodigious degree, creating his own very personal style characterised by free and subtle brushwork and a new manner of interpreting pictorial genres. Most of Velázquez's works, except those of his youthful phase in Seville and those painted on his two journeys to Italy, were produced at the royal court of Spain either for Philip IV himself or for his immediate entourage. They were thus preserved in the Royal Collections, passing eventually to the Prado. From the time of the museum's inauguration in 1819, the prestige of the artist and that of the institution have remained closely linked. It was in its galleries that the world discovered Velázquez. He came to be championed both by those who saw him as the great painter of reality and by those who found in his painting a way to escape from the academic mould.

68
DIEGO VELÁZQUEZ
Seville, 1599–Madrid, 1660

The Adoration of the Magi
1619. Oil on canvas,
203 x 125 cm
P1166

Painted for the Jesuit novitiate of San Luis in Seville, this is the earliest of the three works in the Museo del Prado produced by Velázquez before his arrival at court. Recognisable in it are the features of his early phase in Seville, characterised by chiaroscuro and a meticulous rendering of each object. The painter has created a meditative work whose religious content is clearly and directly conveyed by the expressions and features of the figures, who are situated in the foreground, very close to the viewer. As for his models, it is possible that the work could be a family portrait. The artist may ave portrayed himself as the young king in the foreground, and used his wife Juana Pacheco as the model for the Virgin, his daughter Francisca for the Child, and his father-in-law and master Francisco Pacheco for the oldest of the kings.

Velázquez
Seville and the Early Years at Court

Diego Rodríguez de Silva y Velázquez received his initial training in Seville under his future father-in-law, the painter and treatise writer Francisco Pacheco (1564–1644). There was already evidence then of his immense ability to create highly original work on the basis of the naturalist painting he knew. However, it was at court that he developed his true pictorial personality. Velázquez went to Madrid for the first time in 1622, shortly after Philip IV (reigned 1621–1665) came to the throne. At the summons of the Count-Duke of Olivares (1587–1645), he returned the following year to settle there permanently, and he was named court painter shortly afterwards. This position determined the subjects of his paintings, many of which were therefore portraits, especially during his early years at court. In 1627, he nevertheless won the competition for a painting of *The Expulsion of the Moriscos*, now lost, which was destined for the Salón Nuevo (New Hall) at the Alcázar. This demonstrated his ability to work with a complex composition in a genre, history painting, regarded as a major one. The next year, the king appointed him as usher to the royal chamber. The post marked the beginning of a court career which led to a series of increasingly important positions: bailiff to the royal house and court in 1633, wardrobe adjutant in 1634, superintendent of the royal art works and adjutant to the royal chamber in 1643, and palace chamberlain in 1652. These occupations took time away from his painting, especially in the last decades of his life, but they made it possible for him to ennoble not only himself but the profession of painting as a whole. Velázquez's model was Rubens (1577–1640), who travelled to Madrid in 1628 as an ambassador to negotiate peace between Spain and England. This artist [302 ff.] shared a studio with Velázquez during his stays in Madrid, and it was almost certainly he who urged the Spanish painter to visit Italy. Velázquez also worked with Rubens on the decoration of the Torre de la Parada [77, 78]. Together with the Buen Retiro Palace, this was the most important artistic enterprise of Philip IV's reign.

69
DIEGO VELÁZQUEZ
Seville, 1599–Madrid, 1660

The Venerable Mother Jerónima de la Fuente
1620. Oil on canvas,
160 x 110 cm
P2873

Velázquez painted this portrait of the Venerable Mother Jerónima de la Fuente, mother superior of the convent of Santa Isabel in Toledo, when his sitter was sixty-five years old. She was then waiting in Seville to embark for the Philippines, where she was to found the first convent of nuns on the islands. Velázquez uses a Caravaggesque technique in this picture, which is also an archetypal image of the Spanish clergy of the period.

70
DIEGO VELÁZQUEZ
Seville, 1599–Madrid, 1660

Philip IV
1623–27. Oil on canvas,
198 x 101.5 cm
P1182

Velázquez painted Philip IV
many times in the course of
nearly forty years. This is the
first of the full-length portraits
he made of him. The artist
shows the monarch in an
indeterminate space, achieving
a convincing sense of reality
by means of a limited palette
of browns and greys and a tight,
concise brushwork that was
to undergo a transformation
in his later works. The picture
contains references to the
king's responsibilities through
such traditional symbols as
the Golden Fleece (the symbol
of the Spanish monarchy),
the desk where his hat sits
(representing justice), the
paper he holds in his right hand
(representing administration),
and the sword (for the defence
of the realm). We can also
see some of the modifications
made by Velázquez years later,
when he brought the king's legs
closer together and shortened
the cloak.

71
DIEGO VELÁZQUEZ
Seville, 1599–Madrid, 1660

The Drinkers or *The Feast of Bacchus*
1628–29. Oil on canvas,
165 x 188 cm
P1170

Velázquez, a great reviver of pictorial genres, here takes a mythological subject, rare in Spanish painting, and treats it in a realist manner. It represents the court of Bacchus, the god of wine, but it has almost the appearance of an everyday scene since the characters would not look out of place in the taverns of Madrid. Caravaggio had treated his religious scenes in a similar way, as had Ribera when he painted his philosophers [52]. Rubens may have had an influence on the choice of subject, but the work has none of his idealisation. In Seville,

Velázquez had already worked along these lines in paintings like *Christ in the House of Martha and Mary*, where the religious subject is almost hidden behind an everyday scene. Velázquez here retains his taste for earthy tones, popular costume and leathery faces, but the landscape, the luminosity, the nude body and the magnificent and carefully planned composition of *The Drinkers* indicate that he had by now assimilated the lessons to be learned from the works of Rubens and the Venetian painters in the Royal Collection.

Velázquez
The First Journey to Italy

Velázquez first left for Italy in August 1629. He took with him numerous letters of recommendation and royal permission for two years' leave from the court while continuing to draw his civil servant's salary. The painter visited Genoa, Milan, Venice, Ferrara, Cento, Loreto, and Rome, where he remained for one year. From there he returned to Spain via Naples, where he met José de Ribera. This Italian journey was fundamental for the development of Velázquez's painting and opened up new horizons for him. In Rome, he had the opportunity of seeing not only the masterpieces of antiquity and the Renaissance, but also contemporary masterpieces, of which there were no examples in the Spanish Royal Collections. He was also able to witness the debate between the supporters of the classicism of the Carracci and those who favoured the decorative Baroque of Pietro da Cortona, a controversy that merely reaffirmed his conviction that painting was primarily an intellectual activity. The classicism assimilated by Velázquez in Italy was not of an academic type, and did not distract him from his love of reality. He was also greatly influenced by Venetian colour. His compositions became more ambitious while he was in Italy and he showed a greater interest in the nude and the theory of gestures. The latter is clear from some of the work he produced there, such as *Joseph's Bloody Coat brought to Jacob*, now in the monastery of El Escorial, and *Apollo at the Forge of Vulcan* [74], in the Museo del Prado, which are close to the narratives of Cortona, Reni and Guercino. It was probably on this journey that he painted two *plein air* views of the Villa Medici, where he stayed in the summer of 1630 before his return to Madrid at the end of the year. When he went back to Italy twenty years later, in January 1649, he did so with the king's commission to acquire art works for the decoration of his palaces, and also with the desire to demonstrate his worth as an artist in Rome, the artistic centre of Europe. There are many examples of his success: he was elected to the Academy of St Luke and the Congregation of the Virtuous; he was highly praised for his *Portrait of Juan de Pareja* (now at the Metropolitan Museum of Art in New York); and he was permitted by Pope Innocent X (1572–1655) to paint his portrait, now in the Galleria Doria Pamphilj in Rome. It is one of the most admired and awe-inspiring portraits in the history of art.

72 →
DIEGO VELÁZQUEZ
Seville, 1599–Madrid, 1660

*View of the Garden
of the Villa Medici in Rome*
c. 1630. Oil on canvas,
48.5 x 43 cm
P1210

73 ↓
DIEGO VELÁZQUEZ
Seville, 1599–Madrid, 1660

*View of the Garden
of the Villa Medici in Rome*
c. 1630. Oil on canvas,
44.5 x 38 cm
P1211

These two Roman views are unique in the artist's oeuvre and that of his contemporaries. This is not only because they lack a recognisable subject at a time when landscape was deemed to require the support of a narrative, but also because of their technique of light and vibrant strokes, later seen as precursors of impressionism. Another modern feature that has frequently been remarked on is Velázquez's apparent interest in painting the changing face of nature rather than stressing its immutability, since he shows two moments defined by contrasting atmospheric conditions. Such questions apart, and regardless of whether or not there is a story attached to the figures, the true protagonists of these two small masterpieces are light and the passage of time. They show the gardens of the Villa Medici, where Velázquez, attracted by its sculpture collection and the beauty of its surroundings, stayed for two months.

74
DIEGO VELÁZQUEZ
Seville, 1599–Madrid, 1660

*Apollo at the Forge
of Vulcan*
1630. Oil on canvas,
223 x 290 cm
P1171

This work demonstrates
all the lessons Velázquez
learned from Greco-Roman
statuary, from Michelangelo,
from Roman-Bolognese
classicism, and from the neo-
Venetianism prevailing in
Rome in the early decades
of the seventeenth century.
A passage from Ovid's
Metamorphoses, in which
Apollo visits the forge of
Vulcan to tell him that his
wife Venus has deceived
him with Mars, is turned
into a complex composition
that tells the story through
a remarkable repertoire
of dramatic gestures and
expressions. The setting is
of such verisimilitude that
it seems possible to step
inside it and experience the
space between the bodies,
their carefully rendered
anatomy precisely moulded
by a light that has broken
the bounds of tenebrism.
Palpable too is the space
between the objects, among
which are some fine examples
of still life, such as the armour,
the tools and the red-hot iron.

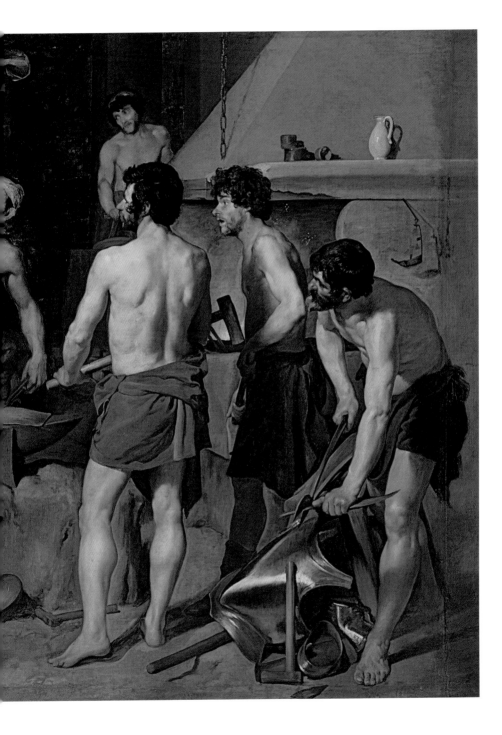

Velázquez
Years of Maturity

The central years of Velázquez's career were spent at court, and this had important consequences for his work. The 1630s were a time of frenzied activity for the Royal Collections. The country had not yet fully plunged into political and economic crisis, and the king, who was still regarded as one of the most powerful monarchs in Europe, made sure he was surrounded by an opulence commensurate with his power. It was then that the commissions were issued for the Buen Retiro Palace and the refurbishment of some parts of the Alcázar. Among the palaces to benefit from this activity was the Torre de la Parada, a hunting pavilion on the heathland of El Pardo that underwent alterations between 1635 and 1638. The pavilion housed one of the most important cycles of mythological paintings of the time, directed by Rubens and with contributions by Velázquez [77], as well as hunting pictures by Frans Snyders and Martin de Vos. Also destined for it, however, were several pictures by Velázquez portraying Philip IV, his brother Fernando and his son Baltasar Carlos as hunters [78], showing that even a palace for the monarchs' leisure and hunting pursuits was to be endowed with representational value.

Besides painting the royal family and some of the courtiers and artists of the time, it was during this period that Velázquez portrayed the Count-Duke of Olivares [79], to whom he probably owed his introduction at court. Significantly, Olivares had himself portrayed in forms and poses that closely resemble the portraits of the king. This indicates the power he came to wield before his fall from grace in 1643, after plunging the nation into a grave political crisis.

Velázquez's links with the court were also largely responsible for the fact that he produced fewer religious paintings than any other Spanish artist of the period. The royal family and the nobility mainly required him to paint portraits or pictures to decorate their palaces, and only on rare occasions was he asked for religious scenes. Although some have seen signs of a lukewarm faith in his dearth of religious compositions, the intensity of those he did paint, and particularly his *Christ on the Cross* [75], has paradoxically led others to consider Velázquez as one of the artists most gifted at conveying profound religious sentiment.

75
DIEGO VELÁZQUEZ
Seville, 1599–Madrid, 1660

Christ on the Cross
c. 1631–32. Oil on canvas,
248 x 169 cm
P1167

This crucifixion scene for the Benedictine convent of San Plácido in Madrid is said by tradition to have been painted at Philip IV's command. The composition is one of great simplicity, showing Christ with four nails, in accordance with the iconographic recommendations of his master, Pacheco. Instead of a background landscape, the cross is placed against a dark green backcloth, rather as if it were a sculpture. On Christ's lifeless but perfectly proportioned body, a nude far removed from the muscular canon of Michelangelo, the marks of his suffering are reduced to a minimum. He is gently moulded by a tenuous light, most pronounced in the halo around his head, while his face is half-hidden by the fall of his hair. The serene beauty of the crucified figure, and the atmosphere of contained silence and meditation achieved by Velázquez, made this work one of the most successful of all Spanish devotional images.

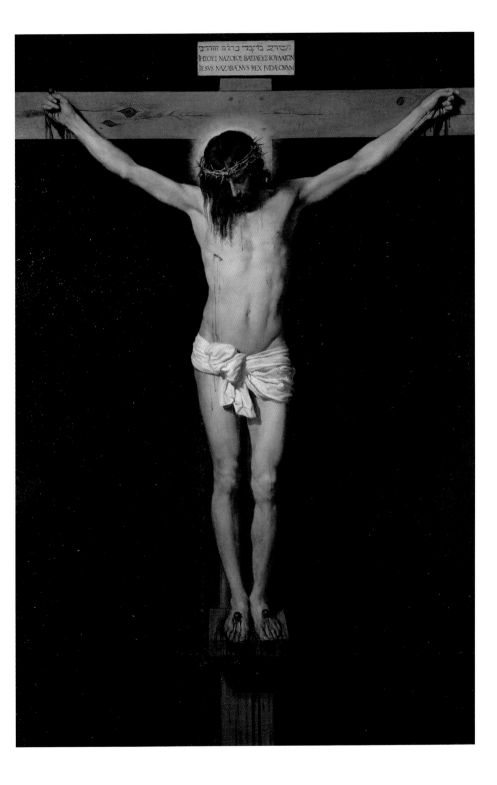

76
DIEGO VELÁZQUEZ
Seville, 1599–Madrid, 1660

*St Anthony Abbot and St Paul
the Hermit*

c. 1633. Oil on canvas,
261 x 192.5 cm
P1169

Painted for the hermitage chapel of San Pablo in the gardens of the Buen Retiro Palace, this work gives considerable importance to the landscape, which occupies more than half the canvas. Perhaps drawing inspiration from canvases or prints by northern precursors of landscape painting, like Patinir [274] or Dürer, it narrates various episodes in the lives of the two saints within a single setting. We see St Anthony asking a centaur and a satyr for directions, St Anthony calling at St Paul's cave, the raven bringing St Paul his daily ration of bread together with an extra one for St Anthony, and finally St Anthony praying before the corpse of his companion. Despite the medieval narrative technique, Velázquez's great freedom and transparency of brushwork infuses the scene with much of the essence of modern painting.

77
DIEGO VELÁZQUEZ
Seville, 1559–Madrid, 1660

Mars

c. 1640. Oil on canvas,
181 x 99 cm
P1208

As in the earlier *Feast of Bacchus* [71], the artist here presents his own version of a mythological subject. Mars, the god of war, is a tired and dejected soldier meditating on the battle, his armour and shield at his feet, and his melancholy gaze turned towards the viewer. It has been suggested that the painting could be seen as a symbol of Spain itself, a country which had dominated the world, and was now beginning a long period of political and military decline. Painted for the Torre de la Parada, it may bear some relation to the paintings of *Aesop* [80] and *Menippus*, which were also destined for the Torre, thus placing the picture in a context of scepticism and disillusionment. Whatever the case, *Mars* demonstrates how efficiently the artist uses his broad and free brushstrokes to render the metallic glint of the weapons and the mature flesh of the god's magnificent nude body.

78
DIEGO VELÁZQUEZ
Seville, 1599–Madrid, 1660

*Prince Baltasar Carlos
as a Hunter*
1635–36. Oil on canvas,
191 x 103 cm
P1189

Velázquez painted three
portraits of members
of the royal family dressed
as hunters: one of the king
himself, another of his brother,
the Cardinal Infante Don
Fernando, and this one of the
young heir to the throne. They
were destined for the Torre
de la Parada, a royal hunting
pavilion on the estate of
El Pardo, just outside Madrid.
This likeness of Baltasar Carlos
is less official in character
than his portrait for the Salón
de Reinos, and there is no
attribute to indicate his royalty.
He is portrayed at the age
of six, but despite his tender
years, he is fully equipped for
hunting, an activity which
was considered basic to a
princely education since it
served as preparation for war.
The young prince, whose
face is depicted with great
verisimilitude and humanity,
is shown against a broad
and luminous landscape, with
the Guadarrama Mountains
in the distance. The portrait
is executed in free and varied
brushwork with a predominance
of silvery tones.

79
DIEGO VELÁZQUEZ
Seville, 1599–Madrid, 1660

Don Gaspar de Guzmán,
Count-Duke of Olivares

c. 1634. Oil on canvas,
313 x 239 cm
P1181

Commissioned by the sitter
himself, this work clearly
shows the power of the Count-
Duke of Olivares (1587–1645),
the favourite of Philip IV.
He has himself painted with
all the attributes of his rank
by the king's own painter
and, moreover, in a manner
resembling the portrait of the
king himself which Velázquez
was shortly to paint for the
Salón de Reinos in the Buen
Retiro Palace [91]. Arrogant
and impetuous, Olivares appears
on a rearing horse, a form of
representation almost exclusive
to the monarchy which signified
the highest expression of
military and political command.
Velázquez situates the horse
obliquely to the canvas, facing
the battle that is taking place
in the background, while the
rider turns his face towards
the viewer in a posture that
allows the artist to disguise his
unprepossessing figure, endowing
it with a force and dynamism that
contrast with the serenity of the
royal portrait.

Velázquez
Philosophers and the 'People of Pleasure'

The so-called 'people of pleasure' – buffoons, dwarfs, and fools – were to be found in most of the courts and noble houses of Europe. They provided entertainment and accompanied the kings and aristocrats of Spain from the reign of Ferdinand and Isabella up until the start of the eighteenth century. By taking them into their households the nobility were able to demonstrate their generosity towards the less fortunate, and their idiosyncrasies and deformities also served as a counterpoint to the supposed elegance and perfection of the aristocracy. There was already a pictorial tradition of portraying them prior to Velázquez, and the Museo del Prado has examples by Anthonis Mor [290], Sánchez Cotán and Juan van der Hamen [96]. It was, however, Velázquez who took them as models most often. Indeed, they became one of his favourite subjects, as the seven examples at the Prado testify. He began to paint them after his first visit to Italy, when he had reached full artistic maturity and was firmly established at court as the king's principal painter. He portrayed them with ever-growing freedom of execution using broad strokes of almost dematerialised paint, and achieving images of great veracity and realism with a remarkable economy of means. With a genius bordering on the magical, Velázquez conjures up an extremely subtle spatial fiction by placing the figures in settings of increasing sobriety. He shows us human nature as he finds it, and with great compassion and affection he endows these singular figures with as much dignity as he gives to royalty. It is possible that these portraits have an allegorical significance, which would be in keeping with the intellectual complexity of Velázquez's painting. This theory is given added weight by the fact that realist portraits with no symbolic content were rare at that time. Furthermore, all the sitters in these portraits bear attributes or perform actions which add meaning to their portrayal.

80
DIEGO VELÁZQUEZ
Seville, 1599–Madrid, 1660

Aesop
c.1638. Oil on canvas,
179 x 94 cm
P1206

Aesop and also *Menippus*, Velázquez's two pictures of 'philosophers', are linked to his paintings of 'people of pleasure' by their pictorial treatment and by the fact that they are not portraits of nobles. Destined for the Torre de la Parada, for which Rubens had already painted the philosophers *Heraclitus* and *Democritus*, these two almost burlesque characters are endowed with the same dignity as Velázquez's dwarfs and buffoons. Aesop is represented as a ragged figure, almost a beggar, in allusion to his origins as a slave. His precedent is to be found in the works of José de Ribera, who had used beggars as models for philosophers of antiquity [52]. The present picture excited particular admiration among nineteenth-century realists because its pictorial values coincided with those sought by the painters of that school.

81
DIEGO VELÁZQUEZ
Seville, 1599–Madrid, 1660

Pablo de Valladolid

c. 1635. Oil on canvas,
209 x 123 cm
P1198

The painter Edouard Manet
(1832–1883) affirmed that this
work was 'perhaps the most
amazing piece of painting that
has ever been painted', which
is a tribute to Velázquez's
astonishing inventiveness.
Here he creates a space
without geometrical reference
to either the floor or the
walls. The figure of Pablo
de Valladolid, who worked
at court from 1632 until his
death, is integrated with
absolute verisimilitude into
a space suggested only by his
shadow and the gradation of
the light. He is shown in an
attitude of declamation, like
an actor on an imaginary stage,
and it is quite possible that
he owed his presence at court
to his comic gifts or acting
talents. The whole piece is
executed with considerable
economy of means, but
also with the sureness
of touch which characterises
Velázquez's mature art.

82 →
DIEGO VELÁZQUEZ
Seville, 1599–Madrid, 1660

Don Sebastián de Morra
c. 1635–40. Oil on canvas,
106 x 81 cm
P1202

Like the 'philosophers',
some of Velázquez's
buffoons were also painted
for the Torre de la Parada.
Two examples are the
portraits of Calabacillas
and Francisco Lezcano,
known as *El Niño de Vallecas*
('The Boy from Vallecas').
Another is that of Sebastián
de Morra, perhaps the
most striking of them.
Velázquez here combines
an intense gaze, partly defiant
and partly melancholy,
with an extremely austere
construction of space.

83 ↑
Francisco Lezcano
c. 1635–40. Oil on canvas,
107 x 83 cm
P1204

84 ↑
The Buffoon Calabacillas
c. 1635–40. Oil on canvas,
107 x 83 cm
P1205

Velázquez
The Last Years

Velázquez died in Madrid on 6 August 1660 of a disease he had contracted shortly after his return from the island of Los Faisanes on the French border, where the marriage of Philip IV's daughter, the Infanta María Teresa (1638–1715), and Louis XIV of France (reigned 1643–1715), had just been celebrated. The painter attended the event in fulfilment of his obligations as palace chamberlain. After his return from Italy in 1651, his courtly duties had taken more and more time from his painting, yet it was in the last years of his life that he painted some of his most amazing pictures. They include two of possibly the greatest masterpieces in the history of painting, *The Spinners (Las Hilanderas)* [88] and, above all, *Las Meninas* [89], both in the Museo del Prado. It was during those last years too that he devoted considerable effort to the long and tiring process of obtaining the title of knight of the Order of Santiago, finally being awarded it in 1658 thanks in part to the support of Philip IV and the assistance of Pope Innocent X, whose portrait he had painted during his second stay in Italy. In *The Spinners* and *Las Meninas*, Velázquez shows his complete command of his pictorial technique and his consummate ability to faithfully reproduce visual experience. In these paintings, so full of life and atmosphere, he creates believable and habitable spaces. His use of colour is extremely sophisticated, and the dazzling lightness of his technique reaches the peak of its simplification and effectiveness. But these are also complex pictures that can be read on many levels. They are more like intellectual projections, or images of an idea, than imitations of the real world. In them, Velázquez once again takes up his concept of painting as a noble and pre-eminently intellectual art.

85
DIEGO VELÁZQUEZ
Seville, 1599–Madrid, 1660

Ferdinando Brandani
c. 1650. Oil on canvas,
50.5 x 47 cm
P7858

During his second stay in Italy, between 1649 and 1651, Velazquez painted some portraits of people related to the papal court. Among them is this one, the subject of which remained unknown for many years. Finally, the person portrayed has been identified as Ferdinando Brandani, a senior official for the Pope's secretary and a person close to Juan of Cordoba, the Spanish agent who helped Velazquez with practical matters in his mission in Rome.
The most characteristic aspect of this work is the lifelike feeling it transmits, thanks to the artist's ability to recreate the delicacy and softness of the ruddy, detailed flesh. Through subtle variations in tone and using brief fills and light touches, he occasionally creates shine, as in the irises of the eyes or the red of the lips, which give greater vivacity and expression to the face. Ultimately, the work is a good example of Velazquez's talent for reproducing reality through a few brushstrokes.

86
DIEGO VELÁZQUEZ
Seville, 1599–Madrid, 1660

Philip IV

c. 1653. Oil on canvas,
69 x 56 cm
P1185

For over thirty years Velázquez
lived under the roof of Philip
IV, one of history's great
collectors and a connoisseur
who was always capable of
appreciating the depth and
novelty of his painting. When he
painted this portrait of the king
with its astonishing economy
of means and profound feeling
for humanity, Velázquez had
reached his full maturity as an
artist. Deeply saddened by the

lack of a male heir and the all-
too-evident decline of the
Spanish monarchy, Philip IV
appears as a weary and rather
elderly man, though he had
not yet reached the age of
fifty. Soberly dressed in black
and placed against a dark
background, the king gazes
despondently out at us with
tired eyes. The artist painted
another very similar portrait,
now in the National Gallery in
London, in which the monarch
wears a suit with gilded buttons,
embroidery on the sleeves,
and a chain with the badge of
the Golden Fleece. However,
it is in the Prado portrait, where
there is no attribute to inform
us of the figure's royal status,
that the personality of the sitter
is conveyed most strongly.

87 →
DIEGO VELÁZQUEZ
Seville, 1559–Madrid, 1660

*Queen Mariana
of Austria*

c. 1652–53. Oil on canvas,
234 x 131.5 cm
P1191

Velázquez painted this
portrait of Mariana of Austria
at the request of her father,
Emperor Ferdinand III, who
wanted to have a likeness
of his adolescent daughter.
It had been arranged that she
would marry Baltasar Carlos,
the heir to the Spanish throne,
but on the prince's untimely
death, she was married instead
to the king himself, her blood
uncle Philip IV. This is a
state portrait, in keeping with
earlier images of the women of
the House of Austria, and so
contains features characteristic
of official portraits, such as the
grand curtain and the imposing
'friar's chair' on which her right
hand rests. Velázquez executed
the work with the rich, loose
technique that characterises
the production of his maturity,
when he succeeded in
perfectly rendering both faces
and fabrics by employing small
brushstrokes on broad areas
of colour.

88
DIEGO VELÁZQUEZ
Seville, 1599–Madrid, 1660

The Spinners, or *The Fable of Arachne*
c. 1657. Oil on canvas,
167 x 252 cm
P1173

For a long time this work was thought to be a genre painting depicting a group of spinners at work in the royal tapestry factory of Santa Isabel in Madrid. This was because Velázquez placed the secondary action in the foreground, while the main scene was played out behind and on a smaller scale. Combined with the fact that more than fifty centimetres were added to the work at the top and thirty-seven on the sides, distorting the original composition, this diverted attention away from the small brightly lit room in the background, which is perceived as more distant. It is there that we find the central motif of the picture, a mythological scene enacted by three figures who stand before a tapestry. Arachne, a simple mortal, has dared to challenge Minerva, goddess of the arts, to a contest. On discovering that Arachne's tapestry is woven with as much skill as the goddess's own, Minerva turns her into a spider. Arachne's tapestry reproduces a painting by Titian, *The Rape of Europa,* which suggests that Velázquez is paying homage to his predecessor by equating his work with that of the goddess. Titian's picture was also copied by Rubens. Velázquez, who knew both versions, has thus created a work which links three of the pillars of the Royal Collection and, ultimately, of the Prado: Titian, Rubens and Velázquez himself.

89
DIEGO VELÁZQUEZ
Seville, 1599–Madrid, 1660

Las Meninas, or *The Family of Philip IV*
1656. Oil on canvas,
318 x 276 cm
P1174

Las Meninas is undoubtedly the best known painting in the Museo del Prado and Velázquez's most famous work. It is also the one which best sums up the characteristics of his art. It is a complex piece that is presented to us like a slice of life, but which hides readings on many levels behind its apparent clarity. In a large room of the Alcázar in Madrid, we see the Infanta Margarita flanked by two maids of honour, or *meninas*. One is María Agustina Sarmiento, who offers the infanta water in a small ceramic jug, and the other is Isabel de Velasco. To her left, and a little further forward, we see the dwarf Maribárbola and a mastiff that is being teased by the midget, Nicolasito Pertusato. Behind, and slightly in shadow, are an unidentified male attendant and Marcela de Ulloa, and on the other side of the composition is Velázquez himself. At the back of the room, we see José Nieto, the royal chamberlain, silhouetted against the light in the open doorway, and a mirror in which the king and queen are reflected. They are therefore standing outside the picture, in the viewer's space. The numerous figures are organised in a balanced composition of such extraordinary depth that it seems to open out of the picture. Velázquez carefully controls both the linear and the aerial perspective, and his treatment of light produces a genuine sensation of space and air. The picture has been interpreted in a number of ways, many of them complementary. The centrality of the infanta Margarita and the reflection of the king and queen in the mirror appear to point to a political and dynastic significance. The presence of Velázquez in the same environment as the king, queen and infanta, and bearing the cross of the Order of Santiago and the chamberlain's key as attributes of his social status, presumably constitutes a validation of his nobility and that of painting itself. He represents himself in an attitude of contemplation, showing that he regards artistic activity as a product of the intellect rather than of manual dexterity. The paintings on the back wall convey the same message. Identified as copies by Juan Bautista Martínez del Mazo of Rubens's *Minerva and Arachne* and Jacob Jordaens's *Apollo and Marsyas*, both are mythological scenes which exalt the nobility and liberal character of painting.

The Salón de Reinos

Building began on the Buen Retiro Palace in 1630 under the direction of the Count-Duke of Olivares (1587–1645), the favourite of Philip IV (reigned 1621–1665). Although initially intended as royal quarters for the monarch's religious retreats at the church of San Jerónimo on the outskirts of Madrid, it eventually became a large pleasure palace for the relaxation and entertainment of the royal family. The exterior of the building was very simple owing to the modest materials used and the speed of its construction, which took only three years. The interiors, on the other hand, were richly and profusely decorated. Of the vast palace complex, nothing remains today except for the gardens, now a public park; the ballroom or *Casón*, which forms part of the Museo del Prado; and the north wing of the main plaza, the home until fairly recently of the Museo del Ejército (Army Museum), which housed the so-called Salón de Reinos, or Hall of Realms. This room was the Buen Retiro's great hall for festivities and ceremonies. In keeping with its important function, it was subjected to a complex decorative programme that evoked the power of the House of Austria. Painted on the ceiling were the shields of the twenty-four realms of the Spanish monarchy, which would give the hall its name, and hung on the walls were twenty-seven specially commissioned paintings: twelve large battle scenes, by different artists [90, 94, 95]; ten scenes from the life of Hercules, painted by Zurbarán; and five equestrian portraits of Philip III and Philip IV, their respective queens and the heir to the throne, Prince Baltasar Carlos, all by Velázquez [91-93]. In this way the Salon de Reinos gave out three parallel and complementary messages. First, the coats of arms of the realms suggested the spread of the monarchy around the world. Secondly, the ten scenes from the life of Hercules showed the virtues the prince must possess, and they also completed the theme of dynastic continuity established by the equestrian portraits, since Hercules was the mythical founder of the Hispanic monarchy. Finally, the battle scenes represented victories achieved in recent years – from 1625 to 1633 – by the Spanish armies, emphasising the military might preserved by a monarchy that was already in sharp decline.

90
DIEGO VELÁZQUEZ
Seville, 1599–Madrid, 1660

The Surrender of Breda

1634–35. Oil on canvas,
307 x 367 cm
P1172

In this work Velázquez gives
another demonstration of
his personal approach to his
subjects. In this case he is faced
with the task of depicting one
of the most important victories
of all those represented in the
hall – the surrender on 5 June

1625 of the city of Breda, the port
of entry to Holland, which
had been besieged by Spanish
troops under the command of
Ambrosio Spínola. Drawing
his inspiration from a play by
Calderón de la Barca, *El sitio
de Breda* (*The Siege of Breda*,
1626), Velázquez does not
celebrate the victory, but rather
places the emphasis on the
magnanimity and clemency
of the Spanish army. The
central motif of the picture is
the gesture whereby Spínola,
who has dismounted, receives
Justin of Nassau, the governor
of the conquered city, as an

equal, refusing to allow him
to kneel. Arranged to their
right and left are Dutch
and Spanish soldiers, the latter
with a row of lances behind
them – a symbol of power
and order that has given the
picture its popular Spanish
name, *Las Lanzas*. Opening
out in the background is
a magnificent landscape.
Especially remarkable is the
evanescent smoke rising up
from the battle and wafting
into the foreground in a
demonstration of Velázquez's
mastery at creating atmosphere
and distance.

91
DIEGO VELÁZQUEZ
Seville, 1599–Madrid, 1660

Philip IV on Horseback
c. 1635–36. Oil on canvas,
301 x 314 cm
P1178

92
DIEGO VELÁZQUEZ
Seville, 1599–Madrid, 1660

*Queen Isabel de Bourbon,
wife of Philip IV,
on Horseback*
c. 1635–36. Oil on canvas,
301 x 314 cm
P1179

93
DIEGO VELÁZQUEZ
Seville, 1599–Madrid, 1660

*Prince Baltasar Carlos
on Horseback*

c. 1635–36. Oil on canvas,
209 x 173 cm
P1180

To symbolise the continuity
of the dynasty, the equestrian
portraits of Philip III and
Queen Margaret of Austria,
the parents of Philip IV, were
arranged on the west wall of the
Salón de Reinos, while on the
opposite wall were those of
Philip IV and his wife, Isabel
de Bourbon [91, 92]. That of

his heir, Prince Baltasar Carlos
[93], was placed between the
two over a door, which explains
the proportions of the horse,
painted to be seen from below.
In the portrait of Philip IV,
Velázquez successfully meets
the challenge of comparison
with the other great equestrian
portraits in the Royal
Collections – that of Charles V
by Titian [213], and that of
Philip IV by Rubens, now
lost. The king appears in strict
profile and dressed as a general,
with the sweeping landscape
of the Guadarrama Mountains
behind him. He controls his
mount with no apparent effort,
thereby symbolising his ability
to rule over his kingdom. In the

portrait of Isabel de Bourbon,
on the other hand, a certain
hardness of line and an excessive
attention to minute detail in
the rendering of the fabrics
recall the northern tradition
followed by artists such as
Pantoja de la Cruz, indicating
that other painters collaborated
with Velázquez on this work.
Even so, Velázquez leaves
proof of his authorship in
outstanding details like the
horse's head. Finally, Baltasar
Carlos, Philip IV's longed-
for first son, is shown with
a general's staff of command,
indicating his readiness to take
up the reins of monarchy. His
early death was to prevent him
from doing so.

94
FRANCISCO DE ZURBARÁN
Fuente de Cantos, Badajoz,
1598–Madrid, 1664

*The Defence of Cadiz
against the English*
1634. Oil on canvas,
302 x 323 cm
P656

Zurbarán painted two pictures
with this subject. This one
shows the Spanish troops
repelling the attack of the
English fleet, which began
on 1 November 1625. The other,
now lost, represented the Indies
fleet, the English objective,
entering Cadiz unharmed.
The work follows the same
composition as the other battle
scenes in the hall, although
the theatrical treatment of space
is slightly more exaggerated.
The differences in the handling
of the foreground and the
battle in the background are
more marked, and the battle
looks like a backdrop. Zurbarán
renders the qualities of the
fabrics and objects with great
skill and chromatic richness,
and there are magnificent
portraits of the city's veteran
governor, Fernando Girón
y Ponce de León, and the other
personages around him. The
governor, immobilised by gout,
gives orders from his chair to
Diego Ruiz, his field marshal.

95
JUAN BAUTISTA MAÍNO
Pastrana, Guadalajara,
1581–Madrid, 1649

*The Recapture of Bahia
in Brazil*

1634–35. Oil on canvas,
309 x 381 cm
P885

Instead of placing triumphant
generals in the foreground,
Maíno shows us a woman
tending a wounded soldier,
so underlining the suffering
of the victims, while relegating
the symbolic representation
of the victory to a more distant
plane. Don Fabrique de Toledo
led the recapture of Salvador
de Bahia, taken by the Dutch
the year before, on 1 May 1625.
He appears on the left of the
composition, directing the
attention of the vanquished
to a tapestry that shows Philip
IV crowned with the wreath

of victory by Minerva and the
Count-Duke of Olivares. Maíno
drew inspiration for this scene
from a play by Lope de Vega,
El Brasil restituido (*Brazil Restored*,
1625), in which the general
addresses a portrait sculpture
of the king to ask him whether
he should spare the vanquished,
to which the monarch replies
in the affirmative. The
painting shows various rotund
figures arranged in a series of
interlocking planes. As is usual
with Maíno, the foreground is
rendered with a great sensitivity
for tactile qualities.

Painters in Seventeenth-century Madrid

The Museo del Prado has several works by Spanish painters born between 1595 and 1615 who worked in Madrid, either occupying a secondary place in the court where Velázquez reigned supreme, or carrying out other commissions, principally for an ecclesiastical clientele. Among those who fall into the second group are Juan van der Hamen [96], a Spanish painter of Flemish origin three years older than Velázquez, who was already working in Madrid when the latter arrived from Seville in 1623; Juan Andrés Rizi [97], a painter and theorist who left the court to enter the Benedictine order; and Antonio de Pereda [98], who took part in the decoration of the Buen Retiro Palace before devoting himself to still lifes and, above all, religious scenes for private clients. Most of these artists developed under the first wave of naturalism and followed a Caravaggesque pattern, maintaining the pictorial styles of the previous generation. However, they did not assimilate the Flemish tradition of Rubens, which clearly separates them from the other painters of the same generation, or in some cases slightly younger, who took the definitive step into High Baroque. Nor did they absorb any influence from Velázquez, who had very little exposure outside the court, perhaps because of his extremely limited clientele and because he had not created any works of a public nature, such as a large altarpiece. He left his mark solely on the portrait, though this was mainly because his works in this genre formed part of an established tradition, and were widely copied by other painters at court. Only in the artists who had a very direct relation with Velázquez is his influence clearly evident. One is his son-in-law, Juan Bautista Martínez del Mazo [99], who succeeded him as court painter and is the one artist who can properly be regarded as his pupil.

96
JUAN VAN DER HAMEN
Madrid, 1596–1631

Portrait of a Dwarf
c. 1626. Oil on canvas,
122 x 87 cm
P7065

Van der Hamen owes his fame to his still lifes and flower pieces, of which the Museo del Prado has some fine examples [42, 43]. However, he was also a consummate portraitist, as this work testifies. Here, as Velázquez was also to do [81-84], he shows one of the so-called 'people of pleasure', then quite a common sight in the courts of Europe, whose function was to entertain members of the royal family. In this picture, one of the few surviving examples of the expertise he attained in the genre, Van der Hamen follows the Spanish tradition of court portraiture established by Alonso Sánchez Coello, giving a detailed rendering of the costume and minutely recreating the textures, a characteristic typical of his still lifes. He bestows great dignity upon his subject, whom he depicts elegantly dressed and with a staff of office in his right hand, thus underlining his air of confidence and the nobility of his features.

97
JUAN ANDRÉS RIZI
Madrid, 1600–Montecassino,
1681

*Don Tiburcio de Redín
y Cruzat*

1635. Oil on canvas, 203 x 124 cm
P887

Tiburcio de Redín, baron
of Bigüezal, was a field marshal
of the Spanish infantry, as
indicated by the two pistols
on the table. The year after
this portrait was painted, the
artist entered the Capuchins
as a lay member, taking the
name of Brother Francisco
of Pamplona. He subsequently
went to America to spread
the gospel, dying at the port
of La Guayra in Venezuela.
Juan Andrés Rizi, the brother
of the painter Francisco Rizi
[101], painted few portraits
because he specialised in
monastic cycles, of which the
Prado holds some examples
that came from the Museo de
la Trinidad.

98
ANTONIO DE PEREDA
Valladolid, 1611–Madrid, 1678

St Jerome

1643. Oil on canvas, 105 x 84 cm
P1046

This work, which came from
the Royal Collections, clearly
shows the range of Pereda's
influences. Here are the taste
for detail of the Flemish
tradition prior to Rubens,
the sumptuous colouring of the
Venetians, and – very evident in

this picture – Ribera's manner
of representing saints [54, 57].
St Jerome hears the trumpet
of the Last Judgement, as
shown in the engraving in the
open book, which is based on
Dürer's print of the subject.
The saint is accompanied by his
characteristic attributes: the
skull and the stone, symbols
of his penitence, and the
books and inkwell, indicative
of his learning and devotion to
writing. Pereda shows great skill
in rendering these objects. Like
Juan van der Hamen, he was
a frequent painter of still lifes.

99
JUAN BAUTISTA MARTÍNEZ
DEL MAZO
Beteta (?), Cuenca, c. 1611–
Madrid, 1667

View of the City of Saragossa
1647. Oil on canvas,
181 x 331 cm
P889

Such is the quality of this picture that it was long regarded, at least in part, as the work of Velázquez, Mazo's father-in-law from 1633 onwards. However, it is securely documented as having been painted by Mazo in 1647 after accompanying Prince Baltasar Carlos on his visit to Saragossa. The city appears in the background of a broad vista that allows us to appreciate Mazo's powers of observation and spatial sense. In the foreground is the animated north bank of the Ebro, peopled with lively little figures.

The High Baroque Painters

Towards the middle of the seventeenth century, there was a transformation in Spanish painting. It had started in the late 1630s and was a response to two main factors. The first was the growing influence of Flemish Baroque, owing to the arrival in Spain of numerous works by Rubens and the dissemination of Flemish prints, and the second was awareness of the changes in the pictorial panorama of Italy, where Roman-Bolognese Baroque had superseded Caravaggesque naturalism. Because of these influences, aspects of Spanish painting that had hitherto been dominant, such as its severity and its taste for concrete reality and direct light sources, were replaced by dynamic compositions and bright and luminous colours. Skies of intense blue became the general norm, and restraint gave way to gesticulation, images of penitence to images of glory, and simple domestic settings to opulent theatrical scenarios. The change was manifest above all in the work of Juan Carreño de Miranda [100, 102, 103] and Francisco Rizi [101], both court painters, and of Francisco de Herrera the Younger [104], their junior, who had trained in Seville. Carreño's portraits embrace the sober Spanish tradition, Velázquez included, but fuse it with the more worldly portraiture of Rubens and Van Dyck. Rizi, the brother of Juan Andrés Rizi, also a painter and theorist, was passed over at court when Carreño was appointed as the king's painter in 1671, so religious paintings account for most of his output. A whole host of younger painters trained under Carreño and Rizi, infusing their Baroque style with greater dynamism and chromatic intensity, and seeking inspiration in the compositions of Rubens and the elegance of Van Dyck. Carreño's disciples, like Mateo Cerezo [109], produced more serene and balanced compositions than Rizi's followers, who were more given to restless movement and had a certain preference for cold colours. One example is Juan Antonio de Frías y Escalante [108], who also shows a profound admiration for Venetian painting, and another is José Antolínez [106], an artist of strong personality and exceptional elegance. Claudio Coello [105], the supreme artist of the Madrid Baroque school, was also apprenticed to Rizi. Herrera the Younger meanwhile took High Baroque from Madrid to Seville.

100
JUAN CARREÑO
DE MIRANDA
Avilés, Asturias, 1614–Madrid,
1685

The Duke of Pastrana
c. 1666. Oil on canvas,
217 x 155 cm
P650

This elegant portrait is one of the artist's best and perhaps the one which most clearly shows the influence of Van Dyck [312] in combination with the light and colour of the Venetian school. The painter here breaks with the traditional Spanish court portrait by introducing greater dynamism and a rhetorical flourish that is lacking in the severe portraits of Velázquez and those inspired by him. This is clearly reflected in the pose of the sitter, Gregorio de Silva y Mendoza (1640–1693), duke of Pastrana and Estremera, prince of Mélito and count of Saldaña, one of the most influential personages in the court of Charles II. It is reflected too in the fact that he is accompanied by two servants – the groom who tends his richly bridled horse, and the page who adjusts his right spur. The result is a composition recalling Van Dyck's portrait of King Charles I of England as a hunter, now in the Musée du Louvre.

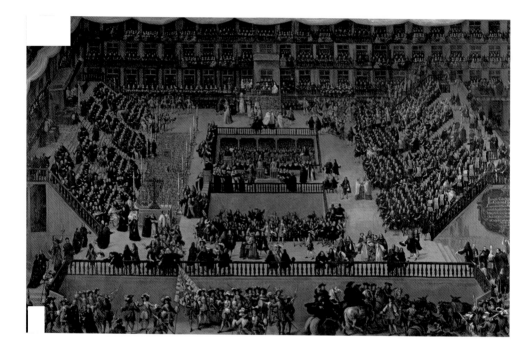

101

FRANCISCO RIZI
Madrid, 1614–El Escorial,
Madrid, 1685

*Auto-da-fé on the Plaza
Mayor in Madrid*

1683. Oil on canvas, 277 x 438 cm
P1126

This work is an unusual one
for its artist, who specialised
in portraiture and devotional
scenes. However, it has a
precedent in a work painted
nearly two hundred years earlier
by Pedro Berruguete, *St Dominic
Guzmán presiding over an Auto-
da-fé*, which is also in the Prado
[13]. Rizi's painting is of great
documentary value, since it
depicts a specific historical
event, the great auto-da-fé held
on 30 June 1680 in the Plaza
Mayor, the main square of

Madrid. Prisoners from all over
Spain were judged in a ceremony
presided over by Charles II,
who was accompanied by his
queen, Marie Louise d'Orléans,
and the queen mother,
Mariana de Austria. Rizi gives
a detailed description of the
scene, showing the complex
ephemeral architecture that
was built for this extremely
important occasion, and taking
the opportunity to paint a vivid
portrait of the Spanish society
of the period.

102
JUAN CARREÑO
DE MIRANDA
Avilés, Asturias, 1614–Madrid,
1685

*Eugenia Martínez Vallejo,
Clothed*
c. 1680. Oil on canvas,
165 x 107 cm
P646

103
*Eugenia Martínez Vallejo,
Nude*
c. 1680. Oil on canvas,
165 x 108 cm
P2800

Unlike his portrait of the duke
of Pastrana [100], Carreño
here remains close to Spanish
tradition and to the portraiture
of Velázquez in both form
and subject [81-84]. Portraits of
people with physical or mental
abnormalities were very much
to the taste of the Spanish
court. In fact, it was Charles II
himself who commissioned
his royal painter to make two
portraits of this girl, who
weighed around seventy
kilos at the age of only six,
and caused a sensation when
she was taken to be admired
at court. In the first painting,
Carreño shows her in a dress
of rich red brocade with silver
buttons, using warm Venetian
colours and brushwork of
great delicacy, and thereby
softening his model as much as
possible. Her expression is one
of annoyance and suspicion.
In the other picture she
appears nude save for some
vine leaves and a crown,
perhaps in allusion to Bacchus,
the god of wine.

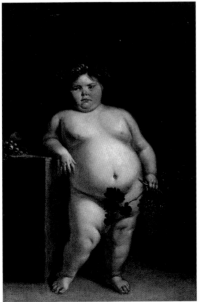

104
FRANCISCO DE HERRERA
THE YOUNGER
Seville, 1627–1685

The Triumph
of St Hermenegild

1654. Oil on canvas, 326 x 228 cm
P833

Hermenegild, the son of the
Visigoth king Leovigild (reigned
572-586), converted to Catholicism
and so came into conflict with his
father. He was beheaded in the late
sixth century after refusing to take
communion from an Arian bishop.
In accordance with the Baroque
aesthetic and the ideology of the
Counter-Reformation, Herrera
does not show the martyrdom of
the saint in his prison cell, as the
followers of the Caravaggesque
tradition would have done, but
instead depicts his triumph.
In this large picture painted
for the high altar of the church

of the convent of the Discalced
Carmelites in Madrid, the saint
rises heavenwards grasping the
crucifix. He is surrounded by
angels who accompany him in his
ascent, and who bear the palm
and instruments of martyrdom
and the attributes of royalty.
Herrera achieves great dynamic
tension and luminosity, employing
audacious back lighting that
leaves Leovigild and the bishop
in shadow while Hermenegild
and the angels, painted with
brushwork of great transparency
and extremely refined colouring,
are brightly lit.

105
CLAUDIO COELLO
Madrid, 1642–1693

*The Triumph
of St Augustine*

1664. Oil on canvas, 271 x 203 cm
P664

This juvenile masterpiece
borrows certain features
from Herrera the Younger's
Triumph of St Hermenegild
[104], including the spiralling
ascent of the saint and the
remarkable dynamism of the
composition. Like Herrera's
work, it is a large altar picture
centred on a monumental
and theatrical image – that
of a saint rising up to glory
– painted with the purpose
of impressing and overawing
the faithful. It was executed
for the convent of Recollet
Augustinians in Alcalá de
Henares, and entered the
Prado after passing through
the Museo de la Trinidad.
The saint is seen ascending
over a beautiful landscape
towards an intensely blue sky,
accompanied in his ascent by
Rubenesque angels carrying
his bishop's crozier. As he
points to heaven with his right
hand, the saint observes his
now defeated enemies, the
infernal dragon and paganism
– represented by a classical
sculpture – upon which an
archangel is bearing down with
his sword of fire.

106
JOSÉ ANTOLÍNEZ
Madrid, 1635–1675

The Magdalene borne by Angels

c. 1672. Oil on canvas,
205 x 163 cm
P591

107
JUAN DE VALDÉS LEAL
Seville, 1622–1690

*St Ambrose denying
Emperor Theodosius
Entry to the Church*
1673. Oil on canvas,
165 x 109.5 cm
P7821

In 2002, the Museo del
Prado acquired four of the
seven paintings on the life
of St Ambrose that were
produced for the Archbishop's
Palace in Seville by Valdés
Leal. They may have been
intended for an altarpiece that
was to be completed with a
Virgin and Child by Murillo,
now at the Walker Art Gallery
in Liverpool. St Ambrose is
represented with the face
of Ambrosio de Espínola
(1632–1684), archbishop
of Seville and patron of the
work, who was the grandson of
the famous general portrayed
several times in the battle
scenes of the Salón de Reinos
[90]. In this picture, the saint
refuses to allow the Emperor
Theodosius, who has been
excommunicated, to enter
and hear mass. A mature
work, it and its companion
pieces have very elaborate
compositions, demonstrating
the artist's skill at narrative.
The energetic brushstrokes
and sketchy and vibrant
execution are here united with
the artist's characteristically
expressive faces.

108
JUAN ANTONIO DE FRÍAS
Y ESCALANTE
Cordova, 1633–Madrid, 1669

*The Triumph of Faith
over the Senses*
1667. Oil on canvas, 113 x 152 cm
P699

This work belongs to a series
of eighteen canvases painted by
Frías y Escalante for the sacristy
of the convent of La Merced
Calzada in Madrid with scenes
from the Old Testament
prefiguring the Eucharist. This
is the only one to represent
an allegory, the subject being
the supremacy of Faith over
the senses. Faith, who holds

the cross and chalice with the
host above it, is accompanied
by five matrons who personify
the five senses. Towards the
top, angels bear a scroll with
an inscription in Latin that
reads: 'May Faith supplant
the defect of the senses'. This
is a verse from the eucharistic
hymn *Pange lingua* by St Thomas
Aquinas.

109
MATEO CEREZO
Burgos, 1637–Madrid, 1666

The Mystic Marriage
of St Catherine
1660. Oil on canvas,
207 x 163 cm
P659

In *The Golden Legend*, Jacobus De Voragine (c. 1228–1298) relates how St Catherine, after converting to the Christian faith, had a dream in which she was mystically married to Christ. It is this dream, and not the traditional scene of her martyrdom, that Mateo Cerezo represents in this work. From his master, Carreño, Cerezo inherited an admiration not only for Titian, reflected here in the colouring and the Venetian sky, but also for Van Dyck, whose painting of the same subject is also in the Prado. Reminiscences of the Flemish painter are apparent in the elegant and fully Baroque composition [314], the rich garments of the saint, and the light and fluid brushwork. Cerezo, an excellent still-life painter, adds to these influences his own aptitude for studies of reality in details like the basket of fruit and the fragment of the wheel on which the saint was tortured.

Murillo

For a long time, Bartolomé Esteban Murillo was the most highly esteemed Spanish artist in Europe, and almost the only one known beyond Spain's borders with the exception of Ribera, who spent nearly the whole of his career in Italy. Murillo's works were already being exported during his lifetime, and his international stature grew still further in the eighteenth century, when he was seen as a precursor of Rococo sensibility. His reputation held firm, especially in England, until the end of the nineteenth century. From that moment on, coinciding with the discovery of the rest of the Spanish school, Murillo fell into discredit owing to the tender and devout nature of his painting, which was judged excessive. His demotion can be said to have lasted until the mid-twentieth century, when his work began to be reappraised, and he once again achieved recognition as one of the greatest and most refined of Spanish painters, and perhaps the most modern of all the seventeenth-century artists, Velázquez excepted. Despite the artist's success during his lifetime, no works by Murillo entered the Royal Collections under the Spanish Habsburgs. However, during the Bourbon court's residence in Seville from 1729 to 1733, Isabella Farnese (1692–1766), the wife of Philip V (reigned 1700–1746), acquired many of the works by Murillo now in the Museo del Prado. Viewed as a whole, these paintings illustrate the artist's development.

He was already working as an independent painter by 1645, and within a few years managed to dominate the market in Seville, a city which he left for only a few months in 1658 to visit the court, where he may have seen the Royal Collections. From the 1660s onwards, he was the most admired painter in Seville. He received many major commissions from its ecclesiastical institutions, as they appreciated his soft, assured and monumental style and his tender religious scenes. Always very personal, his early painting possessed naturalist features, denoting the influence of Juan de Roelas, Herrera the Elder and Zurbarán. These were later replaced by Baroque elements derived from Rubens and Van Dyck, which were introduced to Seville by Herrera the Younger. His last works exhibit a light and transparent style with bright tonalities and a fluid and vibrant brushwork that was much admired by the French and English painters of the eighteenth century.

110
BARTOLOMÉ ESTEBAN
MURILLO
Seville, 1617–1682

Nicolás Omazur
1672. Oil on canvas, 83 x 73 cm
P3060

Murillo was closely involved with the intellectual circles of Seville, one of whose members was Nicolás de Omazur, a Flemish merchant and poet who arrived in Seville in 1669. Omazur became Murillo's principal collector, eventually owning as many as thirty of his works. In 1672 he commissioned this portrait and another, now lost, of his wife. Murillo here follows the Northern Baroque fashion for austere allegorical portraits, placing the merchant inside an oval frame similar to the one he used in his self-portrait at the National Gallery in London. The skull in Omazur's hands alludes to the fragility of life and was paired with the rose, the symbol of the fleeting nature of beauty, which was held by his wife in the companion portrait.

III
BARTOLOMÉ ESTEBAN
MURILLO
Seville, 1617–1682

*The Holy Family
with a Little Bird*

c. 1650. Oil on canvas,
144 x 188 cm
P960

Murillo introduces the viewer to the everyday life of the Holy Family, whom he represents in a modest interior, full of details relating to popular life in Seville at that time. It is an early work, as can be seen from the predominance of browns, the strong modelling of the forms, the firm draughtsmanship and the tight brushwork, as well as from the direct light which picks out the Child and the little dog he is playing with. The Virgin, shown winding wool, looks tenderly at her son, held by St Joseph.

The subject is inspired by *The Madonna of the Cat* by Federico Barocci (1582–1612), now at the National Gallery in London, but Murillo here accords greater prominence to St Joseph, whose cult was promoted from the late sixteenth century onwards when he was held up as an example of generosity, selflessness and discretion. The whole scene exalts family life and a love of work, as Murillo implies through some beautiful still-life details, such as the Virgin's work basket and St Joseph's carpentry tools.

112
BARTOLOMÉ ESTEBAN
MURILLO
Seville, 1617–1682

*The Virgin appearing
to St Bernard*

c. 1660. Oil on canvas,
311 x 249 cm
P978

This subject was also painted
by Alonso Cano but his version,
also in the Prado, differs from
Murillo's in certain important
stylistic and iconographic
respects. Murillo uses
chiaroscuro to emphasise the
darkness of St Bernard's cell
illuminated by the golden light
of his vision. This results in
strong contrasts, especially
between the dark background
and the monk's gleaming white
habit. The Virgin appears in
all her glory, surrounded by
angels and with the Christ
Child in her arms, to reward

St Bernard with her milk for his
devotion and dedication to the
promotion of her cult. Murillo
demonstrates his facility for
relating the supernatural to
the real world, and for creating
large monumental altar pictures.
The popular type of the saint
and his austere cell furnished
with objects like books, writing
materials, an abbot's crozier
and lilies, the symbol of his
devotion to Mary, are rendered
with great mastery and realism,
and the apparition of the Virgin
in a burst of heavenly glory
seems quite natural.

113
BARTOLOMÉ ESTEBAN
MURILLO
Seville, 1617–1682

The Virgin of the Rosary
c. 1650–55. Oil on canvas,
164 x 110 cm
P975

Murillo's devotional images showing isolated figures of saints and, above all, the Virgin and Child, were universally admired, and he was asked to repeat them time and time again. This Virgin and Child was acquired by Charles IV for El Escorial in the eighteenth century and still shows signs of the naturalism which dominated painting in Seville during the first half of the seventeenth century, although the brushwork is looser here, most notably in the Virgin's veil, than in earlier works. The fall of the light extracts the figures from the blackness of the background, emphasising the flesh tones of the Virgin's face and the Child's naked body, while creating deep shadows in the folds of the drapery. The two figures embrace as they look out at the spectator and hold a rosary that intertwines them, thus underlining the importance attached to devotion to the rosary at that period, and stressing Mary's role as intercessor with her son.

114
BARTOLOMÉ ESTEBAN
MURILLO
Seville, 1617–1682

*The Foundation of Santa
Maria Maggiore in Rome
I: The Patrician's Dream*
c. 1662–65. Oil on canvas,
232 x 522 cm
P994

115
*The Foundation of Santa
Maria Maggiore in Rome
II: The Patrician Reveals
his Dream to Pope Liberius*
c. 1662–65. Oil on canvas,
232 x 522 cm
P995

In 1662, Murillo was
commissioned to paint the
decorations for the church of
Santa María la Blanca in Seville,
a former medieval synagogue
which was being rebuilt. These
two works, which formed part of
the decoration, tell the story of the
miraculous foundation of the
Basilica of Santa Maria Maggiore
in Rome. In the first, the Virgin
appears in a dream to John, a
fourth-century Roman patrician,
and his wife. She instructs them
to build a church on the Esquiline
Hill, where they will find the
plan of the building drawn in
the snow. A feeling of languor
infuses the scene, which is
illuminated with the mysterious
light radiating from the serene
apparition of the Virgin, who
is painted with the light and
transparent brushstrokes of the
artist's mature style. The second
canvas shows the patrician John
and his wife relating their vision
to Pope Liberius, who decides to
verify the Virgin's mandate by
leading a procession to the
Esquiline Hill. On the left, the
profile of the pope is seen in
sharp definition against the light
as he listens to the husband
and wife. On the right is a later
part of the narrative, showing
the pontiff hastening with all
his train to the place where the
plan of the future church is
miraculously traced out. Both
works were removed from their
original home during the French
occupation, and were sent by
Marshal Soult to the Musée
Napoléon in Paris, where gilded
decorative corners were added
showing plans and elevations
of Santa Maria Maggiore. There
the paintings remained until
1816, when they were returned
to Spain. They were first kept
at the Academia de Bellas Artes
de San Fernando in Madrid,
then in 1901 passed to the
Museo del Prado.

116 ←
BARTOLOMÉ ESTEBAN
MURILLO
Seville, 1617–1682

The Good Shepherd
c. 1655–60. Oil on canvas,
123 x 101 cm
P962

117 ↓
*The Christ Child and the
Infant Baptist with a Shell*
c. 1670–75. Oil on canvas,
104 x 124 cm
P964

Murillo succeeded in infusing
scenes of children with great
gentleness and verisimilitude,
both in his genre paintings, where
he depicts popular types such as
street urchins and beggars, and
in his religious scenes. Among
the latter, *The Good Shepherd* and
*The Christ Child and the Infant
Baptist with a Shell* are probably
his most successful and widely
known paintings. In the first
picture the artist represents the
biblical allegory of Christ as
the Good Shepherd tending his
flock. The Child looks out at the
viewer while laying his hand on
the back of a sheep, a protective
gesture that tells us that those
who entrust themselves to
him have nothing to fear. In
the background classical ruins
symbolise the triumph of
Christianity over paganism.
In *The Christ Child and the Infant
Baptist with a Shell,* beneath a
group of angels, Jesus gives water
to drink in a shell to his cousin
St John the Baptist, prefiguring
the Baptism on the banks of the
River Jordan. St John is identified
by the camel's hide which covers
him and by the scroll around his
cross of reeds. Written on it is
'Ecce Agnus Dei' ('Behold the
Lamb of God'), in reference to
the Baptist's role as the precursor
of the Messiah. Jesus, with a lamb
by his side, is presented as the
Lamb of God, whose sacrifice
would rid the world of sin.

118
BARTOLOMÉ ESTEBAN
MURILLO
Seville, 1617–1682

*The Soult Immaculate
Conception*
Oil on canvas, 274 x 190 cm
P2809

Murillo painted about twenty
versions of this subject and
the Museo del Prado has
four of them. This is perhaps
the most famous. Spain, and
specifically Seville, was the main
champion of the dogma of the
Immaculate Conception of
Mary, and this found reflection
in the numerous versions of
the theme painted by Seville's
leading artists – Pacheco, Roelas,
Herrera the Elder, Zurbarán and
Velázquez. Although Murillo
was not the first to tackle the
subject, he created the most
succesful images. His Virgins
are less girlish than Zurbarán's
or Velázquez's, but they radiate

beauty and splendour as they
ascend to heaven in a typically
Baroque manner. This *Immaculate
Conception* was commissioned
by Justino de Neve, canon of
Seville Cathedral, who donated
it to the Hospital de Venerables
Sacerdotes, of which he was the
ecclesiastical president. It was
plundered by Soult, Napoleon's
marshal, who had it taken to
his house in Paris. After Soult's
death, it was auctioned in 1852,
when the Musée du Louvre
bought it for the highest price
ever paid until then for a painting.
In 1941, it became the property
of the Museo del Prado through
an exchange with the Louvre.

Eighteenth-century Spanish Painters

The last of the Spanish Habsburgs, Charles II (reigned 1665–1700), died without leaving a direct heir to the throne. He was succeeded by Philip V (reigned 1700–1746), the grandson of Louis XIV of France, who initiated the reign of the Bourbon dynasty in Spain. The change of dynasty also brought a change in taste, since the Bourbon monarchs introduced new and very different artistic models to the Spanish court. They summoned foreign artists to Madrid to paint their official portraits and the decorations for their palaces, and although it took some time for the Bourbon sensibility to spread beyond the court, Spanish painters, who were still imbued with the spirit of the Madrid Baroque of the previous century, were excluded from official commissions. The result was that no Spanish painter attained prominence in the first half of the century, with the exception of Miguel Jacinto Meléndez, who secured a position as portraitist at the court of Philip V [119], and Luis Egidio Meléndez, his nephew, one of the outstanding figures of eighteenth-century Spanish art, who specialised in the still life [125-128]. It was the artists born in the 1740s who finally produced work in tune with the new times, distancing themselves from the Baroque style of Madrid after assimilating the new influences from France and Italy. Working in Madrid at that moment, it should not be forgotten, were the century's three great masters, Corrado Giaquinto, Giovanni Battista Tiepolo and Anton Raffael Mengs, who represented diverse and even contrary styles. The new Rococo style was embraced by some Spanish painters, though they did not acquire the refinement of the French *fête galante*. The chief exponent was Luis Paret y Alcázar [131-133], possibly the most forceful and original figure of the century with the exception of Goya, but there were also others like Antonio Carnicero [130]. Another group of painters, which included Francisco Bayeu, Mariano Salvador Maella and Joaquín Inza [120, 121, 123], were more closely linked to official circles and to the Real Academia de Bellas Artes de San Fernando in Madrid, which was founded by Ferdinand VI in 1752. Their style evolved from the late Baroque of Giaquinto and his disciple Antonio González Velázquez [122] to the severe Neoclassicism of Mengs [355-357].

119
MIGUEL JACINTO
MELÉNDEZ
Oviedo, 1679–Madrid, 1734

Portrait of Philip V
After 1724. Oil on canvas,
82 x 62 cm
P7603

Miguel Jacinto Meléndez was trained in the Baroque tradition of Madrid. However, despite a tendency towards idealisation and denser brushwork, he was one of the first Spanish artists to assimilate the new prototype of royal portrait imposed by the French painters brought by Philip V to the Spanish court. This portrait of the monarch forms a pair with one of his wife, Isabella Farnese, also in the Museo del Prado. It shows the new fashion introduced by the Bourbons for luxurious and elaborate costume, very different from the Habsburgs. Although Meléndez adopts the cold colours of the French portrait, the Spanish tradition persists in the neutral ground framing the monarch, which contrasts sharply with the grandiose palace settings and garden vistas employed by the French artists in their portraits of the Spanish kings.

120
FRANCISCO BAYEU Y SUBÍAS
Saragossa, 1734–Madrid, 1795

The Assumption of the Virgin
1760. Oil on canvas, 137 x 81 cm
P600

The career of Francisco Bayeu, a member of a large family of painters and, from 1773, the brother-in-law of Goya, took him from the late Baroque manner of Corrado Giaquinto to the Neoclassical style of Anton Raffael Mengs. Bayeu, who was a magnificent painter of frescoes, collaborated with Mengs on the most important decorative projects at court. Mengs became his protector, and after his departure for Rome in 1777, he left Bayeu in charge of continuing these projects. This work, a preparatory sketch for a section of the dome of the church of Santa Engracia in Saragossa, was purchased for the Museo Real by Ferdinand VII. It shows the persistence of the influence of Giaquinto and his pupil Antonio González Velázquez in such features as the dense colouring and the dark tonalities contrasting with strokes of white pigment to highlight fabrics and contours.

121
MARIANO SALVADOR
MAELLA
Valencia, 1739–Madrid, 1819

The Immaculate Conception
1781. Oil on canvas, 142 x 74 cm
P7602

Following a path similar to
Francisco Bayeu's, Maella
was trained in the late
Baroque style of Corrado
Giaquinto, but later adopted
the severe classicism of
Anton Raffael Mengs, whose
protégé he too became. This
development allowed Maella
to participate in the main
decorative projects carried
out under royal patronage.
The most important of
them was probably the
decoration for the church
of San Francisco el Grande
in Madrid, instigated by
Charles III, who engaged all
the principal court painters to
work on it. This is the sketch
for the artist's altar painting
for the chapel of San Antonio
in the church. Maella adheres
to the iconographic model
of the Spanish Virgins of the
Immaculate Conception,
but blends the dynamism
of the Baroque tradition with
the cold perfection of Mengs's
work [357]. The latter's
influence is more evident in
the finished work, also painted
in 1781, since the sketch has
more spontaneity.

122
ANTONIO GONZÁLEZ
VELÁZQUEZ
Madrid, 1723–1794

Self-portrait

c. 1775–80. Oil on canvas,
90 x 68.5 cm
P7460

González Velázquez obtained
a pension from the Preparatory
Committee of the Academia de
San Fernando to complete his
apprenticeship in Rome in the
workshop of Corrado Giaquinto,
whose style he introduced
to Spain before the Italian
artist's summons to Madrid
by Ferdinand VI. After his
arrival in Spain, Giaquinto
was appointed director of
the Academia and supported
the nomination of González
Velázquez as court painter,
inviting him at the same time
to collaborate on various artistic
enterprises. This self-portrait,
however, is a late work, and the
Baroque influence of Giaquinto,
who had returned to Naples
in 1770, has been superseded
by that of Anton Raffael Mengs
[355]. The painter portrays
himself in the Neoclassical
style, frankly, unassumingly
and without idealisation, bearing
the attributes of his trade
as he looks out at the viewer.

123
JOAQUÍN INZA
Agreda, Soria, 1736–Madrid,
1811

Don Tomás de Iriarte

1785. Oil on canvas, 82 x 59 cm
P2514

Inza devoted himself mainly to
portraiture, initially following
the style and models of the
French artists Jean Ranc
and Louis-Michel van Loo,
but later inclining towards
the Neoclassical style of
Anton Raffael Mengs. Besides
immortalising the aristocracy
of Madrid, including Manuel
Godoy and Charles III
himself, Inza also portrayed
enlightened intellectuals such
as the poet and dramatist
Tomás de Iriarte, famous for
his *Fábulas literarias en verso
castellano* ('Literary Fables
in Castilian Verse'). In this
portrait, which became widely
known after it was engraved by
Manuel Salvador Carmona in
1792, the writer looks directly
at the viewer, a slight smile on
his lips as he holds one of his
books in his left hand.

124
AGUSTÍN ESTEVE
Valencia, 1753–1820

Portrait of Don Mariano
San Juan y Pinedo, Count
Consort of La Cimera
c. 1813. Oil on canvas,
128 x 89 cm
P2876

In the final third of the
eighteenth century, Esteve
became the favourite portraitist
of Madrid's courtly society
after Goya, with whom he often
collaborated. His compositions
and predominantly cold palette
were clearly influenced by
Anton Raffael Mengs, but his
style gradually took on features
of the portraits of Goya. There

is certainly something of Goya
in the childish candour of this
boy, who was later to marry
María Salomé Mendinueta,
the daughter of Jerónimo
Mendinueta y Múrquiz, first
count of La Cimera (1757–1817).

Meléndez and the Spanish Still Life Tradition in the 18th Century

Luis Egidio Meléndez was an exceptionally gifted artist. However, owing to his father's expulsion from the Preparatory Committee of the Real Academia de Bellas Artes, and perhaps also because of quarrels with his teacher, Louis-Michel van Loo, his academic studies in Spain were curtailed and he was forced to continue his training in Italy. This largely determined his later career, since despite a considerable aptitude for genres like portraiture, he never managed to secure a major court commission. He applied for the post of court painter to Charles III, only to be turned down twice. Among the merits he listed on his second application, in 1772, was the execution of an unfinished series of still lifes that had been commissioned by the Prince of Asturias, the future Charles IV. These paintings, originally at Aranjuez Palace, are now kept at the Museo del Prado.

With their sober compositions and solid draughtsmanship, Meléndez's still lifes are among the finest in the Spanish tradition, and he is a worthy heir in particular to Sánchez Cotán [40] and Zurbarán [64]. However, the importance he attaches to exactitude in the representation of nature reveals a sensibility closer to Enlightenment ideals.

125
LUIS EGIDIO MELÉNDEZ
Naples, 1716–Madrid, 1780

Still Life with a Box of Sweets, Bread Ring and Other Objects
1770. Oil on canvas, 49 x 37 cm
P906

126
Still Life with Chocolate Service
1770. Oil on canvas, 50 x 37 cm
P929

127
LUIS EGIDIO MELÉNDEZ
Naples, 1716–Madrid, 1780

*Still Life with a Piece
of Salmon, a Lemon
and Three Vessels*

1772. Oil on canvas, 42 x 62 cm
P902

These three still lifes form part of the series of forty-four commissioned from him in 1771 by the Prince of Asturias, the future Charles IV, to decorate his Cabinet of Natural History. The painter described the series as 'a representation of every edible species that the Spanish climate produces'. In fact, though, these works have little to do with illustrations of natural history, and a great deal to do with the best in the Spanish still-life tradition. This may be why the Prince of Asturias cancelled the project in 1778 and had the still lifes moved to the Casita del Príncipe at El Escorial, where they would play a more appropriate role as decoration for a rural villa. From there they went to Aranjuez Palace, and later to the Museo del Prado. In all his still lifes, Meléndez arranges his objects in a very stark and almost architectural composition, highlighting them against a dark background which gives them enormous expressive force. In second of the three shown here [126], he depicts a chocolate service, which indicates the great popularity in Spain of this drink from America.

128
LUIS EGIDIO MELÉNDEZ
Naples, 1716–Madrid, 1780

Still Life with Watermelons,
Apples and Landscape
1771. Oil on canvas, 63 x 84 cm
P923

Most of Meléndez's still lifes are of objects arranged on tables in interiors, but he sometimes painted *plein air* compositions with summary landscape backgrounds. In this example, the foreground is occupied by the enticingly fresh fruit. Such a design may have been inspired by the Neapolitan still-life tradition, which Meléndez knew well, but some have also suggested a possible relationship with his panoramic illustrations for the pages of the choir books of the Royal Chapel, where similar devices are employed.

129
BARTOLOMÉ MONTALVO
Sangarcía, Segovia,
1769–Madrid, 1846

Sea-bream
Oil on panel, 51 x 38 cm
P7398

As this *Sea-bream* shows,
Bartolomé Montalvo can
be said to have prolonged
the severe Spanish still-life
tradition of the seventeenth
century well into the
nineteenth. The picture seems
to fuse Meléndez's painstaking
care over surface properties
with the pictorial resources of
Sánchez Cotán [40]. Whilst
Meléndez had employed
animal motifs before, Sánchez
Cotán is clearly the model
for the arrangement of the
fish, which hangs in isolation
against a neutral background.
Because he was a court
painter, Montalvo became
one of the few Spanish artists
whose still lifes hung in the
Prado in the nineteenth
century.

Paret and Cabinet Painting

Luis Paret is perhaps the most original and singular of the eighteenth-century artists, Goya apart, owing to his vast curiosity, his independent character, his broad cultural interests, and his status as the finest representative of the Rococo style in Spanish painting. Outstanding among his production are his cabinet paintings, pictures whose minutely detailed technique and bright colouring were intended for close and attentive scrutiny. Paret was admitted to the Academia de San Fernando when still very young, and by the age of twenty had attracted the attention of the Infante Luis de Borbón (1727–1785), the brother of Charles III, who took him under his protection and financed a three-year stay in Rome that gave him a notably cosmopolitan apprenticeship. His later style, as well as being influenced by Italian painting, was also indebted to two French artists residing in Madrid. From Agustín Duflos, the king's jeweller, he took the minute draughtsmanship proper to a goldsmith, while Charles François de la Traverse gave him the impastoed technique and pastel colours that were to characterise all his work thereafter. His relationship with the Infante, however, eventually had disastrous consequences ending in Paret's banishment by Charles III in 1775 accused of meddling. He lived for three years in exile in Puerto Rico, then settled in 1778 in Bilbao. There he painted religious images for local churches and a series of views of the ports of northern Spain for the decoration of Charles III's country houses. After the king's death, he returned in 1789 to Madrid, where he was appointed vice-secretary to the Real Academia and secretary of its Architecture Committee.

130 ↓
ANTONIO CARNICERO
MANCIO
Salamanca, 1748–Madrid, 1814

*Ascent of a Montgolfier
Balloon at Aranjuez*
1784. Oil on canvas,
170 x 284 cm
P641

Acquired for the Museo del Prado in 1896 at the auction of the estate of the dukes of Osuna, this piece reflects the influence of Paret's style and manner on other artists of the period. As in Paret's *Las Parejas Reales* [133], what is narrated here is a specific event, the Frenchman Bouché's balloon ascent on 4 February 1784 from the gardens of Aranjuez in the presence of King Charles III, his queen, and the entire court. The artist gives a very lively account of this social occasion, which was attended by both the aristocracy and the common people, and he dwells on the variety of costumes and attitudes to be observed among the different groups.

131
LUIS PARET Y ALCÁZAR
Madrid, 1746–1799

Self-portrait in the Studio
c. 1786. Oil on canvas,
39.8 x 31.8 cm
P7701

Before this self-portrait, Paret
had painted an earlier one
in Puerto Rico, where he had
been banished by Charles III
in 1775 on the charge of procuring
women for his patron, the
Infante Luis de Borbón. There,
he depicted himself in Jivaro
costume, bearing bananas
and holding a knife. Here, by
contrast, he adopts the model
of the melancholic artist,
frequently used by the French
and Italian painters of the
period. In a crowded but orderly
composition, Paret indicates
his intellectual leanings through
symbols like the books, the pen
and inkwell, and the two busts,
which refer to his classical
learning. The artist displays
the instruments of his art,
like the palette, and its result,
the picture which serves as the
background to the composition.
However, he shows himself
thinking, not painting, in
vindication of the intellectual
nature of his art. Paret's skill
at creating light effects and
capturing the transparency
of fabrics and the delicacy of
lace is also seen to good effect
in this work.

132
LUIS PARET Y ALCÁZAR
Madrid, 1746–1799

Charles III supping before his Court
c. 1775. Oil on panel,
50 x 64 cm
P2422

In this curious panel, Paret presents an everyday act in the court of Charles III, very much in accord with the Rococo taste for the picturesque. A monarch's meal was a social occasion rather than an intimate domestic moment, and was governed by strict ceremonial in which the principal personages of the court considered themselves honoured to take part. The scene takes place in one of the rooms of the Royal Palace in Madrid, although the artist has altered its proportions, making it larger and higher so as to create a theatrical contrast between the small figures and the monumental setting. Paret has also modified the decoration of the room, showing paintings of mythological subjects and a fresco on the ceiling, rather like the one painted by Giovanni Battista Tiepolo for the Throne Room, none of which tallies with documented fact. The result is a stylish and graceful work with fine brushwork and delicate gleams of golden light.

133
LUIS PARET Y ALCÁZAR
Madrid, 1746–1799

*Las Parejas Reales
(The Royal Pairs)*
c. 1770. Oil on canvas,
232 x 367 cm
P1044

This work, a fine example of the painting which emerged in the eighteenth century in the wake of French Rococo, was commissioned by the Infante Luis de Borbón, Paret's protector. It is a blend of the documentary and the decorative, and represents an equestrian festival held on the Plazuela at Aranjuez Palace on 6 June 1770, one of whose participants was the Prince of Asturias, later King Charles IV. The title refers to the pairs of horses that approach the royal balcony. Bathed in delicate light, the scene is full of vivacity and shows Paret's skill in handling groups of figures.

Goya

When the Museo del Prado first opened in 1819, Goya was still alive. Only three of his works were then on display at the museum: the equestrian portraits of Charles IV and his wife, Queen Maria Luisa [135, 136], who were the parents of the museum's founder, Ferdinand VII, and the *Goader on Horseback*, repainted over the sketch for an equestrian portrait of Charles IV's minister, Manuel Godoy. Since then, the Prado has gone on acquiring works by Goya, whether originating in the Royal Collections or elsewhere. Goya is currently the best represented artist in the museum, which holds nearly one hundred and fifty paintings and five hundred drawings by his hand, as well as his series of engravings – the fullest collection of his work in terms of both number and quality. As with Velázquez, it is impossible to understand Goya without a familiarity with the Prado, which explains why numerous artists have been attracted to Madrid since the nineteenth century out of fascination for his work. Few creators inside or outside the field of art have left such a transcendent legacy. His art has bewitched both artists and art lovers and been analysed by historians, sociologists and psychologists, besides winning a prominent place in literature and the cinema. Goya was treated virtually as a contemporary by the most avant-garde artists of the nineteenth and twentieth centuries, and his ability to break new ground has led to the persistence of his influence in the twenty-first. He was an exceptional witness to a period straddling two centuries and two epochs, the end of the eighteenth century and the beginning of the nineteenth. He lived through the end of Spain's *Ancien Régime*, and was present at the birth of the contemporary world with its legacy of Enlightenment thought and the consequences of the French Revolution. His art anticipated many of the aesthetic and ethical concerns which are still of prime relevance to humanity today. Trained, like many of the eighteenth-century Spanish artists, in Corrado Giaquinto's late derivation of Italian Baroque and in the sophisticated French Rococo, Goya traverses Neoclassical academicism and Romanticism, creating a wholly personal oeuvre centred on man and his vicissitudes. Goya's work presages the development of art in the twentieth century, particularly Expressionism and Surrealism, in the freedom of his response to reality, his inclusion of the world of dreams, and the violently expressive distortions found in much of his work after *Los Caprichos*, published in 1799.

134
FRANCISCO DE GOYA
Fuendetodos, Saragossa, 1746–Bordeaux, 1828

Self-portrait
1815. Oil on canvas, 46 x 35 cm
P723

Goya portrayed himself on a number of occasions, both individually and by including himself in other compositions. This self-portrait, small in size and intimate in character, shows him at the age of sixty-nine. It is recorded in an inventory of his possesions at La Quinta del Sordo drawn up after the artist's death. It dates from a period of anxiety after the return of Ferdinand VII, when the painter felt increasingly insecure about revealing his liberal sympathies at a time when absolutist monarchy was being restored. The artist presents himself with great frankness, wearing the reddish velvet robe traditional for artists but adding no attributes to point to his personality. The composition is focused on his luminous face and intensely reflective gaze, framed by the robe and the black background traced in rapid crossed brushstrokes through which the underlying preparation can be seen. Signed and dated 1815 on the left, while the paint was still fresh, Goya also adds that he is from Aragon and is a painter. The picture was acquired for the Museo de la Trinidad in 1866, passing from there to the Museo del Prado.

135 ↑
FRANCISCO DE GOYA
Fuendetodos, Saragossa,
1746–Bordeaux, 1828

Charles IV on Horseback
c. 1801. Oil on canvas,
336 x 282 cm
P719

136 →
Queen Maria Luisa on
Horseback
1799. Oil on canvas,
338 x 282 cm
P720

These portraits of Charles IV and his wife Maria Luisa of Parma were transferred to the Museo del Prado from the Royal Palace in 1819, and were two of the three works by Goya on display at the museum's inauguration. They are related to the equestrian portraits painted by Velázquez for the Salón de Reinos (Hall of Realms) at the Buen Retiro Palace, also now kept at the Prado [91, 92], of which Goya had made etched copies in 1778. In the first portrait, Goya arranges his figure against a landscape background, but differs from Velázquez, whose portraits of Philip III and Philip IV depict the horse rearing up, in showing the king walking his mount like a governor in time of peace rather than as the leader of his armies. He therefore wears the dress uniform of his own personal *corps de garde*, and sports Spain's highest decorations – the Golden Fleece, the Order of Charles III and the insignia of the four great Orders of Chivalry. He has a serene and good-natured air as he grips the horse's reins, controlling his powerful mount in a clear metaphor for good government. Goya used the same model for the king in this picture as he did for *Charles IV as a Hunter* (Royal Palace). The queen is meanwhile dressed in the dress uniform of a colonel. Behind her are the Guadarrama Mountains, with the palace of La Granja in the distance.

Goya
Tapestry Cartoons

Goya's first work at court was to paint cartoons for tapestries for the royal residences. Before securing this position, he had tried unsuccessfully in 1763 and 1766 to obtain a pension from the Real Academia de San Fernando. The son of a gilder, Goya first trained as a painter in Saragossa with José Luzán (1710–1785), and then with Francisco Bayeu, whose sister Josefa he married in 1773. After his two failed applications to the academy, Goya went off to Italy on his own account, returning to Saragossa in 1771. He then began to win commissions of growing importance, such as those for the vault of the Little Choir in the Basilica of El Pilar and the frescoes in the Charterhouse of Aula Dei. Francisco Bayeu was probably instrumental in persuading Goya to move four years later to Madrid, where his task was to paint cartoons for the series of tapestries produced by the Real Fábrica de Santa Bárbara, a project initiated by Anton Raffael Mengs, chief court painter to Charles III.

Tapestry cartoons fell within the genre of decorative painting, and even their preparatory sketches for presentation were highly appreciated at the time as 'cabinet pictures'. The various series of cartoons painted by Goya served to establish him at court and make him better known. He clearly took advantage of this opportunity, for in July 1780, after presenting his *Christ on the Cross* to the Real Academia de San Fernando, he was unanimously admitted as a member of the academy on merit, and furthermore was invited to contribute to the frescoes on the domes of the Basilica of El Pilar in Saragossa. Goya made tapestry cartoons for nearly twenty years, in the course of which he painted seven series for the palaces of El Pardo and El Escorial. In these works, Goya depicts the subjects typical of Spanish tapestries, which had abandoned Flemish models after 1770, at the instigation of Mengs and in tune with Enlightenment ideas, to draw inspiration from popular life. His first cartoons, on hunting themes, still used the models of Bayeu, but he soon started to execute works of his own invention in which he demonstrated his knowledge of both classical art and the work of his contemporaries, and above all his flair for composition and his facility for providing an accurate new vision of reality. Like his fellow-painters, he used the cartoons to reflect the popular world of the streets, with their *majas* and *manolas*, their taverns and vendors, their games and popular festivals, and all the noisy and bustling life of the alleys and humble quarters of Madrid. Underlying these scenes, however, is a vision of mankind constructed out of small anecdotes of human behaviour, and it is this which lies at the heart of his later work.

137
FRANCISCO DE GOYA
Fuendetodos, Saragossa,
1746–Bordeaux, 1828

The Crockery Vendor
1779. Oil on canvas, 259 x 220 cm
P780

Between 1778 and 1779, Goya painted a series of seven cartoons for tapestries destined for the bedroom of the Prince and Princess of Asturias at the palace of El Pardo. This is one of the most famous of them. Prominent among the numerous figures are the women in the foreground inspecting the vendor's wares, and the mysterious noblewoman looking out at the viewer from the inside of her carriage, who is being admired by the two young men with their backs turned to us. Goya enlivens this everyday market scene by varying the groups of individuals and contrasting the movement of the carriage with the static foreground. The whole scene is bathed in a bright and transparent light and is rendered with great attention to detail, noticeable especially in the pieces of crockery and the glossy fabrics.

138
FRANCISCO DE GOYA
Fuendetodos, Saragossa, 1746–
Bordeaux, 1828

The Threshers, or *Summer*
1786. Oil on canvas,
276 x 641 cm
P794

Among the tapestry cartoons
commissioned from Goya
in 1776 for the Prince of
Asturias's dining-room
at El Pardo is a series on
the Four Seasons, in which
he presents a new vision
of a traditional allegorical
subject through metaphors
of country life. The cartoon
representing Summer is the
largest and most ambitious
of the series. The season is
illustrated by a rural scene
in which the threshers are to
be seen resting, so uniting the
allegorical and the everyday.
The various groups of figures
and horses are organised
harmoniously in a pyramidal
composition. We see the
peasants working, sleeping,
playing or feeding their
children. Imbued with a
golden luminosity, the scene
brims over with natural
exuberance.

139
FRANCISCO DE GOYA
Fuendetodos, Saragossa,
1746–Bordeaux, 1828

St Isidore's Meadow
c. 1788. Oil on canvas,
42 x 90 cm
P750

This is a preparatory
presentation sketch for
one of the cartoons in the
decorative series intended
for the infantas' bedroom
in the palace of El Pardo,
but interrupted by the death

of Charles III in December
1788. It shows the popular
feast of St Isidore, the patron
saint of Madrid, on 15 May, with
all the social classes taking part
in the festivities on the banks of
the River Manzanares. The
brushwork is light and assured,
with small separate touches that
border on the impressionistic.
The background to the
festive gathering is a view
of Madrid bathed in a luminous
and very fine mist, where
buildings such as the Royal
Palace and the great dome
of San Francisco el Grande
are clearly recognisable.

Goya
Religious Painting

Goya is not primarily remembered as a religious painter, but religious subjects were among his earliest works and he returned to them often, though with considerably less frequency after 1790. In the course of his career, Goya evolved from the conventional religious images of popular devotion to a more intimate and emotive approach based on Enlightenment ideas. The earlier paintings, still aesthetically bound to the late Baroque and Rococo styles, include not only small devotional works but also more elaborate compositions, such as the *Adoration of the Name of God* (1771–72) on the vault of the Little Choir in the Basilica of El Pilar, and the *Scenes from the Life of the Virgin* (1772–74) in the Charterhouse of Aula Dei, both in Saragossa. In 1780–81, in a measure of his growing prestige, he was entrusted with the decoration of the dome of El Pilar. It was then that a religious painting tending this time towards Neoclassicism, the *Christ on the Cross* now held by the Prado [141], gained him admission to the Real Academia de San Fernando. In 1798, Goya painted a miracle of St Anthony for the dome of the hermitage chapel of San Antonio de la Florida in Madrid. In this case, he devised a scenic and expressive unity of great originality where the supernatural is made manifest in an everyday setting. Goya returned to religious subjects after the War of Independence, painting large-format pictures like the *St Justa and St Rufina* of 1817 for Seville Cathedral, and the dramatic *Last Communion of St Joseph Calasanz* of 1819.

140
FRANCISCO DE GOYA
Fuendetodos, Saragossa,
1746–Bordeaux, 1828

*St John the Baptist
in the Desert*
c. 1808–12. Oil on canvas,
105 x 90 cm
P7853

This work entered the Museo del Prado in 2003 along with two other religious paintings by Goya, *Tobias and the Angel* and *The Holy Family*. All three were unpublished but mentioned in old documentation, which put them among the works whose whereabouts had been unknown since the nineteenth century. The existence of *St John the Baptist* was known from the inventory made of the goods of Goya and his wife in 1812, where it appears together with a reference to a picture of St Peter, now lost. Goya places the child under a rocky overhang, the usual iconography for hermits. His reed cross bears a scroll with the words 'Ecce Agnus Dei' ('Behold the Lamb of God') signalling him as Christ's forerunner. However, Goya departs from the Spanish tradition of depicting children, seeking inspiration instead from Italian models. His St John is a strong youth with a vigorous body who fervently raises his eyes to heaven while reflecting upon the future Passion of Christ.

141
FRANCISCO DE GOYA
Fuendetodos, Saragossa,
1746–Bordeaux, 1828

Christ on the Cross
1780. Oil on canvas, 255 x 154 cm
P745

In 1780, Goya presented this
work as proof of his mastery
when applying for admission
to the Real Academia de
San Fernando. The painter
was unanimously elected as
a new member of the academy
on merit, and the picture
was sent to the convent
of San Francisco el Grande
in Madrid, a foundation
supported by Charles III.
After the disentailment
of church possessions, the
painting entered the Museo
de la Trinidad, finally passing
to the Museo del Prado in 1872.
One of Goya's most important
religious paintings, it shows
the figure of Christ against
a dark background, in the
tradition of Spanish Baroque
painting [75], though here
re-elaborated in accordance
with the canons of ideal
beauty and classical harmony
established by Anton Raffael
Mengs and Francisco Bayeu
in their interpretations of the
subject.

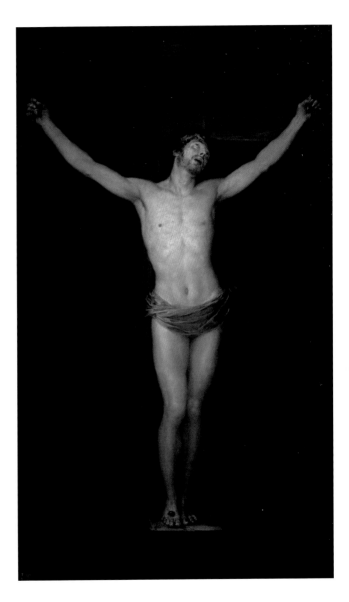

Goya
Royalty, Nobility, the Enlightened and the People of Madrid

In 1789, the year after after Charles IV's accession to the throne, Goya was appointed court painter. After fifteen years of activity at court, he had finally attained a position of prestige. By then he was also one of the most sought-after portraitists of his time, having served the upper echelons of the aristocracy throughout the 1780s and gained important protectors among its members, such as the dukes and duchesses of Osuna and Alba [142]. He also had close relations with the politicians and intellectuals of the Enlightenment, such as Gaspar Melchor de Jovellanos (1744–1811) [143] and Juan Agustín Ceán Bermúdez (1749–1829). Goya shared with them new intellectual, moral and political ideas which found reflection in his work, above all in his series of drawings and etchings. However, two crises were to mark the subsequent course of his life. The first, a personal one, was the serious illness he suffered in 1793, which left him almost stone deaf. This may well have aggravated the artist's critical nature and his desire for independence, of which he had already shown signs. The second crisis, some years later, was the collective one of the Spanish War of Independence (1808–14). Like his enlightened friends, Goya, who served Joseph Bonaparte's government, initially accepted the Napoleonic invasion as a means of bringing the advances of the French Revolution and the new theories of liberty and rationalism to isolated and absolutist Spain. Inevitably, however, the war brought disenchantment with its terrible toll of cruelty and suffering. His disillusion is starkly reflected in the series of prints entitled 'Fatal Consequences of the Bloody War in Spain', better known by its later title, *Disasters of War*, and in the two great canvases painted to commemorate the events of the Second and Third of May, 1808 [151, 152]. After the expulsion of the French and the return of Ferdinand VII (reigned 1813–1833), Goya survived the purge of the palace civil servants and continued to work for a time as court painter. However, after 1816, when he was replaced by the young Vicente López, he started to feel less and less comfortable in a Madrid where his friends were being imprisoned, accused of sympathising with the French or of espousing liberalism. He withdrew to his inner circle of friends and devoted his efforts mainly to two series of etchings, *La Tauromaquia* and *Los Disparates* [374, 375].

142
FRANCISCO DE GOYA
Fuendetodos, Saragossa, 1746–
Bordeaux, 1828

The Duke and Duchess of Osuna and their Children
1787–88. Oil on canvas,
225 x 171 cm
P739

The duke and duchess of Osuna were among Goya's earliest and most constant protectors. From 1786 onwards, they commissioned him to paint family portraits and decorative works for El Capricho, their palatial retreat in La Alameda on the outskirts of Madrid. The duke, Pedro Téllez Girón, and his wife, Josefa Alonso de Pimentel, are seen here with their four children: Francisco de Borja, who inherited the duchy; Pedro de Alcántara, the future prince of Anglona, who became the director of the Museo del Prado during the Liberal Triennium (1820–23); and María Manuela and Joaquina, both of whom Goya was to portray again years later [149, 150]. This type of family portrait is unusual in Spain, and Goya may have been inspired by English models through the numerous prints that were being imported around that time, although the carefully contrived pyramidal composition derives from Mengs. The influence of Velázquez is detectable in the creation of space by means of light and shadow. The delicacy and sympathy with which he portrays the children, as well as the subtle palette, stand out.

143
FRANCISCO DE GOYA
Fuendetodos, Saragossa,
1746–Bordeaux, 1828

Gaspar Melchor de Jovellanos
1798. Oil on canvas, 204 x 133 cm
P3236

Jovellanos, a politician and writer,
and a fundamental figure in the
Spanish Enlightenment, was
a profound admirer of Goya's
work from his early years at court
at the beginning of the 1780s.
The artist presents him in his
bureau, where he is seated before
a rich table of carved and gilded
wood with a classical decoration
of garlands and an ox skull on
the front. There are numerous
papers and documents on top of
the table, for this was the period
when Jovellanos was Minister
for Grace and Justice. Elegantly
attired in a dress coat lined
with lynx fur, and displaying no
official decorations, the politician
turns a serene and intelligent
gaze on the viewer, resting his
head on his hand in a gesture
that traditionally symbolises
melancholy. Goya is perhaps
suggesting the burden of
responsibility that comes
with government, but he may
also be referring to the most
notorious trait of his sitter's
intellectual personality, so much
so that he was called 'Jovino
the Melancholic' by his circle
of poet friends. On the table
is a statue of Minerva, goddess of
wisdom, who holds a shield with
the arms of the Real Instituto
Asturiano, a foundation set up by
Jovellanos in Gijón in 1794 to help
the economic development of
his region, Asturias, through
scientific and technological
study. The portrait, executed in
a technique similar to Velázquez's
and with extremely lively touches
in the materials and the statue,
conveys a sense of immediacy
and verisimilitude.

144
FRANCISCO DE GOYA
Fuendetodos, Saragossa,
1746–Bordeaux, 1828

The Countess of Chinchón
1800. Oil on canvas,
226 x 144 cm
P7767

María Teresa de Borbón y
Vallabriga, fifteenth countess
of Chinchón, was the daughter
of Luis Antonio de Borbón,
Charles III's brother, and María
Teresa de Vallabriga. She was
married at the king and queen's

wish to Don Manuel Godoy,
the Prince of the Peace, who
had been first secretary of state
when Charles IV ascended
the throne. Goya, who had
already portrayed her on several
occasions as a little girl, here
paints her in a high-waisted
dress, the French fashion of
the day, and so emphasises
a pregnancy which is also
symbolised by the ears of corn
in her head-dress, a reference to
the goddess Ceres and therefore
to fertility. She wears a ring
with a miniature, probably
a portrait of her husband,
and her luminous figure stands

out against a dark background
in a studiedly geometrical
composition. Seated in an
attitude of docility and passivity,
the countess smiles timidly,
no doubt at the man who was
her husband, and has a certain
air of helplessness. Her fragile
appearance and the delicacy
imbuing the whole painting are
accentuated by Goya's masterly
rendering of the transparencies
of the subtle white gauze of
the dress, with its tiny flowers,
and his use of light brushstrokes
applied with a precise yet fluent
technique that allows the pink
ground to show through.

145 ↑
FRANCISCO DE GOYA
Fuendetodos, Saragossa,
1746–Bordeaux, 1828

*The Infante Don Francisco
de Paula Antonio*
1800. Oil on canvas, 72 x 59 cm
P730

In June and July 1800, before
embarking on the definitive
composition of *The Family
of Charles IV* [146], Goya
made life studies at Aranjuez
Palace of all the personages
who were to appear in the
painting. The Museo del Prado
has five of the ten sketches
he produced. The figures are
of a similar size to those in the
final painting, and they are
painted on a reddish-orange
ground which can be clearly
seen in this sketch. With deft,
precise and fluent brushstrokes,
Goya here makes a summary
study of the sparkling charm
of the king's youngest son,
whom he treats with the
tenderness characteristic
of his paintings of children,
leaving a testimony of such
vitality that we feel the boy
is standing before us.

146 →
FRANCISCO DE GOYA
Fuendetodos, Saragossa,
1746–Bordeaux, 1828

The Family of Charles IV
1800. Oil on canvas,
280 x 336 cm
P726

This great portrait, a crown
commission, shows the members
of the royal family in an austere hall
whose grandeur is expressed by the
two pictures in the background. In
the centre, the queen stands before
a mythological picture which
represents Hercules, the mythical
founder of the Spanish royal house,
and the nymph Omphale. Maria
Luisa's arm is around her daughter,
Infanta María Isabel, while her
hand holds that of the youngest
of her children, the little Infante
Don Francisco de Paula, who
forms a loving link between her
and the king. Charles IV, on the
right, is placed in the foreground,
which is occupied on the left by
his son and heir, Prince Ferdinand,
whose brother, Infante Carlos
María Isidro, appears behind him.
On the right of the composition
is the group formed by the duke
and duchess of Parma, Luis de
Borbón and his wife, Infanta María
Luisa, who holds their son Luis,
the king and queen's grandchild, in
her arms. Behind the king are his
brother, Infante Antonio Pascual,
and his wife, Infanta María Amalia,

by then already dead. On the left, at the back, is the king's sister, Infanta María Josefa. Of special interest is the female figure seen in profile next to Prince Ferdinand, who is looking at the pictures in the background. Goya almost certainly meant her to represent the fiancée of the heir to the throne, who had not yet been chosen from among the European princesses. Finally, the painter portrays himself in the middle ground

at the left, looking out at the viewer from the shadows in an arrangement recalling Velázquez's self-portrait in *Las Meninas* [89], which is clearly related to this picture both visually and in terms of its significance. Although the painting was at one time interpreted by Goya's biographers as a critique of the royal family, it is in fact a carefully thought out work which seeks to emphasise the dynastic importance and power of the House of Bourbon

in Spain, its French branch having vanished under the guillotine during the Revolution, at a time when Spain was undergoing a period of strained and antagonistic relations with the Consulate and Napoleon. With its wide range of colours, the whole scene glitters and sparkles, lit superbly by the light entering through an invisible window on the left, and producing a sensation of luxury and majesty as befits a royal portrait.

147
FRANCISCO DE GOYA
Fuendetodos, Saragossa, 1746–
Bordeaux, 1828

The Naked Maja
1797–1800. Oil on canvas,
97 x 190 cm
P742

Almost certainly commissioned by Godoy, who had been a staunch patron of Goya's since 1795, this highly singular work – the artist's only female nude at a time when the genre was banned by the Inquisition – is recorded for the first time in 1800, in the palace of the Prince of the Peace, and appears together with *The Clothed Maja* in the 1808 inventory of his confiscated goods. The painting hung in a restricted room of his palace together with two other canvases of nudes, one then attributed to Titian, and the other Velázquez's *Rokeby Venus* (now in the National Gallery, London), both of which had been given to Godoy by the duchess of Alba. Few female nudes have given rise to so much literature as this one, largely owing to the romantic legend surrounding the model's identity. For a time she was thought to be the duchess of Alba herself. Pepita Tudó, Godoy's lover, has also been proposed. What makes the painting so modern is its lack of allegorical purpose, for although Goya's intention, according to the testimony of his son Javier, was to represent Venus, he does so with direct realism, omitting any allusion to mythology and showing her gazing unflinchingly at the viewer.

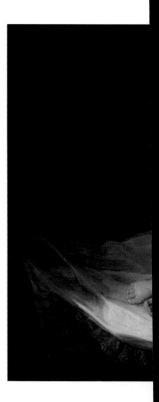

148
FRANCISCO DE GOYA
Fuendetodos, Saragossa, 1746–
Bordeaux, 1828

The Clothed Maja
1800–05. Oil on canvas,
95 x 190 cm
P741

Probably painted later than *The Naked Maja*, this *Maja* appears for the first time in the January 1808 inventory of Godoy's confiscated goods. The white costume clings to the body, hinting at its feminine forms, and the gaze levelled at the viewer is one of teasing merriment. Like the dress, the little jacket with ornamental tassels and the pink sash was typical of the outfits of the Madrid majas, from which comes the later title of this work. In 1815, the Inquisition called on Goya to reveal the name of the person for whom he had painted the pictures, and his motives in doing so, but the artist's reply is not on record. After the confiscation, the *Majas* were deposited at the Real Academia de San Fernando, although only the clothed one was exhibited. They entered the Museo del Prado in 1901.

149 ↑
FRANCISCO DE GOYA
Fuendetodos, Saragossa, 1746–
Bordeaux, 1828

The Marchioness
of Santa Cruz
1805. Oil on canvas,
124 x 207 cm
P7070

Joaquina Téllez Girón y Alonso
Pimentel, marchioness of Santa
Cruz through her marriage to
José Gabriel de Silva y Waldstein
in 1801, was the daughter of the
duke and duchess of Osuna,
and was portrayed by Goya
with her parents and siblings
in a work that is also in the
Museo del Prado [142]. Here,
the painter represents her as one
of the muses, as he was also to
depict her sister, the duchess of
Abrantes, a few years later [150].
Crowned with oak and its small
acorns, symbols of virtue, her
lyre-shaped musical instrument
associates her with Terpsichore,

the muse of dance and song, or
with Erato, the muse of lyric
poetry. The characterisation
refers to her fondness for
the arts, and to the support,
protection and friendship she
gave poets and artists, as well as
expressing the admiration of her
contemporaries for her beauty
and culture. Goya employs a
language close to Neoclassicism
in this portrait, but his use of a
background of purple and mauve
tones to render the velvet of the
divan and the enveloping curtains
stems from his own personal
interpretation of space and
atmosphere.

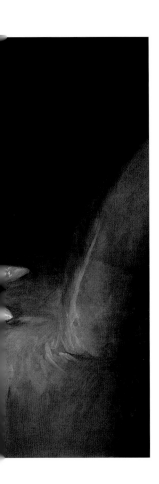

150 →
FRANCISCO DE GOYA
Fuendetodos, Saragossa,
1746–Bordeaux, 1828

The Duchess of Abrantes
1816. Oil on canvas, 92 x 70 cm
P7713

María Manuela Téllez Girón y Alonso Pimentel, the youngest daughter of the duke and duchess of Osuna [142], married Ángel María de Carvajal y Fernández de Córdova, eighth duke of Abrantes, in Cadiz in 1813. Goya painted her eleven years after portraying her sister, the marchioness of Santa Cruz. In both portraits he followed French Neoclassical models, which were much favoured by the upper aristocracy of Madrid. Goya employs a simpler composition here in which the young woman, aged twenty-one, is shown half-length against a neutral background that contrasts with the bold colouring of her dress and ornaments. Looking at the viewer, she seems to be about to sing the notes of the score she holds in her hand, which alludes to her love of song and also bears her identification. The portrait has been seen as an allegory in which Goya represents the duchess, as he had done previously with her sister [149], as a muse. The classical restraint of the picture is combined with absolute technical freedom, visible in the brushstrokes modelling the shawl and the dress, and in the transparency of the lace edging of the neckline, which is constructed from light touches of the brush, almost abstract in nature, revealing the flesh tones beneath.

151
FRANCISCO DE GOYA
Fuendetodos, Saragossa, 1746–
Bordeaux, 1828

*The Second of May, 1808,
in Madrid*
1814. Oil on canvas,
268 x 347 cm
P748

The two pictures entitled
respectively *The Second of
May, 1808* and *The Third
of May, 1808* were painted
for the king between the
spring and autumn of 1814,
at the arrival of Ferdinand
VII. They were almost
certainly commissioned
by the Supreme Junta of
the Regency, which granted
Goya financial aid. They are
registered in a storeroom at
the Prado in 1838, the first to
be exhibited being *The Second
of May*, which is mentioned
by Théophile Gautier in 1845.
The Third of May, on the
other hand, was not shown
until about 1865. In the
first picture, Goya shows
the patriots' attack on the
morning of 2 May 1808 against
the Mamelukes – Egyptian
soldiers incorporated into
Napoleon's Imperial Guard –
and the Empress's Dragoons,
who were escorting the
youngest of the infantes,
Don Francisco de Paula
[145], out of the royal palace.
The work is full of energy,
rage and despair, which the
artist expresses through a
superbly devised composition
and a pattern of colour
that perfectly capture
the horror of the combat
and the violence unleashed
by both sides.

152
FRANCISCO DE GOYA
Fuendetodos, Saragossa,
1746–Bordeaux, 1828

The Third of May, 1808,
in Madrid
1814. Oil on canvas, 268 x 347 cm
P749

On the afternoon of 2 May
1808, and on the night
following the popular uprising
represented in the previous
picture [151], the French
army shot many of the rebels
at various places in Madrid,
such as the Paseo del Prado,
several of the city gates, and
Mount Príncipe Pío, where
this scene is traditionally
supposed to be set. This ended
the revolt of Madrid, which
subsequently endorsed the
French government established
not long afterwards. Goya
presents a terrible scene
of execution that has been
'quoted' in equally impressive
works by later artists, including
Manet and Picasso. The
morning's assailants are now
the victims, either lying dead
in the foreground or begging
for mercy, on the point of being
shot, their faces expressing
their fear, resignation and
despair. Still others are arriving
in groups that have been led out
of the city through the fortified
gate in the background. The
light from the powerful lantern
traverses the damp night air,
illuminating the frightful
details of death in this desolate
and inhospitable place. The
scene is set outside one of
the gates of Madrid, possibly
that of La Vega, behind which
rise the church towers of Santa
María la Real and San Nicolás.

Goya
The Black Paintings and Goya's Last Works

In 1819, Goya bought La Quinta del Sordo (The House of the Deaf Man), a country house with farmland that stood on a rise overlooking the far side of the River Manzanares, on the outskirts of Madrid. The painter, who fell seriously ill shortly after moving there, decorated the walls of the two main rooms on the ground and first floors with mural paintings. As X-ray studies appear to reveal, the walls may have originally been painted with landscapes of the villa featuring bright colours and compositions that were altogether gentler than those we know today. On top of them, he painted what are now called the Black Paintings, enigmatic compositions that could be seen as a continuation and résumé of the prints in *Los Disparates* [375], which date from the same period. The original arrangement of the fourteen pieces is unknown, which makes them difficult to interpret. Their themes appear to be evil, terror, ignorance and death. In 1823, the artist, who was planning to leave for Bordeaux, donated the estate to his grandson Mariano, and after several changes of owner, it was bought in 1873 by Baron Frédéric Émile d'Erlanger (1873–1911), who commissioned Salvador Martínez Cubells, then the restorer at the Museo del Prado, to transfer the paintings to canvas. The baron showed the paintings at the International Exhibition of 1878 in Paris, and he donated them in 1881 to the Spanish state, which assigned them to the Museo del Prado. It is not known whether they were left unfinished when Goya departed for France in 1824, but they are described by Charles Yriarte in his monograph on Goya of 1867, and by Brugada in the inventory of La Quinta del Sordo, whose date is uncertain but which must be subsequent to the artist's death and Brugada's arrival in Spain in 1831. The paintings underwent some modifications during their transfer to canvas and their restoration and it is hard to tell if they followed an iconographic programme, but all the pieces have a tormented and disturbing character. Common to all of them is an exaggeration of gesture and attitude, remarkably free brushwork involving energetic sweeps of the brush, almost splashes in some cases, and strong contrasts of light and colour. Goya painted them with total freedom, no trace of academicism remaining, and endowed them with a deeply felt emotion and a strange beauty that have never ceased to attract and perplex visitors since they were first displayed in the Prado at the end of the nineteenth century. Moreover, the fascination they have exerted on Goya's successors has grown unabated since the nineteenth century, with avant-garde movements like Expressionism and Surrealism.

153
FRANCISCO DE GOYA
Fuendetodos, Saragossa, 1746–
Bordeaux, 1828

Half-submerged Dog
1819–23. Mixed technique
on wall, transferred to canvas,
131 x 79 cm
P767

This possibly unfinished painting, which belonged to the group on the upper floor of La Quinta del Sordo, is perhaps the most enigmatic of all the Black Paintings, and it is impossible to determine what the painter intended. The head of a dog is seen appearing behind a slope, or perhaps sinking into marshy ground. The animal looks upwards with an almost human gaze, producing a deeply unsettling effect in the viewer, which is exacerbated by the vast empty space occupying most of the picture over its head. The sense of anxiety, the sparseness of the motifs and the simplification of the environment have all become a source of inspiration for contemporary artists, and some have regarded its minimalism and almost complete lack of formal organisation as precedents of abstract painting.

154 ↑
FRANCISCO DE GOYA
Fuendetodos, Saragossa,
1746–Bordeaux, 1828

The Witches' Sabbath
1821–23. Oil on wall, transferred
to canvas, 140 x 438 cm
P761

155 ↓
FRANCISCO DE GOYA
Fuendetodos, Saragossa, 1746–
Bordeaux, 1828

Duel with Cudgels
1821–23. Oil on wall, transferred
to canvas, 125 x 261 cm
P758

156 →
FRANCISCO DE GOYA
Fuendetodos, Saragossa,
1746–Bordeaux, 1828

Saturn devouring his Son
1821–23. Oil on wall, transferred
to canvas, 143 x 81 cm
P763

157
FRANCISCO DE GOYA
Fuendetodos, Saragossa,
1746–Bordeaux, 1828

Two Old Men Eating

1820–23. Mixed technique
on wall, transferred to canvas,
49 x 83 cm
P762

Against an almost black
background, an old man appears
to be eating while another
figure, possibly another old
man or perhaps, given his
cadaverous appearance, death
itself, accompanies or stalks
him. The work is painted in free
brushstrokes of great intensity
which deposit the paint in
dense masses, with brown
and grey tones predominating.

Goya represents the figures,
whom he distorts for expressive
effect, with a minimum of
form, filling the whole scene
with a disturbingly nightmarish
atmosphere that is accentuated
by the fact that nobody knows
for certain what the artist meant
by the painting.

158
FRANCISCO DE GOYA
Fuendetodos, Saragossa, 1746–
Bordeaux, 1828

A Manola: Doña Leocadia Zorrilla

1820–23. Oil on wall, transferred to canvas, 145 x 129 cm
P754

Although the figure in this painting has been considered since the nineteenth century to represent Leocadia Zorrilla, there are no firm grounds for this identification. Goya lived with Leocadia during the last years of his life, but it is not clear whether they were lovers. The woman appears to be younger than Leocadia woud have been at the time and may represent beauty and youth in connection with death. The melancholy veiled figure dressed in black rested originally on a chimney mantelpiece, covered by a repaint. She stands out against one of the brightest skies in all the Black Paintings, and presumably her sensual figure is intended to contrast with *Two Old Men Eating* [157], a profoundly dark work, by confronting youth and beauty with gloom, decrepitude and death.

159
FRANCISCO DE GOYA
Fuendetodos, Saragossa, 1746–
Bordeaux, 1828

The Milkmaid of Bordeaux
c. 1825–27. Oil on canvas,
74 x 68 cm
P2899

It is difficult to be sure about the subject of this work, which for a long time has been considered the representation of a young milkmaid. Viewed from below looking upwards, the half body carries a pitcher which bears Goya's name and it has been imagined that she is sitting on an ass which is outside the composition. The theme is related to street trades, a long tradition in art. It has a light colouring in blue tones, illuminated with thick and separated white brushstrokes, tones which have been explained as a new shoot of optimism in the life of the old painter exiled in Bordeaux. Much earlier, Goya had already begun an unstoppable evolution towards a monochrome range, reaching the reduced colours of his last portraits. The painting was offered by Leocadia Zorrilla, who accompanied Goya in his last years, to Juan Bautista Muguiro.

160
FRANCISCO DE GOYA
Fuendetodos, Saragossa,
1746–Bordeaux, 1828

*Don Juan Bautista
de Muguiro*
1827. Oil on canvas, 103 x 85 cm
P2898

Goya spent his final years in
Bordeaux, where he went to live
in 1824 after the liberal interval
of the Constitutional Triennium
had given way to the restoration
of absolute monarchy. His circle
in Bordeaux was principally
made up of exiled French
sympathisers and liberals like
Leandro Fernández de Moratín,
Francisco Silvela and the young
painter Antonio de Brugada. Juan
Bautista Muguiro, merchant and
banker, was also a Spanish exile,
and his appreciation of Goya's
work led to the commission for
this portrait and his acquisition
of *The Milkmaid of Bordeaux* [159].
The painter shows Muguiro

in front of his desk, as he had
depicted Jovellanos years earlier
[143]. This work, however, is a far
cry from the painter's previous
portraits of the aristocracy, not
only because of changing fashions
and the subtle grey and black
tones employed by the painter,
but also because of the sitter's
attitude, which heralds the
triumph of the bourgeoisie.
It is executed in a pure and
synthetic style with sparse but
energetic strokes that merely
suggest material forms. Painted
in May 1827 in Bordeaux, when
Goya was eighty-one years old,
it is possibly the last of the artist's
known works.

Nineteenth-century Painting
Neoclassicism

There has been nineteenth-century art at the Museo del Prado ever since its inauguration in 1819, when a small room was set aside for 'contemporary artists', both living and recently deceased. This collection of modern painting grew in an unsystematic fashion, mainly through legacies and donations, since contemporary art purchased by the state was sent to the Museo Nacional de Pintura y Escultura, more usually known as the Museo de la Trinidad. This museum absorbed the prize-winning works from the National Fine Arts Exhibitions, modelled on the Parisian Salons that were held in Spain from 1856 onwards. The important collection built up in this way passed to the Prado in 1872, when the Museo de la Trinidad was closed down. From then on, the award-winning works from the successive National Exhibitions entered the Prado directly, along with the rest of the state contemporary art acquisitions, until an independent Museo de Arte Contemporáneo was created in 1894. Finally, in 1971, the nineteenth-century painting collections once more became affiiated with the Museo del Prado. The museum thus currently holds the finest and most complete collection of Spanish art from that century.

   The first third of the nineteenth century was marked by the persistence of eighteenth-century academicism. This was the style followed by Vicente López [161], who had been trained by his master, Mariano Salvador Maella, in the Neoclassical canon of Anton Raffael Mengs [355-357]. As principal court painter and director of the Real Academia de San Fernando, Vicente López set the guidelines for official art. In the meantime, another group of painters, only slightly younger than López, received pensions to study in Paris from Charles IV (reigned 1788–1808), and trained in the workshop of the French Neoclassical painter Jacques-Louis David (1748–1825). They then introduced David's Neoclassicism to Spain. One of them was José de Madrazo, not only a fine painter but a figure of prime importance for the development of nineteenth-century Spanish art. José de Madrazo [162], succeeded Vicente López as first court painter and director of the Real Academia de San Fernando, and was also the director of the Museo del Prado itself from 1838 to 1857. He founded a dynasty that would dominate Spanish art and artistic policy throughout the nineteenth century.

161
VICENTE LÓPEZ
Valencia, 1772–Madrid, 1850

Félix Antonio Máximo López, First Organist of the Royal Chapel
1820. Oil on canvas, 100 x 75 cm
P4405

After his appointment as first court painter by Ferdinand VII in 1815, Vicente López became the artist in greatest demand among the aristocracy of Madrid. He painted a large number of portraits for them, exhibiting a polished technique and considerable sensitivity. This half-length shows Félix Antonio Máximo López, the principal royal organist. Dressed in palace uniform, he rests against a pianoforte while holding the score of the most famous of his compositions, *El disparate o la obra de los locos*.

162
JOSÉ DE MADRAZO
Santander, 1781–Madrid, 1859

The Death of Viriatus,
Chief of the Lusitanians
1807. Oil on canvas,
307 x 462 cm
P4469

Trained in the workshop of the French Neoclassical painter Jacques-Louis David, José de Madrazo perfectly assimilated his master's style, following it closely in this ambitiously monumental piece which represents an episode from the ancient history of Hispania. The scene shows the mourning for the death of Viriatus, a Lusitanian chieftain who rebelled against Roman domination and was murdered in his sleep by traitors in the pay of Rome. The central group draws inspiration from a drawing by the English artist John Flaxman (1755–1826) of an episode from the *Iliad*, and Flaxman's linear style is apparent throughout the work. The composition is centred around the soldiers, who are lamenting the chieftain's death or crying out for vengeance. Their markedly sculptural figures, outlined with cold and severe draughtsmanship, seem petrified in the midst of action.

Romanticism

Romanticism reached Spanish painting after some delay, and with a less revolutionary outlook than in other parts of Europe. This was partly because the reign of Ferdinand VII (1813–1833) prolonged the *ancien régime* well into the nineteenth century, but it was also the result of the lack of a strong bourgeoisie, the main public for Romantic art. Like Davidian Neoclassicism before it, Romanticism was brought to Spain by a group of painters who trained in Paris and Rome, one of the foremost being Federico de Madrazo. This artist succeeded his father, José de Madrazo, as the leading figure in Spanish art, and he too became director of the Real Academia de San Fernando, first court painter, and director of the Museo del Prado. Federico, who had studied in Paris under Jean-Auguste-Dominique Ingres (1780–1867), was the chief representative in Spain of a moderate Romanticism that did not challenge the academic system [163]. Besides this purist vein, however, Romanticism also adopted other forms in Spain. Seville became an important regional centre, its chief figure being Antonio María Esquivel, an erudite artist who wrote on art and broke away from narrow local boundaries by moving to court. Esquivel showed the link between Romantic painting and literature in a paradigmatic picture, *Contemporary Poets: A Reading by Zorrilla in the Painter's Studio* [168]. Another path followed by Spanish Romanticism was *costumbrismo*, the painting of local customs, which benefited from the taste of European artists and writers for the romantic image of Spain. This gave rise on the one hand to paintings that exploited Spain's picturesque appeal, and on the other to images whose technique and subject-matter followed in the wake of Goya by depicting the country's backwardness and fanaticism. In this respect, the painters who most successfully assimilated Goya's legacy were Leonardo Alenza [164, 165] and Eugenio Lucas Velázquez. Among the most prominent of the *costumbristas* was Valeriano Domínguez Bécquer, the brother of the Romantic writer Gustavo Adolfo Bécquer (1836–1870), whose most representative work shows the people and customs of Castile with almost anthropological detachment [166].

163
FEDERICO DE MADRAZO
Y KUNTZ
Rome, 1815–Madrid, 1894

*Amalia de Llano
y Dotres, Countess of Vilches*
1853. Oil on canvas, 126 x 89 cm
P2878

Although he also painted religious and historical subjects, Madrazo's principal achievements were in the genre of the portrait. One fine example is this painting, which was bequeathed to the Museo del Prado by the sitter's son. The artist here takes Ingres as a starting point and combines this with his study of Velázquez's technique. Amalia de Llano y Dotres, countess of Vilches by marriage and a keen amateur writer, was a friend of the painter's family. It may be this connection, and the affection in which she was held, which enables Madrazo to convey the grace of the young woman, giving her a subtle sensuality that is absent from his other more sober portraits. The French influence manifests itself in the elegant composition and the naturalness of the expression. The light is centred on the sitter, highlighting the texture of the materials, the superbly rendered glittering jewels, and the delicate skin tones, all executed in a brilliant technique of thin impasto applied in very fine and accurate strokes.

164
LEONARDO ALENZA
Madrid, 1807–1845

The Tooth-puller
1844. Oil on canvas,
38 x 45.5 cm
P7945

165
LEONARDO ALENZA
Madrid, 1807–1845

The Triumph of Bacchus
1844. Oil on canvas, 38 x 45.5 cm
P7946

These two paintings, which were acquired by the Museo del Prado in 2006, are good examples of Alenza's painting and of Spanish Romantic cabinet painting in general, and they demonstrate the influence that the Prado's collections were beginning to exert on Spanish artists in the nineteenth century. The composition, the depiction of humble interiors and the interest in the grotesque can all be related to paintings by Teniers, which Alenza could have seen in the Prado. However, as well as the influence of Flemish and Dutch genre painting, then becoming fashionable all over Europe, these two pictures also demonstrate the importance of the so-called 'Spanish School' for the work of the Spanish Romantic artists. The legacy of Murillo can be seen in specific motifs like the child picking lice in a dark corner in *The Tooth-puller*. The expressive treatment of the faces, the ignoble pursuits and the untidiness of the room – the physical reflection of a moral disorder – all hark back to Goya. Also traceable to Goya is the representation of disturbing scenes in dark interiors lit from the outside. The influence of Velázquez [71], who was also interested in painting low life, likewise finds reflection in these pictures by Alenza. In his *Triumph of Bacchus*, however, the Romantic artist abandons Velázquez's restraint and grotesquely exaggerates the effects of drink on his emphatically burlesque figures.

166
VALERIANO DOMÍNGUEZ
BÉCQUER
Seville, 1834–Madrid, 1870

*The Dance. Folk Traditions
from the Province of Soria*

1866. Oil on canvas, 65 x 101 cm
P4234

This painting, the result of a project instigated by Isabella II, blends the Romantic taste for folklore and picturesque travels with anthropological study. In 1865, the queen granted Bécquer a stipend to paint a series of pictures showing the characteristic folk dresses and customs of the Spanish provinces. The paintings resulting from the project, which was interrupted by the revolution of 1868, were sent to the Museo Nacional de Pintura y Escultura. This one shows a scene set in Villaciervos, a village in the province of Soria, where peasants and woodcutters, young and old, are dancing to a tabor. Despite their activity, the figures have a static quality, as though time had come to a halt, and form a horizontal frieze that gives this scene of popular art a classical and timeless quality.

167
FEDERICO DE MADRAZO
Y KUNTZ
Rome, 1815–Madrid, 1894

The Painter Carlos Luis de Ribera

1839. Oil on canvas, 92 x 73 cm
P7799

Federico de Madrazo and Carlos Luis de Ribera inherited a relationship of friendly rivalry from their fathers, the painters José de Madrazo and Juan Antonio de Ribera, who had introduced Neoclassical painting to Spain. Their sons, the sitter and the painter of this portrait, were prominent figures in Spanish Romanticism. They coincided in Paris in the late 1830s and each made a portrait of the other in what can be considered as both a demonstration of affection and a pictorial contest. In this painting, Federico de Madrazo already displays the qualities which would make him one of the favourite portraitists of Spanish high society, most notably a sense of elegance that combines the influence of David, Ingres and Delaroche, whose work he had encountered in Paris, with the technique of Velázquez. He captures both the physical likeness and the psychology of his sitter, whose melancholy nature combines with his pose, his clothing and his hair to make this a typically Romantic portrait.

168
ANTONIO MARÍA ESQUIVEL
Seville, 1806–Madrid, 1857

*Contemporary Poets: A
Reading by Zorrilla in the
Painter's Studio*
1846. Oil on canvas, 144 x 217 cm
P4299

This impressive work is an
icon of Spanish Romantic art.
It shows the principal writers
of the time at an imaginary
gathering in the painter's own
studio. Esquivel, who was a
writer as well as a painter,
undertook to portray the
most important personalities
of his day in a series of group
portraits in various settings,
of which the Prado holds
this one and another entitled
*Ventura de la Vega reading a
Play to the Actors of the Teatro
del Príncipe*. Employing a
minutely precise technique

that results in a polished finish,
the artist distributes forty-two
characters around the room
with consummate mastery.
He has placed himself in
the centre of the composition,
pausing in his work for a
moment to listen to Zorrilla.
Two of the poets do not appear
in person: Espronceda, who had
died a year earlier, is shown in
a picture on an easel (the original
is in the Prado), and the Duke
of Rivas, who was then the
ambassador to Naples, appears
in a picture hanging on the wall.

History Painting

History painting has been one of the most highly valued genres over the centuries. There are many examples of it in the Museo del Prado, ranging from the battle scenes of the Salón de Reinos in the Buen Retiro Palace [90-95] to Goya's paintings of the War of Independence [151, 152]. The genre acquired even more importance in the nineteenth century with the arrival of Romanticism and the spread of nationalist ideas, though the process was somewhat delayed in Spain by the Carlist wars of succession and the economic crisis that accompanied them. The golden age of Spanish history painting thus fell between 1860 and 1890, long after neighbouring France. This delay explains why the works were Romantic in subject-matter but often closer to realism in their search for verisimilitude in landscape, character and setting, and in the importance given to details. The National Exhibitions, first held in 1856, contributed to the development of the genre in the nineteenth century because history paintings often won the principal awards. This encouraged artists to embark on works whose considerable preparation made them both complex and expensive, and which they might not have undertaken without the incentive of the prizes. History painting also found institutional support, since the genre was seen as a means of enhancing the glories of the nation's past and extracting a moral lesson from it, which was often applied to contemporary politics. Because the prize-winning works from the National Exhibitions were acquired by the state, the finest examples of history painting are now to be found in the Museo del Prado. Especially outstanding are the works of Eduardo Rosales [170, 171], one of the greatest artists of the century, who revitalised Spanish painting with a lively realism that goes back to Velázquez. Of special interest too are the painters Antonio Muñoz Degrain [172], Francisco Pradilla [173] and Antonio Gisbert [169]. The last two were directors of the Museo del Prado.

169
ANTONIO GISBERT
Alcoy, Alicante, 1834–Paris, 1901

The Execution by Firing Squad of Torrijos and his Companions on the Beach at Málaga
1887–88. Oil on canvas, 390 x 601 cm
P4348

During the regency of Queen Maria Cristina, the liberal government of Práxedes Mateo Sagasta commissioned this work from Gisbert, intending it as a denunciation of absolutism. José María Torrijos, the war minister during the Liberal Triennium, had taken refuge in England at the restoration of the absolutist monarch Ferdinand VII in 1823. In 1831, he was tricked into returning to Spain from exile. The ship on which he was sailing to Málaga was boarded, and he and his companions were captured and shot on the city's beaches. The painting depicts the event with sober veracity, reinforced by the precise draughtsmanship and orderly arrangement of the patriots in a receding diagonal. Torrijos takes the hands of the companions closest to him at the moment of greatest tension, just before their imminent death. Their faces reflect their varying emotions, while the violence of the scene is enhanced by its focus on the corpses of those who have already been shot. Foreshortened and cut off by the bottom edge of the canvas, in an extremely modern arrangement, they heighten the dramatic tension of the picture.

170
EDUARDO ROSALES
Madrid, 1836–1873

Queen Isabella the Catholic dictating her Will
1864. Oil on canvas,
290 x 400 cm
P4625

This work, perhaps the most outstanding Spanish history painting of the nineteenth century, led to official recognition for its artist when it was displayed at the National Exhibition of 1864. It also made a great impact on the artistic scene, as its novel atmospheric realism, inherited from Velázquez, influenced much of later Spanish painting. It narrates a key episode in the nation's history: Queen Isabella's will definitively united all the kingdoms of Spain under one crown. Rosales convincingly recreates the setting of the queen's dark chamber in the castle of La Mota, and skilfully arranges the witnesses to the event, who include such recognisable figures as Ferdinand the Catholic, his daughter Joan the Mad, and Cardinal Cisneros. Their faces register a range of different emotions, which contrast with the serenity and calm of the sovereign. Framed by the whiteness of her garments and bedlinen, the queen is the focus of the scene, which is painted in a range of sober colours in a soft and fluid style that combines broad strokes with loose touches.

171
EDUARDO ROSALES
Madrid, 1836–1873

The Death of Lucretia

1871. Oil on canvas, 257 x 347 cm
P4613

After the success of *Queen Isabella the Catholic dictating her Will* [170], Rosales caused another commotion in the genre of Spanish history painting with this canvas. As in the previous picture, he relates the dying moments of a virtuous woman whose demise was to have serious historical consequences. In this case, the suicide of the Roman noblewoman Lucretia, who had been raped by the king's son, hastened the end of the monarchy and the proclamation of the Roman Republic in 510 BC. The scene is set with great economy in the intimacy of the conjugal bedroom, and shows the moment when the lifeless body of Lucretia is discovered by her father, Lucretius, and her husband, Colatinus. Two other figures, presumably Brutus and Valerius, show different reactions to the scene. The first raises his dagger and cries out for vengeance, while the second hides his face, overwhelmed by grief. Although it won the first medal at the National Fine Arts Exhibition of 1871, this painting was surrounded by considerable controversy owing to its disconcertingly modern technique of loose brushwork.

172
ANTONIO MUÑOZ DEGRAIN
Valencia, 1840–Málaga, 1924

The Lovers of Teruel
1884. Oil on canvas,
330 x 516 cm
P4521

A legend set in the city of Teruel in the thirteenth century tells of the ill-fated love of Doña Inés de Segura for an impoverished nobleman, Diego Juan Martínez de Marsilla. The tale inspired romances and other literary works such as Juan Eugenio Hartzenbusch's verse drama, *Los amantes de Teruel*, first performed in 1837, and it was the subject of several nineteenth-century history paintings, of which this is the most important. Awarded the first medal at the 1884 National Fine Arts Exhibition, the painting was also a great popular success. Although Muñoz Degrain was primarily a landscape painter, he here produced one of the crowning achievements of the history genre thanks to the drama he brings to the scene, and the intensity of the pictorial effects, especially his expressive manipulation of the light. He has chosen to depict the most moving moment in the story. Doña Inés, who has just been obliged by her father to marry Don Rodrigo de Azara, dies upon seeing the corpse of her beloved Diego, who had returned to the city with a knight's honours after a five-year journey to seek his fortune and so win the approval of the Seguras.

173
FRANCISCO PRADILLA
Villanueva de Gállego,
Saragossa, 1848–Madrid, 1921

Doña Joan the Mad
1877. Oil on canvas,
340 x 500 cm
P4684

Regarded as Pradilla's
masterpiece, this painting
brought him international fame
when he was just twenty-nine
years old. Rather than narrating
a crucial historical event,
he has depicted a moment of
emotional drama. The subject,
the queen's madness, obsessed
Pradilla, and this aspect of
her personality also fascinated
the nineteenth century. This
Romantic approach to history
is, however, combined with
a fully realist execution. When
her husband, Philip the Fair,
died in 1506, Joan the Mad,
the daughter of the Catholic
monarchs, accompanied his
hearse on its journey from
Burgos to Granada, where
he was buried. Joan, pregnant
with Infanta Catherine
of Austria, is at the centre of a
composition that is structured
in the form of a cross by
the hearse retreating into the
background and the smoke
blowing away from the fire.
With fidelity and restraint,
Pradilla shows the queen's
madness and the expressions
of weariness and compassion
on the faces of her attendants.
The details, from the clothes to
the ruts left by the carts in the
muddy road, are realistically
represented to great decorative
effect. Pradilla was a master
at depicting outdoor scenes
and here he convincingly
conjures up the unstable
weather and atmosphere
of general discomfort.

Realism and its Evolution towards the Fin-de-siècle

In addition to its role in history painting, pictorial realism also spread to other genres such as landscape, which became increasingly prominent in the second half of the nineteenth century until eventually turning into a vehicle for the development of modern art. One figure who was fundamental to the genre in Spain was the Belgian painter Carlos de Haes [177], both because of his own work and because he taught several generations of painters as professor of landscape painting at the Real Academia de San Fernando. The museum has a large collection of his studies, which were donated by his pupils, as well as of the work of Martín Rico [178], another of the principal initiators of modern Spanish landscape painting, who evolved from Romanticism to a realism highly influenced – especially after 1870 – by Mariano Fortuny and Aureliano de Beruete. The latter, one of Haes's pupils, was instrumental in turning the Castilian landscape into the paradigm of Spain [179]. The Prado also holds some outstanding works by Mariano Fortuny, the most valued and internationally renowned of the nineteenth-century Spanish painters, and the one who exerted the greatest influence on his contemporaries despite his early death. Fortuny's early work drew on the Romantic orientalism of the French painter Eugène Delacroix (1798–1863), while he turned in his second phase to the detailed preciosity of the realist trend led by Jean-Louis-Ernest Meissonier (1815–1891) [344]. To all this, he added an interest in life study and the work of Velázquez, and his painting grew more relaxed and spontaneous until it attained the freedom of his last works, such as the Museo del Prado's *The Painter's Children in the Japanese Room* [175]. Fortuny greatly influenced his brother-in-law, Raimundo de Madrazo, who had studied under his father, Federico, and was an exponent of the realist portrait [176]. Finally, the Museo del Prado also preserves works by various artists who followed the path of naturalism into the twentieth century. One example is the Valencian painter Joaquín Sorolla, one of the greatest figures of Spain's *fin de siècle*. Sorolla combined his knowledge of contemporary European naturalism, which he encountered in Paris, with his love of Velázquez and his studies of nature and the effects of light, which were to become the true protagonists of his art [181].

174
MARIANO FORTUNY
Reus, Tarragona, 1838–Rome, 1874

Elderly Nude in the Sun
1871. Oil on canvas, 76 x 60 cm
P2612

In 1870, at the height of his international fame, Fortuny moved to Granada, where he painted a series of pictures executed with great freedom. Among them were various life studies of an old man. This careful and attentive nude study, which entered the Museo del Prado in 1904 as part of the Ramón de Errazu Legacy, is the finest of them. It shows the influence of Spanish Golden Age painting, especially Ribera [54], as well as Fortuny's interest in contemporary realism. Painted in long, loose brushstrokes, the work has various degrees of finish ranging from the sketchiness of the lower part to the more painstaking rendering of the head and the realistic depiction of the play of light on the man's face and naked torso. The artist also captures the feeling of contentment and abandon as the old man feels the warmth of the sun on his skin.

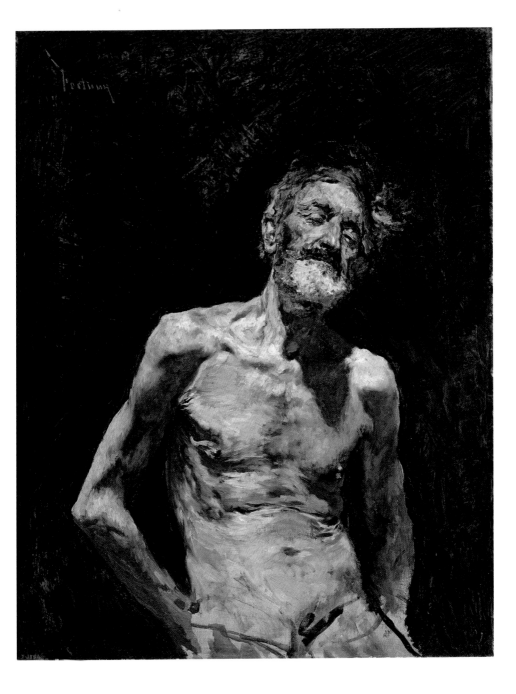

175
MARIANO FORTUNY
Reus, Tarragona, 1838–Rome,
1874

*The Painter's Children
in the Japanese Room*
1874. Oil on canvas, 44 x 93 cm
P2931

This audaciously modern work, which remained unfinished at the artist's death, shows Fortuny's two children, María Luisa (1868–1936) and Mariano (1871–1949). Mariano, who later settled in Venice and became a painter and designer, famous for his fabrics and dresses, bequeathed the picture to the Museo del Prado in 1950. The children are shown on a long divan in the Japanese Room of the Villa Arata in Portici, near Naples, where Fortuny spent the summer of 1874. It is a family portrait free of any commercial constraints, and painted in the artist's most personal style as a gift for his father-in-law, the painter Federico de Madrazo. In the decorative motifs, the exquisite fabrics and the treatment of colour, it shows the influence of the Japanese aesthetic, which was very fashionable in Parisian artistic circles in the second half of the nineteenth century. The chromatic refinement, the freedom of the brushwork and the rapid, loose technique bring a fresh decorative sense to the work without detracting from the impression of reality.

176
RAIMUNDO DE MADRAZO
Rome, 1841–Versailles, 1920

Ramón de Errazu
1879. Oil on panel,
224 x 96.5 cm
P2614

In Raimundo de Madrazo's
painting there are echoes
of the portraits of his father,
Federico de Madrazo, but
also of the portraiture of
the French Second Empire
and of his brother-in-law,
Mariano Fortuny. In the last
quarter of the nineteenth
century, Raimundo became
one of the most sought-after
portraitists in Parisian society.
Ramón de Errazu (1840–1904),
a friend of the artist, was a
businessman living in Paris
who built up an important
collection of Spanish
nineteenth-century art,
including this work, eventually
bequeathed to the Museo
del Prado. Raimundo had
just won the first-class medal
at the 1878 International
Exhibition in Paris, a
success to which Errazu had
contributed by lending several
pieces from his collection.
The influence of Velázquez,
inculcated in Raimundo by
his father, is evident here
in the ambiguity of the
space in which the figure is
placed and the monochrome
elegance of the work. Long
brushstrokes are used for the
background and smaller ones
for the sitter, whose figure
is lengthened and stylised,
thus adding to his distinction,
which is further intensified by
the painting's vertical format.

177
CARLOS DE HAES
Brussels, 1826–Madrid, 1898

*The Mancorbo Canal
in the Picos de Europa*
1876. Oil on canvas, 168 x 123 cm
P4390

Haes made many nature studies
in his striving to recreate the
natural world without artifice,
distancing himself in this way
from the Romantic landscape.
He used these studies to paint
larger and more carefully
executed works in the studio,
such as this one, which entered
the Museo del Prado after
winning a prize at the National
Exhibition of 1876. The painting
depicts the monumental
grandiosity of the Picos de
Europa range and reflects the
artist's love of spectacular
mountain landscapes. The
setting is the Cantabrian rural
area of Liébana, which Haes
had discovered during an 1874
journey with Aureliano de
Beruete.

178
MARTÍN RICO
Madrid, 1833–Venice, 1908

*The Ladies' Tower at the
Alhambra in Granada*
1871. Oil on canvas, 62 x 39 cm
P2623

In 1871, Martín Rico accepted
an invitation from his friend
Fortuny to go to Granada.
He already knew the area, since
he had painted landscapes
of Sierra Nevada in 1857.
In the views and landscapes
he painted from the life upon
his return to Andalusia, his
style grew more brilliant
and luminous under Fortuny's

influence, and his paintings
acquired a crisp atmosphere.
The brushwork became more
vibrant and intense, but Martín
Rico retained the serene
and balanced characteristics
of his own landscape style.
The subject of this work is
the Ladies' Tower, a building
adjacent to the outer wall
of the Alhambra compound,
which gives the artist the
opportunity to integrate the
architecture with nature.
The verticals of the tower
and of the two poplars
dominating the edges of the
composition lend a certain
decorative stylisation to a work
that is otherwise markedly
realist in its depiction of details.

179
AURELIANO DE BERUETE
Madrid, 1845–1912

*View of Madrid from
St Isidore's Meadow*

1909. Oil on canvas, 62 x 103 cm
P4245

The painter has chosen a view of Madrid that closely resembles the one in Goya's *St Isidore's Meadow* of 1788, also in the Museo del Prado [139]. The meadow was a very popular place, and it was there that the feast day of the city's patron saint was celebrated; it also provided a striking view of the city, overlooking the River Manzanares, and including such prominent buildings as the Mount Príncipe Pío Barracks, the Royal Palace and the church of San Francisco el Grande. Painting directly from the life, the artist succeeds in capturing the precise light of the time and place, although his technique was criticised by some as too ragged. His brushwork, however, is not that of the Impressionists, whose work he was familiar with, but is related more to the long irregular strokes of Velázquez, on whom he had published a monograph in 1898.

180
JOAQUÍN SOROLLA
Valencia, 1863–Madrid, 1923

*The Painter Aureliano
de Beruete*

1902. Oil on canvas,
115.5 x 110.5 cm
P4646

Better known for his beach
scenes and for his explorations
of light [181], Sorolla used to
complain about the burden
of having to paint portraits.
Nevertheless, they were
fundamental to his career, and
some of them rank among the
masterpieces in the genre at that
time in Europe. He adopts the
legacy of Spanish Golden Age
painting, assimilating the essence
of Velázquez's atmospheric
realism and adding a pictorial
language of his own. Portrayed
here is his friend, the painter

Aureliano de Beruete. Older
than Sorolla, Beruete was one of
the first to appreciate his artistic
talent, and supported Sorolla
during the difficult period of
his early days in Madrid. Sorolla
shows him in an aristocratic
pose, seated in semi-darkness,
with one of his landscapes
in the background. His face
stands out against the elegant
greys and browns and the
glossy blacks, and his frank
and candid gaze can be seen
as a tribute to his appreciation
and understanding of painting.

181
JOAQUÍN SOROLLA
Valencia, 1863–Madrid, 1923

Young Boys on the Beach
1910. Oil on canvas,
118 x 185 cm
P4648

This is one of the most important of Sorolla's mature works, when the sea and the beach were major motifs. Despite the large size of the canvas, the scene was painted directly from the life on the Valencian beach of El Cabañal, and shows the play of the midday light on the water, the sand and the bodies of the three boys. The true protagonists of the picture are the reflections on the water and the shadows, which the artist represents by broad strokes of yellow, brown and mauve and brief touches of white, achieving a great sense of life and immediacy. The figures are framed so closely that they block out the horizon. Sorolla has created a composition based on diagonals that lead the gaze from the beach to the sea with a progressive intensification of the colouring, the contrasts and the highlights, which are brighter on the figures in the background. It was donated by the artist himself in 1919 to the Museo de Arte Moderno, from where it was later transferred to the Prado.

The Italian Painting Collection

Although poetry in the 'Italian style' was already being written in Spain in Juan II's time (reigned 1406–1454), and Dante was also then being read, Italian innovations in the visual arts arrived relatively late. This was partly due to the tastes of Isabella the Catholic (reigned 1474–1504) who inherited not only her father's important art collection but also his taste for Flemish painting. Despite the affinities between Spanish and Italian art and culture, there was little interest in the latter prior to the sixteenth century, which explains the scarcity of early Italian painting in the Museo del Prado's collection. Spanish military engagements with France on Italian soil, Spanish rule in Milan and southern Italy, and diplomatic travels to Italy, including those of the monarchs themselves, all failed to remedy this shortage in the Royal Collections, the sole exception being Venetian painting, which is well represented in the Prado due to the personal tastes of the emperor Charles V (reigned 1519–1556) and Philip II (reigned 1556–1598). Philip III (reigned 1598–1621) played a relatively small part in the artistic life of Spain during his reign, but Philip IV (reigned 1621–1665) enriched his collections indirectly through gifts or acquisitions at posthumous sales, such as the famous sales of Charles I of England and Rubens, as well as through special envoys, most notably Velázquez during his second trip to Italy. Charles II (reigned 1665–1700) should be remembered for summoning the most important Italian painter of the time, Luca Giordano, to the Spanish court. Giordano left behind examples of his rapid style in a numerous canvases and an important number of frescoes in royal residences.

The Bourbons filled some of the gaps in the Royal Collections. Philip V (reigned 1700–1746) further added to the Italian holdings with the acquisition of over one hundred works from the collection of the painter Carlo Maratta, although more important was the role of Philip's second wife, Isabella Farnese (1692–1766), who was born in Parma and so was already familiar with Italian art. The Italian painters Giaquinto and Amigoni arrived in Madrid around this time and continued to work under Ferdinand VI (reigned 1746–1759). The reign of Charles III (1759–1788) saw an artistic power struggle between Mengs (an Italianate German) and Tiepolo. The Peninsular War halted royal art collecting, and with the foundation of the Museo del Prado in 1819 the Crown focused its attention on developing the new museum.

Renaissance

Following centuries in which European culture had been dominated by theological aspirations, there arose a new spirit in the Italy of the fourteenth and especially the fifteenth centuries that should be understood as an attempt to bring nature closer to man and to grasp it through the senses and through human intelligence. This was a new humanism, which although it aimed to bring about a re-birth of classical antiquity after what were seen as centuries of darkness, went much further in its desire to rationalise man's relationship with the universe. Renaissance art's principal objective was to capture the appearance of the external world in a rational manner. The development of new techniques and devices such as perspective contributed to this end. This conquest of the material world was counterbalanced by another mission of a more abstract nature: the quest for beauty. The tension between the two gave rise to creations of an unprecedented originality and aesthetic beauty. Together with the desire to revive the grandeurs of ancient Rome and the humanist longing for a rational vision of nature, a third factor characterises Renaissance culture: the rise of individual artistic personalities that subsequently passed into history. In fact, the nature of the artist not just as an individual but also as an intellectual and as master of a unique sensitivity is one of the Renaissance's most important contributions to the modern world.

The Italian Quattrocento is generally associated with the opulent mercantile city of Florence, but other cities such as Siena, Mantua, Urbino and Venice also produced major artists. These cities, like the different periods within the Renaissance, are unequally represented in the Prado's collection in a way that reflects the tastes and historical circumstances that influenced the formation of the Spanish Royal Collections. The museum does, however, contain various works of outstanding quality and importance such as *The Annunciation* by Fra Angelico [182], *The Cardinal* by Raphael [186] and *The Story of Nastagio degli Onesti* by Botticelli [185]. The latter work is among the most important twentieth-century additions to the Prado's collections, along with *The Dead Christ supported by an Angel* by Antonello da Messina [184].

182
FRA ANGELICO
Vicchio di Mugello,
1395/1400–Rome, 1455

The Annunciation
c.1425–28. Tempera and gold
leaf on panel, 194 x 194 cm
P15

Fra Angelico (Guido di Piero), a Florentine painter and illuminator who entered the Dominican Order around 1420, painted this altarpiece for the monastery of San Domenico in Fiesole near Florence. The central panel tells the story of man's fall and redemption through two complementary scenes: *The Expulsion of Adam and Eve from the Garden of Eden*, set in a leafy garden, and *The Annunciation of the Archangel Gabriel to Mary*, which takes place in an elegant portico. To emphasise the crucial role of the Virgin, the predella scenes illustrate episodes from her life: her birth and her marriage to St Joseph; the Visitation, in which she visits her cousin Elizabeth; the birth of Christ; the presentation of Christ in the temple; and her death, with Christ gathering up her soul. Fra Angelico, who considered painting a devotional act, combined the late Gothic Italian tradition – evident in the presence of the gold leaf and the interest in minute detail – with the new Renaissance idiom, revealed in his treatment of the architectural space.

183
ANDREA MANTEGNA
Isola di Carturo, 1431–Mantua,
1506

The Death of the Virgin
c.1462. Tempera on panel,
54 x 42 cm
P248

Mantegna was outstanding among the painters of his generation for his knowledge of classical art and his vigorous treatment of figures in space. This painting was executed for Ludovico Gonzaga, second marquis of Mantua from 1444 to 1478. It depicts an episode from the Apocryphal Gospels in which the Virgin Mary, told of her imminent death by St Michael, summons the Apostles to attend her in her last moments on earth. All arrive except Thomas, who was preaching in India.

The composition, derived from a mosaic by Andrea del Castagno, juxtaposes two spaces, interior and exterior, which are defined by a rigorous use of perspective. The window opens onto a view depicting the river at Mantua and is one of the first topographical views in Italian painting. By the time the work entered the Prado it had lost its top third, now in Ferrara, which showed a vaulted structure with Christ receiving the Virgin's soul.

184
ANTONELLO DA MESSINA
Messina, c.1430–Messina, 1479

*The Dead Christ supported
by an Angel*

c.1475–76. Tempera
and oil on panel, 74 x 51 cm
P3092

Vasari stated that it was
Antonello da Messina
who introduced the
Netherlandish technique of oil
painting into Italy. However,
there is no documentary
evidence to prove that the artist
visited the Low Countries and
his knowledge of oil painting
is generally explained by his
training in Naples, the Italian
city which was most influenced
by Netherlandish art, under
the rule of Alfonso V of Aragon
(reigned 1442–1458). Antonello's
style is a fusion of precise
northern handling with the

monumental figure style and
sense of volume characteristic
of Italian art. In 1475 he was in
Venice and in 1476 returned
to his native city in Sicily, where
he remained until his death.
The present panel dates from
this last phase of his career
and can be related to paintings
by the Venetian Giovanni Bellini
with regard to its iconography,
because of the inclusion of
angels, and to its composition,
with Christ in the foreground.
The landscape alludes to the city
of Messina with the church of
San Francesco in the background.

185
SANDRO BOTTICELLI
AND COLLABORATORS
Florence 1444/45–Florence, 1510

The Story of Nastagio degli Onesti

1483

First scene: tempera on panel, 83 x 138 cm
P2838

Second scene: tempera on panel, 82 x 138 cm
P2839

Third scene: tempera on panel, 84 x 142 cm
P2840

These panels formed part of the decoration of a bedroom. They were commissioned from Sandro Botticelli (Alessandro Filipepi del Botticelli) in 1483 by Antonio Pucci to celebrate the wedding of his son Giannozzo to Lucrezia Bini. The coats of arms of both families flank that of the Medici in the third panel. Botticelli was at this point at the height of his career and although he produced the overall design of the work and executed some of the figures, he was assisted by several collaborators, one of whom was Bartolomeo di Giovanni. The subject is inspired by the story of Nastagio degli Onesti in *The Decameron* by Boccaccio. Nastagio, a young man from Ravenna, retired to the outskirts of the city after being rejected by the daughter of Paolo Traversari. In the first panel Nastagio goes into the pine forest after taking leave of his friends and sees an astonishing sight: a rider pursuing a young woman who is attacked by dogs.

The rider, Guido degli Anastagi, had killed himself after being rejected by his beloved. The couple were condemned to hell where they were punished by having to repeat this grim chase in the forest every Friday. On each occasion the young man catches up with his beloved and opens her back to extract her heart and throw it to the dogs. This scene is depicted in the second panel before the horrified gaze of Nastagio who flees in terror while the pursuit is endlessly repeated in the background. The third panel shows the dinner held the following Friday to which Nastagio invites his beloved with her family in order to convince them to change their minds regarding the marriage. Next to a pavilion a maid informs Nastagio of the family's now favourable opinion. The fourth panel, which is in a private collection, shows the wedding banquet. The paintings were donated to the Prado in 1941 by Francesc Cambó.

Raphael

Even in his own lifetime Rafaello Sanzio, also known as Rafaello da Urbino, was considered one of the leading artists of the Florentine and Roman High Renaissance, equalled only by Leonardo, Michelangelo and Bramante. As a result of his remarkable technical abilities, his intense application and his attractive personality, Raphael worked for two of the most important art patrons of his day: Pope Julius II and Pope Leo X. His work represents the ideal of harmonious beauty that characterises the period in which he was active, and his short but brilliant career would profoundly influence later art. Raphael initially trained with his father Giovanni Santi, court painter to the Montefeltro in Urbino, but his principal master was Perugino (c.1452–1523), whose style left a far more important mark on his early output. Around 1504, aged little more than twenty, Raphael moved to Florence where he became familiar with the most recent work of Michelangelo and Leonardo, who had taken Renaissance painting to new levels of dramatic tension. In Florence, Raphael produced a considerable number of portraits and some of his most celebrated images of the Virgin and Child [187, 188]. The composition and iconography of these Madonnas reveal the influence of Michelangelo and Leonardo, but also his emphasis on ideal beauty, even over anatomical accuracy or the faithful representation of nature, which makes his work so distinctive. To achieve this, Raphael made numerous compositional studies and any awkwardness was always compensated by that *grazia* which all his images express and which Giorgio Vasari singled out in his *Lives* (1550 and 1568) as one of Raphael's most remarkable gifts. Around the end of 1508 he was summoned to Rome to work on the frescoes for the rooms in the Vatican palace known as the *Stanze*, along with Perugino, Lotto, Sodoma and others. He soon took charge of this project, which occupied him until his premature death. Raphael's success in Rome was such that he was commissioned not only to produce paintings but also designs and architecture and his studio became one of the principal centres of the Roman Renaissance.

186
RAPHAEL
Urbino, 1483–Rome, 1520

The Cardinal
c.1510–11. Oil on panel,
79 x 61 cm
P299

The Italian humanist and cardinal Pietro Bembo (1470–1547) stated that Raphael painted people 'more real than they are'. In Rome, where he settled in 1508, the artist executed his finest portraits, an extensive body of work if we take into account those included in his frescoes in the Vatican. Some of the figures in these frescoes have been said to resemble the present sitter but this is not clearly demonstrable. In fact, the anonymity of the sitter has led this portrait to be considered the archetype of a high-ranking Renaissance cleric. The pose and enigmatic expression recall Leonardo's *Mona Lisa* but the panel is outstanding on its own merits. The daring juxtaposition of the dark green background with the brilliant red of the cardinal's cape and the white of the sleeve, the subtle three-dimensionality of the face, and the exquisite brushstrokes make this one of the great achievements in portraiture.

188 →
RAPHAEL
Urbino, 1483–Rome, 1520

*The Holy Family
with St Raphael,
Tobias and St Jerome,*
or *The Virgin of the Fish*

c.1513–1514. Oil on panel
transferred to canvas,
215 x 158 cm
P297

Geronimo del Doce
commissioned this painting
for the chapel of St Rosalia in
the church of the Dominican
monastery in Naples. Raphael
executed it while working
on the Stanza d'Eliodoro
in the Vatican. The fact
that the patron's name was
Geronimo explains the
presence of St Jerome, while
the Archangel Raphael's role
as intercessor, as described
in the Book of Tobias, refers
to the chapel's funerary
function. The composition,
whose apparent simplicity
conceals a complex network
of triangles, rectangles and
diagonals, and the expressive
colours relate to the Stanza
d'Eliodoro. Above all,
however, the painting has the
serene beauty characteristic
of Raphael, and for which he
was so highly esteemed. The
Virgin holds the Christ Child
while St Jerome, dressed as a
cardinal and accompanied by
his lion, reads the Bible that
he himself had translated into
Latin. The Archangel Raphael
presents Tobias, who holds
the fish that cured his father's
blindness and which gave this
panel its popular name of
'The Virgin of the Fish'.

187 ↑
RAPHAEL
Urbino, 1483–Rome, 1520

*The Holy Family
with the Lamb*

1507. Oil on panel, 29 x 21 cm
P296

Raphael was highly admired for
his 'Madonnas' or scenes of the
Virgin and Child, which reveal
his classicising approach and his
sensitivity to the mother and
child theme. Represented here
in an idyllic landscape is the
dilemma of Christ's parents,
who have been chosen by God
to protect the Child during his
earthly lifetime. Inspired in
its composition by Leonardo's

preparatory drawing for the
high altar of the Annunziata
in Florence, Raphael slightly
modified the meaning of the
scene. Leonardo's composition
conveyed the doubts
experienced by the Virgin who,
without wishing to prevent
her son's Passion (symbolised
by the lamb), struggles to
accept it. Raphael, however,
presents Mary as tenderly
acknowledging the future of
the Child seated on the lamb
under St Joseph's attentive gaze.
Aware of the premonitory nature
of the moment, both look at
the Christ Child, establishing
an emotional engagement that
distinguishes Raphael's religious
scenes from those of most of his
contemporaries.

189
RAPHAEL
Urbino, 1483–Rome, 1520

Christ on the Road to Calvary
or *Lo Spasimo di Sicilia*
c.1516. Oil on panel transferred
to canvas, 318 x 229 cm
P298

This panel, which was highly admired from the time of its creation, was formerly in the monastery of Santa Maria dello Spasimo in Sicily, from where it derives its popular name. It expresses official doctrine regarding the Virgin's swoon during Christ's Passion, and she is consequently depicted as suffering but conscious rather than as having fainted. The scene, which reveals Raphael's interest in extreme states of mind, is organised around a cross-shaped composition whose spiritual and formal tension converges on the figure of Christ. According to the description in the Prado's inventory of 1857, Christ has fallen under the weight of the cross and announces the destruction of Jerusalem to the holy women, saying, 'Do not weep for me, weep for yourselves and your children'. The expressiveness of the gestures, which seems to prefigure a Baroque sensibility, has been related to prints by northern artists such as Martin Schongauer, Dürer and Lucas van Leyden. Sent to Philip IV in 1661 by Fernando de Fonseca, Viceroy of Naples, the panel was taken to Paris by the French in 1813 during the Napoleonic wars. In Paris it was transferred to canvas before being returned to Spain in 1818.

190
RAPHAEL
Urbino, 1483–Rome, 1520

The Holy Family or *The Pearl*

c.1518. Oil on panel, 144 x 115 cm
P301

Executed at the end of Raphael's career, this work may have involved the collaboration of Giulio Romano, who worked with Raphael from 1514. The overall design is generally attributed to Raphael but it may have been at least partly painted by Giulio. The influence of Leonardo, whom Raphael met again in Rome in 1513 and 1516, is evident in the pyramidal composition and in the contrasts of lighting, as well as in the importance given to the landscape. This is no longer of a generic, idealised type but instead depicts the Roman Campagna with identifiable architectural ruins. In the foreground and sheltered by a vaulted structure that recalls the Basilica of Constantine or the Baths of Diocletian is the harmonious group of the Virgin and Child flanked by St Anne and St John the Baptist. The painting belonged to Philip IV (reigned 1621–1665) and it is said that the monarch referred to it admiringly as the 'pearl' of his collection. Previous owners included the dukes of Mantua and Charles I of England.

The Sixteenth Century in Florence and Rome

The phenomenon known as the High Renaissance was at its height in Florence and Rome in the early years of the sixteenth century. It was a period almost as intense as it was short-lived, spanning slightly less than twenty-five years, from Leonardo's *Last Supper* in Milan to Raphael's premature death in 1520. Raphael, Leonardo da Vinci, Michelangelo and Bramante were the artists who best represent this period in humanist culture that first arose in Tuscany in the previous century. It was soon followed by another trend which came to be known as Mannerism and which, having briefly co-existed with the High Renaissance, then became pre-eminent in central Italy. The term, which is an invention of modern art history, derives from the Italian word *maniera*, and refers to a highly elegant, self-consciously artistic style. (*continues on page 234*)

191 ↓
LEONARDO'S WORKSHOP

Copy of the Mona Lisa
1503-16.
Oil on panel, 76.3 x 57 cm

Up until 2011, the view which extends behind this depiction of the Mona Lisa, lighting up her figure and letting her breathe, remained hidden by a black background added in the 18th century. The cleaning of this copy not only brought to light the limpid landscape we now see, almost conserved intact, but also revealed the close relationship between the copy, documented in the Spanish Royal Collection since 1666, and the original by Leonardo in the Louvre. The technical study has shown that the painting in the Prado was made simultaneously with and in parallel to that of the Florentine maestro, as it shows many of the changes and rectifications present in the original and which today are hidden beneath layers of paint. The style of the more precisely drawn work in Madrid, however, has little in common with the celebrated *sfumato* by Leonardo, and seems closer to that of Francesco Melzi (c. 1493 – 1572/73) or Andrea Salai (1480-1540), two of his disciples. Nonetheless, it may be said to be a careful work, created with noble materials – walnut, lapis lazuli, red lacquer, etc. –, and which cannot be considered as a routine workshop copy.

192
ANDREA DEL SARTO
Florence, 1486–1530

*The Virgin and Child between
St Matthew and an Angel*
c. 1522–23. Oil on panel,
117 x 135 cm
P334

Andrea d'Agnolo, known as
Andrea del Sarto, was trained
in Florence with painters
still committed to classicism
such as Piero di Cosimo and
Raffaelino del Garbo, although
he was soon attracted to the
innovations of Michelangelo,
Leonardo and Raphael. In the
1520s he was drawn to Rosso
and Pontormo, also working in
Florence, who explored directions
that increasingly departed from
classicism. The present work,
which dates from this time,
reflects del Sarto's assimilation
of the art of his day but also
his ability to create a unique
style that remained faithful to
monumental classicism and which
earned him the description of the
'perfect painter'. Commissioned
by the Florentine banker
Lorenzo di Bernardo Jacopi, it
has been interpreted in various
ways. Recently it has been
suggested that the angel on the
right is warning the Virgin and
Child of the Massacre of the
Innocents while the presence of
St Matthew, a tax gatherer and
patron of bankers, is a reference
to the donor. In the background
St Elizabeth seeks refuge for
the Infant St John the Baptist,
following an episode recorded
in the Proto-Gospel of St James
the Greater, an apocryphal
text derived from St Matthew's
Gospel.

(*continues from page 232*) Characterised by a strange unnatural beauty, Mannerism developed in the years between the dramatic fall of the Florentine Republic in 1512, with the assumption of power by the Medici, and the Sack of Rome by the Imperial troops in 1527. This was also the time when the rupture between Catholic and Protestant Europe became increasingly overt. These historical factors are more relevant in an attempt to describe the art of the period as a reflection of a profound spiritual crisis that led artists such as Parmigianino [196-198], Rosso and Pontormo to question some of the principal achievements of Renaissance painting, such as the rational depiction of space, the rigorous representation of the figure and above all the sense of a harmonious relationship between the individual and the universe. However, there were other trends in sixteenth-century Italy, and artists such as Luini [193], Correggio [194, 195] and Andrea del Sarto [191, 192], although aware of the dramatic events of the time, continued the serene, classicising approach to be found in Raphael and in some works by Leonardo and Michelangelo. Mannerism's formal and conceptual complexity did not greatly interest Spanish collectors, who preferred the work of artists who reacted against it. Within the context of sixteenth- and seventeenth-century debates on the primacy of line versus colour, the Spanish monarchs who collected art opted for the latter. This resulted in a preference for Venetian painting but also for the work of artists who followed the Venetians in attaching great importance to colour, such as Correggio and Barocci [203]. The Museo del Prado has outstanding holdings of both these artists. Many of the works from this period come from Spanish and international collections and reflect the criteria of collectors of the day.

193
BERNARDINO LUINI
Luino, 1485–Milan, 1532

The Holy Family
Oil on panel, 100 x 84 cm
P242

Given by Cosimo III de' Medici to Philip II, this panel reveals the influence of Leonardo on Milanese painters, of whom Luini is a prime example. Without deploying all of Leonardo's experimentalism, Luini adopted his forms and models. This is apparent in the present work, which was once thought to have been designed by Leonardo. The subject of the Holy Family with the infant St John the Baptist derives from the *Meditaciones Vitae Christi* by the Pseudo-Bonaventura (fourteenth century), and had been fully developed by Leonardo in *The Virgin of the Rocks*. Luini here presents it as a devotional image particularly suitable for the education of children. He depicts the two infants linked in an embrace that has both an emotional and theological meaning, watched by the Virgin Mary and St Joseph and framed by two vertical elements: the wand of lilies that represents the Virgin's purity, and Joseph's staff, which refers to his advanced years and to the moment when it miraculously flowered and he was chosen to be the Virgin's husband.

194
CORREGGIO
Correggio, 1489–1534

*The Virgin and Child with
the Infant St John the Baptist*
c.1516. Oil on panel, 48 x 37 cm
PII2

This painting dates from the
earliest phase of the career of
Antonio Allegri da Correggio,
before he travelled to Rome
in 1518–1519. In Rome he was
particularly influenced by
the work of Mantegna [183], who
is said to have been his teacher
and the motif of the classical
sandal worn by Mary indicates
this debt. Even more evident,
however, is the influence of
Leonardo, from whom Correggio
derived the cave setting, which

recalls Leonardo's *Virgin
of the Rocks* in the Musée du
Louvre. Also Leonardesque
are the *sfumato*, the Virgin's
hairstyle, and her gesture as
she presents the infant Christ
to St John the Baptist. The
gesture of the infant Christ as
he embraces his cousin as well
as the cross acquires a tragic
and symbolic significance
which is counterbalanced
by the maternal sweetness
of the Virgin.

195
CORREGGIO
Correggio, 1489–1534

Noli me tangere

c.1525. Oil on panel transferred
to canvas, 130 x 103 cm
PIII

This painting depicts
Christ's first appearance
after the Crucifixion. Mary
Magdalene, richly dressed in
sixteenth-century style, kneels
before the gardener whom she
has recognised as the resurrected
Christ. Surrounded by gardening
tools, Christ points to the sky
and says the words which give
the painting its title: 'Touch me
not [*noli me tangere*] for I am not
yet ascended to my Father.' The
painting reveals the influence
of Raphael and Michelangelo
in addition to that of Mantegna
and Leonardo. Synthesising
all these influences, Correggio
formulated a distinctive
classicism that would be
extremely important for later
Italian painting. The detailed
treatment of the natural setting
is a response to the position
of the painting, which was
intended to be seen from close
up in a private chapel. The
composition with its tense
diagonal is particularly striking,
counterbalancing the distraught
figure of the Magdalene with
Christ's monumental serenity.

196
PARMIGIANINO
Parma, 1503–Casalmaggiore, 1540

The Holy Family with Angels
c. 1524. Oil on panel, 110 x 89 cm
P283

Between 1520 and 1524, Parmigianino (Girolamo Francesco Maria Mazzola) assimilated the classicism of Correggio [194], who had moved to Parma to paint frescoes and large altarpieces. The young Parmigianino, however, soon developed a distinctive style that would became highly appreciated and which was endowed with the *grazia* that Vasari considered to be the most important characteristic of sixteenth-century Italian painting. This is evident in the present work, which Parmigianino gave to Pope Clement VII as proof of his artistic merit when he arrived in Rome in 1524. The artist was confident that the painting, which is the first to reveal his mature style although it is still indebted to Correggio in its iconography, would gain him a good position in the competitive environment of the Roman art world. Shortly afterwards and following his study of the work of Raphael and Michelangelo, Parmigianino's classicism evolved into an elegant Mannerism that is already evident in this *Holy Family*. Clement VII gave the painting to his nephew Ippolito de' Medici, then it entered the collection of the Italian sculptor Pompeo Leoni (c.1533–1608), on whose death it passed into the Spanish Royal Collections.

197 →
PARMIGIANINO
Parma, 1503–Casalmaggiore,
1540

Pietro Maria Rossi,
Count of San Segundo
1533–35. Oil on panel,
133 x 98 cm
P279

198 ↓
Camilla Gonzaga, Countess
of San Segundo, and her Sons
c.1533–35. Oil on panel,
128 x 97 cm
P280

The Count of San Segundo
commissioned this portrait
from Parmigianino, who
had returned to Parma in
1530. A celebrated military
figure, the Count had been
in the service of François I
of France, Cosimo de' Medici
and Charles V. He was still
in the service of the latter when
the portrait was painted, which
explains the inclusion of the
word 'IMPERIO' on one of
the books on the right and the
numerous classical references.
The sophisticated gold brocade
in the background may have
been inspired by Raphael's
portrait of Pope Julius II,
a work that Parmigianino had
seen in Rome. However, the
composition, with the elegant
Mannerism of the exaggeratedly
vertical figure juxtaposed
against the tiny sculpture on the
right, suggests that it should be
seen as a secular counterpart
to *The Madonna of the Long Neck*
(1534), one of Parmigianino's
masterpieces. The *Portrait of*
Camilla Gonzaga does not seem
to have been conceived as a
pendant to that of her husband.
Camilla married Rossi in 1523
and she is shown against a sober,
neutral background surrounded
by three of her six sons, Troilo,
Ippolito and Federico, in a way
that suggests a modern image
of the classical *Charity*.

199
SEBASTIANO DEL PIOMBO
Venice, 1485–Rome, 1547

Christ carrying the Cross
c. 1516. Oil on canvas,
121 x 100 cm
P345

This work has numerous
features in common with the
next picture [200], including
the monumentality of the
figures and the expressive use of
colour. It was probably painted
around the same time as *Christ's
Descent into Limbo* and was also
commissioned by Jerónimo Vich
y Vallterra, the ambassador to
Rome of Ferdinand the Catholic
and Charles V, who brought
both paintings back with him
on his return to Valencia. They
remained in his collection
until his great-grandson, Diego
Vich, gave them to Philip IV
in payment of debts. Sebastiano
here takes an unusual approach
to the subject by setting it in an
interior. The scene focuses on
the moment when Christ lifts up
the cross, watched by a soldier
and one of his torturers, and
takes place inside Pilate's palace
rather than on the Via Dolorosa.
The distinctive faces of the two
men reflect the artist's skills
as a portraitist. On the right,
through a large window we see
a group of people setting out in
procession to Mount Golgotha.

200
SEBASTIANO DEL PIOMBO
Venice, 1485–Rome, 1547

Christ's Descent into Limbo
c.1516. Oil on canvas,
226 x 114 cm
P346

Sebastiano del Piombo was
trained in Giovanni Bellini's
workshop in Venice, but
his mature work should be
understood in the context of
Roman art of the first half
of the sixteenth century,
and there are clear echoes
of Michelangelo in the heroic
monumentality of Christ's
body. However, the Venetian
heritage is still evident in the
refined colouring, symbolic
intent and pronounced sense
of drama. The subject of
the painting – the triumph
of Christ over death – was
fundamental for Catholic
dogma, and the painting
was commissioned by
Jerónimo Vich y Vallterra
when he was in Rome as
ambassador. The vertical
format of the painting,
with its notably harmonious
and highly meditated
composition, is due to the
fact that it was the lateral
wing of a triptych whose
central panel showed
*The Lamentation of the Body
of Christ* (Hermitage,
St Petersburg). The other
panel, which is now lost,
depicted *The Apparition of
Christ to the Apostles*, and is
known through a copy by
Ribalta.

201
BRONZINO
Florence, 1503–1572

Don García de' Medici
c.1550. Oil on panel, 48 x 38 cm
P5

Initially trained in the workshop of the Florentine Mannerist painter Pontormo, Bronzino (Agnolo di Cosimo) was noted for his remarkable technical skills. This, together with the sophisticated elegance with which he endowed his sitters, led him to become the preferred portraitist of the Florentine aristocracy. From 1539 he worked for Cosimo de' Medici, Duke of Tuscany (1519–1574), creating the official image of the new regime that had assumed power in Florence after the dissolution of the Republic in 1531. In this work Bronzino depicts García de' Medici (1547–1562), one of the children of Cosimo and Eleonora de Toledo, at the age of around three or four. Bronzino was usually more concerned to convey the sitter's social status than to focus on individual psychology. In this case, however, he clearly shows an emotional engagement with the child, who holds an orange blossom in his right hand and an amulet in his left.

202
DANIELE DA VOLTERRA
Volterra, 1509–Rome, 1566

Portrait of a Nobleman
1550–55. Oil on panel,
101 x 64 cm
P69

The relationship between this portrait and a very similar one in the Museo di Capodimonte, Naples, has allowed the present work to be attributed to Daniele da Volterra (Daniele Ricciarelli da Volterra) rather than to Bronzino or Girolamo da Carpia, to whom it was previously attributed. It is the only known portrait by the artist, as the one in Naples is only a *modello* or *ricordo*. Volterra here creates a typically Mannerist portrait characterised by cold *eleganzia*. Although the sitter was formerly identified as Alfonso II d'Este, Duke of Ferrara, his aristocratic status is established only by the double-handed sword on which he rests his left hand, while the book may refer to his intellectual interests.

203
FEDERICO BAROCCI
Urbino, c.1535–1612

The Nativity

c.1595. Oil on canvas,
134 x 105 cm
P18

Initially trained in Urbino, Barocci became familiar in Rome with the work of Raphael and of the Mannerist artist Taddeo Zuccaro (1529–1566). During a subsequent period in Parma he probably also saw the work of Correggio. In 1567 he painted this work for Francesco Maria III della Rovere, last duke of Urbino. After a period of several years in which he did not paint at all, Barocci reveals a highly individual style in which he has brought together all his earlier influences. He was better able to express his ability in small-format, intimate works. Barocci's art reveals a great sensitivity to the treatment of light, an exquisite colour derived from Venetian painting and a notable realism in the treatment of bodies in space. All these elements result in what has been termed a 'mystic naturalism' which gave his images a poetic quality. Here the focal point is the infant Christ, on whom the kneeling Virgin gazes in rapture. In 1604 the painting was given to Margaret of Austria, wife of Philip III, by Bernardo Maschi, the Duke of Urbino's ambassador in Spain.

Venice

One of the most celebrated features of the Museo del Prado is its extraordinary collection of Venetian paintings, which constitute the largest group of works from this school outside Venice itself. This collection was assembled over centuries as a result of the close relationship between the Spanish monarchs and the leading Venetian painters. During the reign of the Catholic kings (1479–1516) and the first years of Emperor Charles V's rule (reigned 1519–1556) artistic tastes inclined towards the Flemish style that so delighted Isabella the Catholic, but the meeting between Charles and Titian [213, 214] in the early 1520s marked the beginning of a fruitful relationship that would have crucial consequences for the future of the Spanish Royal Collections. Charles's son Philip II (reigned 1556–1598) not only continued this relationship with Titian, although in a slightly different way, but also widened his interests to embrace other leading members of the Venetian school such as Tintoretto [223-225], Veronese [227-229] and the Bassano [230]. As a result, Venetian painting formed the core of the collection in the Alcázar in Madrid, El Escorial and El Pardo, the latter during the reign of Philip III (1598–1621), a moment of transition with regard to the interest in Venice. By the mid-seventeenth century this neo-Venetian trend in art influenced the collecting interests of Philip IV (reigned 1621–1665), who was advised by Velázquez. The artist maintained contacts with the Venetian school during his trips to Italy, and the possession of Venetian works became synonymous with luxury and wealth. The acquisition of works at sales of private collections, and especially at the famous sale following the execution of Charles I of England in 1649, further increased the quantity and quality of the Venetian holdings in the Royal Collections.

This relationship between the Spanish monarchy and Venetian painting was naturally reflected in contemporary art and art theory and the particular development of Spanish painting, especially during the seventeenth century, would be inconceivable without the impressive and fascinating presence of works by the most important Venetian painters in the Royal Collections.

204
GIOVANNI BELLINI
Venice, c. 1430–1516

*The Virgin and Child
between Two Saints*
c. 1490. Oil on panel, 77 x 104 cm
P50

While the authorship of this work has been questioned on occasions, the quality of the colour and the composition, and its relationship with a securely attributed work by the artist in the Accademia in Venice, allow this painting to be set within Bellini's mature output. The figure on the right and the clothes of the saint on the left are different from those in the Accademia. In the Prado version Bellini achieves a balance between his personal interest in form and echoes of Andrea Mantegna [183] and Antonello da Messina [184], in particular in the subtle outlining of the figures against the neutral background.

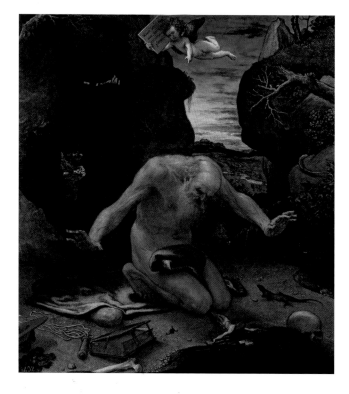

205
LORENZO LOTTO
Venice, c.1480–Loreto,
1556/1557

St Jerome Penitent
1546. Oil on canvas, 99 x 90 cm
P448

The emphasis on penitence
in this work is explained by
the fact it was commissioned
for the Ospedale dei Derelitti
ai Santi Giovanni e Paolo,
a hospital that was one of
the main centres of Catholic
reform in Venice. St Jerome,
here seen emulating Christ's
martyrdom spiritually
and physically, is accompanied
by many of his symbols. The
scourge and skull allude to his
life as a hermit, the red cloak
to the saint's cardinalship,
and the book to his translation
of the Bible, known as the
Vulgate. Finally, the lion in the
background refers to a legend
whereby the saint removed a
thorn embedded in the animal's
paw. Thereafter, the lion always
remained meekly by his side.

206
BERNARDINO LICINIO
Poscanti de Bergamo,
c.1489–Venice, 1560

*Agnese, the Painter's
Sister-in-law*

c. 1525–30. Oil on canvas,
98 x 70 cm
P289

Previously in the Royal
Collections, this is one of the finest
paintings by Licinio, an artist who
specialised in portraiture and group
portraits in particular. Taking
his starting-point from models
developed by Palma Giovane
and Pordenone and to a lesser
extent by Titian and Lorenzo
Lotto, the artist focused on half-
length figures, although without
achieving the skill and mastery of
those artists, and his work retains
a certain provincialism. The lively
and refined depiction of the
face reveals the artist's closeness
to the sitter, his sister-in-law.

207
LORENZO LOTTO
Venice, c.1480–Loreto, 1556/1557

Micer Marsilio and his Wife
1523. Oil on canvas, 71 x 84 cm
P240

This work was commissioned by the textile merchant Giovanni Cassotti, the father of Micer Marsilio, probably with the intention of pointing out to his son the obligations involved in his recent marriage. This is indicated both by the laurel that relates to *virtus* (courage, chastity and eternity) and the yoke over the husband and wife. Lotto subtly refers to the woman's submissive role by locating her on the far right of the canvas leaning towards Marsilio, who places the wedding ring on his wife's hand in a gesture that is significantly not repeated on her part. The scene is thus less a demonstration of the sitters' social status as a recognition of their emotional relationship, and is enriched with references to classical art in the figure of Eros who embraces the pair. He in turn derives from the iconography of *Juno Pronuba* or *Juno Iugalis*, the divinity associated with matrimony which Lotto could have seen on a sculpted funerary stele during his trip to Rome, while the gesture of Eros' outstretched arms derives from contemporary German art.

Titian

For much of the fifteenth century Venetian painting remained rooted in archaic medieval practices, indebted to the Byzantine tradition, and it was not until the last third of that century that it made any progress. In addition to the family and artistic ties that linked the flourishing workshop of the Bellini to Andrea Mantegna, we also find the influential presence of Antonello da Messina from the mid-1470s, whose role would be crucial in the dissemination of the technique of oil painting. Some years later the presence of Leonardo was also crucial, and his importance for Venetian art should not be restricted to his influence on the work of Giorgione. Giovanni Bellini's mastery not only of the rational depiction of space but also, and especially, of a carefully thought-out relationship between perspective, colour and light provided the germ for the development of the remarkable Venetian school, characterised by the pre-eminence of colour over line (the latter characteristic of the Tuscan-Roman tradition). Within this context, the leading role was indisputably played by Tiziano Vecellio, 'Titian'. Trained in the Bellini workshop along with Giorgione, his pre-eminent status is evident in works in the Prado such as the early *Virgin and Child with St George and St Dorothy*, a panel that abandons earlier static compositional formulas; the remarkable canvases for the Gonzaga *camerino* [209, 210], whose public exhibition in Rome in the 1630s encouraged an important neo-Venetian trend in painting of that date; and the late *Self-portrait* of the artist in his old age [222], acquired at the posthumous sale of Rubens, an artist who played a key role in the reception and appreciation of Titian in Spain.

From devotional paintings to mythological scenes and portraits, Titian's work was always central to the Royal Collections. The artist adapted his style with extraordinary facility to the representational requirements of Charles V (reigned 1519–1556) and Philip II (reigned 1556–1598) and to the strictly artistic requirements of the latter. Titian also contributed a specific image of classical antiquity that Philip IV (reigned 1621–1665) and Velázquez adapted to Roman Baroque taste in the Galería del Mediodía in the Alcázar, as well as the vibrantly erotic mythological universe of the so-called 'Titian Vaults', also in the Alcázar.

208
TITIAN
Pieve di Cadore,
c.1489–Venice, 1576

*Venus with an Organist
and a Dog*

c.1550. Oil on canvas,
136 x 220 cm
P420

Titian painted up to five versions of this subject for various clients. In all of them the goddess's body is the principal element. In this example her serene beauty is intruded on only by the dog's innocent playfulness, while her nudity is emphasised by the contrast between the crimson bed cover and the red curtain and still more by the presence of the clothed, sword-bearing musician with his bold gaze, highlighting the eloquent eroticism of the scene. These sensual allusions are also evident in the pleasant garden in which we see a couple strolling, dogs pursuing deer and above all the fountain with a satyr, on which a peacock is perched. The painting has been interpreted as of merely erotic significance but it has also been seen as a Neoplatonic work in which sight and hearing are understood as the ideal vehicles for attaining a knowledge of beauty, although it should perhaps be read in terms of matrimony, as the ring on Venus' right hand seems to indicate.

209 ↑
TITIAN
Pieve di Cadore,
c.1489–Venice, 1576

The Worship of Venus
c.1518–19. Oil on canvas,
172 x 175 cm
P419

210 →
The Bacchanal of the Andrians
1523–26. Oil on canvas,
175 x 193 cm
P418

The Worship of Venus and *The Andrians* were painted for Alfonso d'Este, third Duke of Ferrara, for the *camerino d'alabastro* in his residence in that city. While the meaning of the *camerino* is not totally clear, the celebration of the powers of love and wine through the figures of Venus and Bacchus would seem to relate to the duke's own personality, and Alfonso directed the artists involved not only regarding the themes but also the texts on which their compositions should be based (Philostratus and Ovid). Titian was commissioned to paint *The Worship of Venus* on the death of the painter Fra Bartolommeo in 1517, basing his work on a drawing by the latter, albeit with

significant modifications. His painting includes a great crowd of little putti playing among baskets of apples in a garden presided over by a statue of Venus. The location of the statue on the right presumably relates to the position of the painting in the *camerino* and also allows the viewer's attention to focus on the landscape and putti. *The Worship of Venus* is a hymn to nature's fertility and a celebration of a frank and physical initiation into the labours of love. In *The Andrians* the drunkenness inspired by wine and music becomes a delightful erotic intoxication, as indicated in the musical score on the foreground, which is a canon attributed to the Flemish composer Adriaen Willaert that reads: 'he who drinks and does not drink again does not know what drinking is'. This joyful, Bacchic frenzy is reflected in the rhythm of the composition and in the measured use of colour across the canvas. In addition, Titian combined a refined study of first hand observation with implicit references to classical sculpture and various contemporary works of art, particularly Michelangelo's *Battle of Cascina* and Giovanni Bellini's *Feast of the Gods*, the latter also painted for the *camerino* and with which Titian's canvas establishes a rich dialogue. *The Andrians* was one of the artist's most celebrated and influential works.

212 →
TITIAN
Pieve di Cadore,
c.1489–Venice, 1576

Adam and Eve

c.1550. Oil on canvas,
240 x 186 cm
P429

It is likely that Antonio Pérez,
the ill-fated secretary to
Philip II (reigned 1556–1598),
inherited this painting from
his father, Gonzalo Pérez,
who must have commissioned
it from Titian. Based on
the account in Genesis, it is
inspired by classical Greek
sculpture and contemporary
art such as the fresco of the
same subject by Raphael in
the Stanza della Segnatura,
as well as by Dürer's print of
1504. Titian may have derived
the unusual iconographical
elements from the latter,
including the boy transformed
into a serpent and the fox,
associated with the devil.
The superb colour of the
background landscape
contrasts with a rather
surprising clumsiness in Eve's
pose and in the relationship
between her left hand and
forearm, and with the rather
incongruous placement
of Adam, which Rubens
intentionally modified in his
famous copy also in the Museo
del Prado.

211 ↑
TITIAN
Pieve di Cadore,
c.1489–Venice, 1576

*Federico Gonzaga,
I Duke of Mantua*

1529. Oil on panel, 125 x 99 cm
P408

Son of the celebrated
Renaissance art patron Isabella
d'Este, Federico was raised to a
dukedom by Charles V in 1530.
A leading patron of Titian, it was
Federico who introduced the
painter to the emperor. Given
his dissolute past and in view
of his forthcoming marriage
to Margherita Paleologa,
the wealthy heiress to the
marquisate of Monferrato,
Federico no doubt wanted to
mitigate his doubtful reputation
through the present portrait,
which shows him as courtly
and elegant. He is depicted
wearing a sumptuous doublet of
blue velvet with gold embroidery
and red hose, with a gold and
lapis lazuli rosary around his
neck and accompanied by a
Maltese dog, symbolising piety
and fidelity respectively. With
its fawning recognition of its
master, the dog also conceals
a veiled homage to the painter's
ability to achieve the dazzling
realism evident in this portrait.

Titian and the Habsburgs

One of the most fruitful artist-patron relationships in the entire history of art was the one that linked Titian with the Habsburgs for more than forty years. The painter's work perfectly responded to the Spanish monarchy's requirements for a rhetorical style and Titian adapted his work to the courtly, political and devotional needs of Charles V (reigned 1519–1556) and Philip II (reigned 1556–1598).

The Italianate taste of court circles and the particular interests of the collector and connoisseur Cardinal Granvela (1517–1586) and of Charles's sister, Mary of Hungary, brought Titian into still closer contact with his royal patrons. His portraits responded to the propagandist, political functions required of the artistic image in the Renaissance, and introduced a gravity expressed, in the words of the contemporary art theoretician Ludovico Dolce, through a 'heroic majesty'. Titian thus formulated the prototype of the formal portrait in which the sitter is presented standing and life-size, framed by theatrical curtains or architectural elements that emphasise the expressionless face, itself one of the essential attributes of majesty [214, 215]. Furthermore, the artist also fulfilled Charles's devotional requirements through works such as *The Glory* [220] and *The Burial of Christ* [221], and his re-interpretations of iconographic images such as the '*Virgin Dolorosa*' [219]. The allegorical complexity of his paintings allowed for interpretations that went beyond the apparent simplicity of the subject: for example, the moralising meaning of the so-called 'Furies' [218] still retained its significance in the seventeenth century and these works never lost their admonitory character. In addition, Titian was aware of the value of paintings as works of art destined for private use, such as the famous '*Poesie*' that he painted for Philip II between 1554 and 1562. The '*Poesie*' are primarily noted for their formal qualities, such as the counterbalancing of *Danaë* and *Venus and Adonis* [216, 217], with their explicit references to the Horatian idea of *ut pictura poesis* ('a poem is like a painting') and to the debate on the relative merits of painting and sculpture.

Over the years Titian's work became the central part of the collection of Philip IV (reigned 1621–1665). His paintings occupied the most prominent positions both in the Alcázar in Madrid and in the redecoration of El Escorial in which Velázquez played an important role.

213
TITIAN
Pieve di Cadore,
c.1489–Venice, 1576

Equestrian Portrait of Charles V at Mühlberg
1548. Oil on canvas,
332 x 279 cm
P410

This is possibly Titian's most important portrait of Charles V and is the key to his relationship with the Habsburg dynasty. It was painted to commemorate the victory of the emperor's troops over the Protestant princes of the Schmalkaldic League at Mühlberg on 24 April 1547. In this equestrian portrait, Titian combined the iconography of the classical Roman tradition with that of the Christian knight, his models being the famous equestrian sculpture of Marcus Aurelius on the Capitoline and other more recent interpretations of that work. The political connotations are more overt than the religious ones in order to emphasise Charles's pacific intentions and his qualities as the ruler of an empire, symbolised here by his impassivity despite the prancing of the horse. The references to the battle itself are implicit rather than explicit and the painting is in effect a fusion of pictorial realism and symbolic significance.

214
TITIAN
Pieve di Cadore,
c.1489–Venice, 1576

*The Emperor Charles V
with a Dog*
c.1532–33. Oil on canvas,
192 x 111 cm
P409

It is possible that Titian
painted Charles V during
his trip to Bologna in late
1532 or more probably in
early 1533, basing his work
on the portrait that Jacob
Seissenegger had painted for
Charles's brother Ferdinand
of Austria. This may have been
in response to Charles's own
request, but Titian introduced
significant changes. He made
the emperor's face more
elegant, raising his eyelids and
thus giving him a more lively
expression and also made
his body slimmer and taller.
Charles is located in the
foreground of a space whose
breadth and depth derive from
the use of a low viewpoint, a
device that gives the sitter
a greater monumentality.
This effect is also due to the
masterly use of colour that
envelops the sitter and his
docile hound with a delicate
grace. It is not surprising
that this is one of Titian's
finest portraits and that it
was an important work for
the subsequent development
of the state or formal portrait.

215
TITIAN
Pieve di Cadore,
c.1489–Venice, 1576

Philip II
1551. Oil on canvas,
193 x 111 cm
P411

During his first trip outside the
Iberian Peninsula,the future
Philip II arrived in Milan
between late 1548 and early
1549 where he commissioned
various portraits from Titian.
It seems likely, however, that
this work, Titian's first known
portrait of Philip, was executed
two years later in Augsburg.
The relationship between
painter and patron would last
to the end of Titian's life,
despite the fact that Philip,
who was accustomed to
the detailed style of Flemish
painting, was surprised by the
finished portrait. Unable to
understand the mature artist's
brilliantly loose technique,
he believed the portrait to
have been painted too hastily.
Using a judicious degree of
idealisation, Titian adroitly
conveyed the idea of majesty
by emphasising the presence
of the column, the side table
and the parade armour. These
elements subsequently became
standard ones in state or formal
portraits of the Habsburg
house and were then adopted
by other European royal
houses.

216 ↑
TITIAN
Pieve di Cadore,
c.1489–Venice, 1576

*Danaë and the Shower
of Gold*
1553. Oil on canvas, 129 x 180 cm
P425

217 →
Venus and Adonis
1554. Oil on canvas, 186 x 207 cm
P422

Titian referred to the '*Poesie*' – six canvases on mythological themes painted for Philip II between 1553 and 1562 – as intended for a *camerino* for private use, a room that may or may not have existed in reality. *Danaë and the Shower of Gold* and *Venus and Adonis* formed part of that series. *Danaë* was the earliest in the series and narrates the story of the princess locked up by her father Acrisius, king of Argos, as it had been foretold that her son would kill him. Zeus fell in love with her, transforming himself into a shower of gold to possess her, and their union resulted in the birth of Perseus. Titian replaced

Cupid by an old, avaricious servant in order to create a solid, volumetric composition in which the pearly-skinned, naked young woman passively awaiting her lover contrasts with the ancient, active figure of the servant. *Venus and Adonis* was probably inspired by the *Fable of Adonis, Hippomenes and Atalanta* published in Venice in 1553 by another client of Titian's, Diego Hurtado de Mendoza (1503–1575), given that in the *Metamorphoses* Ovid does not recount this mythological episode in which Venus attempts to prevent her beloved Adonis from going to the boar hunt that will result in his

death. *Venus and Adonis* forms a sensual dialogue with *Danaë* as it depicts the goddess seen from behind in contrast to Danaë seen frontally. The pictorial handling of *Danaë* contrasts with the more sculptural style of *Venus and Adonis*, thus referring to the contemporary debate in Italy that contrasted the merits of painting and sculpture and of Titian and Michelangelo, the leading masters in the two art forms. To contemporary eyes the *Venus* was more erotic, not just because of the goddess's voluptuous bare back but also because of her impassioned restraint of the young Adonis.

218 ←
TITIAN
Pieve di Cadore,
c.1489–Venice, 1576

Tityus
After 1566. Oil on canvas,
253 x 217 cm
P427

This canvas, which belonged
to Íñigo López de Mendoza,
fifth Duke of El Infantado,
is a late replica by Titian
himself of a work in a group
commissioned by Mary of
Hungary, Charles V's sister
and governor of the Low
Countries, to decorate the
Great Hall in her castle
at Binche (Belgium). Based
on the fourth book of Ovid's
Metamorphoses, they depicted
four condemned figures:
Tityus, Sisyphus, Ixion and
Tantalus. The last one was
probably painted by Michiel
Coxcie and was lost together
with *Ixion* in the fire at the
Alcázar in 1734. Traditionally
known as the 'Furies', they
offered a mythological
reading of the fate of those
who rise up against their
ruler. They thus refer to the
potential rebellion of subjects
against Charles or possibly
to his brother Ferdinand's
pretensions to the imperial
throne, which he finally
attained on the death of
Charles. The size of the
figures and their unstable
poses together with the
sombre colours emphasise
their tragic nature, clearly
revealing Michelangelo's
influence on Titian's art and
on these canvases in particular.

219 →
TITIAN
Pieve di Cadore,
c.1489–Venice, 1576

The Virgin Dolorosa
1554. Oil on panel, 68 x 61 cm
P443

220
TITIAN
Pieve di Cadore,
c.1489–Venice, 1576

The Glory

1551–54. Oil on panel,
346 x 240 cm
P432

Charles V commissioned this
panel from Titian during the
court's second period in Augsburg
from 1550 to 1551. The pyramidal
composition gives particular
emphasis to the Trinity and
to the role of the Virgin as
intercessor. She is dressed in
the same blue as the figures
of the Father and Son and walks
towards them, while below
we see various Old Testament
figures. The painting confronts
Protestantism with an exaltation
of the Catholic orthodoxy of
the Habsburg dynasty, some of
whose members are depicted
on the right wrapped in white
shrouds. They include the
emperor himself, his wife
Elizabeth of Portugal and their
son Philip II. Significantly,
the painting does not include
Ferdinand of Austria or his son
Maximilian, a circumstance
that can be related to the
family schism provoked by the
imminent succession to the
imperial throne. The painting
must have been of enormous
devotional importance to the
emperor, who asked for it when
he was dying at Yuste in order
that he might gaze upon it.

221
TITIAN
Pieve di Cadore,
c.1489–Venice, 1576

The Burial of Christ

c.1559. Oil on canvas, 137 x 175 cm
P440

Titian depicted this episode from the New Testament several times, in most cases selecting the moment when Christ's inert body is placed in a classical-style tomb whose reliefs of Cain and Abel (on the left) and the Sacrifice of Isaac (on the right) prefigure the subject of the work itself. In 1557 Titian had a first version with half-length figures sent to Philip II but it was lost in transit. He compensated for this loss two years later with the present version. It has been suggested that the unwonted motif of the Virgin supporting her son's arm was derived from *I Quattro libri de la humanità di Christo* by Titian's friend Pietro Aretino (1492–1556). The present canvas is a key work in Titian's oeuvre as it is the first clear example of the pronounced pathos and drama that would characterise his religious compositions. Another autograph version with numerous differences, given by the Venetian Senate to Philip II's secretary, Antonio Pérez, is also in the Prado.

222
TITIAN
Pieve di Cadore,
c.1489–Venice, 1576

Self-portrait

1562. Oil on canvas, 86 x 65 cm
P407

This is undoubtedly one of the most moving of all self-portraits in art, particularly because of the sober refinement with which Titian painted himself, aged over seventy but still resolute in his desire to be recorded for posterity as a painter. This desire for immortality explains the unusual choice of the profile portrait, a typology derived from classical Roman coins and which therefore has symbolic connotations associated with eternal fame.

The austere palette emphasises the majestic but intimate mood of the portrait. It draws attention to the relationship between the golden chain (which denotes Titian's status as a Knight of the Golden Spur) and the brush that he firmly holds in his right hand and which has brought about his elevation to the nobility, conferred on the artist by Charles V in 1533. Despite his advanced age Titian was still, in Vasari's words, 'ready to paint'.

Tintoretto

In contrast to Titian's close association with the leading members of the Spanish Habsburgs, the relationship between the Spanish monarchy and Jacopo Robusti, known as Tintoretto, was more complex. The extravagant nature of his work, which contemporaries described as *'cosa rara'* and which was only appreciated in certain circles, failed to meet the taste and above all the intentions of Philip II. In the context of the distinctive Counter-Reformatory ambit of the late sixteenth century, Philip was more interested in the clarity of the religious message than in Tintoretto's artistic excesses. Furthermore, various Venetian painters competed to occupy the position in relation to the king left vacant by Titian's death in 1576. This is the context in which we should view the first documented work by Tintoretto in Spain, *The Adoration of the Shepherds* of 1584. Destined for the altar at El Escorial, it was finally installed in a different location because of its disconcerting approach to the subject. His work fared little better with private collectors. Only from the time of Rubens's second visit to Spain between 1628 and 1629 did the situation vary. Rubens, who owned and copied works by Tintoretto, must have inspired Velázquez with an enthusiasm for the artist, and as a consequence Velázquez enriched the Spanish royal collections with copies of paintings by Tintoretto that he himself executed during his first trip to Italy and with original works that he acquired during his second trip.

The changing taste of the Crown was followed by that of private collectors from the time of Antonio Pérez, private secretary to Philip II, to that of the Marquis of Leganés and the Count of Monterrey in the seventeenth century. As a result, more Venetian paintings arrived in Spain. The generous gift that Prime Minister Luis Méndez de Haro made to Philip IV (reigned 1621–1665) included *Christ washing the Disciples' Feet* and *The Rape of Helen* [224, 225], and thus further improved the quality of the Tintoretto holdings in the Royal Collections. Only the collections of the monarch, the Haros and the Enríquez de Cabrera showed any inclination towards the work of Tintoretto, but by the late seventeenth century this situation had changed and the inventory of the Alcázar records forty-three works ascribed to the artist, both originals and copies.

223
TINTORETTO
Venice, 1518–Venice, 1594

The Knight with the Golden Chain
c.1550. Oil on canvas,
104 x 77 cm
P378

This is one of Tintoretto's finest portraits and perhaps the best by the artist in the Prado's collection. The painter succeeds in creating a sense of movement without using exaggerated or complicated devices. The face is the most expressive element, although the depiction of the hands is unusually detailed. The narrow colour range is exploited to its fullest potential and the overall dark tone is subtly broken by the gleams of light on the white shirt and by the glint of the golden chain. The chain, the costly but subdued clothing and the upright bearing of the sitter betray his rank, though he is yet to be identified. The old identifications of Veronese or Leone Leoni have been followed by a more recent suggestion that it shows the Venetian patrician, politician and writer Nicolò Zeno (1515–1565).

224
TINTORETTO
Venice, 1518–Venice, 1594

*Christ washing
the Disciples' Feet*

1547. Oil on canvas, 210 x 533 cm
P2824

Despite recent doubts regarding the commission and the painting's original location, it seems clear that this picture was painted for the Scuola del Sacramento in the Venetian church of San Marcuola. Like the rest of the *scuole*, this confraternity ensured that the Host was properly venerated. Hence the subject of the painting, which is closely linked to the institution of the sacrament of the Eucharist. The subject can also be related to various public ceremonies held in sixteenth-century Venice which reproduced the ceremony of the washing of the feet, a symbol of humility and fraternal love. For this reason, Tintoretto combined idealised elements such as the architectural setting (inspired by Vitruvius' *Tragic Scene*, as reconstructed by Serlio in his treatise) with realistic features, such as the furniture, the figures of the Apostles and the dog. The slanted perspective reveals the artist's interest in the final location of the work: if viewed from the right the depiction of the kneeling Christ can be correctly read.

225

TINTORETTO
Venice, 1518–Venice, 1594

The Rape of Helen
c.1578–79. Oil on canvas,
186 x 307 cm
P399

The painter sets the mythical tale of the Rape of Helen in a contemporary naval context, possibly inspired by the number of images that had proliferated following the Battle of Lepanto in 1571. This combat saw Venice, Spain and the papal troops, allied as the so-called Holy League, battling against the Turkish forces. Tintoretto had already proved his ability in naval battle scenes, such as the outstanding *Fasti Gonzageschi* of the same period, but he is possibly even more successful here. He emphasises the dramatic side of the classical story by placing the main figures in the foreground, silhouetted against the light, and contrasting them with the background figures, who, reduced to mere decoration, almost disappear. Drama also derives from the dynamic mood achieved through the colour, the chiaroscuro, and the relationships between the figures, the principal formal issue that Tintoretto was obliged to resolve here.

226 →
DOMENICO TINTORETTO
Venice, 1560–1635

Lady with Bared Breasts
c.1580. Oil on canvas, 61 x 55 cm
P382

The old attribution to Tintoretto indicates the quality of this canvas, which, however, may well be by the artist's son Domenico. A certain anatomical clumsiness in the depiction of the hands and the rather incongruous relationship between the figure and the setting do not detract from the subtle contrast of the sitter's pink cheeks with the pale softness of her breasts, interrupted only by the double string of pearls that echo the pearls in her hair. The delicacy of her hairstyle, painted with thin, carefully applied brushstrokes, is continued in the soft shadows of the neck and the transparent piece of gauze that frames and emphasises the nudity of this anonymous young woman. She may be Veronica Franco, a famous Venetian courtesan. The portrait would thus fall within the category of depictions of 'Venetians' or courtesans, which proliferated in the mid-sixteenth century and were well represented in the Spanish Royal Collections. Six works of this type are now in the Museo del Prado, depicting the sitters in various degrees of nudity, culminating in the present work.

Veronese

Paolo Caliari, known as Veronese after his native city of Verona, is undoubtedly one of the most celebrated Venetian painters. He moved to Venice permanently in 1553 where he began work on a major series of public commissions. These reveal his Roman style with its rhythms and chromatic notes that were essentially different from the Venetian tradition and which earned him immediate success in Venice. This success was also due to a lack of any reference in his paintings to the social, economic and spiritual crises that were gradually undermining the power of the Serenissima, marking a crucial difference between his work and Tintoretto's. The reconstruction of the Doge's Palace after the fires of 1574 and 1577 resulted in a period of intense artistic activity in which Veronese played an active role. His greatest works date from 1580 onwards and are characterised by the measured relationship between the figures with their calm, dignified gestures, and the architectural backgrounds inspired by contemporary buildings and in particular the work of Andrea Palladio (1508–1580). These characteristics are evident in the paintings by the artist in the Prado, namely *Venus and Adonis* [227], possibly acquired by Velázquez during his second trip to Italy of 1649 to 1651; *The Finding of Moses* [228], which may have belonged to the Marquis de la Torre and which then passed into the Royal Collections; and *Christ among the Doctors in the Temple* [229], which arrived during the reign of Charles II and occupied a prominent position in the Salón de los Espejos in the Alcázar in Madrid. In the 1580s Veronese's links with Spain were more active: the death of Juan Fernández Navarrete, El Mudo, led Philip II's ambassadors to contract Veronese to work on the fresco decorations of the monastery of El Escorial. In addition, the painter Nicolás Granelo (died in 1593) bought an *Annunciation* by Veronese for the high altar of the monastery, along with a *Nativity* by Tintoretto.

227
VERONESE
Verona, 1528–Venice, 1588

Venus and Adonis
c. 1580. Oil on canvas,
162 x 191 cm
P482

Passionately fond of the hunt, Adonis devoted himself to this pursuit and emboldened by his own bravery ignored the pleas of Venus, who feared that he would be devoured by wild animals. One day when out hunting on Mount Lebanon he was pursued by a boar that he had wounded. The boar overpowered him and killed him. Veronese depicts the moment prior to the fateful hunt when the goddess bends over Adonis, as he lies with his head on her lap and a naked cupid seen from behind holds back the straining dog that is anxious to awaken its master. Veronese conveys this blend of premonitory emotions through his use of sensual colours, from Venus' blue and gold damask robe to the glowing orange mantle that covers the still relaxed body of Adonis. The landscape with its evening light acts as an emotional and dramatic backdrop to the forthcoming tragedy. The painting was designed as a pair to *Cephalus and Procris* (Musée de Strasbourg). Both illustrate episodes from Book X of Ovid's *Metamorphoses*, devoted to amorous relationships cut short by the sudden death of one of the lovers.

228
VERONESE
Verona, 1528–Venice, 1588

The Finding of Moses
1560–75. Oil on canvas,
57 x 43 cm
P502

One of the most important Old Testament figures, Moses was born during the reign of a pharaoh who, concerned at the large number of Israelites living in his kingdom, published an edict to bring to an end the prosperity of the chosen people: 'Every son that is born ye shall cast into the river' (Exodus 1, 22). Abandoned on the banks of the Nile at the age of only three months, Moses was rescued by the pharaoh's own daughter. Although based on the biblical account, the scene is presented as if it were simply an episode in the life of a Venetian lady set in the rural surroundings of her Palladian villa. Various versions of this subject are known, including versions in vertical format like those in the Prado and the National Gallery of Washington, and in horizontal format such as the one in the Dresden Gemäldegalerie. This version in Madrid is perhaps the finest of all due to its sparkling brushwork, chromatic richness and the range of formal values characteristic of the artist.

229
VERONESE
Verona, 1528–Venice, 1588

*Christ among the Doctors
in the Temple*
1548. Oil on canvas, 236 x 430 cm
P491

Considered a free copy of a work of the same subject by Jacopo Bassano in the Cure Collection in London, various experts have questioned the date of 1548 that appears on the book held by one of the doctors and have preferred to date it to the 1560s. Whatever the case, this is an outstanding work within Veronese's oeuvre. The architectural background (based on designs by Andrea Palladio) helps to diminish the excessive complexity evident in some of his earlier work,

and the figures and setting relate naturally and smoothly. Both the background architecture with its majestic colonnade and the gestures and gazes of the figures, in particular the central ones seen from behind, focus the viewer's attention on the key element in the composition: Christ's imperious gesture to the doctors who, according to St Luke's Gospel, were 'astonished at his understanding and answers'.

The Bassano

Together with his sons Francesco (1549–1592) and Leandro (1557–1622), Jacopo da Ponte, known as Bassano after his native city, represented one of the leading artistic families in Venice. Their workshop played a key role in the dissemination of Venetian painting from 1570 onwards. Almost industrial in proportion, their output reached all of Europe and in particular Spain, where their works were among the best represented in the Royal Collections after Titian. Between 1590 and 1620 the Bassano became the champions of modern art, a position that was consolidated during the reign of Philip IV (reigned 1621–1665), possibly because their type of naturalism conformed to the stipulations of the Council of Trent and its professed aim to indoctrinate through the vehicle of art. The works of the Bassano were even sent to South America where their compositions offered simple readings of biblical narratives, set in natural settings with the figures engaged in everyday activities surrounded by objects and animals depicted with deliberate naturalism. Widely copied, these paintings represented one of the poles in the debate on the representation of the real. This debate opposed the supremacy of colour with that of drawing, and the undefined with the perfectly finished. The first information on works from the Bassano workshop in Spain dates from 1574, when the Spanish ambassador in Venice sent a *Story of Jacob* to Philip II (reigned 1556–1598), greatly pleasing the king. Some time after this it is recorded that the powerful Duke of Lerma, favourite of Philip III (reigned 1598–1621), owned twenty-nine originals and seventeen copies. Through diplomatic gifts and the energetic efforts of professional art dealers, the number of works by the Bassano increased in the Royal Collections, and by the death of Charles II in 1700 they constituted the largest holdings of such works in Europe. This fact affected the output of Spanish painters and the influence of the Bassano is evident in works by Juan de Roelas, Juan Sánchez Coello and above all Pedro Orrente [49], who is thought to have spent an early period of training with Leandro Bassano.

230
JACOPO BASSANO
Bassano del Grappa, c.1510–1592

God reprimanding Adam

c. 1577. Oil on canvas,
191 x 287 cm
P21

The discovery of Adam's disobedience when he ate the fruit of the tree in the Garden of Eden, encouraged by Eve and disobeying God's orders, is a subject little represented in art. Jacopo Bassano used it as a pretext to show his skill in the naturalistic depiction of animals, a characteristic of his personal style for which he was particularly celebrated. He departed from the biblical text only in depicting God in the sky. The painting was given by Manuel Filiberto of Savoy, Viceroy of Naples, to his cousin Philip IV, undoubtedly because he was aware of the monarch's taste for Bassano's art. From 1636 it was in the Alcázar in Madrid, at one time even hanging in the king's bedroom.

Italian Painters at the Spanish Court

The relationship between Italian artists and the Spanish monarchs was not limited to Titian's long association with Charles V and Philip II. Some artists entered the service of the royal family, such as Sofonisba Anguisciola, who arrived in Spain in 1560 as lady-in-waiting to Elizabeth of Valois and embarked on an important career as a portraitist [231]. Others were summoned for specific projects, such as the decoration of El Escorial, which had to some extent been neglected after the death of Navarrete el Mudo in 1579. Luca Cambiaso, Federico Zuccaro, Pellegrino Tibaldi and the Leoni worked there between 1583 and 1596. Among Zuccaro's assistants was the young Vicente Carducho who would later become the leading artist at court until he was displaced by Velázquez, who settled permanently in Madrid in 1623 and had the support of the king. Velázquez undertook the first negotiations with the Bolognese artists Angelo Michele Colonna and Agostino Mitelli, experts in fresco decoration who came to Madrid in 1657 to paint in the Alcázar and the Buen Retiro. Some time afterwards, in 1692, the most famous fresco painter of the day, Luca Giordano [244, 245], arrived at the court to devote his talents to the exaltation of the Spanish monarchy at El Escorial, the Alcázar and the Casón del Buen Retiro.

With the arrival of the Bourbons, portraiture was monopolised by French artists (Jean Ranc, Louis-Michel Van Loo), while fresco painting continued in the hands of the Italians, many of them summoned by the queen (particularly Isabella Farnese), the Marquis of Scotti or the *castrato* Farinelli (Carlo Broschi, 1705–1782). Andrea Procaccini, Bartolomeo Rusca, Jacopo Bonavia, Jacopo Amigoni [253] and above all Corrado Giaquinto [254] and Giovanni Battista Tiepolo [255, 256] embellished the new royal residences such as the Royal Palace in Madrid or worked on the redecoration of old ones such as the palaces at Aranjuez and La Granja. Decorations for royal celebrations and for theatrical or operatic spectacles as well as work in the royal manufactories, in particular the Royal Tapestry Manufactory, influenced the practice of Spanish painters from Antonio González Velázquez to Francisco de Goya.

231
SOFONISBA ANGUISCIOLA
Cremona, c.1532–Palermo, 1625

Portrait of Philip II
Before 1582. Oil on canvas,
88 x 72 cm
P1036

Sofonisba Anguisciola has here modified a portrait of Philip II of around 1565, possibly with the intention of making it a pair with one of Anne of Austria, the king's fourth wife. Changing her original composition, she gave the monarch a more elegant pose and plainer garments, but left the face as it was in the earlier portrait to disguise the twenty-two years' difference between the king and his wife. The simplicity of the decorative elements, reduced here to the order and chain of the Golden Fleece, the ruff and cuffs, and their contrast with areas of pale flesh tones, give this portrait a marked monumentality in which the private and public aspects of the king's life are perfectly fused. The rosary that he holds in his left hand can be related to the institution of the Feast of the Rosary by Gregory XIII in 1573 after the Battle of Lepanto (1571).

The Bolognese Painters

The new approach that became evident in late sixteenth-century Italian art was characterised by two figurative trends which, although different and even contradictory, had one single aim: that of a return to the real world and to the imitation of nature as basic principles in artistic creation. This process involved a disregard for the academicism, sophisticated virtuosity and exaggerated complexity of Mannerism. Caravaggio is traditionally considered the most revolutionary and daring of these artists, but the brothers Agostino (1557–1602) and Annibale Carracci (1560–1609) and their cousin Ludovico Carracci (1555–1619) made a vital contribution in Bologna with the foundation of the Accademia dei Desiderosi, known from 1590 onwards as the Accademia degli Incamminati. This institution played a crucial role in late sixteenth- and early seventeenth-century painting as it launched the classicising trend in Baroque painting by giving artists complete freedom in the recapture of what the Carracci themselves termed '*il vero naturale*'. In this context, the publication in 1582 of the *Discorso intorno alle immagini sacre e profane* by Cardinal Gabriele Paleotti was extremely important as it called for a reform of religious painting in accordance with the Council of Trent (*continues on page 280*)

232 ↓
DOMENICHINO
Bologna, 1581–Naples, 1641

The Sacrifice of Isaac
c.1627–28. Oil on canvas,
147 x 140 cm
P131

This painting dates from the time of Domenichino's involvement in the church of Sant'Andrea della Valle in Rome and is an excellent example of the idealising classicism that he first learned in the Bolognese studio of Ludovico Carracci and then after 1602 in Annibale Carracci's Roman studio. Domenichino's serene, delicate style, which is significantly indebted to Raphael, was crucial for subsequent artists, including Poussin. The painting depicts an Old Testament episode that is always interpreted as a prefiguration of the Passion of Christ in which Abraham, the first great patriarch of Israel, prepares to sacrifice his son Isaac to comply with God's command, as narrated in Genesis.

233
ANNIBALE CARRACCI
Bologna, 1560–Rome, 1609

Venus, Adonis and Cupid
c. 1590. Oil on canvas,
212 x 268 cm
P2631

In contrast to other works in the Prado that depict the story of Venus and Adonis, in particular those by Titian and Veronese, Annibale Carracci chose the moment when the handsome young Adonis comes across the goddess during the hunt. Venus is still bleeding slightly from the arrow of love that a mischievous Cupid has fired at her. The artist has omitted the narrative and dramatic elements in order to focus on the emotional ones, emphasised by the gestural interplay of the two figures – languid and restrained in the case of the splendid, warmly painted nude Venus, and energetic and dynamic in the case of Adonis. The sensuality of the encounter is conveyed through the three-dimensionality of the volumes and the gentle chiaroscuro, both characteristic of Annibale, which reveal the influence of Correggio [194].

(*continues from page 278*) and a rethinking of iconography as it moved beyond the ideas proposed by the Mannerist painters.

Particularly influenced by Correggio's sensual naturalism and by Venetian painting and with a marked admiration for Raphael, the Carracci adopted an evocative, almost Romantic style in their interpretation of the Italian classical tradition in painting, aiming to make it more comprehensible. Reality in its fullest sense was their model *par excellence* and they introduced subject matter disdained in earlier painting such as scenes of everyday life and even grotesque or ugly subjects. As a result their work, and particularly that of Annibale, reveals an overt tension between realism and idealised classicism. They advocated the continual practice of drawing, a discipline that they consistently recommended to their pupils and followers (hence the name of their academy, the Accademia del Disegno), outstanding among whom were Guido Reni and Domenichino.

234 ↓
GUIDO RENI
Bologna, 1575–1642

St Sebastian
c. 1601–14. Oil on canvas,
170 x 133 cm
P211

Characterised by a tight handling and pronounced chiaroscuro, this painting must date from Reni's period in Rome between 1601 and 1614 due to its affinities with the work of Caravaggio. Reni later abandoned Caravaggio's dramatic approach in favour of a serenity tempered by a lyrical purity closer to the classicist, idealising trend. Reni depicts the saint, a Roman soldier martyred for his defence of Christianity, after he has been wounded with arrows shot by fellow members of the Praetorian guard but before he is found and cured by St Irene. The scene is set in a splendid landscape whose evening light models the saint's naked torso and the shadow projected by his face on his neck, contrasting with the brightly lit area of his right shoulder. Various versions of this composition are known, of which the one in the Musée du Louvre is outstanding. The present canvas was formerly in the collection of Isabella Farnese and was copied on numerous occasions.

235
GUIDO RENI
Bologna, 1575–1642

Hippomenes and Atalanta
c. 1612. Oil on canvas,
206 x 297 cm
P3090

According to the mythological account, an oracle had told Atalanta that she would be in danger if she chose to marry. Obliged to do so by her father, she announced that she would marry whoever was able to defeat her in a race, warning that she would kill anyone who failed. Having got rid of various suitors in this way, she encountered Hippomenes. Every time Atalanta was about to catch up with him, he threw one of the golden apples that Venus had given him. As she paused to pick them up he overtook her and won the race, gaining the young woman's love and her body as his trophy. The painting is a masterpiece of Bolognese classicism and of Reni's art on account of its restrained depiction of the nudes, clear narrative and refined sense of movement. In 1796 it was in the Sala Reservada of the Academia de San Fernando.

Caravaggio and Naturalism

Michelangelo Merisi, known as Caravaggio after the town near Milan where his family came from, was the leading figure in the reaction against the academicism and sophistication of late sixteenth-century Mannerism. A return to a study of the real world and the imitation of nature (rejected by Mannerist artists in favour of the artistic ideal, a principle codified in contemporary treatises by Lomazzo and Zuccari) was one of the starting-points of the Caravaggesque revolution, one of the most important and long-lasting revolutions in the history of painting. The dictates of the post-Tridentine Church, which promulgated a direct, faithful representation of the biblical stories, provided Caravaggio's other reference point. It is true that he initially looked to an earlier naturalist tradition, but his experimental approach took that naturalist trend to its highest point through the depiction of dramatic, key moments in the Bible. He reduced the narrative elements to the essentials, frequently extending the composition into the viewer's space and paying particular attention to emotions expressing states of the soul, whose detailed analysis dates back to Leonardo's Milanese period. The powerful impact that Caravaggio's works had in his own day, and which is still evident today, was also determined by his innovative use of light. This isolates the figures, creating neither space nor atmosphere, and his bold contrasts of light and darkness were intended to be read in moral terms. Tenebrism, as this particular form of painting has been termed, locates the viewer before the divine and its manifestations without intermediaries. This confrontational approach led to some of his works being rejected by his patrons. Caravaggio had no school in the strict sense of the term but he did have a very large number of followers. These artists adopted his figurative models but their works lacked the spiritual content of Caravaggio's own art, which is now so appreciated in the modern age.

236
CARAVAGGIO
Milan, 1571–Porto Ercole, 1610

David and Goliath
c.1600. Oil on canvas,
110 x 91 cm
P65

The story of David and Goliath is taken from an episode in the Bible recounting Israel's struggle against the Philistines. It tells how a young shepherd, using only a sling and five stones, killed the giant Goliath and so brought about the final defeat of the Philistines (1 Samuel 17, 51). The present painting, which may be contemporary with Caravaggio's work in the church of San Luigi dei Francesi in Rome, focuses on a moment not previously represented in art and not mentioned in the biblical account. David is tying up Goliath's hair so that he can carry back the head and present it to the Israelite troops. The monumental composition is highly original, occupying all the foreground and juxtaposing beauty and ugliness, light and dark, serenity and cruelty, with the two heads arranged along a vertical line. The first reference to the work dates from 1794 but it may have been in the collection of G. B. Crescenzi or in that of the Count of Villamediana, both early seventeenth-century collectors.

237
DANIELE CRESPI
Milan (?), 1597/1600–1630

The Pietà

c. 1626. Oil on canvas,
175 x 144 cm
P128

Crespi's restrained naturalism,
evident in the still-life elements
here, and his narrative skill,
marked in this case by highly
expressive pathos, made
him one of the key figures
in Counter-Reformation
art in Milan. His works were
frequently copied, particularly
in Spain, and Ribera's *Pietà* in
the Augustinian convent of
Monterrey, Salamanca (1634),
is a careful interpretation of
this canvas by Crespi, whose
sensitivity always remained
close to the circle of Cardinal
Federico Borromeo and
the short-lived Accademia
Ambrosiana.

238
GIOVANNI SERODINE
Rome (?), 1600–1630

*St Margaret brings
a Young Man back to Life*
c.1620. Oil on canvas,
141 x 104 cm
P246

239
ORAZIO GENTILESCHI
Pisa, 1563–London, 1639

The Finding of Moses

1633. Oil on canvas, 242 x 281 cm
P147

Son of the Levite Amran and his wife Jochebed, Moses was born during the reign of an Egyptian pharaoh who, alarmed at the growing prosperity of the Israelites, issued an edict saying that all recently born male children were to be cast into the Nile. Moses was abandoned on the banks of the river at the age of only three months, but was saved by the pharaoh's own daughter. The scene was painted by Gentileschi during his English period (1626–1639) as a gift for Philip IV, possibly to gain royal support for Gentileschi's return to his native Tuscany or perhaps in a veiled allusion to the birth of Prince Baltasar Carlos on 17 October 1629. Despite being influenced by Caravaggio, Gentileschi did not forget his Tuscan training, which is evident in the reflections and transparent passages of the silks and draperies and in the elegance of the forms, the result of his confident, bold draughtsmanship. The Prado has another version of this subject painted by Veronese some decades earlier [228].

Other Artistic Centres: Florence, Genoa and Ferrara

The presence of the Carracci and of Caravaggio in Rome in the early years of the seventeenth century made the city the centre of pictorial innovation. Outside Rome, local schools of painting continued to flourish and found support in the theoretical art texts of the day, from Carlo Ridolfi (1594–1658) to Cesare Malvasia (1616–1693). In comparison to Roman painting these schools were, however, relatively minor. Overall, the aim of their discoveries was similar to the aim of Caravaggio or of the Carracci: to bring an end to the empty formal emphasis of late sixteenth-century painting. Florentine, Genoese and Bolognese painters gave their work a new emotional vigour which largely derived from a liberation of forms and colours and which fully conformed to the ideals of the Catholic Church.

Elegant line and radiant local colour were the distinctive features of Florentine painting, evident in works such as Furini's with its masterly depiction of the soft sensuality of the female nude [243]. This is perhaps surprising in Furini, given that from 1633 he was prior of Sant'Ansano in Mugello.

The small maritime republic of Genoa continued to maintain its wealth and prosperity due to its highly active banking activities, giving the city a degree of cosmopolitanism reflected in the work of Giacchino Assereto (1600–1649) and Bernardo Strozzi [242]. Both echoed the Caravaggism of Orazio Gentileschi and Simon Vouet (1590–1649) as well as the Flemish colouring of Rubens and Van Dyck.

Guercino's work [240] is distinctive in tone, and in his native Cento, near Ferrara, he developed an innovative style of painting that is rich in warm colours, Baroque movement and striking atmospheric effects. These qualities became more muted in line with his new classicism following his time in Rome between 1621 and 1623 and his definitive move to Bologna in 1642. This classicism would come to impose itself in Rome following the heated disputes between the splendidly Baroque style of Pietro da Cortona (1596–1669) and the more restrained, measured approach of Andrea Sacchi (1599–1661). Sacchi's most distinguished pupil was Maratta [241], who from 1650 opened the way to the subsequent classicism of Anton Raffael Mengs and the writings of his friend Johann Joachim Winckelmann (1717–1768).

240
GUERCINO
Cento, 1591–Bologna, 1666

Susannah and the Elders
1617. Oil on canvas, 176 x 208 cm
P201

This canvas was originally painted for the Ludovisi family, together with *Lot and his Daughters* (now in El Escorial) and *The Prodigal Son* (in the Galleria Sabauda in Turin). In 1664 it was inherited by Philip IV from the estate of Prince Niccolò Ludovisi and by 1667 was in El Escorial. It was moved to the Prado prior to 1843 and became one of the masterpieces of the collection. Guercino harmonises his pictorial and narrative devices to give this work an exceptionally intense emotional charge. The naturalism does not contradict the carefully thought-out composition with its contrast between the agitated, lascivious pose of the elderly men enveloped by the dark background, and the serene, magical beauty of Susannah with her ivory skin. According to Malvasia, the figure of Susannah was apparently inspired by a woman imprisoned in the Episcopal jail in Bologna. True or not, Malvasia's story indicates how Guercino's naturalism followed a direction comparable to Caravaggio's, whose work he may not have known before arriving in Rome in 1623.

241
CARLO MARATTA
Camerano, 1625–Rome, 1713

The Painter Andrea Sacchi
c.1661–62. Oil on canvas,
67 x 50 cm
P327

Andrea Sacchi (1599–1661) was the leading representative of the classicist trend in Roman decorative painting in the mid-seventeenth century which was opposed to the more Baroque style led by Pietro da Cortona. Sacchi is portrayed here by his most important pupil, Carlo Maratta, the most celebrated and sought-after artist in Rome from 1650 onwards. Maratta looked back to the work of sixteenth-century artists and to the innovations of Annibale Carracci and Guido Reni, creating a nostalgic, poetic style. Originally owned by Maratta, it was thought for many years to be a self-portrait.

242
BERNARDO STROZZI
Genoa, 1581–Venice, 1644

St Veronica and the Veil
1620–25. Oil on canvas,
168 x 118 cm
P354

The legend of St Veronica's veil dates back no earlier than the fourteenth century. The name Veronica literally means 'true image' ('*vera icon*'). According to tradition, Veronica approached Christ on the road to Calvary and lent him her veil or handkerchief to wipe the blood and sweat from his face. When Christ returned it to her it was imprinted with his image. Using a bright, harmonious palette and influenced by Rubens and Caravaggio, Strozzi introduced a new, updated approach to Venetian painting in the first half of the seventeenth century with works such as this, which dates from his Genoese period. Such paintings have rich, brilliant colours and vigorous, glowing flesh tones.

243
FRANCESCO FURINI
Florence, 1603–1646

Lot and his Daughters
1635. Oil on canvas, 123 x 120 cm
P144

Ferdinand II (1610–1670), Grand Duke of Tuscany, gave this canvas to Philip IV in 1649 on the occasion of Philip's wedding to Mariana de Austria (1634–1696). The choice of subject may have been deliberate as Lot had incestuous relations with his own daughters in order to continue his line after he had abandoned Sodom and his wife had been turned into a pillar of salt (Genesis 19, 30-38). Similarly, Philip IV married his niece, compelled by the need to secure a male heir. The subject of Lot was traditionally chosen by artists as one of the most appropriate for showing their skill in depicting the female nude and Furini took full advantage of this occasion to contrast the full, rounded flesh of the young women as they encourage their father, and the cold, blue background that reduces the narrative elements to a minimum. Two preparatory drawings for Lot's daughters are in the Uffizi, Florence, and there is a copy of the painting with the addition of a view of Sodom in flames in a Madrid private collection.

Luca Giordano
and Neapolitan Painters

Due to a series of fortunate circumstances, the Neapolitan school became one of the most important schools of the seventeenth century and was enormously influential for the subsequent development of painting. Caravaggio's presence in Naples, first in 1606 when he was fleeing from the Roman authorities, and again between 1609 and 1610, together with the quality of the work that he left there and the fact that José de Ribera settled in Naples permanently in 1616, further animated an already flourishing artistic scene. Painters as open to innovations as Giovanni Do and the Master of the Annunciation to the Shepherds were already established there.

The work of the Neapolitan Luca Giordano combines the ideas of Venetian colour with Pietro da Cortona's epic compositions, of which he was the worthy successor. An itinerant artist who worked in Rome, Florence, Venice, Bergamo and Madrid, Giordano was famously known for his rapid execution and prolific output [244, 245]. Paradoxically, his remarkable stylistic versatility gave rise to his most recognisable style, which was grandiloquent, festive and rhetorical in equal degrees. In 1692 Giordano was made court painter to Charles II (reigned 1675–1700) and executed an outstanding body of work in Madrid and at El Escorial. This work made a profound impression on Spanish artists from Palomino to early Goya, though Giordano's influence also extended to Italian artists of the stature of Solimena, Giaquinto and Amigoni.

Lanfranco trained with the Carracci and was an assistant to Annibale Carraci on the famous Galleria Farnese in Rome. He also produced important work in Naples, including numerous altarpieces and a series of commissions for the Gesù Nuovo, the Charterhouse at San Martino and the Treasury Chapel. He was commissioned by the viceroy in Naples to complete the unfinished decoration of the Buen Retiro palace in Madrid, a project that involved Finoglia, Fracanzano, Falcone, De Leone and Gargiulo, all leading Neapolitan painters. The close links between Spain and Naples also affected the work of Artemisia Gentileschi [246], who abandoned the elegance of her father's style in favour of an innovative Caravaggism. Another artist who worked in Naples was Massimo Stanzione [249]. Bernardo Cavallino can be considered the most refined representative of Neapolitan painting with his atmospherically lyrical and sparkling scenes achieved through an exquisite handling of colour and light [248].

244
LUCA GIORDANO
Naples, 1634–1705

Rubens painting the Allegory of Peace
c.1660. Oil on canvas,
337 x 414 cm
P190

This composition reveals Giordano's versatility in assimilating, adopting, updating and transforming pictorial tradition, in this case with a focus on the work of Rubens. He imitates Rubens's style almost to perfection, confirming the hypothesis that this is a homage to the great Flemish painter. The work has, however, been traditionally interpreted as an allegory of Peace as Rubens is seated over Discord, painting a matron who seems to be putting Fury to flight.

245
LUCA GIORDANO
Naples, 1634–1705

The Prudent Abigail
1696–97. Oil on canvas,
216 x 362 cm
P166

The beautiful and prudent
Abigail was wife of the wealthy
shepherd Nabal of Carmel. One
day he offended David, who was
at that time leader of a band of
outlaws. Abigail prevented the
future king from taking revenge
by going out to meet him with
a large amount of food for his
army, as we see here. Abigail
begged David to punish her
rather than her foolish husband
(1 Samuel 25, 24). She made such
a good impression on David
that when Nabal died of grief

upon learning what his wife had
done, David married her and
she bore his second son, Chileab
(II Samuel 3, 3) or Daniel
(1 Chronicles, 3, 1).

246

ARTEMISIA GENTILESCHI
Rome, 1593–Naples, 1652/1653

The Birth of St John the Baptist

c.1633–35. Oil on canvas,
184 x 258 cm
P149

This work, which is signed on the fictive piece of paper on the left, is one of the artist's masterpieces. It formed part of a series of five paintings on the life of St John the Baptist, painted for a small church dedicated to the saint in the Buen Retiro in Madrid. The other four compositions, all by Massimo Stanzione and all now in the Prado, are *The Announcement of the Baptist's Birth*, *St John the Baptist takes leave of his Parents*, *The Preaching in the Desert* and *The Beheading of St John the Baptist*.

St John was the son of the Virgin Mary's cousin Elizabeth and of Zacharias, a priest at the temple in Jerusalem. Incredulous at the Archangel Gabriel's announcement of the imminent birth of their son when he and his wife were so advanced in age, Zacharias was struck dumb until the day of John's birth. He is depicted on the left writing his son's name. It has been said that this scene, with its magnificent still-life elements, is one of the most delicately painted interiors in seventeenth-century painting.

247 ↑
GIOVANNI LANFRANCO
Parma, 1582–Rome, 1647

Funeral of a Roman Emperor
1634–37. Oil on canvas,
335 x 488 cm
P234

This canvas was part of a major commission comprising thirty-four paintings on the history and customs of ancient Rome that were hung in the recently built Buen Retiro Palace in Madrid. Six are now lost. The agent acting for the Spanish monarch was Manuel de Fonseca y Zúñiga, sixth Count of Monterrey and Viceroy of Naples between 1631 and 1637. The Viceroy spared no efforts to secure the services of the most celebrated Italian artists of the day. The present work has an unfinished appearance, mainly because Lanfranco's principal activity as a fresco painter tended to influence his style, for which he was criticised in the nineteenth century. The symbolism of the Buen Retiro programme has not yet been satisfactorily explained.

248 →
BERNARDO CAVALLINO
Naples, 1616–Naples, 1656

The Martyrdom of St Stephen
After 1645. Oil on canvas,
71 x 93 cm
P7466

This small painting is one of the best examples of the technical elegance and refinement achieved by Cavallino. His starting-point was the Neapolitan realism of Caravaggio and Ribera, to which he added a palette derived from Rubens and Van Dyck. Here the painter represents the death of the first Christian martyr as narrated in Acts 7, 55-60. Stephen was one of the seven deacons who worked with the Apostles. Persecuted by the Jews, he was stoned to death, asking God during his martyrdom to pardon his executioners, as we seem to see here.

249 ↑
MASSIMO STANZIONE
Orta de Antella,
c.1585– Naples, c.1656

Sacrifice to Bacchus

c.1634. Oil on canvas,
237 x 358 cm
P259

Stanzione represents the academic trend in Neapolitan art. He gives a greater sense of narrative and emotion to his works than either Ribera or Artemisia Gentileschi. The present work was commissioned for the Buen Retiro but was in the Alcázar in Madrid by 1666.

It may have formed a thematic pair with *Bacchus' Visit to the Poet Icarus* by Ribera, of which only some fragments survive, and which is known through a copy. Signed on the vessel on the right, the work bears echoes of Titian [210] and Annibale Carracci [233].

Eighteenth-century Italian Painting

In the eighteenth century, Italy continued to be a forum for aesthetic debate, contributing new solutions to modern painting. The country was a complex artistic mosaic as the different states favoured different styles according to their particular artistic inheritance. The resulting diversity ranged from the French influence at the Piedmontese court, evident in the work of Domenico Duprà, to the Roman academicism of Sebastiano Conca or the late Neapolitan Baroque of Solimena, all represented in the Prado. In addition to these native Italian painters there were a number of foreign artists attracted by the Grand Tour. The international art market increased the diversity of pictorial output as new private collectors emerged, with more modern tastes and different requirements from those of the various courts. As a result we see the rise of one of the most prolific genres of the entire eighteenth century: *vedute* or view paintings. Italy became a pictorial motif in itself, transformed into views of ruins, cities or picturesque settings. The genre offered a variety of options, from the grandiose vision of Antiquity in the work of Vanvitelli or Panini in Rome to the technical brilliance of Canaletto and Guardi in Venice. In the eighteenth century Venice was one of the most versatile and avant-garde cities, where early acceptance of the Rococo fused with the traditional Venetian preference for colour, resulting in an unprecedented visual richness that would give an international dimension to artists such as Amigoni or Tiepolo. Spain particularly benefited from this situation thanks to royal patronage. While the new Bourbon dynasty left royal portraiture in the hands of French artists, the decoration of palaces such as La Granja were primarily entrusted to Italians. Isabella Farnese (1692–1766) imposed her particular taste, summoning artists such as Andrea Procaccini, Sani and Rusca to Spain. The Spanish crown acquired important collections of paintings, including that of Carlo Maratti, and also commissioned works from Panini, Conca, Constanzi, Imperiali, Trevisani and Solimena. In addition, the Infante Don Carlos, king of Naples and future Charles III of Spain, sent paintings to the Spanish court. Influenced by the famous singer Farinelli (Carlo Broschi, 1705–1782), Ferdinand VI invited famous artists like Amigoni and Giaquinto and favoured the most Rococo style. Charles III (reigned 1759–88) brought together two trends currently fashionable in Italy: the exuberant colour of Tiepolo and the Neoclassicism of the German painter Anton Raffael Mengs. Heir to this great tradition of patronage and collecting, the Prado thus has an incomparable collection of eighteenth-century Italian painting.

250
POMPEO GIROLAMO BATONI
Lucca, 1708–Rome, 1787

George Legge, Viscount Lewisham
1778. Oil on canvas,
127 x 100 cm
P48

Batoni studied classical art and the legacy of the Renaissance and the Baroque, gaining international fame as a portraitist through his depictions of foreign travellers, producing works that were greatly in demand from those on the Grand Tour. The Grand Tour, in which travellers visited and studied Europe, and especially the classical heritage of Italy, was part of the aristocratic education of the day and is perfectly embodied in this work depicting the English nobleman George Legge, Viscount Lewisham and third Count of Dartmouth. Batoni's portraits, with their faultless technique, featured elements referring to the Tour, in this case the bust of Faustina the Younger and the map of Italy. The artist adapted to the taste of his clients by adopting the English style of portraiture, in itself derived from Van Dyck. The painting was on board the *Westmoreland*, a British ship, when it was captured by the French. In 1783 Charles III acquired part of the cargo, including the two works by Batoni now in the Prado.

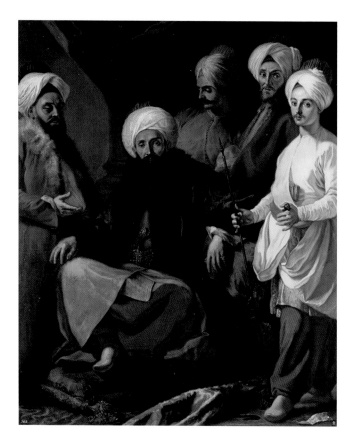

251
GIUSEPPE BONITO
Castellamare di Stabia,
1707–Naples, 1789

The Turkish Diplomatic
Mission in Naples in 1741
1741. Oil on canvas, 207 x 170 cm
P54

Trained in the late Neapolitan Baroque style of his master Francesco Solimena, with echoes of Luca Giordano, Bonito developed a more personal style influenced by Rococo and later by Neoclassicism. His success as a portraitist resulted in his appointment in 1751 as painter to Charles VII of Naples (reigned 1734–1759), the future Charles III of Spain (reigned 1759–1788). The present painting was made a decade earlier, when he was chosen to record one of the most exotic events to have taken place in the new kingdom of Naples. On 30 August 1741 and in response to the visit of a Neapolitan mission made the year before, the Effendi Hagi Hussein, ambassador to the Ottoman Empire, arrived in Naples. Using rich colours and a theatrical composition, Bonito conveyed the details of the dress and un-Italian ways of his sitters that caused so much surprise in Naples. The result is a work that fully responds to the eighteenth-century taste for the exotic, and the painting was sent by the king to Madrid as a gift for his mother, Isabella Farnese.

252
ANTONIO JOLI
Modena, 1700–Naples, 1777

*The Embarkation
of Charles III in Naples*
1759. Oil on canvas, 128 x 205 cm
P232

His training with the perspectival painter Antonio Rinaldi, and then with Giovanni Paolo Panini in Rome, as well as his time in Venice with Canaletto and Belotto, prepared Joli to become one of the most celebrated Italian *vedutisti*. He worked as a theatrical set designer in Germany, London and Madrid, arriving in Naples shortly before Charles III's departure. When Ferdinand VI died in Spain without an heir, Charles VII of Naples (reigned 1734–1759) was the next in line to the throne. He thus renounced the throne of Naples and returned to Spain to be crowned as Charles III (reigned 1759–1788). The Spanish royal squadron arrived in Naples on 4 September and the embarkation took place on 7 October, the moment documented in this canvas. Joli's painting is rigorously topographical, and his viewpoint is from the top of the Castel Novo looking over the port of Naples, from where he depicted a panoramic marine view with Vesuvius in the background. The artist depicted the various elements in great detail, presenting a faithful portrayal of Neapolitan society as it watched the great event.

253
JACOPO AMIGONI
Venice, c.1680/82–Madrid, 1752

The Discovery of the Cup in Benjamin's Bag
c.1748–50. Oil on canvas, 285 x 350 cm
P5260

Amigoni was one of the first Italian painters to exhibit the new Rococo taste. An artist of international scope and a prosperous businessman, he travelled around Europe, entering the service of Ferdinand VI in Spain in 1747 on the recommendation of the singer Farinelli. In Madrid, Amigoni was appointed court painter and was made the first director of the recently created Real Academia de San Fernando. This work and its companion piece,

Joseph in the Pharaoh's Palace, also in the Prado (P5261), were commissioned to decorate the Sala de Conversación in the Royal Palace of Aranjuez. The story of Joseph functions as an allegory of the virtues of a just and virtuous monarch. The architectural setting reveals Venetian influence while the use of pink, pale yellow and sky blue tones reflects the Rococo aesthetic. The sketchy nature of this painting suggests that it remained unfinished on Amigoni's death.

254
CORRADO GIAQUINTO
Molfetta, 1703–Naples, 1766

Justice and Peace
c.1754. Oil on canvas,
216 x 325 cm
P104

Corrado Giaquinto was trained in Naples, influenced by Francesco Solimena's late Baroque and by the artistic legacy of Luca Giordano. He moved to Rome where he worked with Sebastiano Conca and was influenced by a more restrained academicism and by the new Rococo aesthetic. Giaquinto pursued a brilliant international career, not just as a painter on canvas but also as a fresco painter. Following the death of Amigoni and the departure of Louis-Michel Van Loo, he was invited in 1753 to Madrid where the decoration of the new royal palace required the efforts of the best painters in Europe. Appointed court painter and director of the Academia de San Fernando, he executed numerous frescoes and canvases for Spanish royal residences. This allegorical canvas uses a characteristically eighteenth-century palette of pinks, greens and pale yellows, combining echoes of the Baroque with a Rococo elegance and delicacy. Justice symbolically embraces Peace and cupids display the abundance resulting from their union, while others melt down items of military equipment.

The Tiepolo

The new approach to art that had evolved in early eighteenth-century Venice and which combined local tradition with the Rococo, resulted in one of the most attractive styles in Europe. It was adopted by artists such as Jacopo Amigoni, Giovanni Antonio Canaletto, Francesco Guardi and Giambattista Tiepolo. Following his initial training in Gregorio Lazzarino's studio, Tiepolo opted for a tenebrist style of contrasting light and colour and for Giovanni Battista Piazzetta's compositional monumentality. In 1717 he became a member of the painter's guild and two years later married Cecilia Guardi, sister of the *vedutista* Francesco Guardi. Two of his nine children, Giandomenico and Lorenzo, also became painters [256, 370]. Tiepolo's first commissions for local aristocrats, such as the decoration of Ca' Zenobio (1718–1720), reveal his sombre early style with its echoes of Piazzetta. This style is to be seen in the work from this series in the Prado (*Queen Zenobia before the Emperor Aurelian*, P3243). The influence of Sebastiano Ricci was crucial for Tiepolo's move towards a lighter palette as he assimilated the Venetian tradition, particularly that of Veronese. His work in Udine (1726–1728) already reveals the luminosity and light colours that will be characteristic of his mature style. Tiepolo worked in Milan and Bergamo (1731–1732) and was even commissioned to decorate the royal palace in Stockholm, a project he ultimately did not accept. He also worked in the Palazzo Labia in Venice, while in 1750 he collaborated with his sons on the decoration of the Residenz in Würzburg, whose frescoes reveal the splendour of his mature, epic style. Charles III of Spain (reigned 1759–1788) invited him to decorate the State rooms of the new royal palace in Madrid. By now elderly and accompanied by his sons, Tiepolo arrived in Madrid in 1762. Between 1762 and 1766 he decorated various State rooms including the Throne Room, while he was also made court painter and undertook other commissions such as the series for the monastery of San Pascual in Aranjuez. However, the dawn of Neoclassicism in Madrid (and with it the arrival of Mengs) undermined Tiepolo's leading position. On the death of Giambattista in 1770, one of his painter sons, Lorenzo, remained in Spain while the other, Giandomenico, returned to Venice, although he continued to undertake commissions for the Spanish crown.

255
GIAMBATTISTA
TIEPOLO
Venice, 1696–Madrid, 1770

The Immaculate Conception
1767–69. Oil on canvas,
281 x 155 cm
P363

Tiepolo's production in Madrid marks the culmination of both his career and his personal style. This canvas was one of a series of seven commissioned from Tiepolo by Charles III for the monastery of San Pascual in Aranjuez and is one of the artist's masterpieces. The grandeur of Mary's figure derives from the use of a low viewpoint combined with a vertical emphasis. The elegant turn of her body introduces a restrained dynamism, while the density of the colour and the pearly textures make the entire paint surface vibrate. The Virgin's naturalistically painted face is imbued with a profound serenity that contrasts with the liveliness of the angels. In the clouds we see various attributes of the Immaculate Virgin such as the lily, rose, palm tree, mirror, orb, crescent moon and serpent. In 1775 the entire series was replaced by another executed by Mengs and his Spanish followers Maella and Bayeu, revealing how Tiepolo's vibrant, colourful style was by that date considered unsuitable in the new Neoclassical climate.

256
GIANDOMENICO
TIEPOLO
Venice, 1727–1804

Christ Falls on the Road to Calvary

1772. Oil on canvas, 124 x 145 cm
P358

Giambattista Tiepolo's fame initially eclipsed the work of his son, Giandomenico, until the latter returned to Venice in 1770, after which date he formulated a more individual idiom both with regard to style and subject matter. This *Christ Falls on the Road to Calvary* formed part of a 'Via Crucis' of eight episodes that was commissioned from Madrid for the monastery of San Felipe Neri. The scene, which is based on accounts, in the New Testament (Matthew 27, 32-33; Mark 15, 21-22; Luke 23,

26; and John 19, 17), substitutes Giambattista agreeably heroic style for a more dramatic but also more detailed one. The white wood of the cross, soaked in blood, creates a chromatic echo with the body of Christ. Behind Christ we see Simon the Cyrene, who helped him with the cross, the holy women, and the group that accompanied Christ to his place of crucifixion on Mount Golgotha, visible on the left. A preparatory sketch for this canvas is in the Museo Lázaro Galdiano in Madrid.

257
GIAMBATTISTA TIEPOLO
Venice, 1696–Madrid, 1770

Abraham and the Three Angels

c. 1770. Oil on canvas,
197 x 152 cm
P2464

Painted in Madrid for an unknown location, this canvas entered the Prado through a donation in 1924. It is an excellent example of Tiepolo's mature style, depicting the moment when the three pilgrims who visit Abraham and Sarah reveal themselves as angels of God and announce the forthcoming birth of Isaac. The painting creates and combines two different realities through the use of two different viewpoints. The lower level, with the remains of the shared meal, the pilgrim's staff and the kneeling patriarch, corresponds to the moment prior to the revelation. From above and seen in oblique perspective, the clouds reach down to the ground and the angels seem to be descending to earth. Tiepolo succeeds in recreating the moment of the apparition through the use of this double viewpoint with its superimposed angles. The colour helps the narrative, with lighter and more luminous tones for the angels that seem to make them float, and thicker, ochre tones in the lower part of the composition.

The Early Netherlandish and Flemish Painting Collection

With over a thousand paintings and a large number of emblematic works, early Netherlandish and Flemish painting of the fifteenth to seventeenth centuries occupies a very prominent place in the Museo del Prado. Many of these works originate from the royal collections, whose legacy largely accounts for the museum's holdings today.

Flemish painting of the fifteenth and sixteenth centuries is exceptionally well represented in the Prado. The Netherlands became part of the Spanish crown in the sixteenth century, and this political link was further reinforced by the personal interest that Philip II (reigned 1556–1598) took in the early Netherlandish painters. The monarch acquired masterpieces by the most outstanding painters of this school, such as Van der Weyden [262, 263, 265] and Bosch [268-272], but also paintings by later artists such as Patinir. To these should be added those who worked for the monarch, including the great portraitist Anthonis Mor. Indeed, apart from distinguished absentees like Jan van Eyck and Hugo van der Goes, the museum possesses works by the most important artists of this school: Rogier van der Weyden, Robert Campin [259-261], Dirk Bouts [267], Hans Memling [266], Bosch, Joachim Patinir [273-275], Pieter Bruegel the Elder [286] and Anthonis Mor [287, 288, 290]. Most of these paintings came from the royal estates, though some were acquired through bequests, such as Van der Weyden's *Virgin and Child* [262], which entered the museum in 1930 as part of the Fernández Durán Bequest.

The Royal Collection also featured works by major seventeenth-century Flemish painters. This is not surprising given that the southern Netherlands remained under the control of the Spanish monarchy after the northern Netherlands – corresponding to the present-day Netherlands – became independent in 1581. Of paramount importance are the nearly ninety works by Rubens that the Prado owns [302 ff.], many of them outstanding masterpieces, including some he painted in Spain during his two visits to the country in 1603 and 1628. Paintings by his disciples Van Dyck and Jordaens complete the collection of works by the most prominent seventeenth-century Flemish painters, though we also find paintings by Jan 'Velvet' Brueghel [291-293], Paul de Vos and David Teniers [296], who are well represented in the museum.

Southern Netherlandish Painting of the Fifteenth and Sixteenth Centuries

The fifteenth century witnessed the shaping of a new style of painting in Bruges and Tournai, an '*ars nova*', spearheaded by the Van Eyck brothers, Robert Campin and Rogier van der Weyden. Reality took preference over the symbolic and decorative abstraction of the Gothic period, and mastery at capturing the properties of materials, light, space and human emotions led both sacred and worldly themes to be depicted in a lifelike manner. The background to these changes was the wealthy Netherlandish society, the most highly developed in Europe, which made the details of its daily life the timeless setting for works of art. The antecedents of this interest in everyday life were Burgundian court painting and the art of fourteenth-century miniaturists, which took an early delight in depicting contemporary objects and human types. Precise draughtsmanship and the development of oil painting made highly detailed descriptions possible and the range of colours attained a hitherto unknown richness. Using these new techniques, artists modelled the forms and properties of objects, affording them volume and tangibility in space with highly effective illusionistic lighting. Each tiny detail was handled as one of the many individual parts that combined to make a whole: the artistic image. The technical and aesthetic quality achieved by this method reflected a modern, self-satisfied world that possessed a new sensibility to nature and the emotions. And so, together with Italy, the Netherlands became the driving force behind European art of the fifteenth and sixteenth centuries.

From the first quarter of the fifteenth century painters like Memling, Gerard David and Patinir combined this heritage with Italian Renaissance designs. Artists' workshops moved away from Bruges to Antwerp, which became the principal metropolis of Northern Europe in the sixteenth century. The old style gave way permanently to the Renaissance, with artists like Quentin Massys, Jan Gossaert and Bernard van Orley, resulting in a complex art scene that evolved from the elaborate rhetoric of the Mannerists to the naturalism of Peter Bruegel the Elder and the classicism of Michiel Coxcie and Anthonis Mor. The works initially produced for local patricians were soon much sought after abroad, giving rise to one of the first great European art markets. Spain's relations with the Netherlands, at first economic and later political, established a channel for cultural and artistic exchange that tipped the balance of Spanish taste in favour of Netherlandish rather than Italian art.

258
SCHOOL OF JAN VAN EYCK

The Fountain of Grace.
The Triumph of the Church
over the Synagogue
1430s. Oil on panel,
181 x 119 cm
P1511

The subject matter of this panel relates to theological disputes in fifteenth-century Castile, immersed at the time in heated discussions between Jews and Christians. It was painted in Bruges by a follower of Van Eyck. The master himself was then working on the polyptych of the Mystic Lamb for Ghent cathedral. The perfect vertical symmetry and horizontal arrangement of the composition into three staggered terraces add a hierarchical meaning to the painting. At top centre is God on his throne, between Mary and John the Evangelist. At his feet is the lamb from which flows the spring of the Water of Life, an idea taken from the Apocalypse. The stream crosses the second terrace, a lovely garden populated by angel musicians, and springs again from a fountain similar to a tabernacle in the third. The hosts floating in the fountain allude to the Incarnation and Redemption of Christ. The Church on the left, represented by the religious and secular hierarchies, recognises and worships Christ in an orderly fashion. The Synagogue, blinded like the high priest, denies him in a furious, heated debate. While the Christian banner remains erect, that of the Synagogue snaps.

259 ↑
ROBERT CAMPIN (MASTER
OF FLÉMALLE)
Valenciennes, c. 1375–Tournai,
1444

*St John the Baptist and the
Franciscan Master Heinrich
von Werl*

1438. Oil on panel, 101 x 47 cm
P1513

260 →
St Barbara

c. 1435–38. Oil on panel,
101 x 47 cm
P1514

These two panel paintings are the
wings of a triptych whose central
panel is lost. The panel of *St John
the Baptist* is the only dated
work attributed to Campin.
The inscription on the paving
stones refers to the identity of
the person who commissioned
the work and its date of
execution. The inclusion of the
donor in the painting was not a
Netherlandish invention, though
his more intimate relationship
with the sacred events, as shown
here, was. Heinrich von Werl,
professor of theology at Cologne
and provincial of the Order of the
Friars Minor, shares his domestic

environment with St John, who
bears the book and the lamb. The
Franciscan prays before the lost
central panel, which probably
depicted the Virgin, as if a mystic
vision were taking place in the
house. This materialisation of the
supernatural is further enhanced
by the realism of certain details,
but particularly by the mirror,
a borrowing from Van Eyck, in
which we see the reflections of
St John, two Franciscans and a
view of the exterior landscape.
For her part, St Barbara is shown
reading. The irises allude to her
purity and draw a parallel with
the Virgin Mary.

261
ROBERT CAMPIN
(MASTER OF FLÉMALLE)
Valenciennes, c. 1375–Tournai,
1444

The Marriage of the Virgin

c. 1420. Oil on canvas,
77 x 88 cm
P1887

The painting links two related episodes – the miracle of the flowering rod and the marriage of the Virgin – in two parallel and symbolic architectural settings. Inside the Temple of Jerusalem on the left, depicted in an orientalising Romanesque style, Joseph attempts to conceal the flowering of his rod that designates him as the husband God has chosen for Mary. The marriage takes place on the right in the temple's Gothic-style portico, which is under construction. The contrast between the old Romanesque architecture and the new Gothic style symbolises the transition from the Old Law to the New Law. Mary's marriage preannounces Christ's coming, just as the portico under construction marks the beginning of the new temple that will progressively supersede the old one, in allusion to the Church and the Synagogue. The decoration on the capitals and stained-glass windows also illustrates episodes in the Old Testament foretelling the coming of the Messiah.

Van der Weyden and his Circle

Rogier van der Weyden was a key figure in the development and internationalisation of the new Netherlandish painting. The son of a cutler of Tournai, Henri de la Pasture, he began his apprenticeship at the local workshop of Robert Campin in 1427 and qualified as a master painter in 1432. If Campin and the Van Eyck brothers were the pioneers of the 'ars nova', Van der Weyden was their heir. He combined Campin's sculptural volumes with Van Eyck's elegance, sense of space and attention to detail. This was the basis of a personal style that greatly influenced the development of Netherlandish painting and enjoyed huge success abroad. Van der Weyden stripped his works down to the bare essentials in terms of both the composition and the linear handling of the elements, endowing them with an introspective quality and a deep spiritual dimension. He dismissed the virtuosity of the court aesthetic and the anecdotal in favour of a more monumental, focused and eloquent rendering of the subject. His painting has a dramatic quality that gives it a new emotional vibrancy and his humanised manner of expressing sacred drama inspired an intimate feeling of piety in the viewer that was appropriate to modern devotional practices. Van der Weyden settled in Brussels in 1435 and was appointed painter to the city in 1436. He was a prosperous and socially active entrepreneur and represented a new type of bourgeois, city-dwelling painter. He took on large and small commissions from princes, nobles, the clergy and the bourgeoisie, and from his fellow countrymen and foreigners, but he was not attached to the court or to a particular patron. His active workshop spread the popularity of his models and designs throughout Europe; Netherlandish painters like Vrancke Van der Stockt and Hans Memling trained in his shop as well as foreigners such as the Milanese artist Zanetto Bugatto. In the Jubilee year of 1450 Van der Weyden travelled to Rome. His subsequent work has echoes of paintings by artists like Fra Angelico. Rogier van der Weyden earned a high reputation in Italy: the philosopher Nicholas of Cusa described him as 'maximus pictor'; and the humanist Bartolomeo Fazio included him in his De Virus Illustribus. Spain also recognised his genius. In the fifteenth and sixteenth centuries, John II of Castile, Isabella I and Philip II collected and donated works of his to the religious institutions they founded. Modern-day collecting has continued to hold his paintings in great esteem. The Museo del Prado, as the repository of the royal collection and of private bequests, houses some of his most significant achievements.

262
ROGIER VAN DER WEYDEN
Tournai, c. 1399/1400–Brussels, 1464

The Virgin and Child
c. 1435–38. Oil on panel, 100 x 52 cm
P2722

Like an illusionist, Van der Weyden plays at creating a fictitious reality somewhere between sculpture, architecture and painting. The figures of Mary and her Son, positioned on a base that appears to project from the painting, are set inside a Gothic stone niche. The stone has tactile properties that appear to portray Mother and Son as two altar sculptures, but their colour and gestures and the properties of the fabrics and flesh tones make them seem real. This dual effect, which combines the solemnity of sculpture with the vitality of painting, is emphasised by the dark background that converts the stone niche into a picture frame. Despite its apparent naturalness, the scene is infused with symbolism. The Christ Child inexpertly leafs through the Bible while Mary, with a mixture of tenderness and sorrow, meditates on the future Passion prophesied in these pages. An angel descends with a crown of lilies and crosses, the attributes respectively of Mary's virginal purity and her maternal sorrow.

263
ROGIER VAN DER WEYDEN
Tournai, c. 1399/1400–Brussels,
1464

Descent from the Cross
c. 1435. Oil on panel,
220 x 262 cm
P2825

Originally a triptych, this
work is regarded as Van der
Weyden's masterpiece. It
aroused enormous admiration
when it was hung in the chapel
of the archers' guild in the
church of Our Lady Outside
the Walls in Louvain, for
which it was commissioned.
It was later acquired by Mary
of Hungary, governor of the
Netherlands, for her castle
at Binche (Belgium). There
it was seen by her nephew,
the young Prince Felipe of
Spain, the future Philip II,
to whom she bequeathed it
at her death. Tradition has it
that the painting survived a
shipwreck on its way to Spain.
Van der Weyden has created
a reliquary like setting with
figures that imitate painted
sculpture. The minute detail
of the clothing, the flesh tones
and the vegetation heighten its
resemblance to a living theatre,
as do the intense colours and
the careful composition. St
John on the far left and Mary
Magdalene on the right frame
the central scene. The viewer's
gaze descends from the cross
to the body of Jesus and the
figure of Mary, whose diagonal
arrangement establishes a link
between the Passion of Christ
and the sorrow of the Virgin.
The feeling of pity for a mother's
grief is also conveyed by the
expressions of the other figures,
who weep or look on in sadness.

264

VRANCKE VAN DER STOCKT
Brussels, c. 1420–1495

Triptych of the Redemption
Second half of 15ᵗʰ century
Oil on panel, 195 x 172 cm
(central panel), 195 x 77 cm
(side panels)
P1888-P1889-P1891

When closed, the triptych
shows the episode of Caesar's
tribute and, when open, a cycle
alluding to the Redemption.
Van der Stockt sets the scenes
in architectural porticoes in the
manner of his master, Van der
Weyden. The expulsion of Adam
and Eve on the left wing is a
reference to original sin. The arch
displays the six days of Creation
and the spandrels God and the
creation of Eve. The central
panel shows the Crucifixion.
The figure of Christ is positioned
like the mullion of the portico
of a Gothic temple with the
Virgin and St John on either side.
The arch shows scenes of the
Passion and at the ends are six

of the seven sacraments; the
sacrament of the Eucharist is
depicted inside the temple where
a believer takes communion,
administered by a priest. Finally,
the Last Judgement on the
right wing is surrounded by six
of the seven Acts of Mercy,
accompanied by the Burial of
Christ on the spandrels. The
triptych belonged to Leonor
de Mascareñas, governess to
Philip II, who presented it as
a gift to the convent of Los
Ángeles, which she founded.
She arranged to be buried there,
and the theme of the triptych
– salvation of the soul and the
means of achieving it – therefore
has a funerary reference.

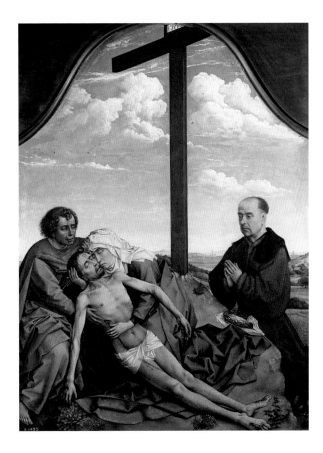

265
ROGIER VAN DER WEYDEN
Tournai, c. 1399/1400–Brussels,
1464

Pietà
c. 1450. Oil on panel,
47 x 34.5 cm
P2540

The success of the models
established by Van der Weyden
led him, and his followers,
to use them repeatedly.
The work is inspired by the
triptych presented as a gift to
the Carthusian monastery of
Miraflores by John II of Castile
(1405–1454). The Pietà was a
very popular theme during the
fifteenth century as it expressed
the new religious sensitivity.
Here Mary, as Mater Dolorosa,
presses her cheek to her son's;
behind them is John the
Evangelist. This tragic moment,
portrayed in a manner that

is both decorous and lifelike,
is observed by the donor.
Identified as a member of the
Broers family, he is present
as a witness to the scene, his
hands joined in prayer in an
act of Christian meditation
on the Redemption. His human
presence is handled in the same
realistic manner as the holy
figures whose space he shares.
Van der Weyden's painterly
skills are also apparent in the
rich palette, which ranges from
the green and blue of John's
robes to the mauve of Mary
and the red of the donor.

266
HANS MEMLING
Seligenstadt, c. 1433–Bruges,
1494

The Adoration of the Magi
c. 1479–80. Oil on panel,
95 x 271 cm
P1557

Memling's elegant, serene style dominated the artistic scene of Bruges in the second half of the fifteenth century. Placed in the oratory of the Casa Real de Aceca (Toledo) by order of Charles V, the triptych shows, from left to right, the Nativity, the Epiphany, and the Purification and Presentation in the Temple. The first two panels share the same architectural setting viewed from two different angles. In the Nativity the angels adore Jesus while Joseph holds a candle, which represents the new light. The symmetrical composition of the Epiphany makes Mary, who is positioned in line with the central column, the symbolic axis. The wooden ceiling framework traces a small cross that foreshadows the Passion. The right-hand panel recreates a Gothic temple. Joseph carries a cage with two pigeons: the offering to God for first-born sons. It has been suggested that the prophetess Anna and the man in black next to Simeon could be portraits of Anne Willemszoon and her son Jan Crabbe, abbot of the Dunes in Koksijde, who may have commissioned the work.

267
DIRK BOUTS
Haarlem c. 1420–Louvain, 1475

*Triptych of the Life
of the Virgin*

c. 1445. Oil on panel,
80 x 217 cm
P1461

This triptych with a central
panel divided in two belonged to
Philip II, who deposited it at El
Escorial in 1584. Although Bouts
borrowed the architectural
structure from Rogier van der
Weyden, his scenes and figures
are more restrained and convey
a calm, contemplative mood.
His handling of the landscape
and of space set a precedent for
later Flemish landscape painting.

In the first panel, showing the
Annunciation, Mary's mantle
invades the portico and the
vaulted ceiling of the room is
an extension of the framing
arch, which shows scenes from
the creation of Eve to the death
of Abel, identifying Mary as
the new Eve. The Visitation
and the Nativity in the central
panel are depicted in a beautiful,
deep landscape setting. The
arches show scenes from the
Passion. In the Epiphany, a hat
again juts out from the portico
and the arch is decorated with
episodes which followed the
Resurrection, alluding to the
universality of Christianity. In
a display of narrative veracity,
the Epiphany and the Nativity
take place against the same
background.

Bosch

A member of the third generation of a family of painters, Bosch (Jeroen van Aken) spent his life in the city of his birth, 's Hertogenbosch, from which his name is derived. His style recalls the elegance of Memling [266], especially in the *Adoration of the Magi* [270], but his sources were chiefly miniatures, the decorative borders of illustrated books, and even the fantastic bestiary of Gothic sculpture. The Prado houses the best collection of works by Bosch in terms of both quantity and quality. Most originate in the Royal Collections and were brought from El Escorial, where Philip II (reigned 1556–1598) housed the first major collection of his works. Philip perpetuated a taste for Bosch developed by his family almost a century earlier. In 1504 his grandfather Philip the Handsome, the husband of Joan I of Castile, had commissioned Bosch to paint a triptych of the Last Judgement, and his great-aunt, Margaret of Austria, possessed a *Temptation of St Anthony* by Bosch in her picture gallery at Mechelen. The Flemish and Spanish nobility followed in their rulers' footsteps: *The Garden of Earthly Delights* [268] was commissioned by Engelbrecht II of Nassau or his nephew Henry III, whose wife, Mencía de Mendoza, also had a copy of the *Haywain*. The inclusion of the Netherlands in the legacy received by Philip II intensified relations with Flanders for the Spanish officials, humanists and nobles who spent part of their lives there and built up small collections. Such is the case with the humanist Felipe de Guevara, whose admiration for Bosch led him to acquire works like *The Removal of the Stone of Folly* [271] and a version of the *Haywain* [272]. Some scholars consider that the select nature of Bosch's clientele may explain the extravagance and complexity of his works, which are so appealing to modern tastes but were incomprehensible to the general public and limited his following to an élite who had the necessary intellectual background to interpret them. But this theory is contradicted by the fact that some of these works were painted for churches like St John's in 's Hertogenbosch, while others, such as the *Garden of Earthly Delights,* are not devotional but designed to inspire moral reflection. Philip II understood this intellectual dimension and acquired as many of Bosch's works as he could. Time blurred the keys to their understanding and led some to believe they were heretical works. But Bosch was an orthodox Catholic and the eroticism of paintings like the *Garden of Earthly Delights*, which may surprise the uninitiated viewer today, should in fact be seen as a moral message, showing that people would be damned if they followed pursuits condemned by the church.

268
HIERONYMUS BOSCH
's Hertogenbosch, c. 1450–1516

The Garden of Earthly Delights
c. 1500–05. Oil on panel,
220 x 389 cm
P2823

The traveller Antonio de Beatis mentioned this work in 1517, describing its figures as 'things so pleasing and fantastic that by no means can they be described to those who have not seen them'. The triptych was then in the palace of Henry III of Nassau in Brussels. In 1568 it was seized by the Duke of Alba, who bequeathed it to his son Fernando. When Fernando died it was acquired by Philip II, who deposited it at El Escorial in 1593. The painting contains a moralising message and analyses, from left to right, the origins of sin and the fate of sinners, from Paradise to Hell. The obverse of the closed wings shows a large sphere representing the world on the third day of Creation, before the beginning of life. When the wings are opened, the Garden of Eden appears on the left. From top to bottom it depicts the first animals, the Fountain of Life in the centre and God offering Adam his latest creation, Eve. The Tree of Knowledge and the serpent announce the original sin and the fall of man. The central panel, with the four rivers of the world on the horizon, situates the scene on Earth. Carnal desire, represented by beautiful naked women and symbolised by an array of red fruit, becomes mankind's driving force. The various earthly pleasures to which mankind yields instinctively and unconsciously are illustrated symbolically or specifically. The right-hand panel shows the consequence: Hell. In the upper part a city in flames receives the groups of condemned people. The specific torments of the gambler, the alchemist and the impious clergymen are shown in the foreground.

269
HIERONYMUS BOSCH
's Hertogenbosch, c. 1450–1516

The Tabletop of the Seven Deadly Sins

c. 1480. Oil on panel,
120 x 150 cm
P2822

The work was acquired by Philip II and deposited at El Escorial in 1574. Its moralising message illustrates the consequences of sin. In the centre Christ as Man of Sorrows emerges from his tomb, an allusion to his sacrifice to redeem mankind. An inscription contains a warning: '*cave, cave, Dominus videt*' ('beware, beware, the Lord sees'). Around it the deadly sins are enacted in seven scenes of everyday life: Anger (peasants quarrelling outside a tavern), Pride (a bourgeois lady spruces herself up before a mirror held by a demon), Lust (lovers amuse themselves with jesters), Sloth (a nun urges a sleeping monk to pray), Gluttony (that of the eater and drinker), Avarice (a judge accepting bribes from the litigants), and Envy (he who desires another's wife, he who envies the nobleman and the dog that wishes for bigger bones). The scrolls at top and bottom with verses from Deuteronomy express God's disappointment. The circles in the four corners depict the Four Last Things: the death of the Christian, the Last Judgement, Hell and Heaven.

270

HIERONYMUS BOSCH
's Hertogenbosch, c. 1450–1516

The Adoration of the Magi
c. 1495. Oil on panel, 135 x 190 cm
P2048

Regarded as one of Bosch's masterpieces, this is his most sophisticated work and the closest to Flemish models. Originally destined for a chapel in 's Hertogenbosch Cathedral, it was deposited at El Escorial in 1574 by Philip II. When closed it shows the eucharistic miracle of the Mass of St Gregory. When open, the wings display the donors and the central panel the Epiphany, all unified by the continuity of the landscape. The work draws a parallel between the adoration of the Corpus Christi during the Mass and the adoration of Jesus in the Epiphany. The Epiphany scene, despite its apparent simplicity, contains a number of Old Testament symbols, such as the sculpture of the Sacrifice of Isaac at Mary's feet, a prefiguration of that of Jesus, and the Queen of Sheba's visit to Solomon, who is identified with Christ, shown on Caspar's shoulder cape. Rather more obscure is the chained and almost nude figure appearing in the doorway, who has been identified in the past with Adam, the Antichrist or Herod.

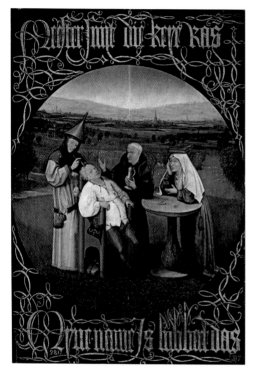

271

HIERONYMUS BOSCH
's Hertogenbosch, c. 1450–1516

*The Removal of the Stone
of Folly*

c. 1490. Oil on panel,
47.5 x 34.5 cm
P2056

In the centre of the panel, set within a circle, is a satirical scene whose meaning is revealed by the surrounding inscription, which has been translated as 'Master, cut this stone out soon, my name is Lubbert Das' (sometimes translated as 'castrated badger'). Seated before a broad landscape, the unsuspecting patient believes that the operation will cure him of madness, which is often taken to be stupidity or ignorance in Flemish proverbs. The surgeon on the left wears an upside-down funnel on his head which appears to allude to his own madness, but also to his avarice, as further reinforced by the money bag hanging from his belt. The friar behind him, who distracts the patient with his conversation, implicates the Church in the deceit and creation of false beliefs. The woman on the right with a closed book on her head may symbolise Science, which is not consulted on this occasion. The tulip on the table like the one extracted from the patient's head is a reference to the money paid for the operation, which indicates that the doctor is a fraudster.

272
HIERONYMUS BOSCH
's Hertogenbosch, c. 1450–1516

The Haywain
c. 1515. Oil on panel,
147 x 212 cm
P2052

Philip II purchased two versions of this triptych, both signed, which hang in the Prado and at El Escorial; the version in the museum is the finest. Its moralising message refers to sin. When closed, it shows a wayfarer on the reverse of the doors. He is the '*homo viator*', the medieval wanderer who renounces possessions and embarks on a spiritual journey where the devil and sin, embodied by the dog and the background scenes of violence and pleasure, lie in wait for him. When open, the left panel shows the origins of sin, from the fall of the rebellious angels to the expulsion from Paradise. The centre panel scrutinises the world of men with an allegorical image based on a Flemish popular saying: 'The world is like a hay cart and everyone takes what he can.' The hay symbolises desire for earthly possessions. Powerful figures like the pope, the emperor and the king follow the wagon in a procession, while the common folk try to clamber on it and are crushed or fight to death in the attempt. Others obtain hay easily, such as the abbess to whom it is brought by her nuns, or through deceit, such as the quack doctor with bulging pockets. On top of the haystack two couples indulge in hedonistic pleasures to the sound of music played by a demon. An angel prays imploringly to Christ the Redeemer, who observes the whole scene from above, showing his wounds. The cart is drawn by infernal beings that drag everyone to Hell, which is depicted in the right-hand panel.

Patinir and Sixteenth-century Netherlandish Painting

Felipe de Guevara, a sixteenth-century Spanish humanist and connoisseur of Netherlandish painting, compared Joachim Patinir to Jan van Eyck and Rogier van der Weyden in his *Comentarios de la pintura* (c.1560), which attests to the enormous prestige Patinir achieved in this period. Albrecht Dürer also dealt personally with Patinir and referred to him as 'the fine painter of landscapes'. Nothing specific is known about Patinir's artistic training, but he was obviously indebted to earlier masters and was in contact with contemporaries like Gérard David [276, 277], Bosch [268, 272] and Dürer himself. Although landscape is granted its own importance in the works of earlier artists such as Jan van Eyck, Petrus Christus, Dirk Bouts and Hugo van der Goes, Patinir is considered the first Flemish landscape artist and the first painter to specialise in the genre, to the point where he often significantly left the figures to other master painters, as in the Prado's *Landscape with the Temptation of St Anthony Abbot* [275]. In Patinir's oeuvre the traditional prominence given to the narrative in the foreground extends to the background, where attention to nature and to distant horizons takes on a fresh importance. And his novel rendering of atmospheric effects, with colour schemes ranging from a beautiful blue to the luminous white of the horizon, attest to a particular interest in the intrinsic values of landscape. Like the paintings of Bosch, some of Patinir's are aimed at a select clientele and incorporate humanistic concepts. Works such as *Charon crossing the River Styx* [273] were a far cry from commonly accepted devotional or social values, and were commissioned by scholarly connoisseurs with modern tastes, such as Lucas Rem, a cosmopolitan merchant linked to the Fugger banking family. This is precisely what the city of Antwerp had to offer as one of the major artistic and intellectual centres of Northern Europe, to whose painters' guild Patinir is recorded as belonging from 1515. It is not surprising that Philip II (reigned 1556–1598) should have acquired all the Patinir paintings available, including those owned by Felipe de Guevara – which are unfortunately lost – but also those now housed in the Prado.

273
JOACHIM PATINIR
Dinant or Bouvignes,
c. 1450–Antwerp, 1524

Charon crossing the River Styx
c. 1520–24. Oil on panel,
64 x 103 cm
P1616

The all-important final choice of the human soul takes place in an extraordinary landscape. The work, which is not documented until 1636, may have been acquired by Philip II and unites Christian and mythological references with a moral purpose, relating it to humanism. In the boat on the river are Charon, the ferryman of the river Styx who leads the dead to Hades, and a soul faced with the dilemma of choosing between the bank of Paradise and that of Hell. Paradise, on the left, has a rugged and swampy bank. An angel points to Eden, where the Fountain of Life flows and the blessed roam. The peacocks and ravens are an allusion to the Resurrection and Redemption. The other side of the river is calmer, with fruits and birds, but deceptive, as revealed by a small monkey, a symbol of the devil. Waiting at the foot of a tower is Cerberus, the three-headed dog who guards the entrance to the underworld, and at the top the first pleas of the damned. The background scenery is arid and in flames. The soul and rudder appear to turn, drawn to the wrong bank.

274
JOACHIM PATINIR
Dinant or Bouvignes,
c. 1450–Antwerp, 1524

Landscape with St Jerome
c. 1516–17. Oil on panel,
74 x 91 cm
P1614.

The painting incorporates two recurrent elements in Patinir's oeuvre: the hermit's life, a particularly popular theme in Northern European devotional works, and the landscape as the main feature. St Jerome was a model of the devout life and his iconography drew on anecdotes taken from Jacobus de Voragine's *Golden Legend*. Patinir's main subject is the moment when the saint removes the thorn from the lion's paw, previously illustrated by Van der Weyden and Memling. However, he clothes the saint as a hermit rather than as a cardinal and sets the scene in a cave, where he includes the skull and cross, instead of in the monastery of Bethlehem, which is shown on a crag. He thus combines a hagiographic source with the Netherlandish tradition. The raising of the horizon line enabled him to develop in depth a natural, human and atmospheric space with magnificent contrasts between the vertical masses and stormy sky on the left and the horizontal lines and luminosity of the right. The landscape with rocky caverns is inspired by the Mosa region where the painter was born and unifies the various episodes of the story. Philip II acquired the painting and had it hung in the Hieronymite monastery of El Escorial.

275
JOACHIM PATINIR
Dinant or Bouvignes,
c. 1450–Antwerp, 1524

QUENTIN MASSYS
Louvain, 1466–Antwerp, 1530

*Landscape with the
Temptation of St Anthony
Abbot*
c. 1520–24. Oil on panel,
155 x 173 cm
P1615

St Anthony, who relinquished his possessions and devoted himself to the contemplative life, was beset by many temptations. In the main group, painted by Quentin Massys, lust embodied by three courtesans attempts to seduce him. The apple, the monkey who knocks it down and the rosary flung to the ground represent temptation, sin and the fall, respectively. Despite the large size of these figures, the landscape enjoys much of the narrative prominence and is the setting for various events in the saint's life. In the middle ground we see the attack of the army of demons on the saint and his hut, and on the right the temptation of the queen and her ladies-in-waiting, some naked in the river and others enjoying a banquet on their barge, served by a toad. In the background, barely visible as two silhouettes, Christ comforts the exhausted saint. In seclusion in a hermitage on a rock the saint reads, again coming under attack from demons in the air. The river and the town in the background evoke the landscape of the Mosa region where Patinir lived. In 1566 the work was owned by Philip II, who deposited it at El Escorial.

276 ↑
GERARD DAVID
Oudewater, c. 1450/60–Bruges, 1523

The Virgin and Child with Two Angels crowning Her
c. 1520. Oil on panel, 34 x 27 cm
P1512

The painting, which belonged to the Royal Collection, is a fine example of the small devotional works that were imported from Flanders. Easy to transport and less costly than triptychs, they provided an affordable solution to the need for images for private worship. The careful rendering of details and the use of gilding made them precious and personal objects. David's Madonnas were influenced by Italian art, and developed a moving and lyrical humanity with a gentler handling of the figures that met with great demand. This work combines Flemish attention to detail with a soft modelling that conveys a feeling of intimacy. Jesus is distracted by the sight of a posy of purple flowers, a harbinger of the pain of the Passion, and his mother watches him while two angels crown her. The positioning of the half-length figure in the foreground emphasises the importance of the emotional impact of the work.

277 →
GERARD DAVID
Oudewater, c. 1450/60–Bruges, 1523

Rest on the Flight into Egypt
c. 1515. Oil on panel, 60 x 39 cm
P2643

Gerard David established himself in Bruges, where he worked on many international commissions. His style incorporated new Italian trends into the Flemish legacy he had inherited, particularly from Van Eyck, and this panel is an excellent example of his style. His figures are more softly modelled and display gentler, more sensitive expressions. The scenery takes on a great significance as human figures are integrated into a narrative and descriptive space that foreshadows Patinir and Flemish landscape art. Mary and Jesus rest on a rock in the centre of the composition. They use the moment to feed the Child; the basket of food and the spoon in Jesus' hand give the scene an everyday air. However, the drama is implicit, for just as Mary feeds Jesus, so will he feed Faith through his sacrifice. In the forest in the background the Holy Family flees to Heliopolis. From the darkness of the grove of trees to the luminous clarity of the horizon, David succeeds in capturing the fleeting effects of light and atmosphere.

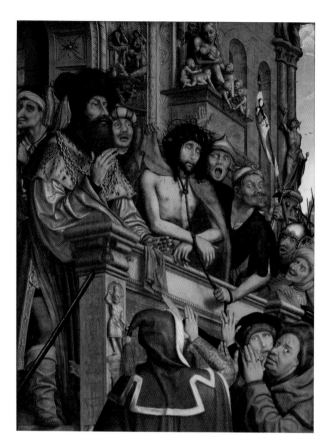

278 ←
QUENTIN MASSYS
Louvain, 1466–Antwerp, 1530.

Christ presented to the People
c. 1515. Oil on panel,
160 x 120 cm
P2801

Christ is presented by Pilate
on the balcony of the Jerusalem
praetorium. The space is wholly
taken up by the figures and the
architecture. Massys employs a
very low viewpoint, placing the
spectator at the same height as
the public who witness the scene
and therefore involving him
in it. This dramatic conception
of the space is combined with
an almost grotesque realism
in the treatment of the Jews
and soldiers, with obvious
satirical intent. Only the
figures of Jesus and Pilate are
calm, although the governor's
indolence contrasts with Jesus'
expression of resigned suffering.
In the background is a sculptural
group representing Charity.

279 →
QUENTIN MASSYS
Louvain, 1466–Antwerp, 1530

The Saviour
1529. Oil on panel, 44 x 35 cm
P1561

The Virgin Mary
1529. Oil on panel, 44 x 35 cm
P1562

These two small panels make
up a diptych in the manner of a
portable altar for prayer or private
devotion. Their intimate nature,
conducive to prayer or reflection,
determines the subject matter,
composition and technique.
Rather like framed portraits,
the figures of Mary and Jesus
occupy the whole surface, without
regard for spatial or anecdotal
considerations. Only the light
sculpts their volumes, which are
beautifully defined by means of
brief strokes and impeccable
brushwork. Every detail of
the robes, flesh tones and hair
is handled in a painstaking,
lifelike manner. This direct and
serene realism is very moving on
account of the tender expression
and gestures of the figures, who
evoke the Christian sacrifice.
Scholars have speculated about
the possibility that they were
painted by the painter's son Jan.
However, Quentin's authorship
is borne out by his signature on
the panel of *The Saviour* and the
outstanding quality of the panels.
They were acquired by Philip II,
who deposited them at El Escorial
shortly before his death.

280
JAN GOSSAERT, MABUSE
Maubeuge, c. 1478–Antwerp, 1532

Christ between the Virgin Mary and St John the Baptist
c. 1510–15. Oil and paper glued to panel, 122 x 133 cm
P1510

The painting, one of the most outstanding in this artist's production, is the central panel of a triptych donated by Philip II to El Escorial. Gossaert was one of the pioneers of Flemish Mannerism, a fusion of the Flemish and Italian traditions which revolutionised the pictorial language of the Netherlands. This work exemplifies his debt to the school of Bruges and specifically to Van Eyck. The figures of Christ, Mary and St John are inspired by those of the *Polyptych of the Mystic Lamb* executed by Hubert and Jan van Eyck for Ghent cathedral. The traditional Deësis, an iconography that shows Mary and John supplicating Christ on behalf of humanity, is portrayed in a novel manner, with bust-length figures. Compared to the original models, Gossaert, influenced by Italian art, handles the subject more naturally, though he continues to display the painstaking Flemish attention to detail in the robes and brocades. While the rich Gothic arches frame the human figures and give them independence, creating a symmetrical hierarchy, the superimposition of the foreground figures unifies the space. A singing angel, inspired by the St Gabriel of the Van Eyck polyptych, emerges from an oculus with a lifelike three-dimensional effect.

281
JAN GOSSAERT, MABUSE
Maubeuge, c. 1478–Antwerp, 1532

The Virgin and Child
c. 1527–30. Oil on panel, 63 x 50 cm
P1930

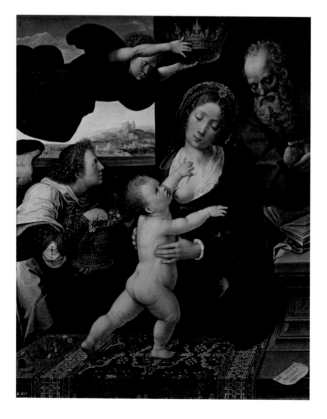

282
BERNARD VAN ORLEY
Brussels, 1488 (?)–1541

The Holy Family
1522. Oil on panel, 90 x 74 cm
P2692

Van Orley had studied Raphael's cartoons of the *Acts of the Apostles* in Brussels, and the influence of Italian classicism is evident in this panel painting, both in the cartouche which contains his signature, which is written in Roman rather than Gothic lettering, and in the overall composition. It shows the Holy Family in an interior setting. A coastal landscape can be seen through an opening. While the Child plays with his mother, St Joseph holds an apple – an allusion to the Garden of Eden. An angel crowns the Virgin as Queen of Heaven, and another presents her with a basket of flowers that symbolises the Passion Jesus will have to undergo in order to redeem mankind. The handling of St Joseph's beard displays a painstaking German technique that recalls Dürer, whom Van Orley had met two years before painting this panel.

283
MICHIEL COXCIE
Malinas, c. 1499-1592

*Death of the Virgin
and the Ascension*
Before 1550. Oil on panel,
208 x 182 cm
P1468

This work is the central panel of a triptych which was completed on the left and the right by two other panels also conserved in the Prado Museum and which respectively depict *The Birth of the Virgin* (P1469) and *The Presentation of the Virgin in the Temple* (P1470). Created for the Saint Gudula Cathedral in Brussels, it was acquired by Philip II, a great admirer of Coxcie, whom he named court painter and from whom he commissioned various works. In 1586, the Spanish monarch donated this triptych to El Escorial Monastery, to which he also bestowed other works by the artist.

Coxcie was trained in Brussels and Rome. As a good Romanist, faithful to what he learned in Italy, he combines the Herculean bodies of Michelangelo with the classical beauty of the school of Raphael, yet without abandoning the realism in the translation of objects and the rich colouring of the Flemish tradition. In this work he takes advantage of the numerous characters to show a complete repertoire of gestures and attitudes, without lapsing into exaggeration, and thus manages to endow this dramatic passage of the life of the Virgin with a spiritual content.

Pieter Bruegel the Elder

Pieter Bruegel was born north of Brabant, and it was therefore natural for him to take an interest in the oeuvre of the most famous painter in the area, Hieronymus Bosch [268-272], who died in 1516. The new artistic hub of the Netherlands was Antwerp, where Bruegel trained, probably in the workshop of Pieter Coecke van Aelst. However, rather than adopt the predominant style, which combined local tradition and Italian classicism, giving rise to a complex and scholarly hybrid style, Bruegel inclined towards naturalism and Flemish popular tradition. In 1551 he qualified as a master artist and by the following year he was in Italy. In Rome he struck up a friendship with Giulio Clovio, a miniaturist in the service of Cardinal Alessandro Farnese and a member of an important intellectual circle. Bruegel travelled around Italy, France, Switzerland and Austria, devoting himself to drawing and landscape painting. He not only continued the tradition of the great Patinir [273-275], but he was also able, through his close friendship with the geographer Abraham Ortelius (1527–1598), to incorporate advances in topographical representation into his bird's-eye views. After returning to Antwerp in 1554, he worked with the engraver Hieronymus Cock (1510–1570), first designing landscapes and later executing moralising works inspired by Bosch. Between 1559 and 1563 he used these images in large-format works such as *The Triumph of Death* [286], which were very popular with collectors like Cardinal Granvelle and the merchant Niclaes Jonghelinck. The intellectual and educational nature of these works connects them to the humanistic circles that Bruegel seems to have frequented judging by his friends, such as the geographer Ortelius and the printer Plantino, and his élite clientele. In 1563 he married Pieter Coecke van Aelst's daughter Maycke and settled in Brussels, where they raised one of the most illustrious families of painters of the seventeenth century. Until his death, the master continued to produce great paintings in which landscape, atmosphere and everyday scenes play a prominent role. His works were greatly in demand and particularly coveted by collectors in the imperial territories. The panel in the Prado was acquired by Queen Isabella Farnese in the eighteenth century. The queen's interest in Flemish art was in keeping with her family's taste. Cosimo Masi, secretary to the Farnese in Brussels, had acquired two important Bruegel paintings for the family during the painter's lifetime. Isabella saw them at Parma and bequeathed them to her son, the future Charles III of Spain, then the king of Naples. She had already acquired one of the versions of the *Tower of Babel*.

284
PIETER BRUEGEL THE
ELDER
Breda, 1525/30–Brussels, 1569

The Triumph of Death
c. 1562–63. Oil on panel,
117 x 162 cm
P1393

Bruegel shares Bosch's moralising tendency, but he has not peopled this allegorical painting with fantastic beings. Instead, he depicts a lifelike battle between the dead and the living. European medieval culture warded off the fear of death through 'Dances of Death', which showed people from all walks of life meeting the same fate. In Italy, Petrarch had proclaimed the victory of Death over Life in his *Triumphs*. In this painting Death gallops on a corpselike horse, cutting down lives with his scythe. A horde of skeletons, protected by coffin-shields, await those who flee, in order to enclose them in an enormous coffin. Throughout the bare, fiery landscape we see the dead attack the living, and executions, gallows and pillories. In the foreground different social types embody specific sins. Such is the case with the king and avarice in the left corner and the lovers given over to sensuous pleasure on the right. The jester, the gambler and the coward, as well as the valiant knight ready to fight in the right-hand corner, will all be slaughtered mercilessly.

285
PIETER BRUEGEL THE ELDER
Breda, 1525/30-Brussels, 1569

*The Wine of Saint
Martin's Day*
1565-68. Tempera on linen,
148 x 1270 cm
P8040

This work depicts the
distribution of the first wine of
the harvest to the village as it was
done on Saint Martin's Day in
Flanders and in the Germanic
countries during the 16th century.
For a long time there were known
to be copies and an engraving of a
Bruegel painting with this subject
whose original was thought to be
lost until this work came to light.
After a thorough study and the
appearance of the handwritten
signature, it entered the Prado
Museum in 2010.
On this linen, the largest of
Bruegel's works to be conserved,
the painter displays his mastery
when it comes to creating a
complex composition in which
he depicts nearly one hundred
figures. Although the saint
appears on the right tearing his
cape, it is neither a religious nor
a profane painting, rather a work
with a moral character, which
reflects the tension between
Saint Martin's charity and the
almost bacchanalian excesses of
the feast which bears his name.
On the outskirts of the city, next
to a hamlet, he has an enormous
barrel around which gather a
crowd of characters in all states
who fight to reach the wine.
Bruegel presents a mountain
made of a humanity dragged
along by the sin of gluttony, a
type of Tower of Babel consisting
of drinkers over which the saint
has no control and he turns his
back on it while he performs
his charity.

286
MARINUS CLAESZON VAN REYMERSWAELE
Reymerswaele, c. 1490/95–
before 1567

*The Money Changer
and his Wife*
1539. Oil on panel, 83 x 97 cm
P2567

Netherlandish society of the fifteenth and sixteenth centuries was depicted in religious and everyday scenes and in individual portraits, but also in corporate images of trades and in group portraits. These generic representations could be laudatory or satirical in intent. It was traditionally thought that this panel by Reymerswaele was a criticism of usury, following a model established by Quentin Massys. Among the apparent evidence for this theory is the disconcerting disorder of the room and the ostentatious clothing and greedy expression of the couple, who concentrate their attention on the weight of a coin. However, this interpretation has been subsequently questioned and the scene is now regarded as one of the first to give prominence to merchants and their activity. After all, it was they who purchased paintings of this kind. Reymerswaele handles every detail with great precision and gives importance to each and every object, including the piece of paper with his signature in the background. His interest in studying space is exemplified by the pencil case on the table, the open lid of which is boldly foreshortened.

Anthonis Mor

Anthonis Mor van Dashort is regarded as one of the great masters of portraiture, a genre that earned him the highest prestige in European courts. The son of the painter Philips Morren van Dashorst, he trained in Jan van Scorel's workshop in Utrecht. This cosmopolitan Romanist painter, a tireless traveller, brought Mor into contact with the Northern European espousal of the Italian Renaissance led by Quentin Massys [278, 279], Jan Gossaert [280, 281] and Bernard van Orley [282]. Mor began to assist his master in 1540, and had joined the Antwerp guild by 1547. Settling first in Utrecht, in 1549 he moved to Antwerp and was involved in the preparations for Philip II's entry into the city. Mor may have made a trip to Italy around this time and come into direct contact with Italian art. The influence of Titian, which is obvious in his work, could stem from this trip or from his relationship with Cardinal Granvelle and Mary of Hungary, the governor of the Netherlands, both of whom owned fine portraits by the Venetian artist. These contacts gave impetus to Mor's courtly career. It was Mary of Hungary who sent him to Lisbon in 1550 to paint the portraits of the Portuguese royal family, one of which, that of Queen Catherine, is in the Prado. During this trip he also painted the likenesses of Maximilian II and Mary of Austria, also in the museum. The official nature of these portraits made it necessary to create an image that was true to life but conveyed the gravity required by royal or imperial majesty. Spanish taste in portraiture had fluctuated between the Flemish style and the Italian style, and Mor drew from both traditions. Taking Titian's imperial portraits [214, 215] as a basis, he introduced Flemish precision and veracity, achieving an image as dignified as it was credible and introspective. His sitters, shown half- or full-length, fill practically the whole picture space. The background fades into dark tones, focusing attention on the person, who is generally arranged diagonally, and clearly and simply lit. The gravity and decorum of the composition are complemented by the painstaking detail of the face, fabrics and jewels, which reveal the individuality and the status of the sitter. Mor travelled to England in 1554 to paint Mary Tudor using this formula [287], and was appointed court painter by Philip II. During his second trip to Spain in 1559 he painted portraits of members of the royal family, such as Joan of Austria, and court personages such as the jester Pejerón [290]. Mor continued to receive commissions from the court and the Flemish élite up until his death.

287
ANTHONIS MOR
Utrecht, 1516/20–Antwerp, 1576/77

Mary Tudor, Queen of England
1554. Oil on panel, 109 x 84 cm
P2108

Mary Tudor, daughter of Henry VIII and Catherine of Aragon, received an excellent education, but the complications arising from her father's various marriages kept her away from the throne until 1553, when her stepbrother Edward VI died without heirs. After her coronation she returned to Catholicism and implemented a harsh anti-Protestant policy that earned her the nickname 'Bloody Mary'. Mary had been promised to her cousin, Emperor Charles V, but remained a spinster at thirty-seven, and it was therefore arranged for her to marry the Prince of Asturias, the future Philip II, in 1554. That year Anthonis Mor travelled to London on the emperor's instructions to paint the portrait now in the Prado. This masterpiece by Mor shows the queen three-quarter length, seated in an armchair but holding herself erect. She bears a rose, the royal emblem of the Tudors, and on a chain round her neck is the jewel that was a gift from her husband. Mor, influenced by the German painter Hans Holbein, made a splendid study of the queen's appearance. The painter delivered the work to Charles V, who took it with him on his retreat to Yuste.

288
ANTHONIS MOR
Utrecht, 1516/20–Antwerp,
1576/77

Portrait of a Married Woman
c. 1554. Oil on panel,
100 x 80 cm
P2114

The Museo del Prado's collection
of portraits by Mor shows the
broad social spectrum of his
clientele. The portraits he made
for the wealthy Dutch, Flemish
and English bourgeoisie are
no less important in number
or quality than those he made
for the court. This portrait is
an eloquent example of the
bourgeois desire to be depicted
in a manner that emulated the
upper classes. In a composition
similar to the portrait of Queen
Mary of England [287], though
here dressed in the severe style
of the Northern European
bourgeoisie, the lady has a little
dog on her lap that symbolises
fidelity.

289
ADRIAEN THOMASZ KEY
Antwerp (?), c. 1544–after 1588

Family Portrait
1583. Oil on panel, 91 x 115 cm
P7614

Key's works are among the
most interesting in the complex
sixteenth-century Flemish art
scene. His realism, technique
and severity recall the pictorial
tradition of Van Eyck and
Memling. However, his adaptation
of this legacy gave rise to a form of
portraiture tailored to suit the
ideals of northern European
bourgeoisie, and in this respect
it was similar to that of Anthonis
Mor. Both the composition and
the objects in the picture have a
symbolic meaning: the skull refers
to the vanity of worldly things;
the clock to the passage of time;
and the rich table cover refers to
the family's social status.

290
ANTHONIS MOR
Utrecht, 1516/20–Antwerp,
1576/77

*Pejerón, Jester of the Count
of Benavente and the Grand
Duke of Alba*
1559–61. Oil on panel,
185 x 93.5 cm
P2107

Mor portrayed the social élite,
including kings and nobles,
but also the people who
were part of everyday life
at the palace and court.
He painted several portraits
of jesters and dwarfs; this
one establishes a significant
precedent in a tradition
that reached its apogee
with Velázquez. It shows a
dignified individual holding a
pack of cards in his right hand.
It is the cards which classify
the sitter as an entertainer,
one of the 'people of pleasure'.
However, like Velázquez
after him [81-84], Mor does
not paint a grotesque portrait
of his subject. The jester
occupies the whole picture
space with great poise, and
the features that reveal his
abnormality, such as his right
hand and legs, are rendered
subtly and without detriment
to his dignity. An inventory of
1600 identifies the sitter
as Pejerón, a famous jester
who served the Count of
Benavente, the Duke of Alba,
Philip II and Prince Carlos.

Jan 'Velvet' Brueghel and Flemish Cabinet Painting

Cabinet painting – small works intended for domestic interiors – became widespread in the Southern Netherlands in the late sixteenth century and remained fashionable throughout the 1600s. The development of collecting in Flanders popularised works of this kind, some of which were executed by great painters of monumental themes like Rubens and Jordaens. Cabinet painting encompassed many genres: landscape, small allegories, kitchen studies and scenes of daily life. Many painters specialised in one or other of these themes, although it was also common for artists to produce a work jointly. Jan Brueghel became the leading specialist in small-format works. The son of Pieter Bruegel the Elder, who had already taken steps in the direction of this type of painting, he was nicknamed 'Velvet' Brueghel (Brueghel de Velours) on account of the elegance and beauty of his output. He worked both in Antwerp, for the governors Albert and Isabella Clara Eugenia, and in Italy, where he enjoyed the protection of Federico Borromeo, archbishop of Milan and a great admirer of his oeuvre. His output was huge and the Museo del Prado has examples from all the genres he embraced. He worked with artists like Rubens [291, 293] and also with Hendrick van Balen or Hendrick de Clerk on allegories of the elements and the seasons in nature settings. In landscape, he developed novel perspectives on the basis of Flemish tradition, sometimes with Joost de Momper [292]. He painted inventive scenes of everyday life, pictures of country folk and ordinary people going about their daily tasks, rendered in a colourful and decorative style and often with a hint of satire. These themes were continued in the work of David Teniers and in the grotesque scenes of Adriaen Brouwer. Jan Brueghel was also the initiator of a new subject matter: devotional images set inside garlands of flowers, in which he could display his skill at depicting nature in minute detail [291]. In fact, his highly realistic pictures of vases of flowers also made him one of the first Flemish painters of still life, a genre that reached its apogee with small kitchen scenes in the first half of the century. Jan Brueghel explored all the possibilities of small-format painting for domestic interiors, which was much sought after by Flemish collectors in the seventeenth century. This phenomenon was in turn reflected by a new genre: scenes of collectors' picture galleries, many of which show Brueghel's own works hanging on the walls [296].

291
JAN 'VELVET' BRUEGHEL
Brussels, 1568–Antwerp, 1625

PETER PAUL RUBENS
Siegen 1577–Antwerp 1640

The Virgin and Child in a Flower Garland
1614–18. Oil on canvas,
79 x 65 cm
P1418

An image of the Virgin and Child, seemingly contained within an octagonal frame, is surrounded by a garland of flowers, fruits and vegetables that hangs from the trees in the background. In the foreground are a number of animals, including such fantastic creatures as the horned hare, which are intended to represent creation as a whole. The abundance and beauty of all the elements depicted are designed as a reflection of the divine nature. Works of this kind were created by Jan Brueghel in the early seventeenth century and were extensively developed by subsequent artists in both Flanders and Spain. On this occasion the figures were executed by Rubens. The artistic, intellectual and religious appeal of these images made them highly popular among the cultural élite of the time.

292
JAN 'VELVET' BRUEGHEL
Brussels, 1568–Antwerp, 1625

JOOST DE MOMPER
Antwerp, c. 1564–Antwerp, 1635

*Market and Washing Place
in Flanders*

c. 1620. Oil on canvas,
166 x 164 cm
P1443

Brueghel's skill at the
detailed description of daily
life and Joost de Momper's
specialisation in the landscape
genre result in a painting that
exalts the simplicity of rural
life in Flanders. Momper
dispensed with his imaginative
panoramic views in favour of
a scene that is much more in
keeping with the real scenery
of the Netherlands. Brueghel's

groups of townsfolk are based
on models disseminated by his
father, Pieter Bruegel the Elder,
in his famous country scenes.
The artist perfectly captures
the bustle of the town market
on the left of the painting, which
is contrasted with the orderly
calm of the washing place on the
right. The open landscape in
the distance infuses the painting
with a feeling of tranquillity.

293
JAN 'VELVET' BRUEGHEL
Brussels, 1568–Antwerp, 1625

PETER PAUL RUBENS
Siegen, 1577–Antwerp, 1640

The Vision of St Hubert
c. 1620. Oil on panel,
63 x 100 cm
P1411

The two Flemish artists here combine their mastery of landscape painting with hagiographic narrative. Hubert, a worldly young man of aristocratic birth, went out hunting in order to vent his anger over his wife's death and came across a magnificent stag. When he was about to shoot it down, Christ on the cross appeared to him between the animal's antlers. The nobleman responded to this vision by converting to Christianity and thenceforward led an exemplary life. The subject of the conversion of the saint, from the city of Liège, was frequently addressed by Flemish painters. Here Hubert is identified as a hunter only by the horn hanging from his waist and by his dogs. Now a repentant believer, he kneels before the divine apparition. The work is a good example of Brueghel's artistic collaboration with Rubens, who painted the figure of the saint.

294
CLARA PEETERS
Antwerp, c. 1594–c. 1659

Table
1611. Oil on panel, 52 x 73 cm
P1620

295
Table
1610–15. Oil on panel,
55 x 73 cm
P1622

Arranged on a table in
the upper panel are a vase
of flowers, a porcelain dish
containing dried fruits
and nuts and a metal dish with
pretzels, as well as a crystal
goblet and some ornate metal
objects. The profusion of
textures and materials attests
to the skill of Peeters at
reproducing different kinds
of surfaces, a facility which
is similarly manifest in the
olives and puff pastries of the
lower painting. Compositions
of this type, known as 'little
breakfast' paintings, illustrated
a pleasing, everyday theme
that was greatly appreciated by
collectors of the time and was
held in high esteem by Flemish
and Dutch painters of the mid-
seventeenth century. Despite
the modernity of the subject
matter, the panels display
obvious links to Netherlandish
tradition. Indeed, the artist,
one of the few female painters
of her time, portrayed herself
on the metal jug, and the
reflection allows the viewer
a glimpse of what lies outside
the picture space.

296
DAVID TENIERS
Antwerp, 1610–Brussels, 1690

Archduke Leopold Wilhelm at his Picture Gallery in Brussels
1647–51. Oil on copper,
104.8 x 130.4 cm
P1813

Depictions of picture galleries were a genre that was very much in vogue among seventeenth-century Flemish art lovers. They were designed to show the cultural and artistic sophistication of their owners, a very important factor in the environment of the Baroque court. Archduke Leopold Wilhelm of Habsburg, governor of the southern Netherlands between 1647 and 1656, wished to be portrayed during his mandate with the magnificent picture collection he had amassed in Brussels and later took to Vienna, where most of these works are housed. On this occasion the task was entrusted to David Teniers, the archduke's court painter, who brought to bear his skill at depicting small figures in scenes of everyday life. The work was commissioned as a gift for his uncle, Philip IV, as a token of their shared love of painting and art collecting.

The Series of the Five Senses

This set of paintings illustrating the senses is one of the most successful collaborations between Peter Paul Rubens and Jan Brueghel. Rubens added the figures of the senses to the magnificent court settings created by Brueghel, and the result is a series of superb quality, with enormous aesthetic and intellectual appeal. The allegorical figures, helped by cherubs, perform actions related to the sense they represent and are accompanied by various objects that facilitate their identification. Sight [298], for example, gazes at a painting, and the whole room is filled with pictures, sculptures and other objects related to vision. Among them are religious paintings such as that illustrating Jesus healing the blind man. Hearing [297] plays a lute and around her are other musical instruments but also paintings whose themes allude symbolically to this sense, such as the story of Orpheus and the animals, which represents the power of music over beasts. Smell [299] is surrounded by fragrant flowers, but also by an angora cat, a symbol of foul odour. A satyr serves a sumptuous meal to Taste [300], who is surrounded by all kinds of delicacies and paintings of banquets illustrating religious and moral themes such as the Marriage of Cana. The personification of Touch [301] is surrounded by various suits of armour and paintings that allude to battles, all related to physical contact. The series attests to Brueghel's prodigious skill at capturing the properties of each object and to Rubens's sensuous rendering of the human body. The set, which was immensely famous in the seventeenth century, was owned successively by the Duke of Neoburg, the Cardinal-Infante Don Ferdinand of Austria and the Duke of Medina de las Torres, before being given by the latter to Philip IV. By 1636 it hung in the Alcázar palace in Madrid.

JAN 'VELVET' BRUEGHEL
Brussels, 1568–Antwerp, 1625

PETER PAUL RUBENS
Siegen, 1577–Antwerp, 1640

297
Sight
1617. Oil on panel, 65 x 109 cm
P1394

298
Hearing
c. 1617. Oil on panel,
65 x 107 cm
P1395

JAN 'VELVET' BRUEGHEL
Brussels, 1568–Antwerp, 1625

PETER PAUL RUBENS
Siegen, 1577–Antwerp, 1640

299
Smell
c. 1617. Oil on panel, 65 x 109 cm
P1396

300
Taste
1618. Oil on panel, 64 x 108 cm
P1397

301
Touch
c. 1617. Oil on panel,
65 x 110 cm
P1398

Rubens

The Museo del Prado owns the largest and one of the best collections of Rubens's paintings thanks to the painter's historical connections with the Spanish monarchy. It illustrates the great versatility of the artist in the different phases of his career and the number of pictorial genres he embraced, which included portraits, landscape, and mythological, history and religious works. Of Flemish origin though born near Cologne, Peter Paul Rubens remained faithful to the Catholic cause during the years of struggle between Spain and the Dutch United Provinces. His educational background provided him with a very high level of courtly and cultural sophistication and after stints at the workshops of various Flemish masters he travelled to Italy. There he studied the great Renaissance artists and furthered his knowledge of classical culture. In 1603, while working for the Gonzaga family in Mantua, he paid his first trip to Spain, as a result of which his first works found their way into the Royal Collection. Back in Antwerp he entered the service of Archduke Albert and Archduchess Isabella, who were embarking on a political and aesthetic reform in the Netherlands. He produced many paintings for them, some of which were conveniently sent to the Spanish king, Philip IV. Active as a painter but also as a courtier and diplomat, Rubens made a second voyage to Spain in 1628–29 in connection with the peace negotiations with England. In Madrid he came into contact with Velázquez, whom he greatly influenced, and achieved the recognition of the Spanish art world. After his departure he received many commissions for paintings and decorative series for the king's palaces. The Alcázar in Madrid, the Buen Retiro and, in particular, the Torre de la Parada were filled with paintings that Rubens and his followers executed in Antwerp and greatly influenced Spanish artists. Philip IV became the greatest Rubens enthusiast of the time, and his taste was imitated by many aristocrats and by Spanish government officials in the Southern Netherlands. As a result of this enthusiasm many of Rubens's works found their way to Spain. In addition to its indisputable artistic quality, Rubens's oeuvre was appreciated for its sensual and cultivated approach to mythology and its celebration of nature and the human figure, but also for the deep devotion conveyed by his religious images. An indefatigable collector and scholar, Rubens amassed a large collection of paintings, both by other artists and his own work. Many of the latter were subsequently acquired by Philip IV and complete the group of Rubens paintings housed in the Prado.

302
PETER PAUL RUBENS
Siegen, 1577–Antwerp, 1640

The Three Graces
c. 1635. Oil on panel,
221 x 181 cm
P1670

According to Hesiod's *Theogony*, there were three Graces: Aglaia, meaning radiant; Euphrosyne, joyful; and Thalia, flowering. Born of Zeus's love affairs, they were pure virgins who lived with the gods, took part in banquets and inspired *joie de vivre*. They were in the service of Aphrodite, the goddess of love, and were never bored. Rubens depicted them by a fountain beneath a garland of flowers with a landscape background. Although the figures are inspired by classical sculpture, the circular rhythm and elegantly undulating movement are common features of the artist's later works, which are steeped in a sensuality that is usually attributed to the happiness of his second marriage. The figure on the left is even directly inspired by his wife, Helena Fourment. The work remained in the painter's possession until his death and was acquired shortly afterwards for Philip IV's collection.

303
PETER PAUL RUBENS
Siegen, 1577–Antwerp, 1640

The Adoration of the Magi
1609 and 1628–29.
Oil on canvas, 346 x 488 cm
p1638

Commissioned by the city of Antwerp in 1609 to commemorate the truce between Spain and the Dutch United Provinces, the painting hung in the city hall until it was presented by the city as a gift to Rodrigo Calderón, who sent it to Spain. After Calderón's death in 1621 the painting passed into Philip IV's collection. It displays Rubens's early style, which was greatly influenced by his recent trip to Italy: vigorous figures, intense use of light and tightly packed compositions. The

painter repainted and enlarged the work to its current size during his second visit to Spain in 1628–1629. In an upper strip he included two angels that reveal Venetian influence and incorporated another strip on the right, in which he left a record of his authorship by portraying himself on horseback. These additions are perfectly visible today, and their inclusion afforded the painting greater breadth, spacing out the initial composition and showing the evolution of Rubens's art.

304
PETER PAUL RUBENS
Siegen, 1577–Antwerp, 1640

*Equestrian Portrait
of the Duke of Lerma*
1603. Oil on canvas,
283 x 200 cm
P3137

Rubens produced this ennobling image of Lerma (1553–1625) during his first trip to Spain in 1603. The duke, the favourite of Philip III and the true ruler of the kingdom, is depicted on horseback holding the baton of command and wearing half-armour in allusion to his status as chief of the armed forces. The scallop shell of the Order of Santiago around his neck is the only aristocratic touch in what is above all a military portrait, as evidenced by the cavalry battle in the background. The painting reveals the force and vigour of the young Rubens's figures and his ability to capture the character of the sitter, in this case the haughtiness and pride of the duke. The artist positioned Lerma frontally, advancing towards the viewer, in the manner of classical sculptures. However, he achieves a modern, more dramatic and Baroque effect by using the palm tree to frame the figure. This image established a model for equestrian portraiture that greatly influenced later artists such as Van Dyck and Gaspar de Crayer.

305 ←
PETER PAUL RUBENS
Siegen, 1577–Antwerp, 1640

St George and the Dragon
1606–10. Oil on canvas,
304 x 256 cm
P1644

According to the *Golden
Legend* by Jacobus de Voragine,
the inhabitants of Silene in
northern Africa were obliged
to appease a dragon's fury by
feeding it a person chosen every
day by lottery. Not even the
king's daughter was exempt.
When making her way towards
this terrible fate, the princess
was seen by St George.
Smitten by her beauty, he
slew the dragon and rescued
her. Rubens produced this
painting during his trip to Italy
and devised a very dynamic
composition with the saint's
horse dividing the scene into
two parts.

307 →
PETER PAUL RUBENS
Siegen, 1577–Antwerp, 1640

Andromeda freed by Perseus
1636–38. Oil on canvas,
265 x 160 cm
P1663

The sea god Poseidon had sent
a monster to the kingdom of
Ethiopia to punish the vanity
of its queen, Cassiopeia, who
considered herself more beautiful
than the Nereids. His fury would
only be placated by the sacrifice
of her daughter Andromeda,
who was duly chained to some
rocks. The painting shows the
moment when the hero Perseus,
having killed the monster, frees
the young woman from her
chains and falls in love with her,
as the presence of Cupid with
his quiver indicates. The figure
of Hymenaeus, god of marriage,
announces their future wedding.
The work was intended for
the New Hall in the Alcázar,
where it was viewed as a political
allegory of the power of the
Spanish monarchy. The hero,
clad in sixteenth-century armour,
would have been regarded as a
metaphor of the monarch himself
and his dominion over evil.

306 ←
PETER PAUL RUBENS
Siegen, 1577–Antwerp, 1640

FRANS SNYDERS
Antwerp, 1579–1657

*The Recognition
of Philopoemen*
1609–10. Oil on canvas,
201 x 311 cm
P1851

According to Plutarch, the famous
Greek general Philopoemen paid a
secret visit to the town of Megara.
His simple, lowly appearance led
him to be mistaken for a servant
by an elderly woman, who ordered
him to perform household chores.
The painting illustrates the
moment when the old woman's
husband realises the true identity
of the visitor. The painting is the
first product of the fruitful artistic
collaboration between Rubens
and Snyders. Rubens, a great
connoisseur of classical culture,
shows the influence of his recent
trip to Italy in his rendering of
the physical characteristics of the
figures. The kitchen scene in
the foreground, with its still life
of vegetables, fruit and game, is
the work of Snyders, a specialist
in this genre. He thus gives the
classical episode a realistic,
everyday aspect that brings it close
to the viewer. The swan and the
peacock reappear in several
of Snyders' thought-provoking
still lifes, which he produced
throughout his career.

308
PAUL BRIL
Antwerp, 1554–Rome, 1626

PETER PAUL RUBENS
Siegen, 1577–Antwerp, 1640

Landscape with Psyche and Jupiter

1610. Oil on canvas,
93 x 128 cm
P1849

Paul Bril was one of the most important Flemish landscape artists of the early seventeenth century. Long based in Rome, where he produced this work, he succeeded in combining the Southern European classicist spirit with the Northern European fondness for detail. Despite its modern, high viewpoint in the middle of the horizon line, the work retains the dramatic quality of Flemish tradition. It also displays a luminosity and order characteristic of the Roman-style landscapes that went on to enjoy such success in the following decades. Rubens, one of Bril's great admirers, added the figures, transforming a mere view of nature into the idealised setting of a mythological story. As a punishment for gazing upon Cupid, her future husband, Psyche was ordered by Venus to fill a flask with water from the treacherous spring of the river Styx. Transforming himself into an eagle, the god Jupiter comes to the young woman's aid by grasping the goblet in his beak and easily filling it among the rugged rocks.

309
PETER PAUL RUBENS
Siegen, 1577–Antwerp, 1640

*The Cardinal-Infante Don
Ferdinand of Austria at the
Battle of Nördlingen*

1634–40. Oil on canvas
335 x 258 cm
P1687

The Cardinal-Infante Don
Ferdinand of Austria, Philip IV's
youngest brother, was appointed
governor of the Netherlands
in 1634. During his trip to
Brussels he confronted the
Protestant armies, defeating
them at the battle of Nördlingen
on 6 September. The portrait
commemorates this victory.
The baton of command and
the red sash refer to Ferdinand's
status as governor. Above
him the allegory of Fury, with
Jupiter's eagle and thunderbolts,
alludes to his strength and
bravery. The clash of the
armies is depicted behind him.
The artist chose an extremely
intense image in which the
horseman's serenity contrasts
with the agitation of his mount.
The horse's rearing stance,
common in equestrian portraits,
is a visual metaphor of the
strength and skills of governors,
whose virtues are listed in
the inscription at the bottom
of the painting. The portrait
was acquired by King Philip IV
and hung at the Alcázar palace
in Madrid as a symbol of the
Habsburgs' dynastic power
in Europe.

310

PETER PAUL RUBENS
Siegen, 1577–Antwerp, 1640

The Garden of Love

1633–34. Oil on canvas,
198 x 283 cm
P1690

The painting depicts a court scene in an idyllic garden setting. In an atmosphere of pleasurable sensuality, women relax or are wooed, while cherubs hover around bearing symbols of marital love, such as the pair of doves and the yoke. The fountains or statues of the Three Graces and the lactating Venus allude to happy marriage and fertility. The peacock is a symbol of Juno, protector of marriage. Rubens was a great connoisseur of classical culture, and here he borrows motifs from Renaissance sculptures and uses the Mannerist portico of his own house in Antwerp as an architectural backdrop. This has led scholars to suggest that the painting was intended as a self-portrait with friends, and it was occasionally called *The Family of Rubens*. Whatever the case, it is an exuberant and exultant allegory of love and marital bliss which Rubens painted as he was savouring the happiness of his second marriage.

311
PETER PAUL RUBENS
Siegen, 1577–Antwerp, 1640

Dance of Mythological
Characters and Villagers
1636–40. Oil on panel,
73 x 106 cm
P1691

A group of country folk dance
boisterously to the sound of
a flute played by a musician
in the tree above them. The
scene takes place in a landscape
that recalls Italy, especially the
country villa in the background.
The presence of satyrs with
naked torsos wearing wreaths
of ivy and bells on their ankles
and the person dressed in
leopard skin, a possible allusion
to the god Bacchus, lend the
scene a certain mythological
air that infuses it with greater

mystery and sensuality.
Rubens masterfully captures
the sensation of circular
movement in a highly dynamic
composition. This impression
is further enhanced by the
dog that moves in parallel
to the dancers. The country
scenes of Pieter Bruegel the
Elder are the precedent of this
painting, which conveys the
happiness of the artist's final
years. It remained in Rubens's
possession until his death, when
it was acquired for Philip IV.

Van Dyck

Born in Antwerp, Anthony van Dyck was an outstanding disciple of Rubens, although by the time he joined his workshop he had almost completed his artistic training. He had learnt the trade with Hendrick van Balen, a painter from a previous generation and a representative of the Italianising trend that transformed Flemish painting at the turn of the sixteenth century. After becoming a master, Van Dyck continued to work with Rubens, taking part in some of his most significant decorative projects. Following a short stay in England which brought him into contact with important patrons and art lovers, Van Dyck spent a second artistic period in Antwerp, where he painted a few portraits and major religious works such as *The Arrest of Christ* [314]. At the end of 1621 he departed for Italy, where he completed the formation of his painting style. Over the next six years he spent time in Venice, Rome and Sicily, but above all in Genoa. There he produced some of the best portraits of the Baroque period, grandiose images that raised the status of his sitters thanks to the dignity he bestowed on them and his command of Venetian colouring. He returned to Antwerp in 1627, entering the service of the Archduchess Isabella Clara Eugenia (1566–1633) and establishing the prototype for official portraits of the governor, now a widow. Some of his finest portraits from this period combine Venetian manners and Flemish fidelity, such as that of the painter Marteen Rijkaert in the Prado [315]. During these years he also worked on important religious works, devotional images infused with a deep spirituality, which were greatly esteemed throughout Europe. In 1632 his fame led him to be sent for by the English king Charles I (reigned 1625–1649) and he travelled to London. There he was much sought after by local enthusiasts, many of them Catholics, who wanted his religious images but also his portraits. A work from this period is the self-portrait with Endymion Porter, now in the Prado [312]. His outdoor portraits revitalised the image of British society and influenced the local school until well into the eighteenth century [359]. His closeness to the king led to a knighthood and a social status similar to that of his master, Rubens. Except for a third period in Antwerp in 1634–1635, where he produced some of the most outstanding portraits of the Flemish bourgeoisie, he lived in London until his death.

312
ANTHONY VAN DYCK
Antwerp, 1599–London, 1641

*Endymion Porter
and Van Dyck*
c. 1635. Oil on canvas.
119 x 144 cm
P1489

An important diplomat of the English court and a great art lover, Endymion Porter (1587–1649) was one of Van Dyck's most loyal supporters during his sojourn in London, and the artist painted this portrait as a token of gratitude. The Englishman is depicted frontally, dressed in white satin, while the painter, in black, is shown in profile and at a lower height so as not to stand above the aristocrat. The unusual nature of this double portrait reflects the affection between the painter and his patron, which is also indicated by the position of their hands on the rock, another symbol of the strength of their friendship. By portraying himself beside an illustrious personage, the artist draws attention to his lofty social status and indirectly dignifies his painter's profession as a noble activity.

313
ANTHONY VAN DYCK
Antwerp, 1599–London, 1641

Christ Crowned with Thorns
1618–20. Oil on canvas,
224 x 197 cm
P1474

This is one of the artist's most moving religious paintings. A group of figures around Christ mock him as King of the Jews, placing on him the crown of thorns and handing him the reed cane that alludes to the royal sceptre. The ignorant violence of those who taunt and ridicule Jesus is embodied by the barking dog. This youthful work displays the powerful influence of Italian art acquired through Rubens. From this source he draws the force of the figures and the Venetian appearance, while the image of Christ is inspired directly by Titian [221]. Also Rubensian is his skilful use of chiaroscuro to create a dramatic atmosphere, although its precedent should be sought in Caravaggio's oeuvre, from which Van Dyck borrows the idea of the two witnesses who contemplate the scene with amazement from behind the barred window.

314
ANTHONY VAN DYCK
Antwerp, 1599–London, 1641

The Arrest of Christ
1618–20. Oil on canvas,
344 x 249 cm
P1477

Van Dyck's *Arrest of Christ* displays the characteristics of his early period, particularly the noticeably Venetian palette and composition. The low viewpoint and use of a single source of light give the painting considerable dramatic intensity. In the darkness of the Mount of Olives, Jesus receives from Judas the kiss that betrays his identity. In the foreground, as described in the Gospel account, Peter cuts off the ear of Malchus, the High Priest's servant, during the violence unleashed by the taunting Roman soldiers. The painting, one of the painter's most appreciated works, is known in several versions which vary only in secondary details. This picture, like the same artist's *Christ Crowned with Thorns* [313], was owned by Rubens, at whose death both were acquired for Philip IV.

315
ANTHONY VAN DYCK
Antwerp, 1599–London, 1641

The Painter Marteen Rijkaert

1627–32. Oil on panel,
148 x 113 cm
P1479

Van Dyck displays his
outstanding skills to the full
in the genre of portraiture.
This work, probably executed
before Van Dyck's trip to
England, is a striking example
of his psychological portraits.
A contemporary of the artist,
the painter Rijkaert had no left
hand. Far from being concealed,
this is ostensibly shown in
the painting, which conveys

the vitality and personality
of the sitter who, unusually,
is positioned frontally. Taking
as his basis the Northern
European portrait tradition
derived from Anthonis Mor, the
painter depicts the sitter against
a deep black background. The
work also displays the influence
of Titian [211], especially in
the use of colour, the rapid
brushstrokes and the pose.

316
ANTHONY VAN DYCK
Antwerp, 1599–London, 1641

Mary Ruthwen,
the Painter's Wife

1639–41. Oil on canvas,
104 x 81 cm
P1495

One of the finest examples of Van Dyck's portraits is that of his wife Mary Ruthwen. Van Dyck had married Mary, who was of Scottish origin, in 1639, and she was to die six years later in 1645. The painter endows the portrait with a sense of intimacy and affection which is enhanced by the gesture of the hands playing with the rosary and by the steadfast gaze. Van Dyck has abandoned the style of the court portraits he was producing in England around this time in favour of a more domestic and private type of painting, which gives the work its special quality.

Jordaens

Jacob Jordaens began his training with the same master as Rubens, the painter Adam van Noort, who was renowned in Antwerp for his history paintings and whose daughter Catharina he later married; such marriages between families of artists were common practice in Flanders. Younger than Rubens, Jordaens soon struck up a working relationship with him and took part in many projects to decorate Antwerp churches, such as those of the Dominicans and the Augustinians. In 1634 he was one of the artists who executed the paintings designed by Rubens to decorate the triumphal arches for the entry of the new governor of the Netherlands, the Cardinal-Infante Ferdinand of Austria. This marked the start of several collaborations between the two artists. One of the most significant was the execution of some of the paintings for the Torre de la Parada, Philip IV's hunting lodge. These were Jordaens' first works to reach Spain. Rubens was responsible for the designs. In 1640, with Rubens dead and Van Dyck working at the English court, Jordaens became the leading Flemish painter. Although he never set foot outside his country of birth, his fame crossed borders and he soon received commissions from some of the principal royal art lovers, such as Christina of Sweden and the Orange family of The Hague. Secretly committed to the Protestant cause, the artist finally converted in 1671, but he continued to paint the Catholic themes commissioned by individuals or religious institutions. Jordaens became a wealthy and socially respectable painter, as he himself conveyed in the portrait of his family today in the Prado [318].

317
JACOB JORDAENS
Antwerp, 1593–1678

Meleager and Atalanta
1620–50. Oil on canvas,
151 x 241 cm
P1546

After hunting down the huge wild boar that was ravaging the kingdom of Calydon, Meleager offered its head to his beloved Atalanta. His uncles, believing themselves to be more entitled to the trophy, snatched it from him and the infuriated hero killed them. The story recounted in Ovid's *Metamorphoses* is illustrated by Jordaens in a composition with two clearly differentiated parts executed at different times. The right-hand side shows the crucial moment when Meleager is about to draw his sword to commence the attack, while the terrified Atalanta tries to deter him. This part still shows the influence of Rubens's monumental figures. Jordaens later added the accompanying group of hunters to set the pace of the composition, as the position of their weapons, the outstretched arm and the movement of the dogs steer the viewer's gaze to the main event. The painting is first documented in 1746 at the palace of La Granja.

318
JACOB JORDAENS
Antwerp, 1593–1678

The Painter's Family
1621–22. Oil on canvas,
181 x 187 cm
P1549

This portrait of Jordaens and his family is set in an elegant garden with animals roaming about freely and a few sculptures which are intended to convey the family's elevated social status. The rich, refined clothing is also suggestive of a certain nobility. The painter rests his hand on an armchair, in a traditional pose, and is surrounded by symbolic elements. The lute he holds represents music, which was seen as a cultivated, aristocratic form of entertainment. The dog is a reference to faithfulness and the servant with a basket of grapes to family prosperity. The work recalls Flemish artists' interest in dignifying their professional activity during the early Baroque period, and in showing themselves to be prominent members of society. It was executed by Jordaens at the beginning of his mature period, when he was at the height of his successful career.

The Dutch Painting Collection

The Dutch school is one of the most distinctive within European Baroque painting. Its separation from the so-called Flemish school was the result of the political separation that took place in the Low Countries, an area ruled by the Habsburg dynasty (to which the Spanish monarchy belonged), which had inherited it from the dukes of Burgundy. Religious differences between the Protestant north and the Catholic south eventually resulted in one of the most prolonged conflicts on mainland Europe. While the independence of the Netherlands was not officially recognised by Spain until the signing of the Treaty of Münster in 1648, in practice the Northern Provinces constituted a nation from the late sixteenth century.

These historical circumstances did not favour artistic relations with Spain, nor did the differing social and religious viewpoints. In Holland subjects such as landscape, sea views and still lifes proliferated and were much sought after by a middle class proud of its lifestyle and its country. In contrast, Spanish collectors generally preferred religious subjects. Nonetheless, while it is generally said that almost no Dutch paintings arrived in Spain in the sixteenth and seventeenth centuries, a number of works that were or could have been Dutch are recorded in the Royal Collections at that time. Among them were still lifes by Jan Davidsz de Heem and various paintings by Dutch artists based in Rome, such as landscapes commissioned from Jan Both and Herman van Swanevelt for the Buen Retiro Palace in Madrid. Some Dutch paintings attributed at the time to Italian artists, like Mathias Stomer's *Doubting Thomas* [322], also came to Spain.

It was only in the eighteenth century, with a change of dynasty in Spain, that Spanish monarchs began to show an interest in Dutch art. Philip V (reigned 1700–1746) and Isabella Farnese (1692–1766) acquired works by Poelenburgh, Van Ostade, Droochsloot, Schoeff and others, including an important group of landscapes by Philips Wouwerman [321]. Charles III (reigned 1759–1788) purchased Rembrandt's *Judith at the Banquet of Holofernes* [319], the jewel of the Prado's Dutch collection. However, it was Charles IV (reigned 1788–1819), the most committed collector of the Bourbon monarchs, who acquired works by Metsu, Breenbergh, Schalcken, Wtewael, Jacop Cuyp, Bramer and Steenwijck [324].

Overall, however, the Dutch paintings that entered the Prado from the Royal Collections constituted a group of varied quality with few works by the great names of this school. Fortunately, subsequent additions have resulted in a considerable increase in the number of artists represented. Through donations and other means of acquisition, the museum has acquired paintings by Potter, Heda and Claesz [323], Van Mierevelt and Koninck, Benjamin G. Cuyp, ter Borch, Moreelse, Netscher and Hondecoeter, among others.

Seventeenth-century Painting in Holland

Social and economic circumstances in the democratic and predominantly Calvinist Holland of the seventeenth century favoured an art that differed in many respects from that produced in Flanders. Calvinism was opposed to the display of religious images in churches. There was no monarchy as such, and the House of Orange, whose function within the republic was largely a military one, was more drawn to Flemish or Italianate artists, for it should not be forgotten that there was a strong Caravaggesque influence on Dutch painters like Gerrit van Honthorst and Hendrick Terbrugghen. All this meant that Dutch artists as early as the sixteenth century were working in a context quite unlike that of the rest of Europe. The result was the appearance of the art market, something which was to have enormous consequences. Despite its wars with Spain, France and England, Holland was an extremely prosperous country on its way to becoming an international commercial power, and its newly enriched burghers soon showed a desire to own paintings. In response to this growing demand, Dutch artists produced pictures of a suitable size for domestic interiors, choosing to represent scenes of everyday life and settings familiar to their clients. The new paintings can be regarded in this respect as a continuation of the fifteenth-century naturalist tradition of the Netherlands, but they also had a characteristic of their own, which was their depiction of the opulence of the society they sprang from. This is evident in the objects and foodstuffs shown in large numbers of still lifes, in the fertility of the landscapes, and in the elegant apparel of the figures, even in paintings of biblical episodes or mythological subjects.

319
REMBRANDT
Leiden, 1606–Amsterdam, 1669

Judith at the Banquet of Holofernes
1634. Oil on canvas,
142 x 154 cm
P2132

Rembrandt Harmensz van Rijn is the great master of 17th century Dutch painting and one of the great Baroque painters. His extraordinary mastery of colour and light, together with his original accuracy of the subjects, are combined in this painting belonging to a group painted between 1633 and 1635 which represent the heroines of Antiquity and the Old Testament.
Until now, this scene was interpreted as Queen Artemis at the moment of drinking the ashes of her husband Mausolo. However, the rich clothing, the luxurious *nautilus* cup, the old lady with the bag and the curtains in the background (visible in an old photograph from around 1887) allow her to be interpreted as Judith at the banquet of Holofernes, which her servant awaits her outside the shop with the bag for the head of the arch enemy (Judith 12, 17-19). The open book is a reference to the Bible. For the Dutch, Judith and Esther were the biblical heroines who best symbolized the patriotic claims against the Spanish. The sitter in this painting has been said to be the painter's first wife, despite her physical traits not fitting with those of existing portraits of Saskia van Uylienburgh.

320
SALOMON DE BRAY
Amsterdam, 1597–
Haarlem, 1664

*Judith with the Head
of Holofernes*
c. 1636. Oil on panel,
89 x 71 cm
P2097

321
PHILIPS WOUWERMAN
Haarlem, 1619–1668

Hunting Hare
c. 1665. Oil on canvas,
77 x 105 cm
P2148

Rustic and hunting scenes were particularly successful within the genre of Dutch landscape painting. Carefully painted animals, especially horses, were always included in these compositions. In his own time Wouwerman was considered the best painter of horses and enjoyed great fame throughout Europe. All the leading European collectors vied to possess his works, which were generally of small format and in which country life is treated with a courtly elegance. In this hunting scene, various mounted courtiers are present at the capture of a hare by a pack of dogs. In the middle-ground other aristocratic figures enjoy a lively picnic in the company of various ladies, while a third group watches the spectacle from the top of a tower. Wouwerman has produced a totally idealised landscape with fantastical monuments, such as the Baroque fountain in the middle of the river, that add a touch of sophistication to the natural setting. The soft, luminous colours add the final pleasing note to this scene in which hunting is presented as a princely pursuit and thus a pastime for the aristocracy.

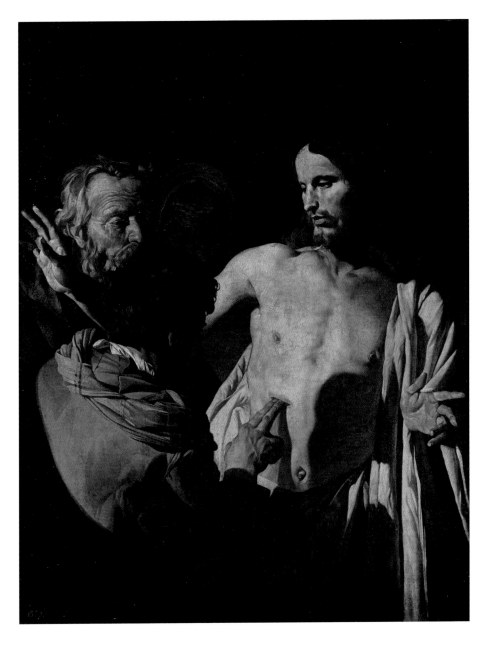

322
MATTHIAS STOMER OR STOM
Amersfoort, c. 1600–Sicily,
after 1652

Doubting Thomas
c. 1641-49. Oil on canvas,
125 x 99 cm
P2094

Stomer did not personally meet Caravaggio but he fully assimilated his approach through his paintings and through those of his northern followers such as Gerrit van Honthorst. In depicting this gospel episode, Stomer therefore uses real, even coarse models, lit by a powerful light so that they stand out from the surrounding shadows. Such a presentation emphasises the drama of the moment when the risen Christ appears to the Apostles. Time seems to stand still as St Thomas touches the open wound on Christ's side in order to prove his identity. The restrained dialogue of gestures and gazes, the unusual placement of Thomas (seen from behind) and the oppressive atmosphere convey the moment of recognition with the maximum sense of realism and tension.

323
PIETER CLAESZ
Berchem, c. 1596-97–Haarlem,
1660

*Still Life with Roemer,
Silver Tazza and Bread*
1637. Oil on canvas, 82,7 x 66,2 cm
P2753

The still life was one of the most successful genres in Dutch painting. The close-up view of the objects and the precise detail in the depiction of textures and forms resulted in highly ornamental compositions which were much sought after by merchants and burghers of the United Provinces for the decoration of their homes. Numerous painters specialised in this field and Claesz was one of the most celebrated and refined within the genre. This painting features all the characteristics of his style. The disordered table is spread with the remains of a banquet. The gleam of the splendid glasses and vessels contrasts with the broken pieces of bread, the decoratively peeled lemon and the nuts. The light is directed from outside the composition in order to emphasise the projection of shadows, which contribute to an effect of three-dimensionality. Overall, the composition challenges the perception of the viewer, who should not be deceived by its exceptionally real appearance.

324
PIETER VAN STEENWIJCK
Delft, c. 1615–[?], after 1650

Emblem of Death
c.1635-40. Oil on canvas,
34,3 x 46 cm
P2137

Within the genre of the still life, so-called *vanitas* paintings refer to the ephemeral nature of all earthly things, inviting the viewer to reflect on the vanity of material objects and to focus on more spiritual ones. This is the significance of this canvas by Steenwijck, an artist of the Leiden school about whom very little is known. The artist arranged the objects to form a rising diagonal but also left a large empty space that emphasises the feeling of solitude and silence. Despite the painting's small size, every element is described in minute detail and given a monumental character. The objects are shown scattered around in disorder, with a confusion of papers, musical instruments, extinguished pipes, the remains of a frugal meal and a casket that probably contains jewels. Everything that gives pleasure to man or distracts him, such as reading, music or smoking, serves for nothing after death, to which the chilling presence of the skull and the spent candle refer.

The French Painting collection

The French School of painting is the fourth in importance in the Museo del Prado's collections after the Spanish, Italian and Flemish Schools. As in the case of Italy and the Low Countries, this group has distinctive characteristics because of the way in which it was formed, a process in which historical circumstances were particularly important. Spain and France were in permanent conflict during the sixteenth and seventeenth centuries, making artistic contact difficult. Furthermore, pictorial tastes at that time were different on the two sides of the Pyrenees. The classicist trend prevailed in France, promoted by the Académie, an institution for which there was no equivalent in Spain until the eighteenth century. Nonetheless, political events brought about some contacts. Over the course of the seventeenth century there were a number of marriages between the two crowns. The Spanish infantas Ana (1601–1666) and María Teresa of Austria (1638–1683) married Louis XIII (reigned 1610–1643) and Louis XIV (reigned 1643–1715) respectively. The consequent exchange of portraits brought works by Philippe de Champagne, Henri and Charles Beaubrun and Jean Nocret to Spain. In addition, other European sovereigns who used French artists had their portraits sent to Madrid, including Christina of Sweden and Charles Manuel II of Savoy, painted by Sébastien Bourdon [331] and Charles Dauphin respectively. While works in other genres were less frequently sent to Spain, the museum has some examples, such as *St John the Baptist* by Pierre Mignard, given to Charles II (reigned 1665–1700) following his marriage to María Luisa of Orléans (1662–1689). Despite this, the *Grand Siècle* in France was barely reflected in Spanish collections. Interestingly, a large proportion of French works that reached Spain arrived via Italy. This was the case with the landscapes by Jean Lemaire, Gaspard Dughet, Poussin and Claude Lorraine commissioned in Rome by agents of Philip IV (reigned 1621–1665) for the Buen Retiro Palace [329, 334], and with *The Martyrdom of St Lawrence* by Valentin de Boulogne [326], which was in the Alcázar in Madrid in 1686 under attribution to Poussin.

When the Bourbons came to the throne in Madrid in the eighteenth century, the gradual acquisition of French paintings from the previous century continued. Philip V (reigned 1700–1746) purchased a notable group of works by Poussin [329,330,332,333] and acquired others by Jacques Stella, Jacques Courtois and the artist known as the Pensionante de Saraceni. Charles III (reigned 1759–1788) acquired a painting of *Susannah* by Antoine Coypel. However, in general, the acquisition of French painting was extremely limited and it was only after the foundation of the Museo del Prado that gaps in these holdings were filled. Thanks to the Brunov Bequest, a biblical scene by Bourdon entered the museum in 1979, while the works by Vouet, Linard, the School of Fontainebleau and La Tour were acquired through purchase [325]. The presence of La Tour was unexpectedly strengthened with the discovery of a previously unknown painting in the Ministry of Employment in 2005 [327].

La Tour and the Beginning of the Baroque in France

The religious wars of the sixteenth century left France in a fragile state economically and politically, from which it was saved by a series of ambitious monarchs, each assisted by an able minister – Henry IV by Sully, Louis XIII by Richelieu and Louis XIV by Colbert. The result was a new age of splendour that would have important consequences for the arts. During the seventy-two years of Louis XIV's reign – from 1643 to 1715 – Paris began to replace Rome as the principal artistic centre in Europe, a position that it would maintain until the nineteenth century.

Nonetheless, in the first half of the seventeenth century, France was notably influenced by Italian art of the day. As in other European countries, Caravaggio was of considerable importance. The work of the first major seventeenth-century artist in France, Georges de La Tour from Lorraine [325, 327], reveals the influence of Caravaggio's realism and dramatic use of chiaroscuro. La Tour's oeuvre, which is extremely small, is unique in its poetic treatment of nocturnal light and of everyday life, which the artist imbued with a mysterious spirituality. While in general it could be said that the Catholic nations and those governed by absolutist monarchs were aware of the emotional appeal of the Italian Baroque, France rejected the formal excesses of southern Baroque and developed a tempered, elegant and classicising style which art historians now hesitate to describe as 'Baroque'. This style's connections with Italy are, however, so evident that it is difficult to avoid the term completely. Paradoxically, the most classicising seventeenth-century French artist, Nicolas Poussin, preferred to live and work outside France in Rome, the very heart of the Baroque.

325
GEORGES DE LA TOUR
Vic-sur-Seille, 1593–
Lunéville, 1652

The Blind Hurdy-Gurdy Player
1610–30. Oil on canvas,
84.7 x 61 cm
P7613

An artist whose career is largely unknown, La Tour produced highly realistic works but ones imbued with a sense of mystery. He is documented as working in Lorraine in the north-east of France and to a lesser degree in Paris. However, the marked influence of Caravaggio on his work has led art historians to propose a hypothetical trip to Italy. His paintings generally depict popular types of a very individualised nature, as in the present work, which shows an old blind musician. La Tour painted this subject on several occasions. The Prado's version must originally have included the figure full-length, which would explain why it now appears to be too tightly fitted into the pictorial space. The figure is shown in profile, with little emphasis placed on his blindness. The rest of the composition is painted in great detail: the deep lines on his forehead, the texture of the wooden instrument and the rough, grey-brown cloak, which all convey his lowly status, age and profession, are combined in an admirably harmonious manner. However, the intention behind the painting is unclear: it could be a simple image of everyday life or a parable with a moral undertone.

326 ↑
VALENTIN DE BOULOGNE
Coulommiers, 1591–Rome, 1632

*The Martyrdom
of St Lawrence*
c. 1621–22. Oil on canvas,
195 x 261 cm
P2346

327 ←
GEORGES DE LA TOUR
Vic-sur-Seille, 1593–
Lunéville, 1652

St Jerome reading a Letter
1610–30. Oil on canvas,
79 x 65 cm
T5006. On deposit from
the Ministry of Employment
and Social Affairs

328 →
SIMON VOUET
Paris, 1590–1649

*Time defeated by Hope,
Love and Beauty*
1627. Oil on canvas,
107 x 142 cm
P2987

The abstract idea of the triumph of the emotions over the passing of time is here given concrete expression as a physical struggle. Each figure represents a classical deity. Time is personified as Saturn, an old man with a beard, holding an hourglass and scythe. Hope and Venus, goddess of beauty, pull him along the ground helped by Cupid, the god of love. Cupid is accompanied by two other little winged putti who trap the elderly Time. The beauty of the young women, their strength and joyful spirit triumph over the inexorable passing of time, although the merciless manner in which they mock Time also suggests the thoughtlessness of youth. Vouet painted this canvas shortly before he left Rome, having been summoned by Louis XIII to become court painter in Paris. The brilliant colouring is characteristic of his mature style, as is the idealisation of the figures and the theatrical organisation of the composition.

Only genre paintings and religious compositions are known by La Tour. Faithful to his artistic vision, the artist depicted beggars and saints with equal realism, as if daily life intruded on the sacred realm. Here St Jerome is depicted as an elderly cardinal who needs glasses to read. His ecclesiastical rank is indicated by his cardinal's cape, whilst the lines on his forehead and his abundant grey hair indicate his advanced age. Although St Jerome was frequently depicted in a moment of inspiration or writing, La Tour chose to show him reading a letter which still retains traces of the sealing-wax with which it was sealed; the sender's handwriting can also be made out. Every detail becomes important as it is emphasised by the strong lighting. As is usual with La Tour, the light comes from two different sources, complicating the interplay of shadows, which are graduated on the face and the folds of the paper and highly pronounced in the background.

Poussin

Within Baroque painting, Nicolas Poussin represents the paradigm of classicism. He initially trained in his native Normandy and in Paris, but his work bcame better known following his arrival in Rome in 1624. From this point onwards his interest in classical antiquity was a constant element in his painting. He combined his study of classical works of art with the study of the great Renaissance painters such as Raphael and Titian. As a result his style is characterised by an almost archaeological evocation of the Greco-Roman world, a quest for balance and ideal beauty, and a study of human passions. In his early years in Italy, Poussin enjoyed the protection of the Barberini family and of the intellectual and art patron Cassiano dal Pozzo (1588–1657), secretary to Cardinal Francesco Barberini. He worked for cultured clients who requested the erudite subjects in which he specialised, both in Rome and France. Because of his fame in his native country he was recalled to Paris by Louis XIII (reigned 1610–1643) and remained there from 1640 to 1642, working on major projects such as the decoration of a gallery in the Palais du Louvre. On his return to Rome, Poussin's work became more measured and restrained, expressing a refined, poetic aesthetic. His art was extremely influential for the subsequent development of French painting.

The Museo del Prado has eight paintings and two drawings by the artist. This is a comprehensive group that covers all the genres in which Poussin worked and includes a number of his masterpieces.

329 ↓
NICOLAS POUSSIN
Les Andelys, 1594–Rome, 1665

Landscape with St Jerome
1637–38. Oil on canvas,
155 x 234 cm
P2304

This painting was commissioned by Philip V's agents in Rome for the decoration of the Buen Retiro Palace in Madrid. It was one of a series of landscapes with hermits painted by artists working in Rome around 1637, resulting in a group of paintings whose religious content assumed a secondary role in relation to the depiction of nature. Poussin played a key role in this development. Landscape became an important element in his compositions and one that reflected the mood of the painting. However, in the present work the wild dramatic setting is in marked contrast to Poussin's usual approach as it is intended to reflect the mysticism of St Jerome, who has taken refuge in a dense forest in order to meditate in solitude. The alternation of light and shade that structures the painting is directly derived from Titian, whom Poussin greatly admired. It has been suggested that the saint depicted is not Jerome but Paul the Hermit.

330
NICOLAS POUSSIN
Les Andelys, 1594–Rome, 1665

Parnassus

c. 1631–33. Oil on canvas,
145 x 197 cm
P2313

Mount Parnassus was the home of Apollo, god of arts and letters. He lived there with the nine Muses, female deities who protected the sciences, theatre and literature. Poussin recreated this idyllic location in a scene depicting nine poets arriving at Apollo's imaginary court. Personified by a nymph, the Castalian Spring spouts the water that inspired all those who drank it. This water is offered to them by various putti from Apollo's retinue. He appears presiding over the event, in which one of the poets is crowned with laurel. The leaves of this shrub were Apollo's symbol and a laurel wreath was reserved for outstanding artists. It has been suggested that the figure being crowned may be Torquato Tasso (1544–1595), author of the epic poem *Jerusalem Liberated*. Poussin looked to classical sculpture in this work as well as to a celebrated fresco by Raphael on the same subject. The soft colouring and harmonious composition are a homage to the Italian artist.

331
SEBASTIAN BOURDON
Montpellier, 1616–Paris, 1671

Queen Christina of Sweden on Horseback
1653–54. Oil on canvas,
383 x 291 cm
P1503

Bourdon exemplifies the classicist style and the influence of Poussin on French painting. This portrait is an eloquent image of power in seventeenth-century Europe. Christina of Sweden (reigned 1632–1654) is depicted during a hunt, and her firm pose is a metaphor for the energy of a ruler. The portrait was given to Philip IV for political reasons, as shortly after it was painted Christina abdicated and converted to Catholicism with the aid of the Spanish monarchy.

332
NICOLAS POUSSIN
Les Andelys, 1594–Rome, 1665

Landscape with Buildings
c. 1648–51. Oil on canvas,
120 x 187 cm
P2310

This landscape offers a good example of Poussin's aesthetic ideals. The figures are depicted on a small scale and the real subject is the broad valley with a river flowing through it. The entire composition is imbued with a sense of calm and harmony, from the luminous colours to the carefully balanced distribution of the different elements. The only bright note is the small touch of red on the clothes of the man talking to two walkers. He could be the Greek philosopher Diogenes of Sinope, who was questioned while walking from Sparta to Athens as to which city he preferred. Poussin here presents an ideal vision of nature, and the buildings and figures are classical in style.

333
NICOLAS POUSSIN
Les Andelys, 1594–Rome, 1665

The Triumph of David
c.1630. Oil on canvas,
100 x 130 cm
P2311

Poussin made use of a classicising mode to represent a subject that does not derive from Greek or Roman tradition. The story of David comes from the Old Testament, but here we appear to witness the triumph of a mythological hero. Rather than depicting the combat between the young shepherd and Goliath, the painter invented a moment that does not appear in the biblical account, making use of allegorical figures that give the scene a different meaning. David, the victor, looks pensively at the spoils piled up next to the mortal remains of his enemy. We can see the wound of the stone shot from a sling with which David killed the giant, as described in the Bible. However, Goliath's armour is more appropriate to a Roman solider than to a Philistine. Similarly classical is the figure of the pagan goddess of Victory, who crowns David with laurel. The putti who accompany her amuse themselves with a harp, an instrument played by David, while another hands Victory a gold crown that presages David's destiny as king of Israel. The classical architecture in the background, painted in elegant grey tones, completes this thoughtful presentation of David reflecting on the consequences of his deed.

Claude Lorraine

334
CLAUDE LORRAINE
Champagne, c. 1600–
Rome, 1682

Claude Gellée, known as Claude Lorraine after the region of France in which he was born, was one of the leading classicist painters. Like Poussin, he spent most of his life in Italy. In 1618 he was in Rome as a student of Agostino Tassi (1566–1644), a painter who specialised in landscapes. Through Tassi, Claude became familiar with the technique of fresco, in which he briefly worked, and above all with the northern landscape tradition. Claude devoted his activities to this genre and became the leading landscape painter of the day. An interest in nature and the study of light characterise his interpretation of landscape, which played a key role in the evolution and reassessment of a genre previously considered inferior. In the 1630s Claude achieved professional success in Roman aristocratic circles and his reputation spread throughout Europe.

Claude's work takes its starting point from direct observation of nature, which he subsequently used as the basis for his harmonious and highly detailed compositions. Around 1640 his landscapes acquired a more classical note and he opted for historical and religious subjects in preference to pastoral ones. His interest in the work of Annibale Carracci [233] and Domenichino [232] influenced this change of direction, as did his humanist contacts in Roman literary circles. Despite being offered academic honours, Claude remained faithful to his art and devoted his life to painting.

The Prado has an outstanding group of ten canvases by Claude. Most were commissioned directly from the artist for the Madrid court. The four he painted for the Buen Retiro Palace [334] have certain features in common. Each of these vertical format compositions, which correspond to four times of day, places all the emphasis on the landscape, which includes a large area of sky, whilst the narrative is confined to the lower part of the painting and seems little more than a pretext for depicting the natural world.

These four paintings were commissioned for the Buen Retiro Palace. In the *Landscape with the Embarkation at Ostia of St Paula Romana*, the imaginary setting is the most striking element. Paula, a noble Roman woman and friend of St Jerome, leaves Rome for the Holy Land accompanied by her daughter, with the intention of living in the desert as a hermit. The setting, which in principle depicts the ancient port of Ostia, highlights the contrast between the civilisation that the two women are leaving behind and the lonely future that awaits them. The real subject of the composition is the study of the dawn light as it bathes the entire scene in delicate golden tones. The second canvas depicts the story of Moses. According to Exodus, pharaoh's daughter rescued the infant Moses from the waters of the Nile, but only the palm tree here suggests the exoticism of Egypt. Claude transfers the scene to a broad Italian plain in which the medieval buildings are idealised according to seventeenth-century eyes. In the third canvas, Claude chose the sad story of St Serapia, using it as a vehicle to depict a landscape with classical ruins. St Sabina, the wife of the senator Valerian, attends the funeral of her maid Serapia, who had converted to Christianity, unaware that she too will be martyred for her new faith. In the fourth canvas, the narrative takes place at dusk. The Archangel Raphael orders Tobias to capture a huge fish whose entrails will cure his father's blindness. The landscape of Mesopotamia has once more been transformed into an idealised version of the fertile Italian countryside.

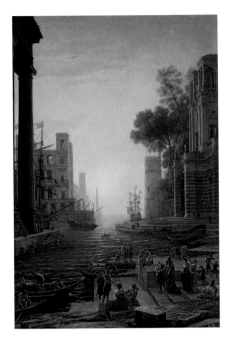

*Landscape with the Embarkation
at Ostia of St Paula Romana*
1639–40. Oil on canvas,
211 x 145 cm
P2254

The Burial of St Serapia
1639–40. Oil on canvas,
212 x 145 cm
P2252

The Finding of Moses
1639–40. Oil on canvas,
209 x 138 cm
P2253

The Archangel Raphael with Tobias
1639–40. Oil on canvas,
211 x 145 cm
P2255

French Painters
at the Spanish Bourbon Court

In 1700, the arrival of the new Bourbon dynasty resulted in dramatic changes in the art and culture of Spain. In 1701 Hyacinthe Rigaud, first painter to Louis XIV (reigned 1643–1715), painted Philip V dressed in the Spanish style. The canvas is now in the Prado. Forty-two years passed between that first image, which still conforms to Spanish taste, and the great family portrait by Van Loo of 1743 [335], sufficient time for the Bourbon royal image to replace the Habsburg one. Historical events as well as the presence of French artists in Madrid were instrumental in bringing about this change. The War of Spanish Succession brought victory to Philip V and with it a free hand to make wide-ranging changes within Spain. In 1712 María Luisa of Savoy (1688–1714), first wife of Philip V, complained to Madame Royale that there were no artists in Madrid to paint her portrait, and it is clear that after the death of Carreño de Miranda in 1685, the quality of Spanish art was not of the highest, although this was primarily an issue of taste. Rigaud's grandiose style and the powerful image that he created of the *Roi Soleil* provided a model for all of Europe that would now be adopted by Spain. Rigaud was too old and celebrated to move there, so it was his followers who arrived in the Spanish capital. The first, in 1715, was Michel-Ange Houasse, whose restrained portraits [336] did not fulfil the requirements of the new royal house, although his genre paintings covered the walls of the small, informal rooms at the palace of La Granja. As a result a second painter, Jean Ranc, arrived in Madrid in 1722. A pupil and nephew of Rigaud, Ranc produced a series of brilliant portraits of the entire royal family in the French style [337, 338]. His death in 1735 meant that a third master had to be found. Louis-Michel van Loo, also sent by Rigaud from Paris, arrived in 1737 and represents the last chapter in this period of artistic renewal. With the aim of creating an institutional framework for this new direction, the Spanish Royal Academies of Fine Arts were founded, and Van Loo was actively involved in the creation of the Academia de San Fernando in Madrid before his return to France in 1752. His influence extended to all the arts and to all genres of paintings and he left his mark on the training of subsequent generations of Spanish painters. However, the influence of Italy, which arrived with Philip V's second wife, Isabella Farnese, and continued under Ferdinand VI and Charles III, undermined the importance of this initial French tendency during the second half of the century.

335

LOUIS-MICHEL VAN LOO
Toulon, 1707–Paris, 1771

The Family of Philip V
1743. Oil on canvas, 406 x 511 cm
P2283

Louis-Michel van Loo arrived in Madrid in 1735 and was court painter to Philip V and Ferdinand VI until 1752, when he returned to Paris. Van Loo's style introduced the rhetoric of the French Baroque into Spanish portraiture. This canvas, which is one of the largest of all family portraits, is among Van Loo's finest achievements. It is the culmination of long-standing plans for a great family portrait of the new dynasty of Bourbons and stands as an epilogue to the reign of Philip V, who died three years later. The entire royal family, richly dressed, are gathered together in an elaborate portico setting. Architecture, gardens, curtains and musicians all emphasise the splendid courtly setting, but despite this formal approach the artist succeeds in capturing the individual personalities. The aged, weary monarch contrasts with the still lively Isabella Farnese. Next to the king, depicted standing, is the future Ferdinand VI, and behind him is his Portuguese wife, Barbara of Braganza, with her step-sister Mariana Victoria, then Princess of Brazil. On the far right we see Charles VII of Naples, later Charles III of Spain, in the company of his wife, Maria Amalia of Saxony. Their daughter María Isabel plays in the foreground with her cousin Isabel, daughter of the Infante Felipe, future Duke of Parma. The Infante rests his hand on the chair of his wife, Luisa Isabel de Borbón. Finally, we see the young Infante Luis behind the queen, and the Infantas María Teresa, future wife of the Dauphin of France, and María Antonia Fernanda, future Queen of Sardinia.

337 →
JEAN RANC
Montpellier, 1674–Madrid, 1735

The Family of Philip V
1723. Oil on canvas, 44 x 65 cm
P2376

Jean Ranc entered Rigaud's
studio in 1697 and was
admitted to the Académie
Royale in 1703. By the time he
arrived in Madrid in 1722
he was already a celebrated
portraitist. The project to
depict the Spanish royal family
in a group portrait was an
innovative idea in Spanish
art. Only this oil sketch has
survived as a record of Ranc's
lost final composition, which
was left unfinished and in
poor condition following the
fire in the Alcázar, the old
Habsburg palace in Madrid,
in 1734. The king and queen
and their children are
presented in a room opening
onto a French-style gallery
in a setting that combines
the domestic and the courtly.
Prince Luis, standing between
the king and queen, and the
infantes, Ferdinand, Charles
and Philip, constituted
the first generation of Spanish
Bourbons.

336 ↑
MICHEL-ANGE HOUASSE
Paris, 1680–Arpajon, 1730

Luis I
1717. Oil on canvas, 172 x 112 cm
P2387

Trained in France in the studio
of his father, René-Antoine
Houasse (1645–1710), Michel-
Ange Houasse lived in Rome
between 1699 and 1705, entering
the Académie Royale in 1706.
It was Jean Orry, Prime Minister
to Philip V, who invited him to
Spain, where he arrived in 1715.
He was portraitist to the Spanish
monarchy for seven years but few
of his portraits have survived.
This image of Luis I is one of his
masterpieces. The ten-year-old
prince is depicted full-length,
posed in the manner of an elegant
courtier. Dressed as a novice
of the Order of the Holy Spirit,
his attire is beautifully painted
in cool, silvery tones that contrast
with the palatial room and the
large red curtain to one side.
Despite the portrait's French
appearance, its abbreviated
style and formal and chromatic
restraint bring it close to the
Spanish tradition. However,
Philip V was interested in a more
grandiose style of portraiture
and Houasse was consequently
replaced as court portraitist by
Jean Ranc in 1722.

338 →
JEAN RANC
Montpellier, 1674–Madrid, 1735

Charles III as a Child
c. 1722–23. Oil on canvas,
142 x 115 cm
P2334

With the intention of creating a
gallery for the palace of La Granja,
Philip V commissioned a series of
family portraits from Ranc, who
had arrived in Madrid in 1722. The
king abdicated in January 1724
and retired to La Granja, and so
the series has both a symbolic and
sentimental value. This portrait of
the Infante Charles, which formed
a pair with that of his step-brother
Ferdinand, also in the Prado, shows
the young prince in his study, where
he is classifying plants. The prince
stands in a room devoted to natural
history, a field that would greatly
interest the sitter after his ascent to
the throne as Charles III (reigned
1759–1788).

The Rococo

After the death of Louis XIV (reigned 1643–1715), the majesty of the French Baroque was followed by a style that emphasised more sensual forms and a more intimate mood. The court moved to Paris under the Regent Philippe d'Orléans and the magnificence of Versailles was replaced by the charm of the city palaces in St-Germain and St-Honoré. Gardens, studies and boudoirs were decorated to conform to a new hedonistic and anti-classical taste. This was the environment in which the Rococo evolved, a style in which the ephemeral and capricious, expressed through pleasing scenes of *galanterie,* succeeded the previous heroic manner. The Rococo was essentially an ornamental style, transforming the surface of mouldings, furniture and porcelain into sinuous, asymmetrical forms. This spirit also extended to painting, and the delicate ambience of courtly life was translated to this medium, together with a delight in nature and rural life. A new emphasis was placed on sensual colour, and there was less interest in design and composition. Pictures became smaller in format in order to fit into the new, more intimate type of room and painting generally became decorative rather than symbolic, losing its grandiose pretensions to become fresh, emotional and anecdotal. The virtues and heroic deeds of the gods were replaced by bacchanals and amorous, erotic episodes involving gods and humans. Masquerades, balls and the *fête galante*, together with aristocratic entertainments in parks and glades, became common subjects, as did evocations of ancient ruins and the newly fashionable Oriental exoticism. Through the work of Watteau, Fragonard and Boucher [339], the Rococo style spread throughout Europe with a creative freedom far removed from academicism.

In Spain, the official character of the new Bourbon art and the continuing importance of the Italian Baroque to some extent limited the influence of the Rococo. Nonetheless, it is evident in the approach to colour seen in some of Houasse's portraits and in his genre scenes (like the Prado's *Bacchanal*), as well as in the decoration of the royal residences. The two paintings by Watteau in the Prado [341, 342] are examples of the modern taste of Isabella Farnese, who was responsible for their acquisition, possibly from her surgeon and art dealer Florencio Kelly. The arrival in Madrid of artists such as Van Loo introduced the Rococo aesthetic into Spanish painting [335], and its influence extended as far as the work of Goya.

339
FRANÇOIS BOUCHER
Paris, 1703–1770

Pan and Syrinx
c.1762. Oil on canvas,
95 x 79 cm
P7066

Boucher's work fully expresses the Rococo aesthetic with its emphasis on the decorative. It also has a sensuality that at times borders on the erotic. A designer, decorator and painter, Boucher enjoyed dazzling professional success at the French court until the advent of Neoclassicism. He was in the service of Louis XV (reigned 1715–1774) and Madame de Pompadour (1721–1764), and from 1765 was director of the Académie. This canvas is representative of his style with its erotic approach to the subject, its deft, loose handling and use of colour. The gods of the eighteenth century were not Jupiter and Apollo but rather Venus and lesser deities who represented nature, beauty and sensory pleasures. This is the case with Pan, the shepherd god and son of Bacchus, who pursued the beautiful nymph Syrinx but saw his desires frustrated when she was transformed into a reed-bed by her sisters and her father, the river Ladon. From one of these reeds, Pan made the famous pipes used by shepherds in the ancient world.

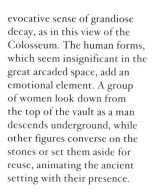

340 →
HUBERT ROBERT
Paris, 1733–1808

The Colosseum
Oil on canvas. 240 x 225 cm
P2883

Views of cities and ruins known as *vedute* became fashionable in the eighteenth century. Because of its classical past and its ruins, Italy produced a large number of view painters or *vedutisti*, but other European artists who travelled around the country also worked and specialised in this genre. One such painter was the French artist Hubert Robert, whose eleven-year stay in Italy allowed him to study its archaeological remains and to meet Giampaolo Panini and Giovanni Battista Piranesi. However, despite his first-hand knowledge of Italian ruins, Robert's approach was fantastical and his exaggeration of their monumentality gave the ruins the appearance of theatrical backdrops. His particular vision and aesthetic imbued these architectural structures with a highly evocative sense of grandiose decay, as in this view of the Colosseum. The human forms, which seem insignificant in the great arcaded space, add an emotional element. A group of women look down from the top of the vault as a man descends underground, while other figures converse on the stones or set them aside for reuse, animating the ancient setting with their presence.

341 ↑
JEAN-ANTOINE WATTEAU
Valenciennes, 1684–
Nogent-sur-Marne, 1721

Fête in a Park
c. 1715. Oil on canvas, 48 x 56 cm
P2354

342 ↓
*The Marriage Contract
and a Country Dance*
c. 1714. Oil on canvas, 47 x 55 cm
P2353

In 1712 Watteau entered the Académie, and in 1717 he was named 'painter of *fêtes galantes*', a category that was introduced to cover the new genre subject invented by the artist. Watteau focused on verdant and poetic natural settings in which he located charming and playful aristocratic scenes. *The Fête in a Park*, which is slightly later than the *Marriage Contract*, is more diffuse and evanescent in style as a result of its use of colour and light. The park in which the *fête galante* takes place has two fountains, one dedicated to Neptune and the other to Ceres, which seem to blend into the surrounding trees, bathed in a golden mist. The figures, harmoniously arranged in elegant groups, devote themselves to conversation or to the contemplation of nature. The fleeting moment depicted is of no consequence in itself, but is rendered beautiful through the poses and delicate colours of the figures and the dreamlike atmosphere. The calm and silence which emanate from these compositions gives them a touch of melancholy which their imitators did not have.

Nineteenth-century French Painting

Nineteenth-century European art is comparatively little represented in the Prado's collection. This is partly because of the history of the museum itself, which, from the year of its opening in 1819, envisaged the acquisition of contemporary works of art as primarily a way of representing Spanish artistic creation. Despite this, the museum's collections now have a number of fine examples of nineteenth-century European painting, some of which are important for their relationship to Spanish painting of the same period and others for their high quality and artistic significance.

In the nineteenth century, there was little interest in Spain in acquiring contemporary French painting, and private collectors were generally more active than institutions. It is thus not surprising that within this area of the museum's holdings, the works bequeathed in 1905 by the private collector Ramón de Errazu (1840–1904) are of particular importance. This group includes works by such celebrated French painters as Baudry and Meissonier [343, 344], along with works by Spanish artists trained in Paris such as Martín Rico, Mariano Fortuny and Raimundo de Madrazo [175, 176, 178]. These works reveal the connection between nineteenth-century French art and Spanish painting of the same period, a connection also evident in the work of other artists such as Juan Antonio Ribera and José de Madrazo [162], pupils of the Neoclassical painter Jacques Louis David (1748–1825), as the corresponding chapter in this guide explains.

343
PAUL BAUDRY
La Roche-sur-Yon, Vendée, 1828–Paris, 1886

The Pearl and the Wave
1862. Oil on canvas, 83 x 175 cm
P2604

Paul Baudry was trained at the École des Beaux-Arts in Paris, settling in the French capital in 1844. Having won the Grand Prix in Rome in 1850, he lived for a lengthy period in that city and subsequently travelled to England, Spain and the Middle East. Baudry's fame brought him commissions to paint decorative works for the Paris Opéra and a number of French palaces. Baudry was an academic painter and his paintings have an immaculate technique and a high finish; many of them also have a notably erotic content, including the present canvas. Exhibited at the 1863 Paris Salon, this nude was considered one of the most beautiful of its day in its representation of a sensual Venus emerging from the foam of the waves, although it was criticised for its excessive hedonism. The painting belonged to the Empress Eugenia de Montijo, the Granada-born wife of Napoleon III. It subsequently entered the Prado as part of the Ramón de Errazu Bequest.

344
JEAN-LOUIS-ERNEST
MEISSONIER
Lyon, 1815–Paris, 1891

Josefa Manzanedo e Intentas de Mitjans, Marchioness of Manzanedo

1872. Oil on canvas, 59 x 49 cm
P2628

Meissonier attained enormous fame under the Second Empire. His realist style, which tended to emphasise the decorative and the exquisite, was in line with the dictates of the French Fine Arts Academies and with bourgeois taste of the day. His paintings, generally small in format, were sold for the highest prices on the international market and official circles uniformly praised his work. Despite this, a number of writers, painters and intellectuals of the day were highly critical of his painting, although that did not prevent later artists such as

Salvador Dalí from admiring it. This portrait is a characteristic example of his work and reveals Meissonier's celebrated interest in detail, as well as his splendid chromatic richness, evident in the interior decoration, which conformed to contemporary taste. Josefa de Manzanedo, Marchioness of Manzanedo, was one of a group of aristocratic Spaniards living in Paris and was also the subject of a portrait by Raimundo de Madrazo. Meissonier gives her the delicate air preferred for female subjects at that date.

The German Painting Collection

The Spanish monarchy's relations with the Germanic Holy Roman Empire were very close during the sixteenth and seventeenth centuries. The two crowns were held by branches of the same family of German origin, the Habsburgs. However, despite this family tie, German works were very scarce in the Spanish Royal Collection. Owing to the international nature of the two courts, exchanges of paintings generally involved works of different provenance. The German paintings that did find their way to Spain continued to be specific acquisitions until well into the eighteenth century, when Anton Raffael Mengs was appointed court painter to Charles III. As a result, German and Central European painting in the Museo del Prado, although notable for its quality, is more sparsely represented than other schools.

The Renaissance is undoubtedly the best represented period. Few museums own four undisputed works by Albrecht Dürer. Three of those held by the Prado are essential for understanding the adoption of Italian forms in Germany [345-347]. The presence of Cranach and Baldung Grien likewise illustrates the blend of the classical world and Gothic expressionism characteristic of German Mannerism [351, 354]. The crisis of the Reformation triggered a major controversy over images. A moralising message can be seen in the works of these masters, and also in Flemish-influenced portraits such those as by Dürer and Amberger. With the exception of Cranach's *Virgin and Child* [351], a recent gift to the museum, all these works were inherited or purchased by Spanish monarchs up until the eighteenth century.

The seventeenth-century paintings are of similar origin, although they were executed by German artists who worked in Italy, such as Adam Elsheimer [350] and Philip Roos. The Czech artist Bartholomäus Strobel [349], who worked chiefly in Poland, is considered part of this group because he was active in Prussia and exemplifies the art of the Habsburg court in Prague. From the eighteenth century are a few examples of the Rococo style – the landscapes of Jan Christian Vollardt, a gift from Pedro Fernández Durán in 1930. Neoclassicism is the other main grouping of the Prado's German collection. Mengs's sojourn in Madrid between 1761 and 1769 explains why he is so well represented in the collection, with nearly forty works, including both paintings on canvas and drawings. Most of them form a portrait gallery of the Bourbons, but the Prado also holds some of his most famous religious compositions [355-357].

Dürer and the German Renaissance

A painter, engraver and writer of treatises, Albrecht Dürer is one of the most prominent figures of the European Renaissance. The son of a goldsmith of Hungarian origin, he was raised in a cultured environment that stimulated his early interest in the arts. He studied at Nuremberg with the painter Michael Wolgemut (1434–1519), and his travels, starting in his youth, played a decisive part in his education. His first travels, around Germany, brought him into direct contact with the art of the period, especially with the work of Martin Schongauer (died 1491). However, it was the trips he made to Italy that gave a new direction to his painting. He stayed twice in Venice: his first sojourn (1494–1495) marked the end of his training, and his second (1505–1507) the height of his artistic maturity. His first-hand knowledge of Venetian painting, and the influence of Giovanni Bellini [204], signified a turning-point in his oeuvre, while Italian artistic literature enabled him to develop his theoretical reflections.

Dürer was acquainted with the leading Northern European intellectuals, headed by Erasmus of Rotterdam (1466/69–1536), and was in the service of Emperor Maximilian I (reigned 1493–1519). He also worked as an engraver in his Nuremberg workshop, combining technical expertise with an astonishing ability to create new and remarkable images. His series of prints on religious themes provided a model for generations of artists. His allegorical compositions are based on his knowledge of Greco-Roman culture and German medieval tradition. His treatises reflect the variety of his artistic and scientific concerns, which ranged from human proportions to fortifications.

345
ALBRECHT DÜRER
Nuremberg, 1471–1528

Self-portrait
1498. Oil on panel, 52 x 41 cm
P2179

As an artist, Dürer was particularly concerned with his own image and made many self-portraits throughout his lifetime. This one shows him at the age of twenty-six, but as a nobleman, not a painter. By depicting himself in rich clothing and an elegant pose, using a model of portraiture reserved for the privileged classes, he vindicates art's noble status. The Renaissance saw the transformation of painters from craftsmen into intellectuals, but also into courtiers. Dürer was the prototype of this new type of artist: he wrote technical treatises, mastered a number of different artistic techniques and enjoyed great success with the powerful figures of his period. In this portrait he displays his ability to depict not just his appearance and dress in minute detail but also the landscape that opens up a broad vista behind him, and he proudly signs his name beneath the window. The value of the painting as a testimony of an illustrious man was especially appreciated by its successive owners. It was a gift from Nuremberg city council to King Charles I of England, and was acquired in 1654 at the sale of his possessions by Don Luis de Haro, who presented it to Philip IV.

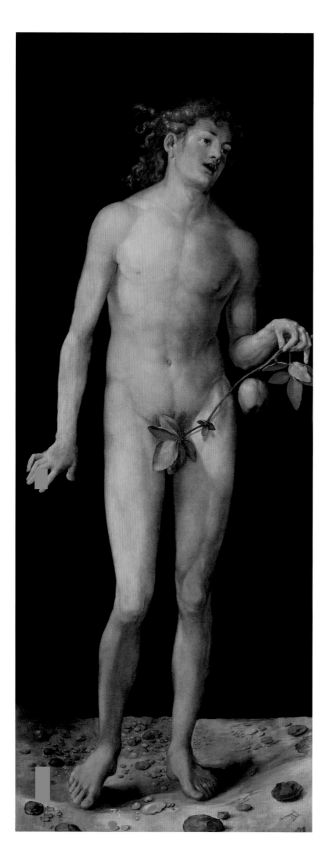

346 ←
Nuremberg, 1471–1528

Adam
1507. Oil on panel, 209 x 81 cm
P2177

347 →
Eve
1507. Oil on panel, 209 x 80 cm
P2178

This depiction of Adam, the
first man, goes beyond the
religious theme. By portraying
him separately, on an almost
lifelike scale and silhouetted
against a black background,
the artist set out to stress
his individuality. Were it not
for the apple he holds and the
proximity of the companion
piece, *Eve*, he could not be
identified as Adam. The
naked figure represents an
ideal of masculine beauty and
harmony, and his attentive gaze
reflects a youthful sensuality,
not realising that his sin will
unleash a dramatic awareness
of nakedness and mortality.
The figure of Eve, in the
meantime, is also portrayed
as a prototype of beauty
based on the same canon
of proportions as her male
companion. Like Adam, she
marks a significant change
from Dürer's earlier ideas
about the nude, exemplified in
the burin engraving of *Adam
and Eve* dated 1504. In her case,
however, the details clearly
reveal her identity, as she is
accompanied by the serpent
that offers her the apple. Her
natural pose and the almost

furtive glance directed at her companion disguise the moment in which they will disregard the prohibition against eating the fruit of the Tree of Knowledge and of Good and Evil. The painter signs the work on a small panel hanging from one of the tree's branches. He also expressly includes a reference to the date on which the Virgin gave birth to Christ. In this way, he relates the first woman to Mary, the first and only woman free of the original sin that mankind inherited from Eve. Eve's apparently innocent gesture will have enormous consequences for all her descendants, and the image is explained in the Christian tradition by means of the written word. Both panels were painted in Nuremberg after Dürer returned from his second trip to Venice, but it is not known for whom they were originally intended. At the end of the sixteenth century, the city council gave them to Emperor Rudolf II. Stolen by Swedish troops in Prague, they were later presented as a gift by Christina of Sweden to Philip IV.

348 ←
ALBRECHT DÜRER
Nuremberg, 1471–1528

Portrait of an Unknown Man

1524. Oil on panel, 50 x 36 cm
P2180

The blend of the Italian and Northern European Renaissance with German tradition is the hallmark of Dürer's paintings. This portrait reveals the influence of Flemish models. Dürer became portraitist to Emperor Maximilian I on account of his shrewdness in capturing not just the physical appearance but also the temperament of his sitter, as in the case of this unknown gentleman. Perhaps painted in Flanders, it might be a portrait of his host there, Joost Pankfelt, or of a high-ranking official, given his costume of rich furs and the roll of paper.

349 ↑
BARTHOLOMÄUS STROBEL
Wroclaw, 1591–Tourum, after
1650

*The Beheading of St John
the Baptist and the Banquet
of Herod*

c. 1630–33. Oil on canvas,
280 x 952 cm
P1940

The composition is designed
as a large frieze in which two
New Testament scenes unfold
successively. Salome presents
King Herod with the head
of St John the Baptist, who has
been executed in the cell that
is depicted separately from the
great banqueting hall. Strobel
used the Gospel story to
portray the luxurious ambience
of an early seventeenth-
century court. He combined
a fantastic setting with real
figures, such as General

Wallenstein and Henri IV
of France, some rendered with
caricature-like features. The
presence of military leaders
of various nations has led some
scholars to attribute a political
meaning to the painting,
interpreting it as an allegory
of Europe's complex political
situation. Strobel is a good
example of German influence
in Central Europe, which was
steeped in the refinement of
the Habsburg court in Vienna
and Prague.

350
ADAM ELSHEIMER
Frankfurt-am-Main,
1578–Rome, 1610

Ceres in the House of Hecuba
c. 1605. Oil on copper,
30 x 25 cm
P2181

351
LUCAS CRANACH THE ELDER
Kronach, 1472–Weimar, 1553

The Virgin and Child with St John and Angels

1536. Oil on panel,
121.3 x 83.4 cm
P7440

As an artist, Cranach was directly involved in the problem of religious images that arose after the Reformation led by Martin Luther (1483–1546). He espoused Luther's religious ideas and was painter to one of the most prominent Protestant princes, the elector John Frederick of Saxony (reigned 1532–1554). However, he continued to produce paintings on themes commissioned by Catholics.

Such is the case of this Virgin, which adapts the model of Italian madonnas to German taste, establishing a prototype that was frequently repeated by the master and his followers. Line is clearly predominant, with a curious combination of broken strokes for the clothing and undulating strokes for the physical features. The idealised appearance achieved using this approach was in keeping with the spiritual needs of his clients. The delicate background landscape is the only reference to real space, recalling Northern European tradition. The gesture of St John, who hands the Child some grapes, is a subtle allusion to Christ's death. From the grapes comes the wine which, according to Catholics, is transformed into Jesus' blood in the Eucharist.

352
LUCAS CRANACH THE ELDER
Kronach, 1472–Weimar, 1553

*Hunt in Charles V's Honour
at Torgau Castle*
1544. Oil on panel, 114 x 175 cm
P2175

Hunting was an activity considered fitting for princes in the *ancien régime*. It was held to be training for war. This panel depicts a hunt organised by Prince John Frederick of Saxony in honour of Emperor Charles V at Torgau Castle (Germany). The two men are shown on the left, by the game they have bagged, preparing to shoot at the deer which the dogs are driving into the water. Cranach raised the horizon line, allowing him to depict numerous simultaneous episodes, opting for an anecdotal rather than a realistic narrative. The scene illustrates the violence of the chase, which contrasts with the composure of the courtiers who wait at their posts among the vegetation. The painting does not refer to a historic hunt. On the contrary, it was a symbolic gift offered by the prince elector to the emperor at a complex political moment in the context of the religious wars. It is the companion piece to the *Hunt in Honour of Ferdinand I, King of the Romans, at Torgau Castle*, also in the Prado.

353 ←
HANS BALDUNG GRIEN
Schwäbisch Gmünd, c.
1484/85–Strasbourg, 1545

Harmony or The Three Graces
1541–44. Oil on panel,
151 x 61 cm
P2219

354 →
The Ages and Death
1541–44. Oil on panel,
151 x 61 cm
P2220

Baldung was one of Dürer's most fervent followers. His work frequently features unsettling themes and symbolism in which German medieval traditions are combined with Renaissance culture. These panels, possibly intended as a kind of diptych, are a good example of this combination, since they clearly seem complementary even though their significance is obscure. The women in the first panel, the artificial elegance of whose anatomical treatment recalls other German painters such as Cranach, may be the Three Graces of classical mythology. Their youth and sensuality and the peaceful setting are in keeping with these personifications of female beauty. However, the musical instruments that accompany them and the music score held by the boy in the foreground seem to suggest an allegory of Harmony. Some elements are moralising, such as the swan that sings the music of the score, a harbinger of death, and the coiled serpent in the tree,

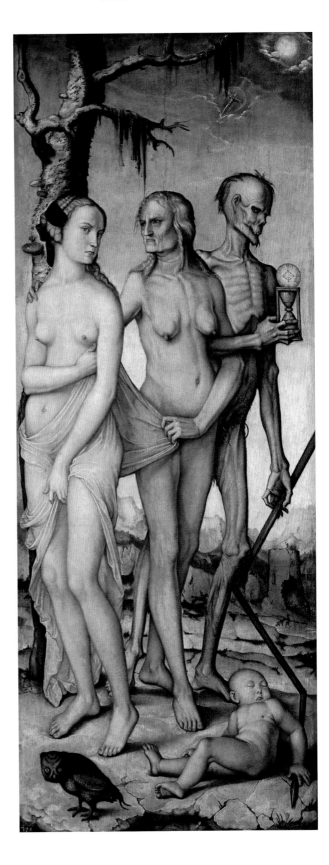

a symbol of sin. In the second panel, the subject is overtly constructed around one of mankind's obsessions, the theme of death. In contrast to its companion piece, it conveys a disturbing message. It depicts the cycle of life, stressing the ravages of time and the irreversible end of existence. It traces a circle that begins with the newborn lying on the ground and ends with the gloomy figure of the decomposing corpse. Both are linked by a broken lance. Youth and Old Age are also interlaced, expressively contrasting their naked bodies. The young woman's gesture of displeasure will be of no avail in avoiding the deterioration brought about by time. The owl symbolises both the slumber from which one awakens at birth and the eternal sleep of death. The scene is set in a desolate, oppressive landscape. Nevertheless, it points out Christian paths to salvation: the Eucharist above the hourglass and the crucified Christ who appears in the heavens.

Anton Raffael Mengs

Mengs is the most important early Neoclassical painter in Europe. The son of Ismael Mengs, painter to the court of Saxony, he trained as an artist in Dresden and in Rome, where he studied the world of antiquity and the great Renaissance masters, particularly Raphael. This classical grounding would become a constant feature in his writing and in his painting. He completed his education at Dresden and came to be the leading painter of Saxony. However, he spent much of his life in Rome. He was a friend of Johann J. Winckelmann (1717–1768), the theorist of Neoclassicism who advocated a return to the models of ancient Greece. Mengs himself wrote an artistic treatise defending his concept of ideal beauty, which was very close to that of Winckelmann but centred on Italian painters of the sixteenth century.

Mengs worked for the Bourbons of Naples and Spain, where he was chief court painter. In Madrid he combined his career as a portraitist with that of a painter of religious subjects. He was also a decorator and fresco artist. His aesthetic theories would have a decisive impact on Spanish art. His influence is evident in the generation of painters of the last third of the eighteenth century, such as Francisco Bayeu, Maella and Goya himself. Mengs also painted portraits for the court of the Grand Duke and Duchess of Tuscany and received various commissions from Rome.

355
ANTON RAFFAEL MENGS
Aussig (now in the Czech Republic), 1728–Rome, 1779

Charles III

1761. Oil on canvas, 154 x 110 cm
P2200

Mengs met the future Charles III in Naples when the king was governing the kingdom as Charles VII and commissioned him to paint a portrait of his family. When his brother Ferdinand VI died without issue, Charles succeeded to the Spanish throne. Mengs entered his service shortly afterwards. So began the artistic supremacy of the Bohemian painter at the Spanish court, where he became chief court painter in 1766. The first works he produced were this portrait of the sovereign and one of his wife Maria Amalia of Saxony, also in the Prado. Mengs shaped an image of Charles III that was in accordance with the conventions of Baroque court portraiture – curtains and an architectural setting that befitted a palace, the grand royal mantle, the chains of the military orders and the sitter's elegant gesture. However, despite the court setting, the king is dressed in armour, with the sword and baton of command. Spain's international policy at the time was to abandon neutrality and become involved in the European wars. This may perhaps explain why Charles is shown as a general prepared to spearhead change.

356
ANTON RAFFAEL MENGS
Aussig (now in the Czech
Republic), 1728–Rome, 1779

Maria Luisa of Parma,
Princess of Asturias
c. 1765. Oil on canvas,
152 x 110 cm
P2189

As court painter to Charles III, Mengs was responsible for portraying the members of the king's family. This portrait is a fine example of his skills and provides an insight into the palace milieu. The sitter is the new Princess of Asturias, daughter of the Duke of Parma, who has just married her cousin, the future King Charles IV (reigned 1788–1808). Maria Luisa (1751–1810), who was only fourteen at the time, is painted in accordance with her status, attired in a luxurious French-style dress and wearing splendid jewels. Some of the jewels emphasise her royal position, such as the Order of the Star-Cross that hangs from the dress and the portrait in the pearl bracelet, most likely of her husband. The princess appears joyful and carefree, confident of a promising future. The portrait was intended as a companion piece to that of her husband in hunting dress (also in the Prado), which explains why both figures are depicted in an outdoor setting. The background scenery recalls the gardens of Aranjuez Palace.

357
ANTON RAFFAEL MENGS
Aussig (now in the Czech
Republic), 1728–Rome, 1779

*The Adoration of the
Shepherds*
1770. Oil on panel, 256 x 190 cm
P2204

Although Mengs is usually more highly valued as a portraitist, he mastered all genres of painting. This *Adoration* is one of his most famous religious works. It was painted in Rome for Charles III, most likely to mark the birth of his grandson, the Infante Carlos Clemente. The composition is inspired by a painting by the Renaissance artist Antonio Correggio, known as *The Night,* in the Gemäldegalerie Alte Meister in Dresden. Like Correggio, Mengs divided the composition into two planes, depicting angels in heaven above the earthly group of figures. But above all he borrowed from

Correggio the motif of the light emanating from the Child, which miraculously bursts through the shadow of the night. The figures have great monumentality, and their arrangement creates the illusion of space without the need for architectural features. The angels and the Holy Family have a serene, idealised beauty which, like the precise technique, is characteristic of Mengs's style. The painter portrayed himself behind St Joseph, pointing at the light that surrounds the object of adoration. He thus not only showed his admiration for past masters but embraced their tradition.

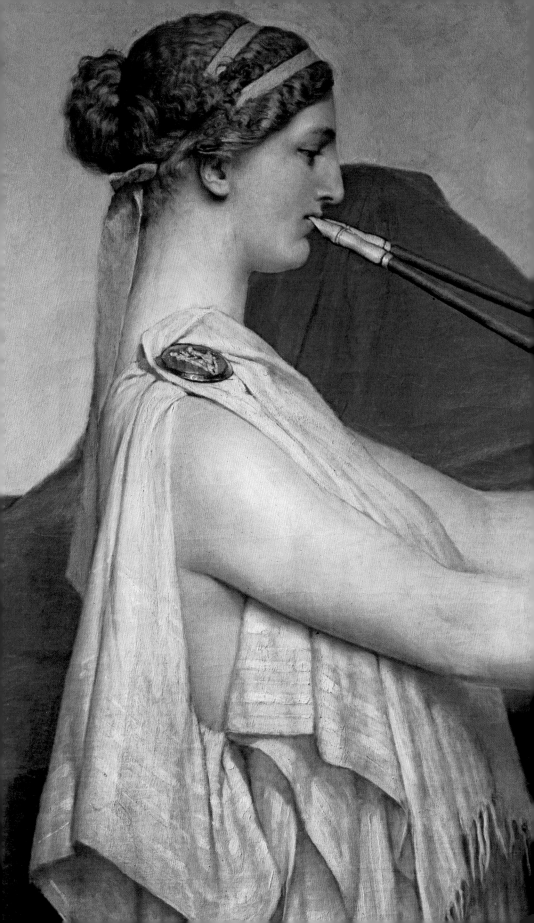

The British Painting Collection

For historical reasons, British painting is the least well represented in the Prado. Whereas Spanish palaces and churches became filled with Italian, Flemish and French works over the centuries as a result of close political, commercial and family ties, political problems between England and Spain following Elizabeth I's ascent to the throne and the country's permanent separation from the Roman Catholic Church complicated the arrival and dissemination of English art in Spain. However, from the eighteenth century onwards, the improvement in political relations and the fact that Spanish aristocrats travelled to Britain resulted in a new interest in the style and models of English art. This is evident for example in the work of Francisco de Goya, whose *Caprichos* can be related to the prints of William Hogarth (1697–1764). Although small in size, the Prado's collection of British painting has works of considerable importance, most of them acquired in the twentieth century. The majority are portraits by artists working in the second half of the eighteenth century and the first half of the nineteenth, including Sir Joshua Reynolds [358], Thomas Gainsborough [360] and Sir Thomas Lawrence [359], who is the best represented. The Prado also has a number of works by David Roberts [361, 362], whose views of Spain promoted an exotic and picturesque vision of the country throughout Europe, as well as influencing the Spanish Romantic landscape painters.

The Apogee of British Painting

The prosperity of eighteenth-century England, largely unaffected by the loss of its American colonies in 1776, led to a period of cultural splendour and the emergence of a school of artists, each with individual characteristics, whose production was largely centred on portraits. With one eye on continental Rococo and Neoclassicism, painters like Gainsborough, Reynolds and the young Lawrence took their lead from the legacy of foreign artists of the past, such as Holbein and Van Dyck, to develop a type of portrait befitting the needs and aspirations of contemporary English society. The beginning of what some historians have called the 'classical' period can be symbolically dated to 1760, the year when a young king with artistic leanings, George III (reigned 1760–1820), ascended the throne, and the Society of Artists of Great Britain held its first public exhibition.

358
JOSHUA REYNOLDS
Plympton, 1723–London, 1792

Portrait of a Clergyman
Second half of the 18th century.
Oil on canvas, 77 x 64 cm
P2858

Trained in England and Italy, Reynolds was one of the most important English portraitists of his time. He became the first President of the Royal Academy in 1768, using the authority the position gave him to bolster his staunch defence of Neoclassicism in England. Taking the work of Anthony van Dyck as his starting point, he reformed the traditional concept of British portraiture by adjusting it systematically to the client and the type of commission. In some portraits, he employs a tenebrism which allows him to concentrate on capturing the sitter's psychology. Reynolds distances himself in this picture from the rhetorical idealisation of his ceremonial portraits, evoking instead the austerity and determination of a person for whom he felt an affinity.

359
THOMAS LAWRENCE
Bristol, 1769–London, 1830

Miss Marthe Carr

1791. Oil on canvas, 76 x 64 cm
P3012

Given Thomas Lawrence's humble
origins, it is perhaps surprising
that he should have become court
painter to George III after the
death of Sir Joshua Reynolds. Son
of a Bristol innkeeper, Lawrence
drew his father's clients and so
acquired the basics of an artistic
training. In 1787 he impressed
critics with one of his portraits. He
entered the Royal Academy in 1791
and the following year began to
work for the king. Lawrence's style
was influenced by Reynolds, but he
went beyond the master's elegantly
academic formality and introduced
a more vital, dramatic and subjective
approach to his sitters that
anticipates Romantic painting.

360
THOMAS GAINSBOROUGH
Sudbury, Suffolk, 1727–London,
1788

Dr Isaac Henrique Sequeira

Late 18th century.
Oil on canvas, 127 x 102 cm
P2979

Gainsborough was one of the
founders of the Royal Academy
in London. His study of Dutch
seventeenth-century landscape
painting inspired his own
landscapes, initiating a genre in
England that reached its apex
with John Constable (1776–1837)
Gainsborough became a leading
portraitist of the aristocracy
and royalty. His portraits were
influenced by Van Dyck [312, 315,
316], but were also a product of
the sensitive, intimate mood of the
eighteenth century. An example
is this portrait of his doctor,
Sequeira, who was born in Portugal
and died in London in 1816.

361 ←
DAVID ROBERTS
Stockbridge, Scotland, 1796–
London, 1864

The Torre del Oro in Seville
1833. Oil on panel, 39 x 48 cm
P2853

362 ↓
*The Castle of Alcalá de
Guadaira*
1833. Oil on panel, 40 x 48 cm
P2852

David Roberts travelled in
Spain in 1832 and 1833, also
visiting Morocco and Tangier.
Upon his return to London,
where he had settled in 1822,
he published *Picturesque
Sketches in Spain during the
Years 1832 and 1833*, which
contained a set of engravings
and lithographs made in
the course of his travels.
The album's success among
a European public with a
growing penchant for the
exotic established Roberts
as a paradigmatic painter
of decorative but dramatic
Romantic landscapes, and was
instrumental in giving form
to the picturesque image
of Spain. Roberts also had a
decisive influence on Spanish
painters like Genaro Pérez
Villaamil, who met the
Scottish artist in Seville.

363
LAWRENCE ALMA TADEMA
Dronryp, Holland, 1836–
London, 1912

Pompeian Scene (The Siesta)
1868. Oil on canvas,
130 x 360 cm
P3996

Born and trained in Holland, Alma Tadema was one of the most celebrated painters of Victorian England. The medieval subject matter of his early works, which were close in style to the Pre-Raphaelites, was followed by scenes of ancient Egypt inspired by his study of collections of ancient art in London. After a trip to Italy in 1863, Alma Tadema focused on subjects from ancient Greece and Rome, which would become an obsessive interest and which brought him international fame. As is evident in the present work, Alma Tadema's painting is highly realistic in both its technique and its historically accurate reconstruction of settings and objects. The table in the foreground displays the equivalent of an archaeological still life with two gold rhytons, a silver Venus, and a red-figure vessel. The profile, hairstyle and clothing of the woman playing the double flute are inspired by the friezes of Phidias. The composition is notable for its precise draughtsmanship, rich and elegant colours and an immaculate, enamel-like finish suggesting the influence of Greek red-figure ceramics.

The Drawing Collection

Although small in size when compared to those of other departments of drawings, the Prado collection – containing some 7,800 works – includes some items of considerable importance. The Spanish school is the best represented, with works from the fifteenth century to the end of the nineteenth, the finest being those by seventeenth-century artists such as Vicente Carducho, Alonso Cano [367], Claudio Coello, Francisco Ribalta, José de Ribera [366] and Juan de Valdés Leal. The eighteenth-century collection is the richest in number and quality, while that of the nineteenth century features important works by Leonardo Alenza, Eugenio Lucas, José and Federico de Madrazo, Eduardo Rosales [369] and Mariano Fortuny. The Italian school is the second most important: there are excellent drawings by Andrea del Sarto, Giorgio Vasari, Luca Cambiaso, Paolo Veronese, Annibale Carracci and Michelangelo [365]. Dating from the seventeenth century are drawings by Guido Reni, Guercino and Luca Giordano, and from the eighteenth, coinciding with the arrival at the Spanish court of Italian artists, works by Giovanni Battista and Lorenzo Tiepolo [370] and Corrado Giaquinto. Although less numerous, the Flemish, French and German schools are well represented by studies by Rubens, Jacob Jordaens and Anton Raffael Mengs. A large number of pieces come from the workshop of the court painters, which produced many of the drawings by eighteenth-century Spanish artists linked to the court, above all Francisco Bayeu – with over 400 works – Mariano Salvador Maella and José del Castillo. Drawings by foreign artists summoned to Spain by the Bourbons, such as Giordano, the Tiepolo and Mengs, also arrived by this route. Another crucial group of drawings, the so-called 'Goya holdings', deserve to be treated separately on account of their number and significance; they consist of the drawings acquired by Román Garreta and sold to the Museo Nacional de la Trinidad in 1866 and those which Mariano Carderera sold to the museum in 1886, together with a number from the bequest of the aristocrat and collector Pedro Fernández Durán (1846–1930), and various more recent additions like the *Italian Notebook* [327] and *The Butterfly Bull*, acquired respectively in 1993 and 2007. Then there are the more than 2,700 drawings by various artists also included in the Fernández Durán Bequest, made to the museum in 1931. Lastly, mention should also be made of the material from the Museo de Arte Moderno, such as the 130 drawings by Carlos de Haes, and the new acquisitions that enrich these holdings year by year.

364
JUAN GUAS
St-Pol-de-Léon, Brittany,
1430–1496

*High Chapel of San Juan
de los Reyes*
Before 1492. Pen on parchment,
1940 x 960 mm
D5526

Guas worked as an architect
for the Catholic Monarchs,
Ferdinand and Isabella, who
appointed him *maestro mayor*
(chief architect) of royal
works. He designed one of his
greatest buildings for them:
the Franciscan monastery
of San Juan de los Reyes
in Toledo. Erected to
commemorate the victory
against Portugal in the battle
of Toro (1476), when Isabella
reaffirmed her rights of
succession against the claims
of her niece Juana, it combines
elements of the Mudejar and
flamboyant Gothic styles. The
drawing, which passed to the
Prado from the Museo de la
Trinidad, is one of the few
architectural designs in Spanish
art and also one of the earliest
known. It shows the project
for the east end of the chapel,
decorated in accordance
with an ambitious scheme
characterised by abundant royal
emblems and including the
monarchs in prayer. Although
the final version differs from
this initial design in many ways,
it nonetheless displays the
same sumptuousness, which
has led scholars to believe that
the monastery was originally
intended as a royal pantheon.

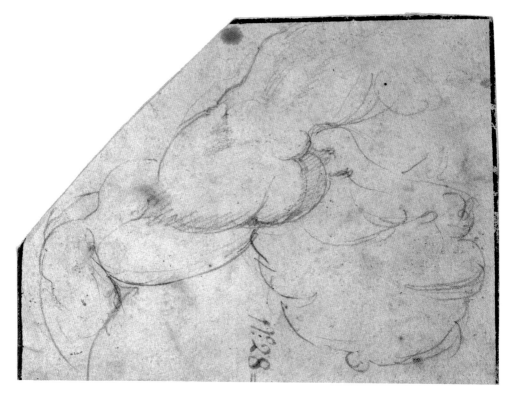

365
MICHELANGELO
BUONARROTI
Caprese, 1475–Rome, 1564

Study of a man's right shoulder, chest and upper arm

1525–50. Pencil on paper,
150 x 115 mm
D1732

In 2003, two drawings previously considered to belong to the school of Michelangelo were correctly identified as anatomical studies for the *Last Judgement* of the Sistine Chapel. This one is a sketch of the shoulder, arm and right-hand side of the chest of one of the demons carrying the bodies of the condemned in the lower right area of the composition. Despite their simplicity and economy – a few vigorous strokes and brief shading – the confidence and tense rhythm of their contours enable them to be attributed with certainty to the master, who instilled life into the demon's powerful, sinewy musculature with only a few lines. These hasty drawings must have played a part in the execution of the fresco, allowing the artist to define and plan the outlines of his figures before applying his brush. The uneven edges of the drawing are probably due to the fact that it was part of a sheet containing other studies; the sheet was probably cut into several pieces by a later owner so that the studies could be sold separately. It was acquired through the Fernández Durán Bequest.

366
JOSÉ DE RIBERA
Játiva, Valencia, 1591–
Naples, 1652

St Cecilia

c. 1645–50. Pen and wash
on white paper, 257 x 210 mm
D6015

Ribera was one of the Golden
Age artists who most cultivated
drawing and has the largest
number of surviving works
of this kind, close to one
hundred. He used them not only
as instruments for working out
and perfecting the compositions
of his paintings, but also as
a medium that afforded him
greater freedom to develop
his ideas and imagination.
Although this drawing, acquired
in 1993, addresses a traditional
theme, it is not related to any
known painting. It shows a
very beautiful, monumentally
rendered saint identified as
Cecilia, the patron saint of
music, playing a music score on
a spinet, while gazing entranced
at the little angels accompanying
her. The delicate clouds, the
flowing robes and the invisible
presence of the music contribute
to the atmosphere of spirituality
with which the scene is imbued.
The work is regarded as one
of Ribera's loveliest and most
balanced drawings and belongs
to his mature period, which
was heavily influenced by the
models of Roman and Bolognese
classicism.

367
ALONSO CANO
Granada, 1601–1667

Female Nude

c. 1645–50. Pen and wash
on laid paper, 163 x 158 mm
D6320

Two independent motifs – an arch
resting on a pilaster and a female
nude – are superimposed in this
magnificent drawing composed
of vivid, nervous strokes, which

was acquired by the Prado in 1997
after passing through various
other collections, including
that of the painter Aureliano de
Beruete. Cano was one of the
most prolific draughtsmen of
seventeenth-century Spain and
regarded drawing as a medium
in its own right, not necessarily
subordinate to the painting
process. Although undated, this
Female Nude is linked to the period
the artist spent at the Madrid
court from 1638, when he came
into contact with the mythological

nudes of painters like Titian
and Rubens [216, 302] in the royal
collections. It is not surprising
that Cano, who possessed a keen
artistic sensibility, should have
wished to measure himself against
these masters and, furthermore,
in a field like the nude, which
had scarcely been explored by
Spanish artists. The woman's
pose of sensual abandonment, her
legs slightly apart, has led her to
be regarded as a Danaë awaiting
the arrival of Zeus, who descended
in the form of a shower of gold.

368
JUAN CARREÑO DE MIRANDA
Avilés, Asturias, 1614–Madrid,
1685

Portrait of a Gentleman

c. 1675. Black pencil and sanguine
on laid paper, 211 x 162 mm
D3809

Despite the inscription that
reads 'Velazqz', which is in fact
a later addition, the drawing is
now attributed to Juan Carreño
de Miranda, one of Velázquez's
successors at the Madrid
court. The anonymous sitter is
portrayed bust length, turning
slightly towards the viewer, in
accordance with a model that
was commonly used in the court
environment of the time. A
painter of extremely vivid and
natural likenesses, as can be
seen in his portrait of the Duke
of Pastrana, also in the Museo
del Prado, in this drawing
Carreño displays his great skills
as a draughtsman, employing a
rich repertoire of strokes.

369
EDUARDO ROSALES
Madrid, 1836–1873

Portrait of a Girl

c. 1861. Pencil on paper,
248 x 183 mm
D5164

Rosales was one of the
most prolific draughtsmen
of nineteenth-century Spain
and employed a wide variety of
techniques and styles. However,
he reserved his most refined and
exquisite strokes for the pencil
drawings with which he often
portrayed people belonging to
his closest circle. This delightful
study of a child is linked to his

trip to Siena in 1861, during which,
in addition to copying works
by fifteenth-century Tuscan
masters, he produced a few child
and female portraits that are
among the most sophisticated
of his entire output. It has been
suggested that the child in this
drawing could be the daughter
of the landlady of the guesthouse
where the painter stayed. Rosales
modelled her delicate features
using fine cross-hatching and
defined the intensity of her gaze
with subtle touches of light and
shadow. The drawing shows
that the artist learned from the
Renaissance painters, particularly
Raphael, whose serene idealisation
is here veiled by a modern
melancholy.

370

LORENZO TIEPOLO
Venice, 1736–Madrid, 1776

*Portrait of the Infanta María
Luisa de Borbón*

1763. Pastel on paper,
705 x 600 mm
D3215

Lorenzo, the youngest of Giambattista Tiepolo's sons, found pastel portraiture to be a medium that was well suited to his artistic skills. It was a lucrative field, formerly dominated by the Venetian artist Rosalba Carriera, who had abandoned it due to her increasing blindness. The young Lorenzo arrived in Madrid with his father in 1762, and produced portraits of the Spanish infantes during his stay at the court. His virtuosity as a pastel artist is evident in this delicate portrait of the Infanta María Luisa, the second daughter of Charles III and Maria Amalia of Saxony, sumptuously dressed, wrapped in an ermine cloak with an eye-catching hat made of fur and feathers. The fragility of the medium and the sense of immediacy conveyed by the sitter, whose direct gaze is a far cry from the strict etiquette of court portraiture, suggest that this was a private work intended for the family.

Drawings and Prints by Goya

With nearly five hundred drawings, the Prado can pride itself on being the institution with the best resources in the world for studying Goya's achievements as a draughtsman, perhaps the aspect of his art which is most intimately linked to his life and thought. The lion's share of this collection comes from the albums that the artist began to use in 1796 during his stay in Sanlúcar de Barrameda. The first of them, known as the *Sanlúcar Album* or *Album A*, records the peaceful days spent with the Duchess of Alba and her female companions, whom Goya captured in intimate, sensuous poses in drawings of great freshness. Although the particular sensibility of this album extends into the first pages of the *Madrid Album* or *Album B*, produced around 1796–1797 between the end of his stay in Sanlúcar and his return to Madrid, a shift to more critical themes that foreshadow the *Caprichos* series soon becomes apparent. Executed during the years between the Peninsular War and the three-year Liberal interlude known as the Triennium (1808–1823), albums *C* and *F* reflect Goya's concerns and fears in this turbulent period in Spanish history, with violence being one of the main themes. Albums *G* and *H*, which display considerable expressive freedom, are centred on street motifs with a powerful presence of the absurd and the grotesque [373], and date from his period in Bordeaux (1824–1828). Most of these drawings were acquired by Román Garreta, brother-in-law of the then director of the Prado, Federico de Madrazo, and sold in 1866 to the Museo de la Trinidad, from where they passed to the Prado. Mention should also be made of the so-called *Italian Notebook*, acquired in 1993 [372]. Begun in Italy around 1771, it contains the earliest drawings attributed to Goya as well as annotations relating to his life and artistic tastes. In addition to this collection are the 284 preparatory drawings for his four sets of prints, *Caprichos* [371], *Disasters of War*, *Tauromaquia* [374] and *Disparates* [375], which are executed with a freedom that is not always preserved in the related engravings, aimed at the public at large. They come from the collection of the painter and historian Valentín de Carderera, who acquired them from the painter's direct descendants, and whose heir, Mariano Carderera, sold them to the Prado in 1886. (*continues on page 434*)

371
FRANCISCO DE GOYA
Fuendetodos, Zaragoza,
1746–Bordeaux, 1828

Dream 1: Universal language. The author sleeping
1797. Pen, ink and black pencil on laid paper, 247 x 172 mm
D3923

(*continues from page 432*) In the 1960s, the presence in the museum of this superb corpus of drawings prompted Tomás Harris, an eminent Goya collector and scholar, to donate a large number of prints, which had hitherto been absent from the museum holdings. Since then the Prado has striven to build up the presence of Goya the printmaker. Accordingly, in 1990, the museum acquired a lot consisting of thirteen artist's proofs and four printer's proofs of the *Caprichos;* in 1991, Plácido Arango donated a complete first edition of the *Caprichos;* in 1992, using funds from the Villaescusa bequest, the museum purchased a set of the *Disparates* consisting of eighteen prints made around 1854; also a first edition of the *Disasters* in 2000 and, lastly, one of the *Tauromaquia* [374] in 2002.

372
FRANCISCO DE GOYA
Fuendetodos, Zaragoza,
1746–Bordeaux, 1828

Italian Notebook: The Fall of Adam and The Expulsion from Paradise
1770–86. Pen and sanguine on laid paper, each sheet
186 x 128 mm
D6086 (P. 23) and D6090 (P. 29)

373
FRANCISCO DE GOYA
Fuendetodos, Zaragoza,
1746–Bordeaux, 1828

Album G: I'm still learning
c. 1825–28. Black pencil on laid
paper, 191 x 145 mm
D4151

374
FRANCISCO DE GOYA
Fuendetodos, Zaragoza,
1746–Bordeaux, 1828

Tauromaquia 20:
The Agility and Audacity
of Juanito Apiñani
1815–16. Sanguine on laid paper,
183 x 277 mm
D4307

375
FRANCISCO DE GOYA
Fuendetodos, Zaragoza,
1746–Bordeaux, 1828

*Disparate 13: A Way
of Flying*
1815–24. Etching, aquatint
and drypoint on paper,
245 x 360 mm
G749

The Sculpture
and Decorative Arts Collection

Those who regard the Prado solely as a picture gallery forget that it houses a valuable collection of over nine hundred sculptures, which trace the history of the genre and complement and enrich the viewing of the museum's paintings, with which they shared space and vicissitudes on more than one occasion in the past. As in the case of the paintings, the Royal Collection is the origin of many of these pieces which once adorned the palaces, gardens, churches and private chapels of the Spanish monarchs. The initial core of the holdings was formed in the first half of the sixteenth century, during the reign of Charles V. To him is owed an outstanding group of works: the family likenesses the emperor commissioned from the Milanese sculptors Leone and Pompeo Leoni, which are among the finest accomplishments of late Renaissance sculpture. In the second half of the century, his son Philip II also received a few noteworthy pieces as diplomatic gifts, specifically several sets of busts of Roman emperors and a few works from the collection of the writer and diplomat Diego Hurtado de Mendoza (1503–1575). Later on, in the seventeenth century, during the reign of Philip IV, the collection was supplemented by such important sculptures as the *Apotheosis of Claudius* [386], a gift from Cardinal Girolamo Colonna. It was also during this period that the king, through the agency of an outstanding ambassador, the painter Diego Velázquez, commissioned bronze castings of the most famous Roman classic statues to decorate the galleries of the Alcázar palace. The advent to the throne of the Bourbons in the eighteenth century marked a turning point in the formation of the collection. Philip V and Isabella Farnese were responsible for the purchase of two splendid collections assembled in Rome during the Baroque period. One is that of Queen Christina of Sweden, then owned by the Odescalchi, which provided the museum with some of its finest classical pieces, such as the *Diadumenos* [88], the *Muses from Hadrian's Villa* [383], the *Faun with Young Goat* [376], the *San Ildefonso Group* [384] and the *Bacchic Altar,* which belonged to the painter Rubens. The other is that of the Marquis of Carpio, Gaspar de Méndez de Haro y Guzmán (1598–1661), then in the possession of the Duke of Alba. Under Charles IV, the number of classical sculptures grew with the incorporation of the collection belonging to the enlightened diplomat José Nicolás de Azara (1730–1804), who was particularly interested in portraits of famous Greeks. In the twentieth century, together with a few specific gifts such as El Greco's *Epimetheus and Pandora* in 1962, mention should be made of the donation of two private sculpture collections: that of the Mexican artist and collector Marius de Zayas (1880–1961) in 1944; and that of the Chilean painter Claudio Bravo (born 1936) in 1999. The great majority of the Prado's nineteenth-century sculptures came from the Museo de Arte Moderno, whose contents passed to the Prado in 1971.

The museum's holdings also include a rich decorative arts collection centred on the Dauphin's Treasure, and valuable collections of *pietre dure* and medals.

Ancient Sculpture

The collection consists of over 250 pieces, including portraits, mythological figures, reliefs, burial urns and animal representations. Most were brought from Italy between the sixteenth and nineteenth centuries. Many of them originate from the major collections assembled in Italy during the Renaissance and Baroque periods, which were enriched by the great archaeological discoveries that took place, mainly in Rome and the surrounding area, which give the collection a certain unity. In that period, as in the Roman Empire, the aesthetic ideal was characterised by a return to the models of Greek classicism; this explains why a considerable number of examples of Greek art of the fifth century BC can be viewed in the Prado through Roman copies – some of very fine quality, such as that of the *Diadumenos* of Polyclitus [380], and Phidias' *Athena Parthenos* [379] – together with several examples from the fourth century, such as the *Resting Satyr* and *Head of Aphrodite of Cnidus* by Praxiteles (390–320 BC) and the *Leda* of Timotheos (active 370–350 BC). The collection also includes a small but select group of Roman copies of Hellenistic works such as the *Faun with Young Goat* [376], the *Venus with Dolphin* [385] and *Hypnos* [381], and a group of Roman portraits, mainly from the imperial period, that is significant both in number and quality. Despite its admiration for these works, Baroque and Renaissance taste, however, neglected the more severe appeal of the Greek archaic period and of the great civilisations of the Near East, which are more poorly represented in the museum's holdings. It is no coincidence that we must wait until the twentieth century, which witnessed a new appreciation of the art of the earliest periods in human history, to find pieces from sixth-century Greece, like the *Kouros* [437] and the *Horse* [377], all from the collection of the Mexican Marius de Zayas, who frequented European and American avant-garde circles. These works also attest to a new way of looking at things that emerged in the contemporary world, in which ancient sculpture was appreciated without restoration or retouching, valued for its formal properties and as a vestige of lost civilisations. The other side of the coin is found in the sculptures of the collection of Christina of Sweden [376, 383, 385], which were freely restored and completed in the humanistic environment of the Renaissance and Baroque periods, which felt a close and natural link with Antiquity.

376
Faun with Young Goat
Roman copy of c. AD 130–150
of a Hellenistic original dating
from 160–150 BC
Marble, 155 cm high
E29

The piece was discovered by chance together with other statues and utensils in a workshop of the Roman period when a street in Rome was being laid out around 1675. It may represent a faun or Pan, woodland creatures characterised by their pointed ears, small horns and tail. The figure carries on his shoulders a young goat to be sacrificed to Dionysius and gazes skywards in amazement, as if entranced by the presence of the god. The statue forms a pyramid shape – a characteristic device of the Hellenistic school of Pergamon – which accentuates the dramatic tension of the gesture, infusing the figure with grace and sensuality. Left unfinished by the Roman sculptor, as can be seen by the barely outlined pipes hanging from the tree, and incomplete, it was judiciously restored in the seventeenth century by a disciple of the Italian Baroque sculptor Bernini. That same century Queen Christina of Sweden purchased it for her palace in Rome. Her collection was later acquired by Philip V and Isabella Farnese, which explains why the piece is now in the Museo del Prado.

29.

377 ←
Horse
Fragment of a Greek work
of c. 520–510 BC
Marble, 109 cm high
E438

Dating from the Greek archaic period, this impressive sculpture has been linked for its style to some horses of the Athens Acropolis that were used as votive offerings. The horizontal furrow on the neck suggests that it originally had metal reins similar to those held by the famous *Charioteer of Delphi*. This detail, together with the extreme slenderness of the neck when viewed frontally, suggests that it was juxtaposed with similar horses that drew a chariot and was probably intended to decorate a pediment. The piece is part of the gift made to the museum in 1944 by Marius de Zayas, who shared the early twentieth-century avant-garde artists' passion for the formal purity of the art of the early civilisations.

378 →
Crater depicting centaurs fighting
Roman, c. 50 BC, with reliefs copied from an Attic original dating from c. 430–420 BC
Marble, 64 cm high
E303

This piece is related to the taste for large ornamental vessels, designed to decorate the gardens of the richest villas, which emerged in Rome in the first century BC. Although most of these pieces displayed Bacchic motifs that reminded their owners of the pleasures of wine and abundance, other themes – possibly intended for more discerning collectors – gained ground in the market. A good example is this crater illustrating the battle between Lapiths and centaurs, a theme that symbolised the struggle of civilisation against barbarity, particularly after the wars against the Persians. The finely crafted reliefs display an appealing dynamism and dramatic force which culminates in the scene showing the two opponents engaged in a fight with their teeth. They may have originated from the reliefs illustrating the same theme carved on the shield of Phidias' *Athena Promachos*, which are known from literature.

379 →
Athena Parthenos
Roman copy of c. AD 130–150
of an original by Phidias
dating from c. 440 BC
Marble, 96 cm high
E47

This fine miniature copy of
the statue created by Phidias
for the Parthenon of the
Acropolis in Athens is
one of the sculptural gems
that the Museo del Prado
owes to the collection of
Charles III. We know from
ancient testimonies and
from surviving copies that
this image of the goddess
of wisdom and protector of
Athens lacks some of her
most striking attributes, such
as the rich crest of her helmet
which was once decorated with
fabulous animals, of which
only the sphinx – a modern
addition – remains. The
shield, the lance, the Victory
in the palm of her right
hand, and the numerous
serpents that adorned the
aegis are also lost. Even so,
the harmony and slenderness
of her proportions and the
refinement of the style, which
can be appreciated in details
like the hairstyle and the
folds of the drapery, give a
hint of the splendour of the
lost original, a twelve-metre-
high colossus crafted from
gold and ivory that was the
wonder of Antiquity.

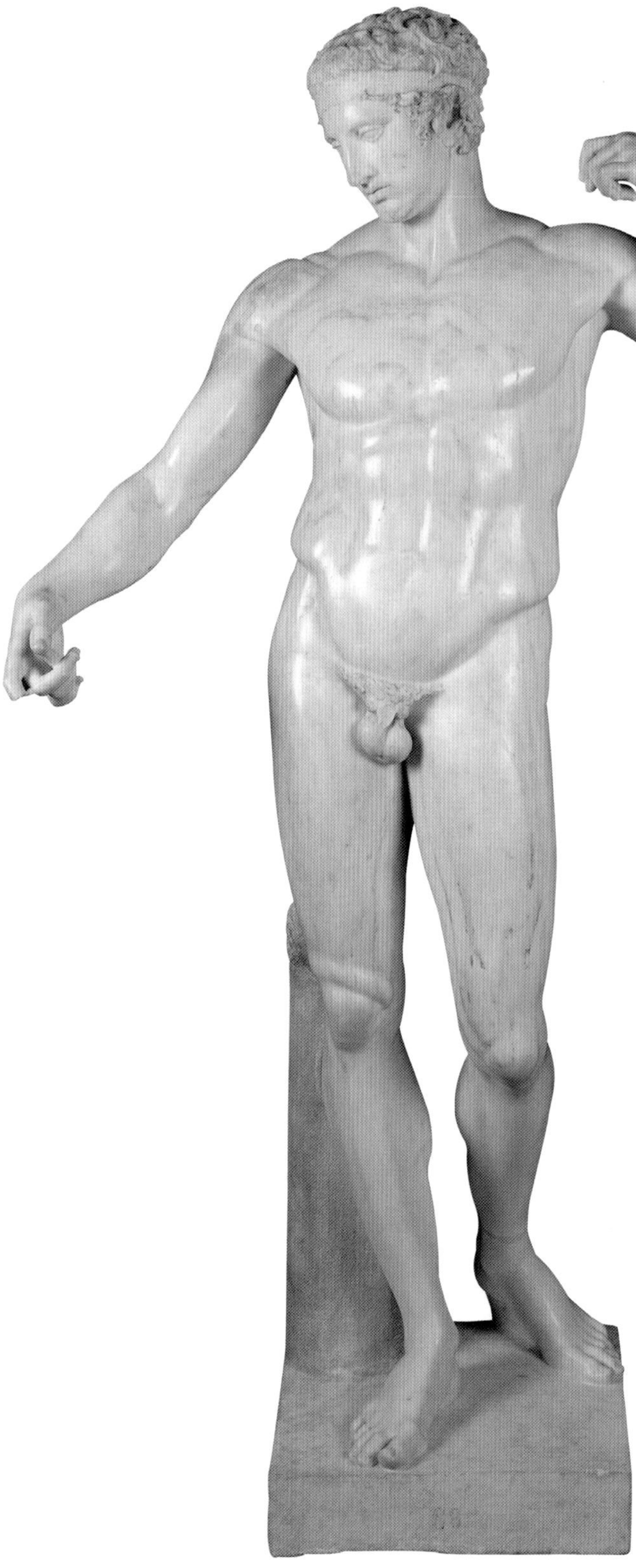

380
Diadumenos
Roman copy of c. AD 140–150
after an original by Polyclitus
dating from c. 420 BC
Marble, 202 cm high
E88

This replica of a lost bronze
original by Polyclitus may
be considered the finest of all
those that are preserved to
this day, despite the Baroque
restoration that modifies the
original position of the right
arm. In this work, produced
towards the end of his career,
Polyclitus varies the canon
that is exemplified by the
Doryphoros, the paradigm of
ideal male proportions.
The trunk is inclined to the
left, while the supporting
leg is suspended. To
provide a counterweight,
the right shoulder and arm
are positioned lower than
those of the opposite side,
thereby balancing the forms
and affording rhythm and
harmony to the mathematical
perfection of the canon.
The sculptor gives the
hair more naturalness and
movement than in his
previous statues.

381
Hypnos
Roman replica of AD 120–130
of a classical model dating
from 150–125 BC
Marble, 150 cm high
E 89

He 'comes softly and is sweet for men', according to the description provided by the Greek poet Hesiod (eighth century BC) of Slumber, the son of Night and brother of Death, who 'roams the earth and the width of the sea's broad back'. This piece, a Roman copy of a late Hellenistic original, conveys the lightness of a movement halfway between flight and walking. The trunk is a Roman addition and interferes with what must have been the main view of the Greek original – that showing the movement of the body from the left, with the head in profile, the expressive diagonal traced by the right leg and arm, and the torso inclined. The rendering of the flesh is particularly effective, although the figure has lost part of the wings on the temples and part of the arms, one of which would have been outstretched holding a small horn containing a sleep-inducing substance. The figure can now only be completed in the mind of the viewer, who must imagine the sleeping figure at which the god's oblique gaze is directed.

382 ←

Neptune
Roman, c. AD 130–140
White marble with blue veins,
236 cm high
E3

Much larger than life size,
this representation of the god
of the seas is an example of
the Roman classicism which
flourished during the period
of the empire and advocated the
merge of elements from various
Greek schools to achieve novel
results. The broad, robust body
of the god and his dishevelled,
vigorous locks recall the forces
of nature that he personifies,
while the blue veins of the marble
enliven the surface of his flesh.
The figure was discovered in
the eighteenth century in the
Corinth region, where statues
of Neptune were abundant,
as the isthmus was consecrated
to him. It was subsequently taken
to Rome and acquired by Charles
III for the new Royal Palace in
Madrid. From the Greek writer
Pausanias we know that the
incised inscription on the head
of the dolphin, indicates that
the sculpture was an offering
'to the [god] of the Isthmus'
by the priest Publius Licinius
Priscus, and was displayed
at the sanctuary of Palaemon
in Isthmia.

383 →

Muses from Hadrian's Villa
Roman copies of c. AD
130–140 after Greek originals
dating from 150–100 BC
Marble, 152 cm high
E37, E38, E40, E41, E61, E62, E68
(Clío illustrated) and E69

Among the first pieces found
at the villa of the Emperor
Hadrian at Tivoli in about 1500
was a group of eight muses that
must have adorned the palatial
architecture of the stage of
the Odeon. They were later
acquired by Queen Christina of
Sweden, who had them restored
by Ercole Ferrata, a disciple of
Bernini, and installed them in
one of the halls of her palace in
Rome. The group was completed
with a modern sculpture
of Apollo and the portrait of
the queen herself, a typically
Baroque device to illustrate her
role as patron of the arts and
sciences. Daughters of Zeus
and Mnemosyne (Memory),
the muses entertained the
gods with their talent, and also
inspired artists. They are shown
here seated on rocky ledges, all
very similarly dressed and with
graceful bodies and arms. Only
two of the heads are ancient;
the others were added in the
Baroque period along with many
of their attributes, which makes
their identification difficult.
Possibly made in two different
workshops, one more traditional
and one more innovative,
they are Roman copies of
Hellenic originals.

384
Orestes and Pylades or
The San Ildefonso Group
c. 10 BC
Marble, 161 cm high
E 28

The figures represented in this sculpture are identified as Orestes and Pylades, legendary models of friendship, who are making a sacrifice to Apollo after returning from Tauris (now Crimea) with the votive statuette of the goddess Artemis. By this act Orestes sought to atone for the murder of his mother, Clytemnestra, who was responsible for the death of Orestes' father, Agamemnon. The piece is original, without known replicas, and is a magnificent example of the eclecticism of the period of Augustus, combining Polyclitus' more compact canon, embodied by the torch bearer, with the more curved lines of Praxiteles. It was completed in the modern age with a Roman portrait of Antinous and the archaic-style goddess. Following its discovery in Rome in 1623 the sculpture was coveted by numerous collectors and passed through various hands before being acquired by Philip V, who installed it in the royal palace of La Granja de San Ildefonso, after which it is named.

385
Venus with Dolphin
Roman copy of c. AD 140–150
of an early Hellenistic original
dating from c. 280–250 BC.
Marble, 200 cm high
E31

The *Venus with Dolphin*
belongs to a long tradition
of representations of Aphrodite
that was established in the
mid-fourth century by
Praxiteles, who revolutionised
the traditional conception of
the goddess of love by sculpting
her completely naked, her
beautiful form unconcealed
by drapery. Her body is inclined
forward slightly and her arms
are positioned in a gesture of
modesty. This particular version
in the Prado is based on the
very widely copied *Capitoline
Venus* in Rome, though it
includes original elements
such as the soft curls tumbling
on her shoulders evoking the
waves from which she emerged.
It rests on the dolphin, which
recalls her marine origins and
was partially restored in the
Baroque period. The statue
was found in a Roman villa and
acquired by Queen Christina
of Sweden in the seventeenth
century.

386

Apotheosis of Claudius

Trophies of the burial
monument of M. Valerius
Messala Corvinus c. AD 20;
pedestal c. 1620
Marble, 184 cm high
E 225

This hybrid piece consisting
of both ancient and more recent
elements was a gift to Philip IV
from Cardinal Girolamo
Colonna, and was held in high

esteem while in the Alcázar
palace in Madrid. The eagle
on top of a pile of arms is an
ancient fragment restored
during the Baroque period;
the sculptor Orfeo Bosselli
added a bust of the Emperor
Claudius around the same
time. The bust was lost in the
eighteenth century and replaced
by another in about 1830.
The sculpture is almost
certainly part of the burial
monument of Valerius Messala
Corvinus, a general and

companion at arms of Augustus,
and was found at his country
villa near Bovillae, south-east
of Rome. The trophies probably
allude to battles and victories
over the enemies of Augustus,
while the eagle clutching
Jupiter's thunderbolt symbolises
the triumph of the Romans.
The pedestal, made in 1620
for the Italian prince Alberico
Cybo Malaspina, is decorated
with a swan, an emblem of
the family, and several eagles,
and is laden with symbolism.

Modern Sculpture

The main groups of modern sculptures are those which were commissioned by the Emperor Charles V from the Milanese sculptor Leone Leoni in 1549 and completed by his son Pompeo some years later, around 1564. They form a set of full-length figures, busts and reliefs that represent the emperor himself and his closest relatives: his wife Isabella, who died in 1539 [389]; his sisters Eleanor and Mary; and his son Philip [387]. While Titian realised with his brush the ideals of majesty and separateness upheld by the Habsburgs [213-215], Leoni did so through sculpture, making the most of two particular materials, bronze and Carrara marble, which were ideal vehicles for expressing the values of nobility and eternity. There has been much debate about the possible destination of these works, which remained unfinished in the Leonis' Madrid workshop when the emperor died in 1558; one sculpture in this group, entitled *Emperor Charles V and the Fury* [388], stands out for its sophistication and technical mastery. Another aspect of royal portraiture, the equestrian model, can also be studied at the Prado thanks to works like *Philip IV* by Pietro Tacca (1577–1640), *Charles II* by Giovanni Battista Foggini (1652–1725) and *Philip V* by Lorenzo Vaccaro (1655–1706). The replicas and versions of Greco-Roman works made during the Renaissance and Baroque periods provide another interesting group of sculptures. The major archaeological discoveries made in Italy stimulated the enthusiasm for antiquities, which soon spread to the leading European courts, disseminated through copies, drawings and prints. Several busts of Roman emperors and pieces such as *Antinous* (by an anonymous sixteenth-century Italian sculptor) belong to this category, as well as the *Venus* by Bartolomeo Ammannati (1511–1592), made for the gardens of the palace of Aranjuez; and the *Ariadne* (anonymous eighteenth-century Italian sculptor). Special mention should be made of the assignment given by Philip IV to Velázquez on his second trip to Italy, around 1651–1653, to commission casts of some of the most admired ancient sculptures of the period, such as the *Spinario*, the *Venus of the Shell* and the *Hermaphrodite,* one of the sources for Velázquez's *Toilet of Venus.* During this trip the artist also commissioned the Italian Matteo Bonarelli (active between 1630 and 1654) to make the gilt bronze lions that now support several *pietre dure* table tops displayed in the museum. Outstanding pieces from the height of the Late Renaissance are the *Allegory of Francis I* by Giambologna (Giovanni da Bologna) [390] and El Greco's *Epimetheus and Pandora,* one of the rare examples of mythological nudes in Spanish art.

387
LEONE LEONI
Arezzo, 1509–Milan, 1590

POMPEO LEONI
Venice (?), c. 1533–Madrid, 1608

Philip II
1551-64 . Bronze, 171 cm high
E272

388
LEONE LEONI
Arezzo, 1509–Milan, 1590

POMPEO LEONI
Venice (?), c. 1533–Madrid,
1608

*Emperor Charles V
and the Fury*
1551-64. Bronze, 251 cm high
E273

The *Fury* is the most
ambitious of the sculptures
commissioned by Charles
V (1500–1558) from Leone
Leoni in 1549. The emperor,
dressed in Roman armour, is
portrayed as a magnanimous
Greek hero. At his feet,
on a pile of trophies, is the
writhing Fury, personified
as a chained slave in allusion
to the emperor's victories
and his role as a peacemaker.
Leone, in a very typical
display of Mannerism,
designed the sculpture
and the armour, which were
cast separately, so that they
could be taken apart, allowing
the emperor's naked body
and the rich armour crafted
with jewel-like precision to
be admired. Leone studied
models from Antiquity as
well as the achievements
of his most talented
contemporaries such as
Donatello and Michelangelo.
It is uncertain for whom the
piece was originally intended.
Indeed, before reaching
the Museo del Prado it passed
through the Madrid palaces
of Aranjuez, Buen Retiro
and Buenavista and the Plaza
de Santa Ana.

389
LEONE LEONI
Arezzo, 1509–Milan, 1590

POMPEO LEONI
Venice (?), c. 1533–Madrid, 1608

The Empress Isabella
1564. Bronze, 177 cm high
E274

The Empress Isabella of Portugal, who died in Toledo in 1539 at the early age of thirty-six, was the first and only wife of Charles V, who loved her deeply. In order to recreate her likeness years later, Leone resorted to a portrait painted by Titian, now in the Museo del Prado, which shows her dressed in very similar attire, with her hair worn in a double plait, and a robe with voluminous, richly embroidered sleeves and divided overskirt. The sculpture, of which there is an almost identical version in marble, also in the Prado, left Leone's Milan workshop in 1556 but did not arrive in Spain until 1562. Once there, the sculptor had the Spanish goldsmiths Felipe Jusarte and Micael Méndez complete the details of the dress. The frontal pose, and the majesty and solemnity of the sculpture, have led scholars to point out the heavy influence of the sculptures decorating the tomb of Emperor Maximilian I in Innsbruck, specifically that of his aunt, Margaret of Austria, which deeply impressed the emperor.

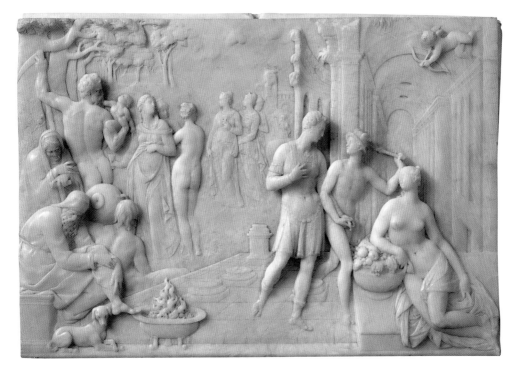

390
GIAMBOLOGNA
Douai, Netherlands,
1529–Florence, 1608

*Allegory of Francesco I
de' Medici*

1560–61. Alabaster,
31 x 45.8 x 5 cm
E296

Among the works that
Giambologna made for
Francesco I de' Medici is this
magnificent alabaster relief,
of which several replicas survive.
On the right the young prince
is introduced by Mercury to
a female figure who has been
identified as either Ceres, Hope
or the city of Florence. Hovering
above the group is Cupid, armed
with his bow and about to
shoot an arrow. On the left are
several allegorical figures related
to the passage of time, among

them two young women with
hourglasses. Made in accordance
with the canon of elongated
proportions that is characteristic
of Mannerism, the work excels
in details like the delicate
landscape and the classical
architecture. Giambologna
may have executed it as a token
of gratitude to the prince for his
appointment as court sculptor
and it has been interpreted
as a symbol of the promising
future that awaited Francesco I
as Grand Duke of Tuscany.

Nineteenth-century Sculpture

The formation of the Prado's collection of nineteenth-century sculpture began in 1826, when José Álvarez Cubero, the chief court sculptor, selected a number of pieces of Neoclassical art for the museum. These were later joined by commissioned works, namely pieces sent by scholarship holders and sculptures that Ferdinand VII chose by artists such as José Ginés, Antonio Solá, Ramón Barba, and Álvarez Cubero himself, including the posthumous portrait of Isabella II and the *Defence of Zaragoza*. A few contemporary sculptures were placed on display in the museum in 1826 alongside classical sculptures, and the inventory of 1834 mentions most of the Neoclassical sculptures that make up the collection. Significantly, the institution is referred to in the 1843 catalogue as 'His Majesty's Royal Museum of Painting and Sculpture'. The setting up of the room devoted to Isabella of Braganza in 1853 – where the painting *Las Meninas* is currently displayed – led to a large number of sculptures being placed on exhibition. The balustrade from which they could be viewed from another perspective survived almost until the establishment of the Museo de Arte Moderno.

The next few years saw the arrival at the museum of various sculptures that were sent by artists on a scholarship in Rome (José Piquer, Sabino de Medina and José Pagniucci, among others), cast in permanent material, or acquired by the state,

391
AGAPITO VALLMITJANA
Barcelona, 1833–1905

Recumbent Christ
1872. Marble, 73 x 210 x 48 cm
E815

Prominent among the eclectic art produced in Spain in the third quarter of the nineteenth century is that of the brothers Venancio and Agapito Vallmitjana in Catalonia. Regarded as a masterpiece on account of its contained serenity and sophisticated craftsmanship, Agapito's *Recumbent Christ* is linked to a Spanish tradition of suffering Christ figures, such as those of Gregorio Fernández, but also draws on the legacy of classicism and on works like Michelangelo's *Pietà*. All these influences are

interpreted with a romantic sensibility that chooses to portray 'Christ the man' – the incarnation of the tragic, solitary hero – rather than the 'triumphant Christ'. Shown at the Vienna exhibition of 1873 and at the National Exhibition of 1876, the work aroused contradictory reactions: some praised its beauty and realism, others criticised its excessive sensuality. It seems that Vallmitjana's model was his painter friend Eduardo Rosales, then seriously ill, who died in 1873.

having won awards at the National Exhibitions of Fine Arts, such as the *Recumbent Christ* by Agapito Vallmitjana [391]; *Tradition* and the large relief of *St Francis healing the Lepers* by Agustín Querol; and Ricardo Bellver's *Fallen Angel*, now in the Retiro Park. Other acquisitions had been shown at the national exhibitions but failed to receive awards. The collection also grew with the addition of works of mainly Italian provenance acquired from important Spanish collectors like the Marquess of Salamanca and the Duchess of Osuna. Living sculptors therefore enjoyed a similar presence to contemporary painters, in accordance with the official policy of the time.

Owing to the museum's pressing problems of shortage of space, in 1897 most of these sculptures – except for *Isabella of Braganza* by Álvarez Cubero [392], which remained at the Villanueva building – became part of the holdings of the recently established Museo de Arte Moderno, which was officially opened in 1898 at the Palacio de Bibliotecas y Museos. This museum continued to take in new nineteenth-century sculptures until it was dissolved in 1971, at which point they returned to the Prado and were installed in the Casón del Buen Retiro. Also around this time, and for several years, the Museo del Prado made arrangements for dozens of works from this collection to be placed on deposit at other institutions, mainly provincial museums.

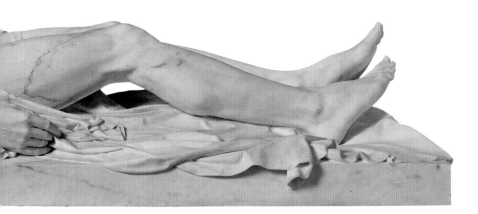

392
JOSÉ ÁLVAREZ CUBERO
Priego, Córdoba, 1768–Madrid,
1827

Isabella of Braganza
1826. Marble, 145 cm high
E1

Isabella of Braganza, the
second wife of Ferdinand VII,
whom she married in 1816, was
bound by particularly close
ties to the Museo del Prado,
which she enthusiastically
supported. This portrait, which
originates from the Royal
Palace and was executed after
her death, was one of the last
works produced by Álvarez
Cubero in Rome after he was
appointed chief court sculptor.
It combines references to the
sculpture of Antonio Canova
and Bertel Thorwaldsen with
echoes of the portraits of
the painter Jacques-Louis
David and of Roman statues
of grand seated matrons. The
queen is dressed in 'Greek
style', in accordance with the
elegant and discreet imperial
fashion, wearing a high-
waisted dress and sandals,
and her hair is gathered
in a chignon, revealing the
back of her neck. The work
is a perfect example of
Neoclassical ideals on account
of its technical excellence, its
serene and idealised beauty,
and its lifelike portrayal
inspired by the legacy
of Antiquity.

393
CAMILLO TORREGIANI
Ferrara, 1820–1896

Isabella II veiled
1855. Marble, 96 cm high
E525

Torreggiani intended this
portrait of Isabella II, a superb
example of virtuosity, to be
his introduction to the Madrid
court. Borrowing from the
Italian eighteenth-century
tradition of veiled sculptures,
it attests to his mastery
of the wet drapery technique
and allows the viewer to
appreciate the different
textures and surfaces of the
queen's face, her crown and
necklace and the jewel she
wears. Torreggiani also crafted
the base for the bust, which
bears the coat of arms of
Spain, and a pedestal with plant
and allegorical decorations,
including references to the
crown. Torreggiani worked
on the piece for over a
year. It was acquired with
a recommendation from
the Real Academia de Bellas
Artes de San Fernando and is
currently the reference work
of this sculptor, who specialised
in portraits and was chiefly
active in Florence and Ferrara.

The Dauphin's Treasure

From very early times, especially beautiful stones were believed to possess curative, magical and protective powers. The remoteness of the mines, the difficulty of extracting the stones and the extremely careful handling they required made them particularly coveted objects that were the exclusive preserve of a privileged few, whose prestige and distinction they enhanced. Known in early inventories as the 'Dauphin's Jewels' (*Alhajas del Delfín*), the Dauphin's Treasure comprises nearly one hundred and fifty precious vessels from the collection of the Grand Dauphin of France, the son of Louis XIV and father of Philip V, the first Spanish Bourbon monarch. When he died in 1712, Louis XIV wanted his grandson to inherit a selection of the finest pieces on display in his father's apartments in Versailles, which are recorded as being deposited at the royal residence of La Granja de San Ildefonso in 1724. In 1776, the enlightened concerns of King Charles III (reigned 1759–1788) led him to develop a scientific interest in the collection and to donate it to the Royal Cabinet of Natural History. During the Peninsular War against France (1808–1814), several pieces were lost and many others were damaged. Installed again in the Royal Cabinet in 1839, the treasures were given by Isabella II to the Real Museo de Pinturas, the future Museo Nacional del Prado, thereby giving priority to their artistic value over their mineralogical interest.

394
ANONYMOUS

Rectangular casket with cameos
1630–40. Agate, amethyst, chalcedony, carnelian, lapis lazuli, onyx, fire opal, gold, gilt silver and sardonyx.
12·5 cm high
O31

395
ANONYMOUS

Goblet with gold mermaid
Paris (?), third quarter of
16th century. Agate, partially
enamelled gold, rubies
and diamonds, c. 17.5 cm
O1

This goblet or vase is formed
by a golden-skinned mermaid
with a double tail enamelled
in blue, green and red.
The slender arms of the figure,
whose head is adorned with
a feathered crest and whose
body is decorated with various
jewels, hold a small agate plate
that may have been used to
contain salt. The mermaid
is supported by another piece
of agate with a richly adorned
base held up in its turn by four
dolphins. The piece, which
has been linked to the famous
Salt cellar by Benvenuto
Cellini (1500–1571) in the
Kunsthistorisches Museum
in Vienna, was probably made
by a French workshop of the
first half of the sixteenth
century familiar with Italian
models.

The vessels that make up the Treasure may be divided into two groups: those made of colourless rock crystal, and those crafted from so-called *pietre dure* or 'hardstones' including jade, agate, chalcedony, lapis lazuli, jasper of several colours, quartz and alabaster. Precious stones like diamonds, sapphires, emeralds and rubies and semiprecious stones like turquoise, amethysts and garnets are also abundant, as are pearls of all sizes. The mounts, made by prestigious workshops such as that of the Toutain, are generally gold and often adorned with rich enamelwork. The iconographical sources are very varied, ranging from Ovid's *Metamorphoses* to the Old Testament, and the rich decorative repertoire encompasses sources from Antiquity to the Renaissance, including Byzantium and the Middle Ages. Significant among the workshops involved in their manufacture are those of the Milanese Miseroni and the Sarachi, masters in rock crystal carving, and that of Giambattista Metellino, though some pieces were brought from Persia, China, Turkey and Mogul India. Nearly all have individual transport cases (most of which are deposited at the Museo de Artes Decorativas, Madrid) made of wood and decoratively covered in fine skins or luxury fabrics.

The *Pietre Dure* Collection

In the mid-sixteenth century Rome and Florence witnessed the revival of a rare and costly technique that had reached its apogee in the period of the Roman Emperor Augustus (31 BC–AD 14): the so-called *opus sectile* or coloured marble and hardstone inlay. Although it was above all the popes and a few powerful families like the Medici who encouraged the fashion for this ancient technique, they were soon followed by the great European monarchs. The special relationship between Spain and Italy during the sixteenth, seventeenth and eighteenth centuries and the fact that these pieces were presented as gifts by kings, high-ranking nobles and members of the ecclesiastical hierarchy led to the incorporation of a large number of them into the Spanish Royal Collections. In most cases these panels inlaid with pieces of marble, alabaster, onyx, jasper, coral, mother-of-pearl, lapis lazuli and malachite served as sumptuous ceremonial table tops and were placed on stands of carved stone or finewoods. One of the earliest examples, and one of the largest, in the Prado [396] dates from the period of Philip II. It is dominated by geometrical motifs and was a personal gift from Cardinal Alessandrini, the nephew of Pope Pius V. In the seventeenth century, the

396
ANONYMOUS

Table top of Philip II
Before 1587. Gilt bronze and pietre dure,
246.2 x 116.5 cm
O452

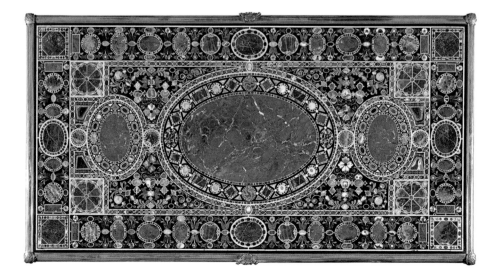

397
FRANCESCO GHINGHI
Florence, 1689–Naples, 1766

Writing desk

1749–63. Marquetry and *pietre
dure*, 95 x 150 x 105 cm
0466

reign of Philip IV saw the arrival of the so-called '*Writing
desk of Nuncio Máximo*', a gift from the papal nuncio Camilo
Massimi exemplifying the distinct style of Florentine
craftsmen, who tended to draw inspiration from nature and
use bird, flower, fruit and insect motifs in their designs. In
the seventeenth century the fashion for *pietre dure* panels
spread to the nobility, and the Prado has pieces from the
collections of Rodrigo de Calderón, Pedro Téllez Girón
and Alfonso Enríquez de Cabrera. However, the main
driving force behind the spread of this technique in Spain
was Charles III, who, not content with importing *pietre
dure*, promoted their manufacture. As king of Naples and
Sicily, he founded the Real Laboratorio delle Pietre Dure in
1737, directed by the great gem engraver Francesco Ghinghi
[397], and later in Spain, as Charles III, he set up the Real
Laboratorio de Piedras Duras of the Buen Retiro in 1762.
The latter workshop produced seven beautiful console tables
now in the Prado. Based on works by painters like Luis
Paret y Alcázar, Charles-Joseph Flipart and Gaspar van
Wittel, they illustrate the complexity of this technique in
the eighteenth century.

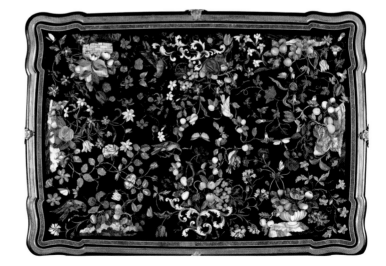

The Medal and Miniature Collection

The collection of medals comes almost entirely from the generosity of the collector Pablo Bosch y Barrau (1862 – 1915), who in 1915 left a group of some nine hundred pieces from the principal European workshops and mints from the 15th to the 20th centuries. The oldest examples from the middle of the 15th century are of Italian origin by the first creators of the genre: Matteo de Pasti, Andrea Guazzalotti and Cristoforo di Geremia. The best catalogued collection is that of the Spanish medals, which begins with the first pieces which the Austrias commissioned to Italian artisans such as Leone Leoni, author of the commemorative medal of Charles V's victory in Mühlberg; Jacopo Nizzolo da Trezzo, responsible for those of Mary Tudor of England and of Philip as king and prince of Spain; and Giampaolo Poggini, who created several of Philip II. At the end of the 16th century, the proclaiming and swearing-in of kings types of medals erupted, and of which a good example is the proclamation of Philip III in Granada. Rutilio Gaci, who introduced the Baroque medals, is well represented with pieces such as those of Philip III and Margaret of Austria and that of Philip IV. In the 18th century, Spanish authors already stand out, such as Isidro Párraga, author of the medals of Philip V and Marie Louise of Savoy, and of Philip V and Elizabeth Farnese.

398
JACOPO NIZZOLO DA TREZZO
Lombardy, 1515/19–Madrid, 1589

Medal of the architect Juan de Herrera
1578. Bronze, 50.5 mm Ø
01003

399
DUCKER, GUILLERMO
Holanda, doc. 1799-1813

*Pedro Alcántara
Téllez-Girón, IX duque
de Osuna*
h. 1805. Marfil. 72 x 50 mm.
0821

In the reign of Charles III, Tomas Francisco Prieto, Pedro González of Sepúlveda and Jerónimo Antonio Gil, creator of the engraving school in Mexico and one of the founders of the San Carlos Royal Academy, stand out.

Additionally, the Museo del Prado conserves an important collection of small portraits and miniatures comprised of one hundred and seventy nine pieces from various bequests and purchases, the largest group being comprised of those acquired from the heirs of Arturo Perera in 1980.

The small portraits, painted in oil on copper plate and card, are few but they stand out for their quality. Particularly notable among them are those painted by Francisco de Goya and Michiel Jansz van Mierevelt. For its part, the group of miniatures, tempera or gouache on vellum, paper or ivory, offer an evolution of this pictorial genre from the second half of the 18th until the end of the 19th centuries. The school best represented is the Spanish one with works by Guillermo Ducker, a Dutch miniaturist working in Spain, José Alonso del Rivero, Luis de la Cruz y Ríos, Florentino Decraene, Cecilio Corro, Juan Pérez de Villamayor and Antonio Tomasich, although there are good examples of French, English and Austrian miniatures.

Index of artists and works

A

Alenza, Leonardo 196, 198, 425
The Tooth-puller 198
The Triumph of Bacchus **198**

Alma Tadema, Lawrence 423
Pompeian Scene (The Siesta) **423**

Álvarez Cubero, José 454, 455, 456
Isabella of Braganza 455, **456**

Amigoni, Jacopo 219, 276, 290,
296, 300, 301, 302
*The Discovery of the Cup
in Benjamin's Bag* **300**

Anguisciola, Sofonisba 276
Philip II 276, **277**

Anonymous Castilian Franco-
Gothic,
St Christopher Altarpiece 28, **29**

Anonymous Hispano-Flemish,
St Michael the Archangel **34**

Antolínez, José 132, 137
The Magdalene borne by Angels **137**

Arellano, Juan de 70, 73
Flowers in a Crystal Vase **73**

B

Baldung Grien, Hans 403, 412
The Ages and Death **412**, **413**
Harmony or *The Three Graces* **412**

Barocci, Federico 14, 141, 234, 243
The Nativity **243**

Bassano, Jacopo da Ponte 52, 56,
244, 273, 274, 275
God reprimanding Adam **275**

Batoni, Pompeo Girolamo 296
George Legge, Viscount Lewisham
296, **297**

Baudry, Paul 400
Pearl and the Wave **400**

Bayeu, Francisco 148, 150, 151, 166,
171, 302, 414, 425
The Assumption of the Virgin **150**

Bellini, Giovanni 223, 241, 245,
248, 251, 404
*The Virgin and Child between
Two Saints* **245**

Bermejo, Bartolomé 36
*St Dominic of Silos enthroned
as Bishop* 36, **37**

Berruguete, Pedro 23, 35, 38, 39,
134
*St Dominic Guzmán presiding
over an Auto-da-fé* **39**, 134

Beruete, Aureliano de 210, 214,
215, 216, 429
*View of Madrid from St Isidore's
Meadow* **215**

Beuckelaer, Joachim 337
*Christ in the House of Martha
and Mary* **337**

Bolonia, Juan de (Jean de
Boulogne; Giambologna) 450, 453
Allegory of Francesco I de' Medici
450, **453**

Bonito, Giuseppe 298
*The Turkish Diplomatic Mission
in Naples in 1741* **298**

El Bosco (Hieronymus Bosch;
Jeroen van Aken) 94, 307, 320,
321, 322, 323, 324, 325, 326, 338
The Adoration of the Magi **323**
The Garden of Earthly Delights
320, **321**
The Haywain 320, **325**
*The Removal of the Stone of
Folly* 320, **324**
*The Tabletop of the Seven Deadly
Sins* **322**

Botticelli, Sandro 220, 224
*The Story of Nastagio degli
Onesti* 220, **224**, **225**

Boucher, François 396, 397
Pan and Syrinx **396**, **397**

Boulogne, Valentin de 381, 384
The Martyrdom of St Lawrence
381, **384**

Bourdon, Sébastien 381, 388
*Queen Christina of Sweden on
Horseback* **388**

Bouts, Dirk 12, 307, 319, 326
Triptych of the Life of the Virgin
318, **319**

Bray, Salomon de 376
Judith and Holofernes **376**

Bril, Paul 360
Landscape with Psyche and Jupiter
(with Pedro Pablo Rubens) **360**

Bronzino (Agnolo di Cosimo) 242
Don García de Médicis **242**

Bruegel, The Elder, Pieter 307,
308, 336, 337, 338, 339, 344, 346,
363
The Triumph of Death **336**, **337**
The Wine of Saint Martin's Day
338, **339**

Brueghel de Velours, Jan 307, 344,
345, 346, 347, 350, 352
*Market and Washing Place in
Flanders* (with Joost de Momper)
346

The Series of the Five Senses
(with Pedro Pablo Rubens):
Hearing **350**, **351**
Sight 350, **351**
Smell 350, **352**, **353**
Taste **352**, **353**
Touch **353**

*The Virgin and Child in a Flower
Garland* (with Pedro Pablo
Rubens) **344**, **345**
The Vision of St Hubert (with
Pedro Pablo Rubens) **347**

C

Campin, Robert ('Master of
Flémalle')12, 307, 308, 310, 311, 312
The Marriage of the Virgin **311**
St Barbara **310**
*St John the Baptist and the Franciscan
Master Heinrich von Werl* **310**

Cano, Alonso 84, 86, 90, 92, 93,
142, 425, 429
*The Dead Christ supported by
an Angel* **93**
Female Nude **429**
The Miracle of the Well 90, **92**
The Virgin and Child 90, **91**

Caravaggio (Michelangelo Merisi)
64, 67, 76, 77, 84, 99, 278, 280,
282, 285, 286, 287, 288, 290, 294,
366, 377, 382
David and Goliath **282, 283**

Carnicero, Antonio 148, 158
*Ascent of a Montgolfier Balloon
at Aranjuez* **158**

Carracci, Annibale 13, 100, 278,
279, 280, 286, 288, 290, 390, 425
Venus, Adonis and Cupid **279**

Carreño de Miranda, Juan 132, 135,
139, 392, 430
The Duke of Pastrana **132, 133**
Eugenia Martínez Vallejo, Clothed
135
Eugenia Martínez Vallejo, Nude
135
Portrait of a Gentleman **430**

Cavallino, Bernardo 290, 294
The Martyrdom of St Stephen **294,
295**

Cerezo, Mateo 132, 139
*The Mystic Marriage of
St Catherine* **139**

Claesz, Pieter 373, 378
Still life **378**

Coello, Claudio 132, 137, 425
The Triumph of St Augustine
137

Correa de Vivar, Juan 46
The Annunciation **46**

Correggio, Antonio Allegri 234,
236, 237, 238, 243, 279, 280, 417
Noli me tangere **237**
*The Virgin and Child with
the Infant St John the Baptist*
236

Coxcie, Michiel 260, 308, 335
*Death of the Virgin and the
Ascension* **335**

Cranach, The Elder, Lucas 403,
410,411, 412
*Hunt in Charles V's Honour
at Torgau Castle* **411**
*The Virgin and Child with St John
and Angels* **410**

Crespi, Daniele 284
The Pietà **284**

D

Dauphin's Treasure 458:
Goblet with gold mermaid **459**
Rectangular casket with cameos
458

David, Gerard 38, 308, 326, 330,331
Rest on the Flight into Egypt 326,
330, 331
*Virgin and Child with Two Angels
crowning Her* **330**

Domenichino (Domenico
Zampieri) 13, 278, 280, 390
Sacrifice of Isaac **278**

Domínguez Bécquer, Valeriano
196, 199
*The Dance. Folk Traditions from
the Province of Soria* **199**

Ducker, Wilhelm, 462, 463
*Pedro Alcántara Téllez-Girón, IX
Duke of Osun* **463**

Dürer, Albrecht 13, 54, 82, 90,
106,130, 230, 252, 326, 403, 404,
405, 406, 407, 408, 412
Adam and Eve **406, 407**
Portrait of an Unknown Man **408**
Self-portrait 13, **404, 405**

Dyck, Anthony van 90, 132, 139,
140, 286, 294, 296, 307, 357, 364,
366, 367, 368, 369, 370, 420, 421
The Arrest of Christ 364, **367**
Christ Crowned with Thorns 366, 367
Endymion Porter and Van Dyck
364, 365
Mary Ruthwen, the Painter's Wife
369
The Painter Martin Rijkaert **368**

E

Elsheimer, Adam 403, 409
Ceres in the House of Hecuba **409**

Espinosa, Juan de 70
*Still life with Apples, Plums,
Grapes and Pears* **70**

Esquivel y Suárez de Urbina,
Antonio María 196, 201
*Contemporary Poets: A Reading
by Zorrilla in the Painter's Studio*
196, **201**

Esteve, Agustín 153
Portrait of Don Mariano San Juan

*y Pinedo, Count Consort of La
Cimera* **153**

Eyck, school of Jan van 308, 309
*Fountain of Grace, the Triumph
of the Church over the Synagogue*
308, 309

F

Fernández de Navarrete, el Mudo,
Juan 50, 52, 74, 270, 276
The Baptism of Christ **52**

Fernández, Alejo 44
The Flagellation **44**

Fernández, el Labrador, Juan
70, 71
Two Hanging Bunches of Grapes **71**

Flandes, Juan de 38, 40, 41
The Crucifixion 38, 40, **41**
The Resurrection of Lazarus 38, 40

Florentine workshop of 16th
century 460
Table top of Philip II **460**

Fortuny y Marsal, Mariano 210,
212, 213, 214, 400, 425
Elderly Nude in the Sun 210, **211**
*The Painter's Children in the
Japanese Room* 210, **212**

Fra Angelico 220, 221, 312
The Annunciation **220, 221**

Francés, Nicolás 28, 31
*Altarpiece of the Life of the Virgin
and of St Francis* 28, **31**

Frías y Escalante, Juan Antonio
de 132
*The Triumph of Faith over the
Senses* **138**

Furini, Francesco 286, 289
Lot and his Daughters **289**

G

Gainsborough, Thomas 419, 420,421
Dr Isaac Henrique Sequeira **421**

Gallego, Fernando 32
Pietà, or the Fifth Sorrow **32, 33**

Gentileschi, Artemisa 290, 293, 295
The Birth of St John the Baptist **293**

Gentileschi, Orazio 64, 285, 286
The Finding of Moses **285**

Ghinghi, Francesco 461
Writing desk **461**

Giaquinto, Corrado 14, 148, 150,
151, 152, 162, 219, 276, 290, 296,
301, 425
Justice and Peace **301**

Giordano, Luca 219, 276, 290, 291,
292, 293, 298, 301, 425
The Prudent Abigail **292, 293**
*Rubens painting the Allegory
of Peace* **290, 291**

Gisbert Pérez, Antonio 202, 203
*The Execution by Firing Squad of
Torrijos and his Companions on the
Beach at Málaga* **202, 203**

González Velázquez, Antonio 152
Self-portrait **152**

Gossaert de Maubege, Jan
(Mabuse) 12, 308, 333, 334, 340
*Christ between the Virgin Mary
and St John the Baptist* **333**
The Virgin and Child **334**

Goya, Francisco de 14, 23, 54, 94,
148, 150, 153, 158, 162, 163, 164,
165, 166, 167, 168, 170, 171, 172,
174, 175, 176, 177, 178, 180, 181,
182, 183, 185, 186, 190, 191, 192,
193, 196, 198, 202, 215, 276, 290,
396, 414, 419, 425, 432, 434, 435,
436, 437
*The Agility and Audacity of
Juanito, Apiñani (Tauromaquia 20)*
436
Album G
Caprichos 162, 432, 434
Charles IV on Horseback **164**
Christ on the Cross 166, 170, **171**
The Clothed Maja **178, 179**
The Countess of Chinchón **175**
The Crockery Vendor 166, **167**

Disparates 172, 186, 432, 434, 437:
A Way of Flying **437**

Don Juan Bautista de Muguiro **193**
*Dream 1: Universal Language. The
author sleeping* **432, 433**
The Duchess of Abrantes **181**
*The Duke and Duchess of Osuna
and their Children* 172, **173**
*The Fall of Adam and the Expulsion
from Paradise* **434**
Family of Charles IV 176, **177**
Gaspar Melchor de Jovellanos **174**
I'm still learning (Album G) **435**
I'm still learning **435**
*The Infante don Francisco de Paula
Antonio* **176**
Italian Notebook 425, 432, 434
The Marchioness of Santa Cruz
180, 181

The Milkmaid of Bordeaux **192**, 193
The Naked Maja **178, 179**

The Black Paintings:
A manola: doña Leocadia Zorrilla
191
Duel with Cudgels **188**
Half-submerged Dog **186, 187**
Saturno devoring his Son **189**
Two Old Men Eating **190**, 191
The Witches' Sabbath **188**

Queen Maria Luisa on Horseback
164, **165**
*The Second of May, 1808, in
Madrid* **182, 183**
Self-portrait **162, 163**
St Isidore's Meadow **168, 169**
St John the Baptist in the Desert
170

Tauromaquia 172, 432, 434, **436**
*The Agility and Audacity of
Juanito, Apiñani* **436**

The Third of May, 1808, in Madrid
184, 185
The Threshers or *Summer* **168**
A Way of Flying (Disparate 13) **437**

El Greco (Domenicos
Theotocopoulos) 23, 48, 54, 55,
56, 57, 58, 59, 60, 61, 62, 63, 64,
74, 82, 94, 439, 450
The Adoration of the Shepherds
54, 60, **63**
Aged Gentleman **58**
The Annunciation **56**
Fable **57**
The Flight into Egypt **56**
Jerónimo de Cevallos **58**
*The Nobleman with his Hand on his
Breast* **59**

High Altar of the College
of Doña María de Aragón:
The Annunciation 60, **61**, 62
The Baptism of Christ **62**
The Trinity 54, **55**

Greek workshop of Archaid
Period 440, 442
Horse from the Archaic Period 440,
442

Grien, Baldung (see Baldung
Grien)

Guas, Juan 426
*High Chapel of San Juan de los
Reyes* **426**

Guercino (Giovanni Francesco
Barbieri) 14, 100, 286, 287, 425
Susanna and the Elders **287**

H

Haes, Carlos de 210, 214, 425
*The Mancorbo Canal in the Picos
de Europa* **214**

Hamen, Juan van der 66, 68, 69,
110, 128, 130
Portrait of a Dwarf **128, 129**
*Still life with Artichokes, Flowers
and Glass Vessels* **69**
*Still life with Sweets and Glass
Vessels* **68**

Herrera, The Elder, Francisco
de 84, 85
*St Bonaventure receives the Habit
from St Francis* **85**

Herrera, The Younger, Francisco
de 132, 136, 137, 140
The Triumph of St Hermenegild **136**

Hiepes, Tomás 70, 72
*Delft Fruit Bowl and Two Vases
of Flowers* **72**
Two Fruit Bowls on a Table **72**

Houasse, Michel-Ange 392, 394,
396
Luis I **394**

I

Inza, Joaquín 148, 152
Don Tomás de Iriarte **152**

J

Joli, Antonio 299
*The Embarkation of Charles III
in Naples* **299**

Jordaens, Jacob 307, 344, 370, 371, 425
The Meleager and Atalanta **370**
Painter's Family **371**

Juanes, Juan de 14, 47, 74
The Last Supper **47**

K

Key, Adrien Thomasz 342
Family Portrait **342**

L

La Tour, Georges de 381, 382,
384, 385
The Blind Hurdy-Gurdy Player
382, 383
St Jerome reading a Letter **384**

Lanfranco, Giovanni 290, 294
Funeral of a Roman Emperor **294**

Lawrence, Thomas 419, 420, 421
Miss Marthe Carr **421**

Leonardo's Workshop 232
Copy of the Mona Lisa **232**

Leoni, Leone 264, 276, 450, 451, 452, 462
Emperor Charles V and the Fury (with Pompeo Leoni) 450, **451**
The Empress Isabella (with Pompeo Leoni) **452**
Philip II (with Pompeo Leoni) **450**

Leoni, Pompeo 238, 276, 439, 450,451, 452
Emperor Charles V and the Fury (with Leone Leoni) 450, **451**
The Empress Isabella (with Leone Leoni) **452**
Philip II (with Leone Leoni) **450**

Licinio, Bernardino 246
Agnese, the Painter's Sister-in-law **246**

Loo, Louis-Michel van 152, 154, 276, 301, 392, 393, 396
The Family of Philip V **393**

López, Vicente 194
Félix Antonio Máximo López, First Organist of the Royal Chapel **194**

Lorena, Claudio de (Claude Gellée) 390, 391
The Archangel Raphael with Tobias **391**
The Burial of St Serapia **391**
The Finding of Moses **391**
Landscape with the Embarkation at Ostia of St Paula Romana **391**

Lotto, Lorenzo 226, 246, 247
Micer Marsilio and his Wife **247**
St Jerome Penitent **246**

Luini, Bernardino 234
The Holy Family **234, 235**

M

Machuca, Pedro 45, 46
The Descent from the Cross **45**

Madrazo y Agudo, José de 16, 194,195, 196, 200, 400
The Death of Viriatus, Chief of the Lusitanians **195**

Madrazo y Garreta, Raimundo de 210, 213, 400, 401
Ramón de Errazu **213**

Madrazo y Kuntz, Federico de 196, 200, 212, 213, 425, 432
The Painter Carlos Luis de Ribera **200**
Doña Amalia de Llano y Dotres, Countess of Vilches **196, 197**

Maella, Mariano Salvador 148, 151,194, 302, 414, 425
The Immaculate Conception **151**

Maíno, Juan Bautista 64, 127
The Adoration of the Kings **64, 65**
Portrait of a Gentleman **64**
The Recapture of Bahia in Brazil 64, **127**

Mantegna, Andrea 41, 222, 236, 237, 245, 248
The Death of the Virgin 13, **222**

Maratta, Carlo 13, 219, 286, 288,296
The Painter Andrea Sacchi **288**

Martínez del Mazo, Juan Bautista 120, 128, 131
View of the City of Saragossa **131**

Masip, Juan Vicente 44, 47
The Visitation **44**

Massys, Quentin 44, 308, 329, 332, 335, 340
Christ presented to the People **332**
Landscape with the Temptation of St Anthony Abbot (with Joachim Patinir) 326, **329**
The Saviour **332**
The Virgin Mary **332**

Master of San Baudelio in Berlanga 24, 25
Mural paintings from San Baudelio in Casillas de Berlanga (Soria): *Hare Chase* 24, **25**

Master of Santa Cruz de Maderuelo 24, 27
Mural paintings from the chapel of Santa Cruz de Maderuelo (Segovia): *The Creation of Adam* and *The Fall of Adam and Eve* **26, 27**

Master of Sopetrán 34
The First Duke of El Infantado **34**

Master of the Virgin of the Catholic Monarchs 35
The Virgin of the Catholic Monarchs **35**

Meissonier, Jean-Louis-Ernest 210, 400, 401
Josefa Manzanedo e Intentas

de Mitjans, Marchioness of Manzanedo **401**

Meléndez, Luis Egidio 148, 154, 155, 156
Still life with a Box of Sweets, Bread Ring and Other Objects **154**
Still life with Chocolate Service **154**
Still life with a Piece of Salmon, a Lemon and Three Vessels **155**
Still life with Wattermelons, Apples and Landscape **156**

Meléndez, Miguel Jacinto 148
Portrait of Philip V **148, 149**

Memling, Hans 38, 307, 308, 312, 318, 320, 328, 342
The Adoration of the Magi **318**

Mengs, Anton Raphael 14, 148, 150, 151, 152, 153, 166, 171, 172, 194, 219, 286, 296, 302, 403, 414,416, 417, 425
The Adoration of the Shepherds **417**
Carlos III **414, 415**
María Luisa of Parma, Princess of Asturias **416**

Messina, Antonello da 220, 223, 245, 248
The Dead Christ supported by an Angel 220, **223**

Metsys, Quentin (see Massys, Quentin)

Miguel Ángel (Michelangelo Buonarrotti) 427
Study of man's right shoulder, chest and upper arm **427**

Momper, Joost de 346
Market and Washing Place in Flanders (with Jan Brueghel de Velours) **346**

Montalvo, Bartolomé 157
Sea-bream **157**

Mor, Anthonis (Antonis Mor van Dashorst) 12, 50, 94, 307, 308, 340, 342, 343, 368
Mary Tudor, Queen of England **340, 341**
Pejerón, Jester of the Count of Benavente and the Grand Duke of Alba **343**
Portrait of a Married Woman **342**

Morales, Luis de 48, 49, 74
The Birth of the Virgin **48**
The Virgin and Child **49**

Muñoz Degrain, Antonio 202, 207
The Lovers of Teruel **207**

Murillo, Bartolomé Esteban
14, 23, 76, 81, 86, 90, 138,
140, 141, 142, 143, 144, 146,
147, 198
*The Christ Child and the Infant
Baptist with a Shell* **146**
*The Foundation of Santa Maria
Maggiore in Rome I: The
Patrician's Dream* **144**, **145**
*The Foundation of Santa Maria
Maggiore in Rome II: The
Patrician Reveals his Dream to
Pope Liberius* **144**, **145**
The Good Shepherd **146**
*The Holy Family with a Little
Bird* **141**
Nicolás Omazur **140**
*The Soult Immaculate
Conception* **147**
The Virgin appearing to St Bernard
142
The Virgin of the Rosary **143**

O

Orley, Bernard van 308, 334, 336, 340
The Holy Family **334**

Orrente, Pedro 74, 274
The Crucifixion **74**

P

Pantoja de la Cruz, Juan 52, 53, 125
Queen Margaret of Austria **53**

Paret y Alcázar, Luis 14, 148, 158,
159, 160, 161, 461
*Charles III supping before his
Court* **160**
The Royal Couples, 158, **161**
Self-portrait in the Studio **159**

Parmigianino (Girolamo
Francesco Maria Mazzola) 46,
234, 238, 239
*Camilla Gonzaga, Countess of
San Segundo, and her Sons* **239**
*The Holy Family with an
Angel* **238**
*Pietro Maria Rossi, Count of San
Segundo* **239**

Patinir, Joachim 12, 106, 307, 308,
326, 327, 328, 329, 338
Charon crossing the River Styx
326, **327**
*Landscape with the Temptation of
St Anthony Abbot* (with Quentin

Massys) 326, **329**
Lanscape with St Jerome **328**

Peeters, Clara 348
Table (1611) **348**
Table (1610-1615) **348**

Pereda, Antonio de 128, 130
St Jerome **130**

Piombo, Sebastiano del
(Sebastiano Luciani) 42, 44, 52,
74, 75, 240, 241
Christ carrying the Cross **240**
Christ's Descent into Limbo 240, **241**

Poussin, Nicolas 13, 278, 381, 382,
386, 387, 388, 389, 390
Landscape with Buildings **388**
Landscape with St Jerome **386**
Parnassus **387**
The Triumph of David **389**

Pradilla Ortiz, Francisco 202, 208
Joan the Mad **208**, **209**

R

Rafael (Rafael Sanzio) 13, 14, 42,
44, 46, 47, 90, 220, 226, 228, 230,
231, 232, 233, 234, 237, 238, 239,
243, 252, 278, 280, 334, 336, 386,
387, 414, 430
The Cardinal 220, **226**, **227**
Christ on the Road to Calvary
or *Lo Spasimo di Sicilia* **230**
The Holy Family, or *The Pearl*
13, **231**
*The Holy Family with St Raphael
Tobias and St Jerome*, or *The
Virgin of the Fish* **228**, **229**
The Holy Family with the Lamb **228**

Ramírez, Felipe 66, 68
*Still life with Cardoon, Francolin,
Grapes and Lilies* 66, **68**

Ranc, Jean 152, 276, 392, 394, 395
Charles III as a Child **395**
The Family of Philip V **394**, 395

Rembrandt (Rembrandt
Harmensz van Rijn) 373, 374
Judith at the Banquet of Holofernes
373, **374**, **375**

Reni, Guido 14, 64, 100, 280, 281,
288, 425
Hippomenes and Atalanta **281**
St Sebastian **280**, 281

Reymerswaele, Marinus Claesz
van 339
The Money Changer and his Wife
339

Reynolds, Joshua 419, 420, 421
Portrait of a Clergyman **420**

Ribalta, Francisco 14, 74, 75,
241, 425
Christ embracing St Bernard **75**

Ribera, José de 14, 23, 76, 77, 78,
79, 80, 81, 82, 83, 86, 94, 99, 100,
130, 140, 210, 284, 290, 294, 295,
425, 428
Democritus **77**
Isaac and Jacob **78**, **79**
Jacob's Dream **81**
The Magdalene **83**
The Martyrdom of St Philip **80**
The Resurrection of Lazarus **76**
St Cecilia **428**
St James the Elder **78**
The Trinity 23, **82**

Rico, Martín 210, 214, 400
*The Ladies' Tower at the Alhambra
in Granada* **214**

Rizi, Francisco 130, 132, 134
*Auto-da-fé on the Plaza Mayor
in Madrid* **134**

Rizi, Juan Andrés 128, 130, 132
Don Tiburcio de Redín y Cruzat **130**

Robert, Hubert 398
The Colosseum **398**

Roberts, David 419, 422
The Castle of Alcalá de Guadaira **422**
The Torre del Oro in Seville **422**

Rodríguez de Toledo, Juan 28, 30
*Altarpiece of Archbishop Sancho
de Rojas* 28, **30**

Roman workshop 439, 447
Orestes and Pylades or *The
San Ildefonso Group* 439, **447**

Roman workshop 439, 449
Apotheosis of Claudius 439, **449**

Roman workshop 442
Crater depicting centaurs fighting
442

Roman workshop 446
Neptune **446**

Roman workshop of Greek
originals 439, 446
Muses from Hadrian's Villa 439, **446**

Roman workshop of an original
by Phidias 440, 443
Athena Parthenos, 440, **443**

Roman workshop of an original
by Polyclitus 440, 444
Diadumenos 440, **444**

Roman workshop of a Hellenistic
original 439, 440
Faun with Young Goat 439, **440**,
441

Roman workshop of a Hellenistic
original 440, 445
Hypnos 440, **445**

Roman workshop of a Hellenistic
original 440, 448
Venus with Dolphin 440, **448**

Rosales, Eduardo 202, 205, 206,
425, 430, 455
The Death of Lucretia 206
Portrait of a Girl 430
*Queen Isabella the Catholic
dictating her Will* 204, 205, 206

Rubens, Pedro Pablo 13, 70, 94,
96, 99, 104, 110, 118, 120, 125,
130, 132, 140, 219, 248, 252, 264,
286, 288, 290, 294, 307, 344, 347,
350, 353, 354, 356, 357, 358, 359,
360, 361, 362, 363, 364, 366, 367,
370, 425, 429, 439
The Adoration of the Magi 356
Andromeda freed by Perseus 359
*The Cardinal-Infante Don
Ferdinand of Austria at the Battle
of Nördlingen* 361
*Equestrian Portrait of the Duke
of Lerma* 357
The Garden of Love 362
Landscape with Psyche and Jupiter
(with Paul Bril) 360
The Recognition of Philopoemen
(with Frans Snyders) 358, **359**

The Series of the Five Senses
(with Jan Brueghel de Velours):
Hearing 350, **351**
Sight 350, 351
Smell 350, **352**, 353
Taste 352, 353
Touch 353

St George and the Dragon 358
The Three Graces 354, **355**
Villagers' Dance 363
*The Virgin and Child in a Flower
Garland* (with Jan Brueghel de
Velours) **344**, 345
The Vision of St Hubert (with Jan
Brueghel de Velours) **347**

S

San Baudelio in Casillas de
Berlanga (Soria) (see Master
of San Baudelio de Berlanga)

San Leocadio, Paolo de 38
*The Virgin of the Knight of
Montesa* 38

Sánchez Coello, Alonso 12, 50, 51,
52, 53, 128
*The Infantas Isabella Clara
Eugenia and Catherine Micaela* 50
Prince Carlos 50, **51**

Sánchez Cotán, Juan 66, 67, 68,
69, 70, 71, 74, 110, 154, 157, 274
*Still life with Game, Vegetables
and Fruit* 67

Santa Cruz de Maderuelo
(Segovia) (see Master of Santa
Cruz de Maderuelo)

Sarto, Andrea del 14, 232, 233, 234, 425
The Sacrifice of Isaac 232
*The Virgin and Child between
St Matthew and an Angel* 233

Serodine, Giovanni 284
St Margaret revives a Young Man
284

Snyders, Frans 359
The Recognition of Philopoemen
(with Pedro Pablo Rubens) 359

Sorolla, Joaquín 210, 216, 217
The Painter Aureliano de Beruete 216
Young Boys on the Beach **217**

Stanzione, Massimo 290, 293, 295
Sacrifice to Bacchus **295**

Steenwijck, Pieter van 373, 379
Emblem of Death 379

Stockt, Vrancke van der 312, 316
Triptych of the Redemption 316, **317**

Stomer (o Stom), Mathias 373, 377
Doubting Thomas 373, **377**

Strobel, Bartholomäus 403, 409
*The Beheading of St John the
Baptist and the Banquet of Herod*
408, **409**

Strozzi, Bernardo 286, 288
St Veronica and the Veil **288**

T

Teniers, David 198, 307, 344, 349
*Archduke Leopold Wilhelm at his
Picture Gallery in Brussels* 349

Tiepolo, Giovanni Battista 14,
148, 160, 219, 276, 296, 302, 304,
305, 425, 431
Abraham and the Three Angels 305
The Immaculate Conception 302, **303**

Tiepolo, Giovanni Domenico
304, 425
Christ Falls on the Road to Calvary
304

Tiepolo, Lorenzo 425, 431
*Portrait of the Infanta María
Luisa de Borbón* **431**

Tintoretto (Jacopo Comino
Robusti) 13, 56, 94, 244, 264, 267,
268, 269, 270
Christ Washing the Disciples' Feet
13, 264, **266**, 267
*The Knight with the Golden
Chain* 264, **265**
The Rape of Helen 264, **268**

Tintoretto, Domenico 269
Lady with Bared Breasts **269**

Titian (Tiziano Vecelio) 12, 50,
52, 54, 56, 90, 94, 118, 125, 139, 178,
244, 246, 248, 249, 250, 251, 252,
254, 256, 257, 258, 259, 260, 261,
262, 263, 264, 274, 276, 279, 295,
340, 366, 368, 386, 429, 450, 452
Adam and Eve 252, **253**
The Bacchanal of the Andrians
250, **251**
The Burial of Christ 254, **262**
Danaë and the Shower of Gold **258**
*The Emperor Charles V with a
Dog* 256
*Equestrian Portrait of Charles V
at Mühlberg* 254, **255**
*Federico Gonzaga, I Duke of
Mantua* 252
The Glory 254, **261**
Philip II 257
Self-portrait 248, **263**
Tityus 260
Venus and Adonis 254, **258**, 259
Venus with an Organist and a Dog
249
The Virgin Dolorosa 254, **260**
The Worship of Venus 250, 251

Torregiani, Camillo 457
Isabella II veiled **457**

Trezzo, Jacopo Nizzolo da 462, 463
*Medal of the architect Juan
de Herrera* **462**

V

Valdés Leal, Juan de 138, 425
*St Ambrose denying Emperor
Theodosius Entry to the Church* **138**

Vallmitjana, Agapito 454, 455
Recumbent Christ **454**, **455**

Van der Hamen, Juan (see Hamen, Juan van der)

Van der Stockt, Vrancke (see Stockt, Vrancke van der)

Van der Weyden, Roger (see Weyden, Roger van der)

Van Dyck, Anton (see Dyck, Anton van)

Van Loo, Louis-Michel (see Loo, Louis-Michel van)

Van Orley, Bernard (see Orley, Bernard van)

Van Reymerswaele, Marinus Claesz (see Reymerswaele, Marinus Claesz van)

Van Steenwijck, Pieter (see Steenwijck, Pieter van)

Velázquez, Diego 13, 14, 23, 54, 64, 76, 84, 86, 90, 92, 94, 96, 98, 99, 100, 102, 104, 106, 108, 109, 110, 112, 113, 114, 116, 118, 120, 122, 123, 125, 128, 131, 132, 140, 147, 162, 165, 172, 177, 178, 198, 200, 210, 213, 215, 216, 219, 244, 248, 254, 264, 270, 276, 337, 343, 354, 439, 450
The Adoration of the Magi **94, 95**
Aesop 14, 107, **110, 111**
Apollo at the Forge of Vulcan 100, **102, 103**
The Buffoon Calabacillas **113**
Christ on the Cross 23, **104, 105**
Don Gaspar de Guzmán, Count-Duke of Olivares **109**
Don Sebastián de Morra **113**
The Drinkers, or The Feast of Bacchus **99**, 107, 198
Ferdinando Brandani **114**
Francisco Lezcano **113**
Las Meninas or The Family of Philip IV 94, 114, **120, 121**, 177, 454
Mars **107**
Pablo de Valladolid **112**
Philip IV (1623-27) **98**
Philip IV (h. 1653) **116**
Philip IV on Horseback **124**
Portrait of a Man, called The Pope's Barber 114, **115**
Prince Baltasar Carlos as a Hunter **108**
Prince Baltasar Carlos on Horseback **125**
Queen Elizabeth of France on Horseback **124**
Queen Maria Anna of Austria **116, 117**

The Spinners or *The Fable of Arachne* 114, **118, 119**
St Anthony Abbot and St Paul the Hermit **106**
The Surrender of Breda **123**
The Venerable Mother Jerónima de la Fuente **96, 97**
View of the Garden of the Villa Medici in Rome **100, 101**

Veronese (Paolo Caliari) 13, 244, 264, 270, 272, 273, 279, 285, 302, 425
Christ among the Doctors in the Temple 270, **273**
The Finding of Moses 270, **272**
Venus and Adonis 270, **271**

Volterra, Daniele da 242
Portrait of a Nobleman **242**

Vouet, Simon 286, 381, 385
Time defeated by Hope, Love and Beauty **385**

W

Watteau, Jean-Antoine 396, 398
Fête in a Park **398, 399**
The Marriage Contract and a Country Dance **398, 399**

Weyden, Roger van der 12, 307, 308, 312, 315, 316, 317, 319, 326, 328
Descent from the Cross **314, 315**
Pietà **317**
The Virgin and Child 307, **312, 313**

Wouwerman, Philips 373, 376
Hunting Hare **376**

Y

Yáñez de la Almedina, Fernando 42
St Catherine **42, 43**

Z

Zurbarán, Francisco de 23, 70, 76, 84, 85, 86, 87, 88, 89, 90, 122, 126, 140, 147, 154
Agnus Dei **88, 89**
Bodegón **89**
The Defence of Cadiz against the English **126**
Painter before Christ on the Cross, A **87**
St Elizabeth of Portugal **88**
St Peter the Apostle appearing to St Peter Nolasco **86, 87**